Daily Devotions for Superintendents

Kerry Roberts,
Pauline Sampson &
Jeremy Glenn

STEPHEN F. AUSTIN STATE UNIVERSITY PRESS
NACOGDOCHES ★ TEXAS

Manufactured in the United States of America.

For information, contact:
Stephen F. Austin State University Press
1936 North Street LAN 203
P.O. Box 13007
Nacogdoches, TX 75962
936.468.1078
sfapress@sfasu.edu
sfasu.edu/sfapress

ISBN: 9781622880331

Distributed by Texas A&M University Press Consortium
tamupress.com

∾ CONTENTS ∾

Forward

Many books have been written about the superintendency and all aspects of it. Additionally, "standards for superintendents" has been written by the American Association for School Administrators (AASA). These eight standards deal with *Leadership and District Culture, Policy and Governance, Communications and Community Relations, Organizational Management, Curriculum Planning and Development, Instructional Management, Human Resource Management,* and *Values and Ethics of Leadership.*

States have standards that mirror these. Texas, for example, put the standards into three domains: *Leadership of the Educational Community*; *Instructional Leadership*; and *Administrative Leadership.* Within these three domains are listed the eight competencies which reflect AASA's eight standards. This devotional covers many of the standards but really hones in on Competency 1 which reads, *"The superintendent knows how to act with integrity, fairness, and in an ethical manner in order to promote the success of all students."* In writing this devotional, the King James Version was used as our source for the bible verses.

Writing a devotional for superintendents has been a dream of ours. We understand the situation of today coupled with the many stresses and pitfalls. There are high and lows in the profession of the superintendency and there are times we have to feed our spiritual person just like we feed the physical person.

We recognize that God is the source of our strength and a comfort in the time of storms. We've been through the good, the bad, and the ugly. One thing that we recognized was that it was the Lord who brought us through. He took our hand and led us on. As we were discussing this, we came to the conclusion that this would be a real help and assistance for superintendents and even other school administrators.

In writing the devotional we endeavored to look at all areas of the superintendency and write a devotional about it out of every book in the Bible. Some books, such as Psalms and Proverbs, we tended verses more often than from other books and that was because they were written to help the spiritual man. We also recognize that the Bible is the infallible word of God and it directs us in all areas of life. Presidents, businessmen, leaders, and laymen understand that they need God in their lives and that they could not make it without His help and guidance.

We come from three different walks of life. We all received our doctorates in three different states and in three different decades. Dr. Roberts was raised in the northwest whose father worked on the railroad. Though his roots were meager, it was rich in love and Godly instruction. His father taught him how to live, how to be a good citizen, and most of all, how to love the Lord. He was raised in Assembly of God churches in western Montana, the panhandle of Idaho, and eastern Washington.

Dr. Sampson was raised in a farming family in Iowa and is currently the chair of the superintendent program at Stephen F. Austin State University. She learned from her family that family, God, and faith were important principles to cherish and build on. Helping your fellow man, giving, and always doing what was right were three tenants that were instilled in her. She was raised in the Lutheran church and is currently a member of the Methodist church.

Dr. Glenn was raised in Texas and is currently the superintendent of Central Heights ISD. He knew what he was destined to be and was focused on that goal. He enjoys and played athletics. He understands that the discipline it takes to be successful at any level and this has transferred over to his success as a superintendent. He was raised in the Southern Baptist churches.

As you can see, there are three different generations, three different walks of life, and three different denominations which came together because of their one commonality, their love for God and the Bible. We all recognized that God is the source of our strength and we need to plug into that source daily.

—Dr. Kerry Roberts, Dr. Pauline Sampson, Dr. Jeremy Glenn

Biography

Kerry L. Roberts is an associate professor in the superintendent program at Stephen F. Austin State University. Kerry received his Ph.D. from Washington State University in 1983 with a major in school administration and a minor in tests and measurements. His administrative work has been mainly in the mid-west. He has over 20 years of administrative experience and over 10 years of superintendent experience which has been in Minnesota, Kansas, and Oklahoma. In addition to his work in public education he has worked as an administrator in private education, an associate dean of distance learning at Oral Roberts University, and an assistant professor at Arkansas Tech University. David Roberts, Dr.Roberts' son, an aero-space engineer for Lockheed Martin, wrote two devotionals.

Pauline M. Sampson is an associate professor and chair of the superintendent program at Stephen F. Austin State University. She received her Ph.D. from Iowa State University in 1999 with a major in educational leadership. Her administrative experience has been in Iowa as a teacher, principal, consultant, special education director, and superintendent. She conducted over seven school audits for school districts.

Jeremy Glenn was born in Fort Hood, Texas, and attended public schools in nearby Marble Falls, Texas. Upon graduation from Marble Falls High School in 1995, Jeremy attended Tyler Junior College where he received an Associate of Arts in General Studies. Jeremy then transferred to the University of Texas at Tyler where he received a Bachelor of Science in Political Science and later a Master of Education in Educational Administration. Jeremy was the first in his family to receive a college degree. In May, 2006, he entered the doctoral program at Sam Houston State University. Jeremy has worked in education for twelve years.

He began his career as an English teacher in the Mineola Independent School District in Mineola, Texas. At the age of 25 he became a principal and later the interim superintendent for the Oakwood Independent School District in Oakwood, Texas. In 2008, Jeremy became the superintendent for Central Heights Independent School District in Nacogdoches, Texas. Jeremy remains an active member of various local and state organizations including the International Lions Club, Texas Association of School Administrators, and the Family, Career and Community Leaders of America.

January

A New Start

Remember ye, not the former things, neither consider the things of old. Behold, I will do a new thing; now it shall spring forth; shall ye not know it? I will even make a way in the wilderness, and rivers in the desert. **Isaiah 43: 18-19**

The wilderness and the solitary place shall be glad for them; and the desert shall rejoice, and blossom as the rose. It shall blossom abundantly, and rejoice even with joy and singing: the glory of Lebanon shall be given unto it, the excellency of Carmel and Sharon, they shall see the glory of the LORD, and the excellency of our God. **Isaiah 35:1-2**

There are times in my life that have felt barren and brown, just like my lawn when the grass has turned brown and leaves cover it. After high winds, many branches fall onto the brown lawn and leave a very unattractive yard. But when I rake up the leaves and bundle the branches, the yard starts to look less messy. Then, in the spring, new sprouts of grass show through the brown. This new growth provides me the hope for a fresh new lawn, free of debris and weeds.

New school years and even new semesters give a chance for a similar type of renewed hope. We can encourage our students who have not done well to put their past behind them and consider ways to change for a new start. Additionally, leaders can encourage others to reach out and find ways to help those who are struggling. Everyone needs that sense of renewed energy where fresh goals have a chance to be developed, new ways to meet the goals, along with plans on how to get rid of the old ways that were not helpful.

Spring brings a new feeling of life just as new semesters bring new chances for a fresh start. We need to surround ourselves with people who can help us with our goals as well as hold us accountable as we attempt to reach those goals. This renewed hope can falter easily if there is no one to help us. Old habits creep back unless we continue with a clear focus of our goals and a commitment to others, including asking God's support.

I'll have a new home of glory, where the redeemed of God shall stand
There'll be no more sorrow, there'll be no more strife.
Raised in the likeness of my Savior ready to live in Paradise
I'll have a new body, Praise the Lord, I'll have a new life.
—Hank Williams

Therefore, if any man be in Christ, he is a new creature:
Old things are passed away, behold all things have become new.
II Corinthians 5:17

When the Lights Go Out

Then spake Jesus again unto them, saying, I am the light of the world: he that followeth me shall not walk in darkness, but shall have the light of life. John 8:12

I was working in my office when the lights went out. I didn't know the electricity was going to be shut off because the university administrative memo said the electricity wasn't going to shut off until that evening. It went pitch black, and I lost everything on my computer. A couple of other professors came out of their offices and wondered what had happened. We collected our items and went outside into the light.

As a superintendent, you will sometimes have the "lights turned off on you." But there is one stronger than you who will help you and "lead you into the light." Don't let circumstances get you down and put you in the prison of despair. Jesus will turn the lights back on by giving you inner peace, spirit led direction, bringing the right people into your life, or a host of other ways.

I had the lights turned off on me in one of my superintendent positions. I was in despair. My blood pressure went out of sight. Everything seemed hopeless. I spent many hours in prayer and tears. Then, Jesus turned up just in time and turned the lights back on again. I was offered a position in another state, after many months of searching.

Before we started to follow Jesus, we walked in darkness. Jesus came along, turned on the lights, and we started walking in the light. Jesus cares for everything and will always turn the lights back on when we turn to Him for help.

Brightly beams our Father's mercy,
From His lighthouse evermore
But to us He gives the keeping
Of the lights along the shore.
−P. P. Bliss

Trust in Him and the lights will be turned back on.

Rejected

He is despised and rejected of men; a man of sorrows, and acquainted with grief: and we hid as it were our faces from him; he was despised, and we esteemed him not. **Isaiah 53:3**

Michael Jordan, arguably the best basketball player of all time, was cut from his high school basketball team when he was a sophomore. They said he was too short. Henry Ford, known for his innovative assembly line and American-made cars, wasn't an instant success. Five times he floundered before the Ford Motor Company became a household name. Harland David Sanders, who later was known as Colonel Sanders, of KFC, had a hard time selling chicken. His famous secret recipe received 1,009 rejections before a restaurant saw its potential. Abraham Lincoln's life wasn't easy. In his youth, he went to war a captain and returned a private.

The Diary of Anne Frank was rejected. One publisher said it was hardly worth reading. Joseph was rejected by his brothers and sold into slavery in Egypt. Job felt the whole world was coming down on him when even his wife said, "curse God and die."

Education is no stranger to rejection. When a bond issue fails or a board negates contract extensions, superintendents feel rejection. When a "thank you, but no thank you" letter comes from a peer-reviewed journal or conference, professors feel rejection. When a peer turns their nose to a student, that student feels rejection.

Rejection is hard, but as a Christian, we know we have someone who never strays from acceptance. As a superintendent, you can't let rejection overtake you. Failure is inevitable, just remember, you have a friend guiding your steps.

What a friend we have in Jesus,
All our sins and griefs to bear
What a privilege to carry,
Everything to God in prayer!
O what peace we often forfeit
O what needless pain we bear
All because we do not carry
Everything to God in prayer!

–Scriven and Converse

A rejection is nothing more than a necessary step in the pursuit of success.
–Bo Bennett

Deep Cleaning

Let us draw near with a true heart in full assurance of faith, having our hearts sprinkled from an evil conscience and our bodies washed with pure water. **Hebrews 10:22**

There are times along our journey when the Lord asks us to reexamine ourselves, a deep cleaning per se. He asks us to dig into the dark depths of our souls and look closely at past decisions. He wants us to ask forgiveness. This is no easy task; yet we are willing to do it because it will bring us closer to our God.

In my house, "Spring Cleaning" requires a multitude of cleaning supplies, as well as time and energy. I gather paper towels, soap, a vacuum cleaner, scrub brushes, pails, etc. I first must prioritize. For example, cleaning the ceiling fan blades after I've vacuumed the floor is counter-productive. All I have done is knock dust onto a clean floor. A sense of satisfaction washes over me when my house is thoroughly cleaned. Every closet and cupboard is pristine. While these days of deep cleaning leave me exhausted, I know it is worth it because the end product looks fantastic.

Sometimes God's request is required for some Christians to remember forgotten sins. These are the sins that need cleansing. It is humbling to have the Lord show you areas that are not clean.

The only way to expunge these sins and thwart the Devil in his attempt to take advantage of us is to ask for the Lord's forgiveness. Once asked and granted, we can throw away wrongs just like Jesus when he forgave us. He threw our sins into the sea of forgetfulness. A clean relationship with our Lord allows us to shine like a deeply cleaned home. A daily relationship helps us keep a close spiritual connection and prevents us from needing a deep cleaning. It is a daily repenting of our sins that gives us a renewed spirit that can shine daily.

> *Search me, O God, and know my heart today;*
> *Try me, O Savior, and know my thoughts, I pray.*
> *See if there be some wicked way in me;*
> *Cleanse me from every sin and set me free.*
> —J. Edwin Orr

Create in me a clean heart, O God; and renew a right spirit within me. Psalm 51:10

Fighting the Good Fight

I have fought the good fight, I have finished the race, I have kept the faith. **II Timothy 4:7**

When we talk about "fighting the good fight," nowhere is this more important than in our spiritual life. As school administrators, sometimes we are faced with the challenge of making decisions that are not always easy or popular. This requires fighting. Fighting is a way of life; it is how we thrive; it has a direct correlation to our spiritual lives.

In Jim Collins' book *Good to Great*, great leaders are described as those who blend humility with intense personal will. They exhibit a commitment to doing what is best for their organizations regardless of what challenges might arise. They exhibit the ability to "fight" for their beliefs.

Collins goes on to list other qualities of leadership including: (1) relying on high expectations rather than a charismatic personality, (2) hiring quality people and putting them in positions which they can succeed, (3) having discipline in the organization, (4) dealing with the realities of their organization, and (5) facing difficult questions regarding the future of their organization (Collins 2001). Each leadership quality reflects an aspect of servant leadership which can be applied to our daily lives.

Christians are often faced with dilemmas that not only affect our personal and professional lives, but our spiritual lives as well. As we look to establish a closer relationship with God, let us first acquire the knowledge and faith that will allow us to "fight the good fight" and "finish the race." Life's trials can be difficult, but "the God of all grace, who called you to his eternal glory in Christ, after you have suffered a little while, will himself restore you and make you strong, firm, and steadfast" (I Peter 5:10).

Always fighting for what is right
Will keep you in God's light
Jesus is the way the truth and the life
Therefore, keep on fighting the good fight.

A man who has nothing for which he is willing to fight,
nothing which is more important that his own personal safety,
is a miserable creature and has no chance of being free
unless made and kept so by the exertions of better menthan himself.

–John Stuart Mill

An Angry Man or Woman

Make no friendship with an angry man; and with a furious man thou shalt not go: Lest thou learn his ways, and get a snare to thy soul. **Proverbs 22:24-25**

Kevin Nelson (1996) wrote in The *Golfer's Book of Daily Inspiration:* "A dad sat down and talked with his son. Listen, you're a great player for a 16 year old. If I was your age and had your talent, I would be thrilled. But I need to tell you is your attitude is killing you. Pouting, mouthing off, sulking after a miss-hit, blaming others for your mistakes, tyrannically demanding perfection from every swing, and then erupting in rage if you don't meet this impossible high standard are characteristics of an immature golfer. This golfer will never achieve his maximum potential until he grows up or changes his attitude or both. Sorry to pull rank on you there. But I have lived considerably longer than you, and while I don't know everything I do know that nobody likes a kids with a chip on his shoulder. I love you and care about you. I want the best for you. That is why I am talking to you like this. You will never be the player you can be until you stop fighting yourself and everyone around you."

Angry people usually justify their anger, saying "it is someone else's fault they are angry." The Bible repeatedly warns us about giving in to anger when we are upset by our neighbor's words or actions. When you give in to anger, you focus on your own welfare, comfort or happiness. Instead, you should be primarily concerned about your neighbor's welfare and being a good witness for God.

There are many Bible verses warning us about anger, some are:

Refrain from anger and turn from wrath; do not fret it leads only to evil (Psalm 37:8). *Reckless words pierce like a sword, but the tongue of the wise brings healing* (Proverbs 12:18). *A wise man fears the Lord and shuns evil, but a fool is hotheaded and reckless* (Proverbs 14:16). *A patient man has great understanding, but a quick-tempered man displays folly* (Proverbs 14:29). *A gentle answer turns away wrath, but a harsh word stirs up anger* (Proverbs 15:1). *A hot-tempered man stirs up dissension, but a patient man calms a quarrel* (Proverbs 15:18). *A man of knowledge uses words with restraint, and a man of understanding is even-tempered* (Proverbs 17:27). *A fool gives full vent to his anger, but a wise man keeps himself under control* (Proverbs 29:11). *An angry man stirs up dissension, and a hot-tempered one commits many sins* (Proverbs 29:22). *But now you must rid yourselves of all such things as these: anger, rage, malice, slander, and filthy language from your lips* (Colossians 3:8). *My dear brothers, take note of this: Everyone should be quick to listen, slow to speak and slow to become angry, for man's anger does not bring about the righteous life that God desires* (James 1:19-20).

Glorify God and curb your tongue or it will curb your career.

Righteousness and Meekness

Seek ye the Lord all ye meek of the earth, which have wrought his judgment; seek righteousness, seek meekness: it may be ye shall be hid in the day of the Lord's anger. Zephaniah 2:3

Meekness is defined as the feeling of patient, submissive humbleness. It represents the humbling of our life to God's rule. Think of the wild, untamed stallion that bucks at any attempt to be broken, meanwhile, the meek, trained horse, has as much power but it's under the authority of an outside force.

Jesus is looking for people who are meek. He wants their will completely submitted to Him. This is done by dying to self and by openly acknowledging that He is Lord.

Righteousness is defined as adhering to moral principles. It speaks of the sphere of the will. Righteousness completes Jesus' goals. God is instilling a total obedience to His law. Jesus summarized the law when He commanded us to love God with all our heart, soul, and mind, and to love our neighbor as our self.

When our lives agree with God's will, that is righteousness. Righteousness speaks to what we say, think and do and translates the principles of God into our daily lives. Romans 6:19 speaks about this when it says our bodies are slaves of righteousness.

Seek to be meek and moral. Don't let yourself be swayed by temptations and lures to your integrity. I have a motto that I follow which goes like this: *If it illegal, unethical, or immoral then don't do it.* Not only will righteousness and meekness save you in this world, but it will save you on your job and your name will become a legacy. Die to self and follow God's moral principles and you will survive the storm!

> *My hope is built on nothing less,*
> *Than Jesus' blood and righteousness;*
> *I dare not trust the sweetest frame,*
> *But wholly lean on Jesus' name.*
> –William Bradbury

Meekness is love and school, at the school of Christ.
–James Hamilton

Compassion to the Bereaved

Jesus wept. John 11:35

Counseling and helping people through a difficult time in their lives is our duty as Christians and superintendents. We need to help provide healing to the bereaved. Even when you are prepared for the death of a loved one, it can take years to work through the grieving process. Grieving is a necessary part of healing.

While working in a school district as the superintendent, in the span of a year, the Director of Special Education's husband committed suicide, the secretary in the personnel office passed away from a blood-clot, and two other secretary's husbands were killed in automobile accidents. Everyone was affected by the tragedies of that year. The only thing I knew to do was to have compassion toward the grieving spouses and their families. In one of the cases, I remember that the husband of the secretary was so very grateful for our compassion and understanding that he asked me to be a pallbearer.

In another district, my assistant superintendent lost both her parents within the span of two months. They were sick and elderly. Their deaths were expected, but the grieving process was still necessary. Around the same time, I lost my father. The assistant superintendent told me, "I can only comfort myself by knowing that my parents are home in the arms of Jesus." I had the same comfort.

We have to remember the pain doesn't end after the funeral. It is only after the family goes home that reality of the loss sinks in. Shock becomes denial, and denial becomes pain when you realize life must go on without your loved one. I truly understand that as I still miss my father and he's been gone for over eight years.

Superintendents can help by reminding the grieving they are not alone, by simply sending a card, typing an e-mail or making a phone call. Even though Christians have the hope of a resurrection, grief is still a normal reaction to death. God is deeply touched as even Jesus wept at Lazarus's tomb.

Precious father, loving mother, fly across the lonely years;
And old home scenes of my childhood, in fond memory appears.
Precious memories, how they linger, how they ever flood my soul;
In the stillness of the midnight, precious, sacred scenes unfold.
-J. B. F. Wright

When we are in pain, there is a merciful God who is moved by our pain.

—Christina Quick

Condemnation

There is therefore now no condemnation to them which are in Christ Jesus, who walk not after the flesh, but after the Spirit. **Romans 8:1**

What does condemnation mean? It means to be judged, to be found guilty, and to be sentenced. Before Christ came, we were found guilty. He forgave us when Jesus, his only son, paid the price for our sins by going to the cross. Instead of judgment, God gives mercy. "God sent his son to the world not to condemn the world but that the world through Him might be saved" (John 3:17). God loves you and is not condemning you. The Holy Spirit convicts but doesn't condemn.

So where does condemnation come from? Condemnation comes from the accuser, Satan, the father of all liars. Satan is telling you that you are no good and that God will never forgive you. His lying voice tells you that you've crossed the line. You're just too wishy-washy; God will not forgive you. God doesn't even love you. Turn off your ears to the voice of the devil!

Two stories come to mind: Bob went to his pastor, Rev. Kevin, and said, "I can never be saved as I've done too many bad things and everyone in the church knows it." The pastor said, "I don't know it so right there, not everyone knows it." Bob was listening to the father of all liars. Have you ever said everyone knows it and I can't be forgiven? One thing is for certain, not everyone knows. God will forgive if we ask for forgiveness.

Dr. Tom, a superintendent, found one of his employees blatantly breaking a school policy and, in fact, could have been fired. Before this superintendent made a judgmental decision, he thoroughly investigated the matter. He found out that the sorrowful, repentant employee was facing some real difficult life challenges. Instead of firing the individual, the superintendent granted him mercy. The employee paid his debt and has been a model employee ever since. Remember God offers mercy, Satan condemns.

> *I was guilty with nothing to say,*
> *They were coming to take me away*
> *When a voice from Heaven was heard that said*
> *Let him go, take me instead.*
> *I should have been crucified,*
> *I should have suffered and died,*
> *I should have hung on the cross in disgrace,*
> *But Jesus, God's son took my place.*
> —Oak Ridge Boys

The church is not in the condemning business but in the saving business.

Fear God

Let us hear the conclusion of the whole matter; Fear God and keep his commandments; for this is the whole duty of man. **Ecclesiastes 12:13**

Your life is recorded in the book of God in heaven. Every sin you have committed is registered. Every regret for sin, every tear of repentance, every confession of guilt, and the forsaking of every sin, is recorded. When the Book is opened on God's judgment day, every case will have to stand the test of the law of God.

When you take God out of society, everything runs rampant. You end up with Cambodia's Pol Pot, Communist Russia, Communist China, Nazi Germany, Iran, and the degeneration of society morals. Without Christ, there are no morals; life is purposeless and intolerable to the human spirit.

There is a movement in the United States to take God out of our society. Frivolous lawsuits about the Ten-Commandments in the court house, Christmas at schools, reading the Bible in school, state approved same-sex marriages, broken homes, and abortions are examples of what happens when Church separates from state. People think only about themselves and satisfying their own lusts and desires.

Taking God out of the school has created an institution that is wreaking havoc on our society. **Proverbs 22:6** says, "Train up a child in the way he should go and when he is old he will not turn from it." When the evilness of society started taking over our schools, society started to change. Pray that the Lord will give you the wisdom and guidance to lead your school district during these perilous times. Pray that the Lord will put a hedge about you and your family to keep you from these evils. Pray for your school district and the parents of your school's children that the Lord will open their eyes. Remember to fear God in everything!

What does it mean to fear the Lord?
It seems a very important concept.
It seems at the heart of serving God.
Awe comes to mind as a related word to this phrase.
When you fully encounter God,
How can you do anything but fall at his feet and worship?

A parent receives an "A" in parenting
when they've taught their child to fear God.

Finding a Bargain

For which of you intending to build a tower, sitteth not down first, and counteth the cost whether he have sufficient to finish it? **Luke 14:28**

Everyone loves to get a bargain. But it is important to remember that an initial lower cost may not mean a long term bargain. If something only lasts for a short time because of poor construction, the reality is that it was not a bargain. An example of a questionable bargain is airplane tickets. There used to be hidden fees after the supposed low price. This made the original low fee not much of a bargain.

Leaders have to closely examine costs and benefits in many of their decisions. As leaders look to purchases, there are many factors to consider. Many products have a life expectancy for the product and these needs to be taken into consideration along with the price. Additionally, many leaders like to check with their colleagues to get recommendations on the durability and quality of products. What may seem like a bargain at the front end of a decision may not be the best choice.

Our lives have several decisions. The devil would have us believe that his way is easy and a better bargain to life. But it is extremely temporary and there are many hidden sorrows and consequences when we try that way. The bargain way to that path is full of deception.

The Lord's way provides quality way of life and offers a relationship that lasts for eternity. Quality relationships lead to a true and abundant life. We are told to seek Him in order to make good decisions; we need to increase our knowledge of His word by reading our Bible daily and holding His word in our heart. Proverbs encourages us to seek other Christians when we need to make decisions. We need to look long-term in all our decisions to make sure they give God the glory, will benefit the school district, and bring us closer to the Master.

Christian friendship and counsel is needed,
We only need to make certain that it's heeded,
It will help us make the right decision
That is why God's map is so essential for our provision.

Ointment and perfume rejoice the heart;
so doth the sweetness of a man's friend by hearty counsel. Proverbs 27:9

God's GPS

Thy word have I hid in mine heart, that I might not sin against thee. Psalms 119:11

A couple of weekends ago, my wife and I were driving through Henderson, Texas, and we needed to mail a letter. Not knowing where the post office was located, my wife looked it up on our GPS. It took us into the middle of town and as we got past the town square, the GPS said, "Turn left."

We went a few blocks and my wife said, "I think the GPS took us the wrong way. I think I see the post office over there." She insisted I turn right. I did and we ended up at a church. I then said, "We need to follow the GPS." The GPS took us around the block and put us back on the original street. We stayed on that street and sure enough, a quarter of a mile up the road, on the left, was the post office, hidden by trees.

I have to use the GPS when I visit principal-interns and superintendent-interns. It is tremendously helpful when I have to find my way around a large city. After I've been in that city several times, I can find my way around okay because I've hidden the directions in "my heart."

Life is like a road trip in need of a GPS. You have the guide, the Bible, which helps you travel through life. Times will come when you think you have made a wrong turn or the GPS is wrong. The good news is when you've gone the wrong way and haven't followed God's GPS, the Bible will get you back on the right road.

G. B. Towner recognized this when he wrote in his song, "When we walk with the Lord, In the light of His word…He abides with all who will trust and obey." Our children are taught this in children's church when they sing the song called the BIBLE.

> *The B-I-B-L-E,*
> *Yes that's the book for me,*
> *I stand alone on the Word of God*
> *The B-I-B-L-E*

The Bible is your GPS for life and will always lead you to the correct place!

Helping in the Time of Need

If thy whole body therefore be full of light, having no part dark, the whole shall be full of light, as when the bright shining of a candle doth give thee light. **Luke 12:36**

One foggy Tuesday morning, I got in my car to drive to work. I wanted to arrive early because I had a busy week coming up. An unexpected, high-priority task from my boss on Monday consumed my entire day and put me behind.

I had scarcely gotten out of our residential neighborhood and come to the first light – a red light, no less – when I heard the screech of tires followed by the sickening crunch of metal and plastic. A red minivan plowed into the white pickup behind me and swerved to my right. By the look of the front of the red minivan, I could tell it was more than a mere fender-bender.

When the light turned green, my first impulse was to drive away. After all, my car had not been hit, and besides, I was a day behind in my work. I justified to myself why it was okay to leave the scene. But then I remembered a time only a few years past when I was in a minor accident at a stoplight, and some stranger stopped to offer me a business card as a witness to the event. With that in mind, I decided to do the right thing—put on my hazard lights, get out to check on the other drivers, offer my name as a witness and call the emergency response team.

I thought about my decision to stop as I drove away. I thought of the parable about the good Samaritan, which, if you recall, featured several players – a Levite, a priest, and a Samaritan. Ironically, the two characters society would view as "most likely to do a good deed," – the priest and the Levite – came upon the beaten man in the road and walked past and did nothing, while the character that society would view as "scum of the earth" – the Samaritan – stopped and offered assistance.

I wondered why the priest and Levite would walk past. Perhaps, it was the same reason many of us have the impulse to pass by when bad events happen. Maybe they had a very busy week ahead. Maybe they reasoned that because they didn't have proper training to care for a badly injured man, there was nothing they could do, and therefore stopping would be of little value. The Bible does not record their reasons. All we know is that they failed to stop. They failed to help. They failed to perform a good deed when it was in their ability to do so.

I was also reminded of James 4:17: "Therefore, to one who knows the right thing to do and does not do it, to him it is sin." We often think of sin as doing something that is wrong. How often do we fail to see the other perspective – neglecting to do what is good? Inaction, when good action is required, is a sin.

Lord, let us not become so wrapped up in the business of our lives
That we neglected to do good when unplanned events occur in our lives.
Let us not choose the easy course of inaction
When good actions are necessary.

There is no better way to thank God for your sight
than by giving a helping hand to someone in the dark.
–Helen Keller

I Can't Wait Until the Weekend

And they shall build houses, and inhabit them; and they shall plant vineyards, and eat the fruit of them. They shall not build, and another inhabit; they shall not plant, and another eat; for as the days of a tree are the days of my people, and mine elect shall long enjoy the work of their hands. They shall not labour in vain, nor bring forth for trouble; for they are the seed of the blessed of the Lord, and their offspring with them. Isaiah 65:21-23

Many times I hear people talk about their desire for the weekend. They seem overworked during the week with the responsibilities of their job and their families. It seems that my staff and even the students wish the week away so they can quickly get to those weekend activities. Perhaps they have special plans, or perhaps people feel it is a chance to do whatever they wish to do. The implication is that they find no joy or contentment from their job.

We miss the wonderful opportunities to see what the Lord has for us each day if we wish the day away. There is no guarantee we will even be here for the weekend. I believe our Lord wants us to enjoy every day. We can ask ourselves and the Lord at the beginning of each day to help us be open to His beauty and ways we may help others. If we look for the Lord's wonders each day, we won't miss those great things our Lord desires for us.

There is beauty in watching a student learn something well enough to share it with another student. There is wonder in watching a master teacher presenting a new concept to the students. I marvel at the kindness I see as a secretary patiently helps a new family complete forms. It is inspiring to observe the sensitivity and generosity of others when they hear about students' needs and with their own resources pay for those needs.

Behold that which I have seen; it is good and comely for one to eat and to drink, and to enjoy the good of all his labour that he taketh under the sun all the days of his life, which God giveth him; for it is his portion. Every man also to whom God hath given riches and wealth, and hath given him power to eat thereof, and to take his portion, and to rejoice in his labour; this is the gift of God. Ecclesiastes 5: 18-19

If you keep waiting for the weekend you will miss out on the other five days of the week and what God has to offer us in each of those days.

Jesus Calms the Storms

And he saith unto them, Why are ye fearful, O ye of little faith? Then he arose, and rebuked the winds and the sea; and there was a great calm. **Matthew 8:26**

The year was going very well and the new superintendent was enjoying the "honeymoon" period. New and innovative changes were being made. He truly wanted to help the students learn and succeed. Around Christmas time, the school board president's son was in trouble for attending a school dance under the influence of alcohol.

The board president wasn't pleased and put pressure on the new superintendent to "undo" his son's punishment. Since it was the athletic director who caught the student under-the-influence, he administered the policy as he had done to all students. Because the athletic director wouldn't back down from the punishment, he was reassigned to other duties by the new superintendent.

That decision started a "fire-storm" in the community. The new superintendent was quickly fighting for his own job. He apologized in the newspaper. After a lengthy and packed board meeting, the superintendent reinstated the athletic director. He was beaten but not knocked out because the Lord brought him through.

These storms will come. As a superintendent, unexpected storms will cause you to fight for your "very career." It is during these storms that you need to remember you have an anchor in Jesus. He will see you safely through. You will get battered and scarred, but you will come safely through the storm. You will never get rid of the scars but they serve as a reminder that Jesus helped you and for you to continue trusting him.

When you start trusting in yourself, any storm that comes will quickly remind you that your only hope is in Jesus. Always keep your eyes and trust on Him and He will calm the storm.

The anchor holds
though the ship is battered,
the anchor holds
though the sails are torn,
I have fallen on my knees
as I faced the raging seas,
the anchor holds
in spite of the storm.
—Ray Boltz

Jesus is your only help in the time of a storm.

Major Remodel

For we are His workmanship, created in Christ Jesus unto good works, which God hath before ordained that we should walk in them. **Ephesians 2:10**

When I watch renovation shows on television, I am always amazed by the transformations made by designers and carpenters. They must envision the project's potential before they start their renovations. It amazes me when you see the before and after pictures. Renovation can be very messy and can take time, but the end result is always worth the wait.

Some have a great vision of how a school can be remodeled, making it amazing. A remodel increases the value of a school. It allows for more efficient and energy saving products. The cost of the renovation requires an understanding of all the details. and that a saving may be made for the long term, even if the upfront cost is more with a more efficient and energy saving product.

Therefore, if any man be in Christ, he is a new creature. Old things are passed away, behold al things are become new. II Corinthians 5:17

The Lord is in the construction business just like many superintendents are part of renovation projects or new construction. The Lord can take the most fallen down and broken person and transform that person into a beautiful person again. The Lord has a vision of what people can become and all they have to do is believe in Him and submit to his design.

The Lord makes people beautiful beyond their imaginations. His burden is light and he makes it easy. His renovation on us only requires us to trust Him and allow Him to create His vision for us. *And be not conformed to this world, but be ye transformed by the renewing of your mind that ye may prove what is that good and acceptable and perfect will of God. Romans 12:2*

> *I praise Thee, Lord, for cleansing me from sin:*
> *Fulfill They word, and make me pure within;*
> *Fill me with fire, where once I burned with shame:*
> *Grant my desire to magnify Thy name.*
> —J. Edwin Orr

You are God's master piece and he continually makes you over until He welcomes you to your eternal home.

Overwhelmed

***From the end of the earth will I cry unto thee, when my heart is overwhelmed: lead me to the rock that is higher than I.* Psalms 61:2**

It was a bright sunny winter day, and we were sitting in a principal department meeting at the university. We were the only university in the state being visited by the state department of education to audit our program. Needless to say, stress levels were high as the semester had just started up, and now we had to prepare for a visit that was coming in four weeks. Though it was sunny outside, it was "gloomy and misty" inside.

As I contemplated this, I thought about Moses who led the children of Israel out of Egypt. Moses and the children of Israel were in the desert, and they had to be fed. Feeding two to three million people takes a lot of food. According to the Army, Moses would have needed 1500 tons of food each day. In today's terms, that would require two freight trains, each a mile long, to provide that food. To top it off, they were in the desert and would have needed firewood for cooking. This would take 4000 tons of wood and a few more freight trains, each a mile long, each day. They lived out there for 40 years and were always in transit.

As you know, you need water. If they only had enough to drink and wash a few dishes, that would take 11,000,000 gallons each day and a freight train with tank cars, 1800 miles long, just to bring the water! Then, they had to cross the Red Sea at night. If they went double file, the line would be 800 miles long and would require 35 days and nights to cross the Red Sea. So Moses had to find a place at least 3 miles wide, so they could walk 5000 abreast to get over in one night. Another problems was this: where would they camp each day as that would take up a campground two thirds the size of Rhode Island or a total of 750 square miles? Finally, what about the latrines?

Do you think Moses figured all of this out before he left Egypt and took the children of Israel with him? No! The difference was that Moses believed in God, and God took care of these things for him. Do you think God has any problem taking care of all your needs, whether as a superintendent or in your personal life? Remember, our God is an awesome God!

When the road you're traveling on
Seems difficult at best
Just remember, keep on praying,
And God will do the rest.

See that a pilot steers the ship in which we sail, who will never allow us to perish even in the midst of shipwrecks, there is no reason why our minds should be overwhelmed with fear and overcome with weariness.

—John Calvin

Peacemaker

Blessed are the peacemakers: for they shall be called the children of God. Matthew 5:9

The *Colt Single Action Model P. Peacemaker* is a single action revolver that was designed for the U.S. government as a service revolver in 1872 by Colt Manufacturing Company. The revolver was popular with ranchers, lawmen, and outlaws. The name of this gun is a "play on words" as a gun is not a peacemaker. A gun is used for killing, gathering food, and target practice. It is used by the good, the bad, and the hideous.

A peacemaker is one who turns hostility into lasting amity. This is important as everyone needs peace: the office, the home, the business, the country, the school, and the world.

As a child of God, you can be the one who brings calm and peace to the situation and to those who seriously need it. People around you will see the love of Jesus mirrored in your life and you will reflect this calm back to them. Healing and peace come from God's love mirrored through you. Unlike the gun which brought peace through death and destruction, you will bring peace through the gift of God living in your life and in your actions.

Be the peacemaker in your community, school district, board, family, and church. A peacemaker strives to do the following: a.) To make peace with God; b.) To make peace with others; and c.) To make peace between others. If you feel that you are not a real peacemaker, pray that the Lord will make you a peacemaker.

What a treasure I have in this wonderful peace, buried deep in the heart of my soul;
So secure that no power can mine it away, while the years of eternity roll.
Peace! Peace! Wonderful peace, coming down from the Father above;
Sweep over my spirit forever, I pray, in fathomless billows of love.
—W. G. Cooper

If we are to be peacemakers, we first must make our peace with God.
—Billy Graham

Rebates

According as his divine power hath given unto us all things that pertain unto life and godliness, through the knowledge of him that hath called us to glory and virtue. **2 Peter 1:3**

It oftentimes seems difficult and unnecessary to buy something that the sale price requires you to mail a proof of purchase and receipt with a form in order to get a rebate. I wish the company would just allow the product to be sold at a discount price so I would not have to go through the extra steps required to get that sale price. Is it to the customer's advantage or the company's advantage to require the rebate process?

Perhaps that is one reason I am always amazed by the grace of God. It would seem that His advantage would be to just cut us off and say we were not redeemable. We have all sinned and seem to continue to sin and come short of His glory numerous times, yet He continues to give the ultimate customer service.

God forgives us over and over again. He kindly and gently corrects us and guides us to a clear path. Do we give others that same service? We expect others to help us or forgive us when we do something hurtful. But we may not be as open to help them or forgive them when they do something less.

I see this happen at appointment times. We are running late because of the need to complete something, making us late for the appointment. We expect others to understand our tardiness. Are we as tolerant when others are late for an appointment with us or when the doctor can't see us on the appointed time?

God gave the ultimate price that requires only that we accept that Jesus died for our sins. It does not require any proof of purchase or receipt. It is a free gift. It is the ultimate customer service for eternal life. "Every good gift and every perfect gift is from above, and cometh down from the Father of lights, with whom is no variableness, neither shadow of turning" (James 1:17).

> *Jesus paid it all,*
> *All to him I owe,*
> *Sin had left a crimson stain,*
> *He washed it white as snow.*
> —John Grape

The rebate for giving up a sinful life is eternal life.

Rock Your World

And it shall come to pass, if thou shalt hearken diligently unto the voice of the LORD thy God, to observe and to do all his commandments which I command thee this day, that the LORD thy God will set thee on high above all nations of the earth. **Deuteronomy 28:1**

The life of Jesus is miraculous. He shows us the ultimate in what we can do when we give everything to the Lord. You'll be the "head and not the tail." He "rocked his world" and you can "rock" yours. I found a list of all the miracles of our Lord and Savior, Jesus Christ, and the following list that came up:

- Born of a virgin
- Changed the water into wine
- Healed the royal official's son
- Healed a demon possessed man in Capernaum
- Healed Peter's mother-in-law
- Healed the sick during the evening
- Showed the fishermen where to catch a "boat load" of fish.
- Healed the leper
- Healed the centurion's servant
- Healed a paralyzed man
- Healed a withered hand
- Raised a widow's son from the dead
- Calmed the stormy sea
- Healed a demon-possessed girl
- Healed the demon-possessed man at Gerasene
- Healed many at Gennesaret
- Healed a woman of internal bleeding
- Raised Jairus' daughter from the dead
- Healed two blind men
- Healed a demon-possessed man who could not hear
- Healed a deaf man with a speech impediment
- Healed a man who was crippled for 38 years
- Fed 5000 men and their families
- Fed 4000 men and their families
- Healed a blind man in Bethsaida
- Healed a man born blind
- Healed a boy possessed by a demon
- A fish was caught with a coin in its mouth
- Healed a blind and deaf man who was demon-possessed
- Peter walked on the water
- Healed a woman with an 18 year infirmity
- Healed a man with dropsy
- Healed 10 men suffering from leprosy
- Raised Lazarus from the dead
- Healed Bartimaeus of blindness
- Withered the fig tree so it would not yield fruit

- Restored a severed ear
- Resurrected from the dead

This is amazing. If all was written about what Jesus did, there would not be enough books to contain His miracles. My brother, Rev. Del, changed his own world. He said to me, "I want to be totally submerged in the presence of the Lord." When he took that stand, his church exploded. People knew he was "for real."

Well I've been reading, and I've been feeding, upon the precious Word of God.
Marvelous story, so full of glory; It is the path that Jesus trod.
He was man's deliverer, and sin forgiver, every problem He understood.
Everywhere He went, my Lord was doing good…doing good.
–Unknown

Put Christ first in everything and you will change your world.

Strategic Listening

I am the good shepherd, and know my sheep, and am known of mine. John 10:14

My sheep hear my voice. I know them, and they follow me. John 10:27

Strategic listening is a process that is taught in school administration classes to students as they prepare to become principals and superintendents. When we truly listen, our staff and students feel like we care wholly for their well-being. The strategic listening process consists of:

Listening between the words
Providing supportive feedback
Clarifying messages through second-guessing
Adjusting to problems of poor listeners
Learning to tolerate and enjoy silence
Improving memory
Using excessive thinking time productively
Understanding and committing to the listening process
                    (O'Hair: The strategic listening process 1998)

When we take these points and put them into practice, our school and our home will be much better. The Lord speaks to us. We must listen. **Isaiah 50:4** (NIV) says, "[…]he wakens my ear to listen[…]." Sometimes we have to be quiet to listen, and sometimes we have to ask the Lord what he is saying. When we truly listen to the Lord, he will guide our steps. The following is an example of strategic listening when a young soldier called his parents coming home from the Vietnam War:
"Mom and Dad, I'm coming home, but I've a favor to ask. I have a friend I'd like to bring home with me."
"Sure," they replied, "we'd love to meet him."
"There's something you should know," the son continued, "he was hurt pretty badly in the fighting. He stepped on a land mine and lost an arm and a leg. He has nowhere else to go, and I want him to come live with us."
His parents listened strategically and opened up their hearts and home to this wounded soldier.
Strategic listening is effective listening. Strategic listening is listening to the voice of the Lord.

Speak, my Lord, speak, my Lord,
Speak, and I'll be quick to answer Thee;
Speak, my Lord, speak, my Lord,
Speak, and I will answer, "Lord, send me."

I like to listen. I have learned a great deal from listening carefully.
Most people never listen.
—Ernest Hemingway

Sing A Song of Triumph

Then sang Moses and the children of Israel this song unto the Lord, and spake, saying, I will sing unto the Lord, for he hath triumphed gloriously: the horse and his rider hath he thrown into the sea. **Exodus 15:1**

Moses and the children sang this song when the armies of Pharaoh were drowned in the Red Sea. God was with the children of Israel and led them by using a pillar of fire by night and a cloud by day to protect them. They came to this unforgivable barrier. There was no way they could escape the armies of Egypt. Everything seemed hopeless, then God did the unforeseeable, he separated the Red Sea and the children of Israel walked through on dry land.

How many times in your life has a huge, gigantic, impossible barrier been put in your path? At least, that is what you thought when you saw it. After much fasting, prayer, and tears, the Lord came along at the right moment and helped you get through that barrier.

I attended a superintendent's monthly meeting and they were afraid, befuddled, scared, angry, and downright confused. The state was in a huge budget crisis, just like the majority of the states, and cuts had to be made. The superintendents had come to this barrier and didn't quite know how to get through it. Follow God's word and He will provide a way of escape at the right time.

When God provides a passage through the barrier, sing a song of praise to him. Psalms 22:3 says God inhabits the praises of his people. Many times we forget to give God praise. Don't dread the future, but thank God for the answer. The lyrics of one song goes like this, "I will sing unto the Lord for He has triumphed gloriously, the horse and rider fell into the sea."

> *Dread not the things that are ahead*
> *The burdens great, the sinking sand,*
> *The thorns that o'er the path are spread,*
> *God holds the future in His hand.*
> —James Vaughan

All glory to Him I bring! With gladness to Him I cling. With perfect delight, by the day and by night this wonderful song I sing.
—G. W. Sebren

Blessings From our Mistakes

Take with you words, and turn to the Lord: say unto him, Take away all iniquity, and receive us graciously. **Hosea 14:2**

Many times a leader makes a decision when a better choice could have been made. This reminds me of someone cooking soup and forgetting one of the ingredients. Sometimes, adding the ingredient later fixes the problem, while other times a new creation is made when that one ingredient is left out. Most cooking mistakes are not made on purpose, but made because of distractions.

How do you handle a mistake once you realize you made it? Did you run from a decision because you didn't want to confront someone? Did you forget to bring some important data for a meeting? Were there many distractions in your day before you went to the important meeting? Many of these moments are the "Jonah" moments: we head the wrong direction either intentionally or because of an error.

The Lord can turn a wrong into a blessing like He did with Jonah. The other sailors on the ship were not Christians. They believed in many gods. Jonah did not confess immediately about his wrong decision and his running from God until he came under the sailors' questioning. The sailors realized the power of God when the storm was silenced and they showed their reverence for the Lord.

Then the men feared the Lord exceedingly and offered a sacrifice unto the Lord and made vows. Jonah 1:16

The Lord took Jonah's wrong decision and made a blessing for the other sailors to see His power. It would not be appropriate to intentionally do wrong or run from the Lord with tough decisions, but it is important to know that the Lord can make a blessing or a new creation even from our wrong actions. Many times, it takes a look back at those wrong times to see how the Lord was able to create something amazing.

*That he who blesseth himself in the earth shall bless himself in the God of truth; and he that sweareth in the earth shall swear by the God of truth; because the former troubles are forgotten, and because **they** are hid from mine eyes. For behold, I create new heavens and a new earth; and the former shall not be remembered, nor come into mind. Isaiah 65:16-17*

I shall forever lift my eyes to Calvary
To view the cross where Jesus died for me
How marvelous the grace that caught my falling soul
He looked beyond my fault and saw my need.
—Dottie Rambo

God can always make lemonade out of a lemon.

January 24

The Paradox of Persecution

Blessed are they which are persecuted for righteousness' sake: for theirs is the kingdom of heaven. **Matthew 5:10**

There is a paradox in persecution. The more the children of Israel were oppressed, the more they multiplied and spread (Exodus 1:12 NIV). Horrible suffering equals purity plus power plus growth. How does this compare to today's persecuted believers. They are extremely faithful (Daniel 1:11-15). They are totally truthful (Daniel 4:24-27). They are always courageous (Daniel 6:10). Trials bring out the best in you as you have to totally 100% put your trust in God.

You can pray for today's persecuted Christians. Pray for governments to work for justice. Pray for the church to grow in the midst of persecution and that the believers will have strength, courage, and peace. Pray for the persecutors that they may be saved like Saul who later became Paul. Finally, praise God for his faithfulness. Remember that God is in control. Ephesians 6:10 says, "Be strong in the Lord and in his mighty power."

In the world today, the ten top nations with persecution towards Christians are North Korea, Iran, Saudi Arabia, Somalia, Maldives, Afghanistan, Yemen, Mauritania, Laos, and Uzbekistan. If you think you have it hard as a Christian superintendent, then remember the Christians that are in these nations. You will say, "Dear Lord, I'm sorry but my trials don't even compare to theirs."

When persecution and trials come, keep your eye on the Lord because he will see you through. Remember, nothing can separate you from the love of God.

> *Lord, make me an instrument of thy peace.*
> *Where there is hatred, let me sow love;*
> *Where there is injury, pardon;*
> *Where there is doubt, faith;*
> *Where there is despair, hope;*
> *Where there is darkness, light;*
> *Where there is sadness, joy.*
> —St. Francis of Assisi

Remain faithful and trust in the Lord, the one who conquered the fiercest enemies of all, sin and death.

Vigorously Pursue Quality Relationships

A man that hath friends must show himself friendly: and there is a friend that sticketh closer than a brother. **Proverbs 18:24**

I no longer call you servants, because a servant does not know his master's business. Instead, I have called you friends, for everything that I learned from my Father I have made known to you. **John 15:15**

As a former superintendent, I quickly learned that problems and tragedies happen. Get up in the morning and welcome the day and I guarantee you some problems will arise, something will go wrong that is totally out of your control: your car may not start, you may have developed a case of the flu, a principal or assistant superintendent will not show up for work, your secretary is running late because of an unplanned emergency, a school bus forgot to pick up a child, a parent is angry with the coach and waiting for you.

You must come to realize these situations (personal or professional) will happen. You must also realize you need to make good things come your way. How is this done? It is by pursuing, with effort, those relationships that make life worth living. You need to initiate the relationship process and work at making the relationship work. Examples of how this is done are as follows: by making an extra phone call, by going out of your way to meet people and being approachable, or by joining an organization because of its philosophy and membership.

Satisfaction and a sense of living take effort on your part by initiating a proactive role in meaningful relationships. These relationships become the foundation for your satisfaction and help to reduce stress. They can become the support network that assists you in a crisis and consoles you in times of distress.

Christ vigorously pursued you and gave his life for your salvation. He is a friend that sticks closer than a brother. When things go wrong, which they will, take the problem to the Lord in prayer. Call close friends and have them pray with you because Jesus said "where two or three are gathered together in my name, there I am in the midst" (**Matthew 18:20**).

Almighty God, the Great I Am, Immovable Rock, Omnipotent powerful, Awesome Lord
Victorious Warrior, Commanding King of Kings, Mighty Conqueror
And the only time I ever saw Him run was when He ran to me
And took me in His arms.

–Benny Hester

Beginning today, treat everyone you meet as if they were going to be dead by midnight. Extend to them all the care, kindness, and understanding you can muster, and do it with no thought of any reward. Your life will never be the same again.

–Og Mandino

Wet Pants

This is a faithful saying, and worthy of all acceptation, that Christ Jesus came into the world to save sinners; of whom I am chief. **I Timothy 1:15**

I read an anonymous story on the internet and it was so applicable to our situation as superintendents. Come with me to a third grade classroom where there is a nine year old boy sitting at his desk. All of a sudden there is a puddle between his feet and the front of his pants are wet. At the start of class, he'd asked the teacher if he could use the restroom, but she wouldn't let him. She said, "you can wait until the end of the period." He thinks his heart is going to stop because he can't possibly imagine how this has happened. He's never wet his pants before and he knows that he will be unmercifully ridiculed when the students find out. The boys will never "let him live it down," and the girls will never speak to him again.

Ashamed, he puts his head down and prays this prayer, "Dear God, this is an emergency! Five minutes from now I'm dead meat!" He looks up from his prayer and here comes the teacher with a look of utter disdain in her eyes that says he's been discovered. As the teacher walks towards him, a class mate, named Debbie, is carrying a goldfish bowl that is filled with water. Debbie trips in front of the teacher and inexplicably dumps the bowl of water on the boy's lap.

The boy pretends to be angry, but all the while is saying to himself, "Thank you, Lord! Thank you, Lord!"

Now instead of being the object of ridicule and scorn, the boy is the object of sympathy. The teacher rushes him downstairs and gives him gym shorts to put on while his pants dry out. All the other students are helping to clean up the water around his desk. The sympathy is wonderful but as life would have it, the ridicule that should have been his has been transferred to someone else—Debbie.

She tried to help, but they tell her to get out of the way. She is called a "klutz" and "calamity Jane." Finally, at the end of the day, as the students are waiting for the bus, the boy walks over to Debbie and whispers, "you did that on purpose, didn't you?" Debbie whispers back, "I wet my pants once too." May God help us see the opportunities that are always around us to do good.

> *If you could go with me back to where I started from*
> *I'm just a sinner saved by grace*
> *When I stood condemned to death He took my place*
> *How I live and breathe in freedom with each breath of life I take.*
> –Bill Gaither

Jesus looks beyond our imperfections and sees our heart.

Who Holds the Title of the Earth?

Thou are worthy, O Lord, to receive glory and honor and power, for thou has created all things, and for thy pleasure they are and were created. Revelations 4:11

God created the earth, and the devil tried to steal it. God gave his Son, claiming the earth as His own.

When we buy property, we often do a title search to make sure there are no liens, it has a clear title, and to find out to whom the property once belonged. I had a title company going out of business and since I owned my home, they sent the deed to me. It listed all of the owners of the house, as well as the property before the house was built in 1940. It was interesting to see all the owners' names as well as who had built the house. I held the title to this piece of property, and yet I understood it was only temporary.

This was an earthly possession, meaning it held no eternal value by itself. It was our home, and my children were raised with the values of the Christian faith in that home. But the house itself would not be eternal like the values given to my children.

When we look at the earth, we know that God owns it as he created it. He holds the title to the earth as it belongs to Him. He is the designer, the builder, and the owner of this earth. He owns me. As a superintendent, the community and the district owns all of the buildings, equipment, and supplies. You are the guardian of the community's property. "And they sang a new song saying, Thou are worthy to take the book, and to open the seals thereof: for thou was slain, and has redeemed us to God by the blood out of every kindred and tongue and people and nation" (**Revelations 5:9**).

> *Worthy is the Lamb, let men and angels sing,*
> *Worthy is the Lamb, let hallelujah's ring,*
> *And when life is past, upon the golden shore,*
> *Worthy is the Lamb, we'll shout forevermore.*
> –Johnson Oatman, Jr

He holds the whole world in His hands
and we are only caretakers of His creation.

Rimrocked

Cast thy burden upon the Lord, and he shall sustain thee: he shall never suffer the righteous to be moved Psalms 55:22

Do you ever feel that your burden is so great that there is no way out? You are so unnerved by your load that you are afraid you will never get out from underneath it. This means you are "rimrocked." Rimrocked is when you climb up to a spot from which you are too frightened to descend. Many climbers find it easy to scramble *up* the ladder-like layers, but going down can be quite unnerving. Having this overwhelming burden leaves you feeling like the rimrocked climber.

In the old west, an explorer or cowboy would find himself gazing at the canyon floor below their feet. Their only choice was to go back if they could and find another way down. If he were on horseback, it is possible that he did a stupid thing and came down a very steep piece of rock and the horse isn't going to back up so now you are stuck. That's the kind of rimrocked I'm talking about.

A superintendent told me that he felt like he was "rimrocked" in his community. It was so unnerving that his health started to deteriorate as his blood pressure sky-rocketed. To make matters worse, his close acquaintances and colleagues avoided him like the plague. He had done nothing illegal, unethical, or immoral. He recommended the demotion of a director who was sexually harassing an employee. This director happened to be friends with the local newspaper editor and president of the teacher's union. The lies being perpetuated were unbelievable. The superintendent's only way out was to resign and start fresh somewhere else. It took him a year before he could get another job.

Another superintendent made some unwise decisions and is now "rimrocked" in all decision making. Everything he does in that community is questioned and closely scrutinized. He can survive, but he'll have to start looking for another position. When you are "rimrocked" reach out to Jesus. He is a friend who sticks closer than a brother and will help you find a way out.

Is the life you're living filled with sorrow and despair?
Does the future press you with its worries and its care?
Are you tired and friendless,
Have you almost lost your way?
Jesus will help you, just call on Him today.
He is always there hearing every prayer faithful and true
Walking by our side in His love we hide, all the day through.
When you get discouraged just remember what to do,
Reach out to Jesus, He's reaching out to you.
                                                    –Ralph Carmichael

You may think you are "rimrocked" and can't move,
but that is a lie perpetuated by the devil.
As a Christian you always have a way out
and that is through Jesus.

Directionally Challenged

The proverbs of Solomon, the son of David, King of Israel. To know wisdom and instruction, to perceive the words of understanding. To receive the instruction of wisdom, justice, and judgments, and equity. to give subtlety to the simple, to the young man knowledge and discretion. A wise man will hear and will increase learning and a man of understanding shall attain unto wise counsel. **Proverbs 1: 1-5**

God has a plan for our lives, and he gives us the choice to follow His plan or follow our own. Our life will be more fulfilled if we follow God' plan. So how do we know what God's plan is for our life? Do we listen to the small whispering of the Holy Spirit when we might be going the wrong way?

I often follow driving directions best by landmarks, not the mile markers or road signs. For example, I might turn right at an old gas station, go about two miles to the large white church, then turn left going two more miles. That would be my preferred way to get and give directions. My son doesn't understand why I would choose to use those directions. He wants clear directions: road sign names, highway numbers, and street names. His premise is that those signs don't change where my landmarks might change. Road construction can also block your use of a road and you will have to follow the detour signs. But either way of following directions can get a person to their desired location.

God's way is very clear. The book of *Proverbs* has been a clear guide for me. There have been many times when the direction doesn't immediately have a correct answer and those are the times as a leader, I need to remember to be patient and wait for the Lord's answer. My focus needs to remain on the direction that pleases the Lord most, not the direction that might be easiest for me. The only way I will know what pleases the Lord most is to read his Word and talk with Him daily. A leader who wants to follow God's directions must know God's word and voice. I also need to remain open to listening for the voice of the Holy Spirit guiding me along God's way. A person can sense when they are not going the right way. Things just don't seem right. It is time to stop and look for God's way through the Holy Spirit. You may need to turn around and find a different way when that happens in your life. It is important to know that the Lord will direct your ways.

Is any of you afflicted? Let him pray. Is any merry? Let him sing psalms. Is any sick among you? Let him call for the elders of the church and let them pray over him, anointing him with oil in the name of the Lord. **James 5: 13-14**

> *Jesus is the way-maker, Jesus is the way-maker One day he made a way for me,*
> *When I was lost in sin; No hope, no peace within*
> *On day, He made a way for me.*
> –Unknown

Where He leads me I will follow and go with Him all the way.
–Ernest Blandy

One More Soul

Let your light so shine before men, that they may see your good works, and glorify your Father which is in heaven. **Matthew 5:16**

Her dying father-in-law was scared to die. He looked at her and asked what he should do. It was the opening she needed. She responded that he just needed to confess his sins and ask for Jesus to save him. What a comfort for the daughter-in-law to watch him accept Christ.

She knows that her father-in-law will soon join his late wife. She saved a soul, and he will live eternally in heaven. It is a great comfort for her to know that he will be in a beautiful place with those who preceded him. Now that is an outstanding witness.

How many times do we get the opportunity to make sure we will have those we love with us eternally and be assured that they will have a blessed life? I know I am so excited to think of the people I will get to be with again in heaven.

As a leader of a school, you may not feel you are allowed to witness about your faith or tell someone how to be saved eternally. But it is really about showing your personal faith through your actions and how you decorate your office. If people see a Bible or a cross on your desk or a Christian picture on your wall, this will say you are a Christian. People watch your actions to see if you are genuine.

What a day that will be
When my Jesus I shall see
And I look upon His face
The One who saved my by His grace
When He takes me by the hand
And leads me through the Promised Land
What a day, glorious day that will be.
–James Hill

The best witness for Christ is your life.

Knocked Down but Not Out

We are pressed on every side by troubles, but we are not crushed. We are perplexed, but not driven to despair. We are hunted down, but never abandoned by God. We get knocked down, but we are not destroyed. **II Corinthians 4:8-9**

In 1960, Tom Landry became the coach of the Dallas Cowboys. During his first season as head coach, Landry went 0-11-1. Many in Cowboy's management lost confidence in Landry and wanted him fired. In Texas, there are high expectations for football, especially in Dallas.

When the season ended, the Cowboys' general manager recommended to Clint Murchison, the Cowboys' owner, that Tom Landry be dismissed. Murchison decided to take the weekend to think it over. When he returned to work Monday morning, he surprised everyone by giving Landry a 10-year contract. Landry would reward Murchison's faith by winning 270 games, two Super Bowls, five NFC titles, and 13 Division titles.

The moral of this story is good things take time. In today's society, many individuals look for instant gratification. In fact, I am willing to bet no NFL coach would be rewarded with a ten year contract after a no win season. At some point, in our fast paced, technological society, we have forgotten that long term, sustainable success takes time.

I have seen many superintendents come into districts with big ideas ready to make sweeping changes, but they forget building relationships with teachers and the community must come first. They want instant gratification, but they are unwilling to make long term sacrifices. These superintendents bounce from district to district never finding fulfillment in their job, and certainly never making a positive impact on a school district.

As you move forward with your day, remember that good things take time. God is with us even when we are "pressed on every side by troubles," and no matter the situation we are "never abandoned by God." As you deal with the struggles of daily life, remember that you are building a foundation for a brighter future. Keep your priorities in order: take time to pray, spend quality time with your family, and lead those around you by example.

I've struggled through this life
and have been knocked to the ground,
I know I'll get back up and not stay down
Because my father taught me oh so well,
How the Lord helped me so I could tell.

An intent person will stay the course and go the distance.
He or she will concentrate on objectives with determination,
stamina, and resolve. Intentness is the quality that won't permit
us to quit, even when our goal is going to take a while to accomplish.
–John Wooden

FEBRUARY

Contentment

But godliness with contentment is great gain. **I Timothy 6:6**

*W*ebster's Dictionary defines contentment as "the state of being contented." Contented is "a feeling satisfaction with one's possession, status, or situation." I have known people who are never contented with what they have or who they are. They are always trying to impress someone or are depressed about their status.

Sometimes, I feel that superintendents need to be more content. I feel that the main reason for their lack of contentment is their lack of status in the eyes of their peers and their earthly possessions. I remember when my brother passed away. All of his earthly possessions were either given away or thrown away. Then I thought to myself, "Why am I so proud of my earthly possessions?" Is this truly contentment? Am I really just trying to keep up with everyone else and have deceived myself into thinking that "all of these things" will make me content and will impress others? I had to ask the Lord to search my motives and then ask Him for forgiveness. Since that day, I've been happier and more content than I've ever been in my life. I have given it all to the Lord and said, "Not my will but thy will be done."

There are many Bible verses that talk about being contented and the following were selected to bless and guide you. Psalms 37:7 says, "Fret not thyself because of him who prospereth in his way." Psalms 37:16 says, "A little that a righteous man hath is better than the riches of many wicked." Finally, Proverbs 16:8 reads, "Better is a little with righteousness than great revenues without right."

> *I have set my heart on a pilgrimage with God – a journey.*
> *At the end of the road, God waits.*
> *By my side, He walks.*
> *His glory shining a light to show the path,*
> *His presence to encourage, comfort, and protect,*
> *His joy to add delight along the way.*
> *I trust in You, O Lord, and persevere.*
> *I put one foot in front of the other,*
> *keeping my eyes on You.*
> *And You, O Lord, do not disappoint,*
> *but always keep Your promises to me.*
> *I praise you, God for Your unfailing love*
> *and Your wonderful gifts of blessing.*

–Carlyn Sullivan

**I have held many things in my hands, and have lost them all;
but whatever I have placed in God's hands, that I still possess.**
–Martin Luther

Losing Courage

And as soon as we had heard these things, our hearts did melt, neither did there remain any more courage in any man, because of you: for the LORD your God, he is God in heaven above, and in earth beneath. Joshua 2:11

Moses sent twelve spies into the promise land to scout it out. They brought back the fruit of the land but ten brought back bad reports. They told the people there were giants with iron chariots.

The people became extremely fearful. Only two had given a good report but they listened to the 10 who gave the bad report. They had forgotten how God had helped them through the wilderness for 40 years, helped them escape Egypt, provided food and water for them in the desert, and totally sustained them.

Have you ever lost courage because of a bad report from your administrators or someone you trusted? Did you lose courage? Did your stomach turns into a knot? Were you on the edge of developing an ulcer? Did you feel like you just wanted to quit and get out?

Did you feel like everyone was against you and the board was breathing down your neck? Did you just have a closed-door meeting with the board president and it did not go well? He told you that you were lazy and didn't fit in the district. He forgot all about the good you've done for the district. Under your leadership, buildings were built, test scores improved, and teacher morale was up. The board president forgot those "wins" when he was out in the community and listened to a "few giants" who were jealous of the superintendent.

When you are downhearted and on the verge of losing courage, take it to Jesus in prayer. Put all of your cares on him and remember, Jesus has everything under control. He is with you in your time of trial and will safely see you through

> *See the mighty host advancing, Satan leading on;*
> *Mighty ones around us falling, courage almost gone!*
> *Hold the fort for I am coming, Jesus signals still;*
> *Wave the answer back to Heaven, By thy grace we will.*
>   –Philip Bliss

Don't lose heart and don't lose courage. Jesus has your back!

When You Can't Be Refreshed

***The Lord give mercy unto the house of Onesiphorus; for he oft refreshed me, and was not ashamed of my chains.* II Timothy 1:16**

I was visiting Glacier National Park and traveled on the *Road to the Sun* to a lodge at the top of the pass. The road was steep. I had to pay attention because it was a long way down if I went over the edge. We arrived at the lodge and then decided to hike about two miles to this glacial lake that was on the Continental Divide. At the far end of the lake was a glacier touching the water.

It was a hot July day, and there was not a single cloud in the sky. By the time we reached the lake, we were hot and sweaty. The water was crystal clear and looked so refreshing. I thought that it would be so nice to wade in to refresh myself, but when I stuck my foot in the water, it was so cold that I quickly pulled it out. It felt like someone had put my foot in a vice grip and was applying pressure. I didn't know the water was frigid cold and probably about one degree above freezing.

There I stood sweating, but I couldn't be refreshed because the water was extremely frigid. There are times as a superintendent, you are "sweating" because of some issue or problem and at the end, you see a "light" and you feel you will be refreshed. When it doesn't come, disappointment sets in. Hang on because the Lord has calmed the storm!

There are situations when you can't be refreshed. Find those people who will refresh you like Onesiphorus did for Paul even though he was in chains. Sometimes our situation will drive people away from us because they don't want to be associated with us. Understand this, the Lord will refresh you and there are people whom the Lord will bring into your life who will "refresh" you.

> *I thirsted in the barren land of sin and shame*
> *And nothing satisfying there I found*
> *But to the blessed cross of Christ one day I came*
> *Where springs of living water did abound*
> *Drinking at the springs of living water*
> *Happy now am I, my soul is satisfied*
> *Drinking at the springs of living water*

**Let us touch the dying, the poor, the lonely and the unwanted
according to the graces we have received and
let us not be ashamed or slow to do the humble work.**
–Mother Teresa

Focus On Significance

Don't copy the behavior and customs of this world, but let God transform you into a new person by changing the way you think. Then you will learn to know God's will for you, which is good and pleasing and perfect. **Romans 12:2**

Have you ever stopped and thought about your leadership style? Would others view you the way you view yourself? I Corinthians 12:5-6 says, "There are different kinds of service, but we serve the same Lord. God works in different ways, but it is the same God who does the work in all of us." The Bible provides us with some wonderful examples of both good and bad leadership. The foundation of all leadership lies within our relationships with others.

As Christians, we know that relationships are ultimately what matter most. Our relationships with others and our relationship with God are the keys to our success as a superintendent. When we lose sight of the people in our lives we often lose sight of God. No matter your position in life, every platform provides us with a unique opportunity to change the world by changing people's lives. Even in prison the apostle Paul gave glory to God and shared with others the story of salvation through Jesus Christ.

Never forget as long as you have breath, God has a purpose for your life. It is only when we start making excuses and conforming to worldly things that we lose focus and create bad habits. By focusing on God, we can gain more fulfillment and energy in our relationships, on the job, and in other important pursuits. When we focus on God, we can begin to live a life of significance!

"This book of the law shall not depart out of your mouth, but you shall mediate on it day and night, that you may be careful to do according to all that is written in it; for then you shall make your way prosperous, and then you shall have good success" (Joshua 1:8). When you pause to think about your leadership style, or the leader you want to become, let me first challenge you to think about your purpose. Is your focus on God?

When we focus on God, He promises to make our way "prosperous" so that we might have "good success." Additionally, when we focus on God, we place greater value on the relationships we have with those around us. This allows us to look for ways to serve others, which ultimately benefits us, those we care about, and our organization.

Turn your eyes upon Jesus,
Look full in His wonderful face,
And the things of earth will grow strangely dim,
In the light of His glory and grace.
–Helen Lemmel

Preach the gospel at all times; when necessary, use words.
–St. Francis of Assisi

Save Others by Pulling Them from the Fire

Keep yourselves in the love of God, looking for the mercy of our Lord Jesus Christ unto eternal life. And of some have compassion, making a difference. And others save with fear, pulling them out of the fire, hating even the garment spoiled by the flesh. **Jude 21-23**

If you see your employees doing things in error, is your first reaction to fire them? Or do you want to help them grow by providing them training and extra professional development opportunities? Of course it matters if the error is illegal or an act that would harm others, then you may need to ask the employee to resign or even file for potential charges. There are many times it would be easy to ignore some problems rather than tackle the problems in an open and direct manner with the person who has erred.

The conversations that need to be made may not be comfortable, but a person will not learn or understand the need for change without them. The style of the conversation needs to be chosen carefully based on the needs and emotional style of the listener. Some people need to be told bluntly what they are doing wrong, while others need a more gentle approach. Strong leaders understand people and situations. They are able to adjust their own conversational style based on those situations.

Leaders understand they have the responsibility to save people from the fire. They also understand people are more willing to listen and follow a leader's suggestions when there is already an established rapport based on a leader being respectful and honest. A leader that has already shown himself/herself to be of a high moral character will find it easier to work with people. This does not mean that the moral leader uses high character as a religious zealot, but rather as a humble servant.

Let nothing be done through strife or vainglory; but in lowliness of mind let each esteem other better than themselves. Philippians 2:3

When you find the need to talk with an employee about an error, it is important to check your facts and make sure you have planned how and what you will say to the employee. There are times the employee will want to cover up or blame someone else for the error. Again, here is where it is important to have your facts. You need to present the facts very straightforward. It is also important to be specific about the change that you expect and then follow up on the actions. All of these actions are the leader's attempts to make sure this employee is not doomed to eternal damnation.

**And they went up on the breadth of the earth, and compassed
the camp of the saints about, and the beloved city;
and fire came down from God out of heaven
and devoured them. Revelations 20:9**

Accepting Gifts

***The king by judgment establisheth the land: but he that receiveth gifts overthroweth it.* Proverbs 29:4**

Many states have laws prohibiting superintendents from accepting gifts from vendors. Why do you think this is so? The reason is illustrated by the following example:

A private birthday party at an upscale steakhouse, Houston Rockets playoff tickets, checks totaling $30,000, and the offer of a personal loan for an undisclosed sum were given to Houston Independent School District employees by private companies seeking millions of dollars worth of technology contracts with the school system, public records show.

These practices brought federal sanctions, costing the district around $1 million in direct costs and the loss of another $105 million in federal technology funding. In addition, it cost the administrators their jobs. In one school district, an official is serving prison time.

I know of a superintendent who had vendors—insurance companies, technology companies, service companies, etc.—give him gifts. Early in his career, he accepted the gifts, he then found out he was breaking the law.

What was he accepting? They were small gifts, but nevertheless they were gifts. He was given a leather folder, steak dinners at up-scale restaurants, and a box ticket at a major university for a basketball game. He thought it was okay, as there were other superintendents with him. When he found out that he was breaking the law, he stopped. He said he was blinded by the cordiality of the vendors and justified it by saying, "We don't have a contract with these people, they are just being nice." His conscious pricked him and he asked the Lord to forgive him.

This type of practice is extremely deceitful and clouds the mind of the superintendent in regards to accepting bids and companies to do certain work for the district. The devil works the same way. He'll promise you riches untold and fame but his payoff is death, hell, and the grave. Don't let your values be compromised. Keep your eyes on Jesus and ask him to protect you from the temptations. Jesus is your guiding hand.

Jesus, Savior, pilot me,
Over life's tempestuous sea!
Unknown waves before me roll,
Hiding rock and treacherous shoal
–Unknown

The temptations of the "freebie" will get you a free ticket from your job and possible free ticket in a state penal institution.

Allow Me to Hate

Alexander the coppersmith did me much evil: the Lord reward him according to his works. II Timothy 4:14

In the movie, *The Count of Monte Cristo*, Dantes said to his bride when they married fifteen years later, "If you love me, allow me to hate." He had been unjustly accused of treason by his best friend and was sentenced to the notorious prison Chateau d'If. After his escape, hate and vengeance drove him as he planned revenge on his friend and the two other people who falsely accused him. The friend who betrayed him was driven by envy and jealousy. He wanted everything Dantes had, but most of all he wanted Dantes' betrothed bride for himself. At the end of the movie, Dantes bought the Chateau d'If with the intention of tearing it down, and he was able to put the hate and vengeance behind him. He kept the notorious prison and proclaimed that his wealth will be used for good.

As a superintendent, you will have people come into your life who will falsely accuse you of things and try to assassinate your career. Their envy and hate towards you is so great that they don't care what they do to you and your family. Your mind will play scenes of how you can get revenge and get even with them over and over again. But you have to let it go and remember, "God has everything under control" and "greater is he that is within you, than he that is within the world." In Romans 12:19 (NIV), Paul wrote, "Do not take revenge [...] but leave room for God's wrath, for it is written: 'It is mine to avenge; I will repay,' says the Lord." The only one who will suffer will be you because of the hate driving you.

I've been around superintendents who have been unjustly treated who can't seem to get past it. They always bring up the past and retell the story. It reminds me of Mr. Ed, a principal I worked for in Washington state. He was unjustly fired. It took him two years of court battles to get his job back. Mr. Ed was a very nice man but he could never get past how he was treated even though he was reinstated. Every time you saw Mr. Ed, he would talk about the past. If this is you, ask the Lord to cleanse your mind; don't let that evil take hold of your heart.

> *Create in me a clean heart, oh God,*
> *And renew a right spirit within me.*
> *Cast me not away from Thy presence,*
> *Restore unto me the joy of Thy salvation*
> –Unknown

Don't allow your adversary to put a "ring in your nose" and lead you around which is what happens when their actions drive you to vengeance and hate.

Authority

Wherefore neither thought I myself worthy to come unto thee, but say in a word, and my servant shall be healed. For I also am a man set under authority, having under me soldiers, and I say unto one, Go, and he goeth, and to another, Come, and he cometh, and to my servant, Do this and he doeth it. Luke 7:7-8

We obey laws because it is the right thing to do. Many laws are established in order to protect people. We have lower speed limits near schools so people slow down and watch for children. We have seat belt laws so that people will have more protection if there is an accident.

As leaders, we give directions we believe to be good for our employees or are law, and we expect others to follow our directions. We don't have to check on everyone to ensure directions are followed. People, who work for us, may not always agree with our decisions, but the position calls for respect. Leaders do not want employees who undermine their decisions. They want employees to be sincere and try to understand why decisions have to be made in regards to state and federal laws. But employees also want leaders to be fair in their decisions. Therefore, the respect for authority has requirements for both the leader as well as the employees.

The leader in the bible reference was a centurion who wanted his servant healed. He had sent friends to ask Jesus to heal his servant. He did not feel worthy enough to have Jesus come to his home but he understood Jesus' authority to heal. He did not believe Jesus had to come in order for that authority to work. The centurion believed in Jesus' word.

The role of a leader is usually defined with expectations from their boards. The roles give certain levels of authority while also restricting other areas of authority. For example, many superintendents may be granted authority to make purchases for a school district to amounts up to $25,000. However, any purchase higher requires a board vote and thus the leader is restricted to a certain amount. A leader's decisions should be examined for fulfilling the requirements and expectations that serve the best interest of an organization. A leader's word holds the most power when the power is used in a fair manner that serves others.

Servants, be obedient to them that are your masters according to the flesh, with fear and trembling, in singleness of your heart unto Christ: Not with eye service, as men pleasers; but as the servants of Christ doing the will of God from the heart; With good will doing service, as to the Lord and not to men; Knowing that whatsoever good thing any man doeth, the same shall he receive of the Lord, whether he be bond or free. And ye masters, do the same things unto them, forbearing threatening; knowing that your Master also is in heaven; neither is there respect of person with him. Ephesians 6:5-9

Because power corrupts, society's demands for moral authority and character increase as the importance of the position increases.

–John Adams

Helping Widows

Rejoice with them that do rejoice; and weep with them that weep. **Romans 12:15**

One of the hardest experiences to handle for a leader is the death of an employee or an employee's spouse. Whether expected or unexpected, as a leader, you must communicate factually with other employees while being sensitive to the needs of the surviving spouse. This requires you to meet with the survivor so to better understand their wishes. You should help support the survivor with the immediate needs as well as following up later with continued support. It is important to find ways to help and comfort them.

There are a variety of ways to help, home repair or lawn maintenance, locating volunteers with their needs, but one of the most important ways to help is to check with them often and listen to them. There may be times that they want to talk about their deceased spouse. Or there may be times they want a distraction from the death. Either way, if you listen to them, that should guide the conversation.

Some other ways to help is to provide snacks and quick meals. Often survivors don't feel like eating, or they simply forget to eat. Inviting them out allows for time with others and gets them out of their house.

There are no short term fixes when people lose their spouse. This will be a long journey for them. At times, they seem fine and other times they may have many needs. Jesus provided several examples of helping those in need. He understood the pain of death. He also understood how others could help in times of loss. We must find the ways to help our employees and especially in times when there has been a death of a spouse.

Two widows from Bible days long ago,
Forgotten by name, but not by deed,
Both teach us how we should respond whenever God shows us a need.
In plenty we're all quick to give, but slower when cupboards are bare.
God, move us to share in your work to show by our gifts that we care.
–Mary N. Keithahn

Pure religion and undefiled before God and the Father is this,
to visit the fatherless and widows in their affliction,
and to keep himself unspotted from the world. James 1:27

Interdependence

And let us consider one another to provoke unto love and to good works; not forsaking the assembly of ourselves together, as the manner of some is, but exhorting one another: and so much the more, as ye see the day approaching. **Hebrews 10: 24-25**

God created us to be with each other and not to live in isolation. His creation of a man was followed by Eve so man would not be alone. People need each other for their emotional and spiritual well-being and thus their physical well-being.

The church community is a place where relationships are established to help each other. The relationships with family, friends, and coworkers take time, but it is time well spent so that you will be able to help each other when you see a need or an opportunity. Many people believe others are strong when they are independent. Yet, throughout the Bible, we get a sense that we are meant to be connected with each other for our strength.

We are meant to depend on our Lord. We are stronger with each other because we all have different strengths and gifts. We can help each other in our daily Christian walk as we help meet each other's needs. Our unique gifts were granted so that we must work together. Our gifts were given to be shared and not kept to ourselves. It does us very little good to have a gift and then not use it in God's honor.

Our interdependence does not mean we rely on others to support us or fulfill our needs without doing anything. We are expected to work but the expectation is not to fulfill ourselves but rather to have something to share with others. The words of the Bible are clear: we should work hard and not be lazy. This independence is not to be seen as working in isolation. We remember that we all rely on God and our work should bring glory to God. Leaders are often able to help guide a community and foster strong relationships that encourage each other to find ways to support each other and be interdependent.

For life in its fullness, put love in control
Love God with your heart, with your body and soul.
And see all your neighbors? Go love them as well,
And care for each one as you care for yourself.
                                        –Ken Bible

Bear ye one another's burdens, and so fulfill the law of Christ. Galatians 6:2

Leadership

Thus saith the Lord, thy Redeemer, the Holy One of Israel; I am the Lord thy God which teacheth thee to profit, which leadeth thee by the way that thou shouldest go. Isaiah 48:7

Many leaders read a lot of books and attend professional development seminars to improve their leadership skills. I often wonder if leaders spend as much time studying the leadership in the Bible.

Jesus provided a wonderful example of leadership. He knew the word of God and was prepared to discuss this with scholars of His day. He used many examples that people could relate to, such as nature, farming, and soldier type examples. These examples were understood by the people. He answered questions that were meant to trap him.

I have realized that when people want to challenge me for the sack of embarrassment, often it is better to respond with questions. They respond less aggressively. The Bible models other leadership skills through many people. Joshua was one of those strong leaders who learned from Moses and God. He followed Moses and courageously scouted lands before going in to conquer them. He followed God's directions and thus was able to have success.

As leaders, we are expected to be knowledgeable about our jobs. Our boards, community members, and faculty want us to lead them and answer their questions and concerns. There is an expectation that we have the vision to guide the organization to success. This requires our constant attention to details.

Leaders must watch changes in the law. They are responsible for following all the rules and regulations that impact the organization. It is the leader's responsibility to guide others so they understand all the regulations. Leaders must manage the resources of an organization so that growth is possible. Additionally, leaders must involve many people from different agencies and organizations to enlist the help of the entire community in support of the organization.

> *Lord, you are the rock and there is no other,*
> *A tower of strength, You are my shelter*
> *Lord, You are my hope eternal*
> *You are the rock that is higher than I.*
> *Lead me to the rock.*
> –Paul Baloche

**But sanctify the Lord God in your hearts and be ready always
to give an answer to every man that asketh you a reason
of the hope that is in you with meekness and fear. I Peter 3:15**

Make the Most of Your Time

But one thing is needful: and Mary hath chosen that good part, which shall not be taken away from her. Luke 10:42

My wife and I were sitting at the breakfast table planning a trip to visit our children and grandchildren over Spring break. Our son called the night before and asked if we were going to be arriving Friday night or Saturday morning. We talked about it, called him back later that evening, and said we'd be getting in around 10:30 p.m. on Friday night. He was extremely happy. He said he could take me to a men's prayer breakfast and then we could all go watch his kids' soccer and basketball games. He didn't tell us his plans earlier because he didn't want to be disappointed if we told him we couldn't make it until Saturday.

The next day, as we sat down to eat our breakfast, my wife started to sob. She was holding back the tears, but could no longer contain them. I said, "What's wrong?" She replied, "I want to make the most of my time with my kids. I remember when we were visiting our son at the Naval Academy and he asked if we were going to attend church with him the Sunday before we left to go home and I said I don't know because we might be sleeping in. We woke up earlier than anticipated and went to church and there was our son sitting alone." She went on to say how that has bothered her for a long time and from that time forward, she had purposed in her heart that she would always make time for her kids as time on earth is so precious and fleeting.

How often as a superintendent do we say to our family, "I don't have the time to spend with you?" Or we say, "Not now, but later." Our spouse and our children, most likely will say, "Ok" but, inside they will be hurting. We only get to spend quality time with our children once when they are little and when they are grown and out of the house, it'll be too late. Don't let the job become more important than God and your family. If you've done this, or you can see that you are going down this path, then change your focus of what is important. It will be healthy to your faith, family, health, and career.

Dear Lord, Jesus, please forgive me if I've not prioritized my life correctly.
Help me always to put you first in my life,
Let my family always be second in my life after You.
Help me to always place my job last after my family.

To find favor with the Lord, put him first in your life
and your job last and your family will be ever grateful.

Mentors

And when Saul was come to Jerusalem, he assayed to join himself to the disciplines; but they were all afraid of him, and believed not that he was a disciple. But Barnabas took him, and brought him to the apostles, and declared unto them how he had seen the Lord in the way, and that he had spoken to him and how he had preached boldly at Damascus in the name of Jesus. Acts 9:26-27

When I was a teacher leader, I found people who were willing to help, answer questions, and support me when I made mistakes. I found this to be true also when I became an administrator. Many other administrators stepped up to help me feel comfortable in my new leadership role. They answered multitudes of questions while making me feel like I was able to do the job. After years of administrative leadership, I hope I have been able to help others new to the field. Any mentorship opportunities with new administrators were welcomed. I wanted other new leaders to feel the same support I had been given.

And he said to his disciples, "Therefore I tell you, do not be anxious about your life, what you will eat, nor about your body, what you will put on. For life is more than food, and the body more than clothing. Consider the ravens: they neither sow nor reap, they have neither storehouse nor barn, and yet God feeds them. Of how much more value are you than the birds! And which of you by being anxious can add a single hour to his span of life? If then you are not able to do as small a thing as that, why are you anxious about the rest? Luke 12:22-34

I wonder if the disciples felt mentorship from Jesus. Jesus let them ask questions. He shared many examples and made connections to stories that would help them understand concepts of leadership. When they went out on their own and did not find success, it was Jesus who guided them to understand. He constantly showed his disciples they needed to trust in God. Jesus also taught them to determine the most important issues, which have eternal significance.

As you think about mentorship, you may decide at times to be the mentor and other times to be the mentee. Mentorship takes time. One of the most important elements of mentoring is building a trusting relationship. There needs to be a give and take. It is wonderful when you find a person that is willing to help you grow as a professional and who also gains value from you.

> *Mentor me, O God, and know my heart today,*
> *Teach me, O Savior, know my thoughts, I pray;*
> *See if there needs to be some adjustments made in me;*
> *Please, open my mind to your mentoring and develop me.*
> –James Orr

And when he had found him, he brought him unto Antioch.
And it came to pass, that a whole year they assembled themselves
with the church, and taught much people.
And the disciples were called Christians first in Antioch. Acts 11:26

Real Love

Greater love hath no man than this, that a man lay down his life for his friends.
John 15:13

A few nights ago, I was watching a program about wild animal babies. It was so interesting because of the instinct God built into those animals to care for their young. They showed what musk oxen do when one of their young is threatened by a hungry wolf or bear. The entire herd gets together, shoulder-to-shoulder, with their horns facing outwards with the calves in the middle. The predator gets the point in a hurry that they aren't going to get one of those calves. They are protected. The mother bear fights to the death to protect her cubs. The lioness fights to the death to protect her cubs. In fact, almost all of the animals have a protective instinct. Even alligators keep by their young for a while to keep away predators.

One species of spider caught my attention. This mother has many baby spiders who are aggressive and eat each other. As they grow larger, they crawl upon the mother and start eating her. She gives her life for her little baby spiders!

I know, as a parent, I will give my life for my children. I will, as the saying goes, "go to the mat for them." This bond and love is so strong it transcends all feelings. A soldier has such great love for his country and fellow soldiers that he will give his life to save theirs. These soldiers are then usually given a great honor posthumously. God loved the world so much that He gave His only begotten son (John 3:16). How many of you would give your child to be sacrificed? God did! He did this for our salvation!

Could we with ink the ocean fill,
And were the skies of parchment made,
Were every stalk on earth a quill,
And every man a scribe by trade,
To write the love of God above,
Would drain the ocean dry.
Nor could the scroll contain the whole,
Though stretched from sky to sky.
                                        –Fredrick Lehman

God loves each of us as if there were only one of us.
                                        –St. Augustine

February 15

Now is the Best Time

So teach us to number our days, that we may apply our hearts unto wisdom.
Psalms 90:12

As a superintendent, you need to know the best time for many situations, one example being board packets for your board meetings. Board packets of information must be prepared and sent to board members with enough time for them to read prior to the meeting. You must also know your board members' schedules so you know when it is best to contact them in order to determine if they have any questions.

Knowing the best time to start a bond campaign is another example of timing. Leaders need to have a clear vision of the readiness and capability of a community to support a bond. There is an emotional commitment as well as a financial commitment that is needed for a bond passage.

These are just a couple of examples for knowing the best time for school leaders to take actions. But it is even more important to understand when it is the best time to accept Jesus and follow His ways and plans for our lives. In order to fully enjoy life on earth as well as to have eternal life, we must know that the time is now to make sure you are right with the Lord. Only Jesus can provide a truly contented and purposeful life. You don't want to miss the opportunities the Lord has planned for us.

The Lord has planned outstanding things for each of us who follow Him. Now is the best time to follow Jesus. There is no guarantee of tomorrow or even another minute. The best time to ask for His forgiveness is the instance we find out that we have not followed His narrow path. The best time to do what is right is immediately. Many times we wait too long when we know what the Lord expects from us. Is your heart right with God?

> *Now is the time to seek the Lord,*
> *Arise and Him obey;*
> *Why will you not believe His word?*
> *O hasten, don't delay!*
> —Elisha Hoffman

Therefore to whom that knoweth to do good, and doeth it not, to him it is sin. James 4:17

Service with Compassion

Then shall the King say unto them on His right hand, come, ye blessed of my Father, inherit the kingdom prepared for you from the foundation of the world. For I was hungred, and ye gave me meat, I was thirsty, and ye gave me drink. I was a stranger, and ye took me in. Naked, and ye clothed me. I was in prison, and ye came unto me. Then shall the righteous answer him, saying, Lord, when saw we thee hungered and fed thee? Or thirsty, and gave thee drink? When saw we thee sick, or in prison, and came unto thee? And the King shall answer and say unto them, Verily I say unto you, Inasmuch as ye have done it unto one of the least of these my brethren, ye have done it unto me. **Matthew 25:34-40**

As superintendents, we often have the opportunity to see people in our community who may be struggling from a multitude of different circumstances. We can marshal the help of others in order to serve the people who have needs. When we guide others to help with acts of compassion, it is important not to take extra credit for our work. Compassion comes from our inward desire to have strong concern for others' welfare. The desire is not egocentric or an attempt to make ourselves look good.

But whoso hath this world's good, and seeth his brother have need, and shutteth up his bowels of compassion from him, how dwelleth the love of God in him? My little children, let us not love in word, neither in tongue, but in deed and in truth.
I John 3: 17-18

Another way to help others is to guide children to learn about the strong character traits of compassion. This can be done by requiring children to participate in service projects, such as collecting food for a local food pantry, grooming and walking shelter dogs, picking up garbage at parks or along roadways, making cards for those in the hospital, collecting coats and clothing, reading to younger children, visiting elderly people, or playing with a child who has disabilities. There are many other possible service projects. Most don't require any money, rather the requirement is time and compassion.

The benefits are not just for those receiving the help. The benefits are for the children to learn strong compassion with humility. Another benefit is seen as many college admission criteria and scholarship criteria have components of service. College admission administrators and scholarship grantors want to see students who have participated well in service in addition to their academic achievements. That can't be the reason for completing the service projects, but it can be a by-product of serving others with compassion. Christ had compassion on the multitudes!

Love sought me, mercy found me
But it was grace, that set me free.
Love saw my teardrops, mercy had compassion
But it was grace that set me free.

Finally, all of you, live in harmony with one another; be sympathetic, love as brothers, be compassionate and humble. I Peter 3:8

Standing up for the Truth

For we can do nothing against the truth, but for the truth. **II Corinthians 13:8**

Lily Tomlin said, "After all, what is reality anyway? Nothing but a collective hunch." This statement echoes Howard Bloom's article that's titled, "Reality is a Shared Hallucination." Lily Tomlin and Howard Bloom are clueless on what the truth is or are ignorant about the matter. And when people say, "Perception is reality," as Stephen Baldwin said, "They're just too lazy to find out the truth."

A trait school boards desire in their superintendent, more than anything else, is honesty. I was sitting in a school board meeting the other day listening to a deputy superintendent and technology director "spin" the truth so the board would vote positively on a technology request. What they said wasn't wrong so much as what was they left out that intrigued me. They forgot to do their homework or even identify how this request would improve student achievement.

The mainstream media tells stories and distorts the truth by doing journalistic somersaults. The problem is once an article gets printed the public thinks it's the truth and it's harder to defend the truth. This is how media shapes opinion. With advanced technological devices and social media, such as Facebook, Twitter, Skype, Texting, iPads, Smartphones, and so forth, false rumors get out faster than lightning. As a superintendent, I always marveled at how fast false rumors spread in a community or school, and this was before advanced technology. When this "lie" was spread, you ended up spending a lot of precious time putting out the unnecessary fire and getting the truth out.

It is necessary for a superintendent to stand up and speak the truth. The superintendent has to have courage. It will be healthy to your career and your health. If you have a hard time with being truthful or feel pressured by political groups to be untruthful in certain matters, then pray this prayer as King David prayed, "You desire truth in the inner being; make me therefore to know wisdom in my inmost heart" (Psalms 51:6).

There are times the truth is hard to hear,
It's questioned, before it reaches our ear.
When truth's been disguised, it's difficult to recognize,
But when revealed it's a surprise.
The place to go for real truth to discover,
Is God's Word, as it's contained between the covers.
God gave His word to man so he will live a truthful life,
While dealing with events that cause him trouble and strife.

It is taught, throughout the Bible,
that you should always tell the truth,
don't lie, and don't be a false witness.

Substitute

For he hath made him to be sin for us, who knew no sin; that we might be made the righteousness of God in him. **II Corinthians 5:21**

One of the hardest jobs I ever had was as a substitute teacher. As a substitute teacher, every time you come into a new classroom, you are faced with a new environment and a new group of students. The students know each other, but they know they may never see you again. The classroom climate varies by the way their regular teachers have established classroom expectations, rules, and procedures. Even in the most disciplined of classrooms, there is new content at a variety of grade levels that are expected of the substitute. It was helpful if I brought some of my own activities that could be used when the teacher's regularly planned activities were completed. This helped me have control in the classroom if there was additional time to fill.

My role as a substitute teacher helped me in my own classroom. It was important for me to prepare my students well so that they would show respect and be able to help the substitute teachers. Additionally, it was important that substitute teachers feel comfortable with the class and want to return to the class.

My role as a substitute teacher also helped me as a building principal. I felt it was my role to help all substitute teachers to feel welcome on my campus. It was important that they knew where to get information and supplies, as well as where to locate the restrooms and break rooms. Many times my administrative assistant would help with this. I encourage all the teachers to help a substitute. Additionally, each teacher had developed a substitute folder with information about their class, procedures, material, and students.

The idea of a substitute shows up in the Bible also. Jesus was the substitute for our sins. It was John the Baptist that led the way to Jesus prior to the arrival of Jesus. He was telling others about Jesus.

> *Jesus paid it all,*
> *All to Him I owe;*
> *Sin had left a crimson stain,*
> *He washed it white as snow.*
> –Elvina Hall

The next day John seeth Jesus coming unto him and saith,
Behold the Lamb of God, which taketh away the sin of the world. John 1:29

The Sudoku Puzzles

The fear of the Lord is the beginning of knowledge: but fools despise wisdom and instruction **Proverbs 1:7**

Have you ever played the Sudoku puzzles? There are different levels which usually range from one for "very easy" to four for "very hard." I got myself into the habit of trying to play and complete these mind-challenging puzzles. It has become a competition for me to see how many I can complete. I am now at the point where I can complete the level one and two puzzles with relative ease, even the level three doesn't give me much trouble, but the level four puzzles are a challenge. If I can successfully complete half the puzzles, I will feel very good.

The other day, I was working on a level four puzzle and came to a point where I was stuck. I had this one square of numbers completed except for two blanks. I knew that four and seven would complete that box but I didn't know where to put the four or seven. I had a fifty/fifty chance. So after much consideration, I guessed. The puzzle fell into place and I felt happy with myself that I had guessed correctly until I got to the very end. That is when I found out I guessed wrong. I made so many decisions based on that one wrong decision, and I ended up with numerous errors. It was next to impossible to fix the puzzle without looking at the answer.

This is an example of what happens when you leave Jesus out of your decision making, personal life, and/or professional life. One mistake piles upon another and it gets to the point that you can't fix the mess you're in. You then must turn to the book of answers, the Bible, to help you out of your predicament. The same also happens with your job. If you don't do your homework thoroughly and operate by "the seat of your pants," you will make mistakes that will be impossible to correct, and it will cost you your job. If you don't know what to do, call your colleagues, research the literature, and most of all, ask the Lord for WISDOM.

> *Wisdom and knowledge are intertwined*
> *They safeguard against mistakes*
> *When you guess you take down the alarms*
> *And the failure you experience will do you harm.*

When you guess, your answer is not blessed because you left Jesus out.

The Body

But in fact God has arranged the parts in the body, every one of them, just as he wanted them to be. I Corinthians 12:18

An effective body has all its parts and works in harmony. All parts can't be the same. Paul specifically mentioned this when he said, "if the whole body were an eye, how would you hear? Or if your whole body were an ear, how would you smell anything?" (I Corinthians 12:17). So it is in the school. There are many parts and they are all crucial to the effectiveness of the school. No one part is more important than another.

If we were all math teachers, who would teach science? If we were all teachers, who would be the attendance clerk? If we were all secretaries, who would be the bus driver? As you can see, the parts are many and each is needed. The bus driver brings children to school and takes them home. The secretary keeps records and correspondence up-to-date while making a great welcoming presence for the school. The cook provides the meals to feed the kids so they can learn. The janitor keeps the bathrooms and halls clean, takes out the trash, and so forth so there is a quality clean learning environment. Administrators keep the school and district running in their various functions. All parts are essential.

The same is true in sports. In basketball, all can't be a guard or a forward or a center or a trainer. There needs to be a team that is fine-tuned with all parts working together. The same is true with us. Wherever you are, make your strengths strong, and minimize your weaknesses. If, as a superintendent, you are strong in finance, hire an administrator who is strong in curriculum. Don't allow yourself to get to the point where you hire more than "one nose" because the other "nose" is lazy or incompetent. That is as bad as not having a "nose" at all. Everyone has their role and every position is important. Be that sunbeam in your job for Jesus!

Jesus wants me for a sunbeam
To shine for Him each day;
In every way try to please Him,
At home, at work, at play.

You may never have proof of your importance
but you are more important than you think.
                                                    –Robert Fulghum

The Evilness of Envy

Wrath is cruel, and anger is outrageous; but who is able to stand before envy?
Proverbs 27:4

Envy begins when we believe we have failed. We think we should have gotten a position or job because we're entitled to it. When someone else gets that position, we slowly become filled with resentment. This then manifests itself in us by giving us a "bad attitude."

Envy shows itself in stages. The first stage is regret. You were in competition for a superintendent position and despite your best interview effort, you saw someone else, possibly your friend get offered the job. You have nothing to be ashamed of. If you are gracious, you will congratulate the new superintendent and wish him, or her, well. Losses are good for us because they build character.

The second stage is resentment. This is harmful to you, your body, and your career. Rancor can be expressed by ill will, such as wishing the new superintendent receives bad press, poor evaluations, or makes a bad decision. This is harmful because it festers in your soul like a sore. Antisthenes wrote over 2,400 years ago, "As iron is eaten away by rust, so the envious are consumed by their own passion." Malicious acts originate from thoughts, making the second stage harmful. It leads to the third stage: hateful actions. This is why envy is taken seriously in the Bible. "A sound heart is the life of the flesh: but envy is the rottenness of the bones" (Proverbs 14:30). Also, Exodus 20:17 states explicitly that you should not covet anything of your neighbors. This leads to spreading hateful rumors, lying, tormenting ourselves and ultimately to crimes committed because of hate.

Do you envy a fellow superintendent? Then be a friend and express your admiration for his or her accomplishment. He or she will be happy to pass on their tips to you. Use your negative emotions to help you grow and develop into something useful. If someone is envious of you and treats you coldly, be compassionate and friendly back. If you extend your hand in friendship, you may have the power to change their life by your own example. Be like Jesus and treat them good!

Envy and jealousy, they make me so small
Envy and jealousy cause me to fall
Jesus is my only hope to be saved from this torment
Lord please free me from this bondage of sin

Envy is the mud that failures throw at success.

The Jericho Road

If I then, your Lord and Master, have washed your feet; ye also ought to wash one another's feet. **John 13:14**

The Jericho Road is 17 miles long, connecting Jerusalem to Jericho. It is a windy, steep, and narrow road, circling around a large mountain. The elevation drops 3,600 feet. This road was a haven for robbers and hooligans. Jesus used this road when he gave an illustration on being a neighbor.

While traveling from Jerusalem down to Jericho, a Jewish man was attacked by bandits. They stripped him of his clothes, beat him up, and left him half dead beside the road. By chance, a priest came along. When he saw the man lying there, he crossed to the other side of the road and passed him. A Temple assistant walked over, looked at him lying there, and he, too, passed by on the other side. Then, a hated Samaritan came along. When he saw the man, he felt compassion for him. Going over to him, the Samaritan soothed his wounds with olive oil and wine and bandaged them. He put the man on his own donkey, took him to an inn, and cared for him. The next day he handed the innkeeper two silver coins, telling him, "'Take care of this man. If his bill runs higher than this, I'll pay you the next time I'm here.' 'Now which of these three would you say was a neighbor to the man who was attacked by bandits?' Jesus asked. The man replied, 'The one who showed him mercy.' Then Jesus said, 'Yes, now go and do the same'" (Luke 10:30-37 NLT).

There are several lessons superintendents can learn from this parable. The first lesson is an attack against non-involvement. If you don't get involved in your community, you will waste your talents. There is a new sickness spreading across America at warp speed and it's called "non-involvement." The second lesson is that you always "do good," no matter the circumstance. This parable is about people who don't get involved with people who are hurting because of safety, money, time, inconvenience, and busyness. Pray, dear Lord, please don't let me fall in the trap of not helping others. Remember the Lord has compassion and mercy on us.

As we travel along on the Jericho Road
Does the world seem all wrong and heavy your load
Just bring it to Christ your sins all confess
On the Jericho Road your heart will be blessed
On the Jericho Road there's room for just two
No more and no less just Jesus and you
Each burden He'll bear, each sorrow He'll share
There's never a care for Jesus is there

All of us need to have hearts of love for anybody who is hurting on any of the Jericho roads of life.

Three Blind Mice

Children, obey your parents in all things: for this is well pleasing unto the Lord.
Colossians 3:20

Have you heard the story of the three blind mice? Their names are Max, Minerva, and Marvin. Mr. and Mrs. Mouse, their parents, remind me of parents who warn their children against the dangers of life. First these parents tell Max that he should never drink whiskey. But Max is blind to the dangers of drinking. He ignores the advice of his parents and begins to drink. He says, "I'm not afraid because whiskey can't hurt me!" But very soon he's caught in a trap and he's become an alcoholic.

Next, they talk to Minerva and tell her of the dangers of the suggestive and sensuous dances. But she is blind and says, "I'm not afraid to dance suggestively and provocatively with boys as I can take care of myself." She, too, is caught in a trap and her life is spoiled by lecherous men and boys.

Marvin tells his parents that he sees no harm in violent and X rated shows. His father and mother tell him of many boys who have been ruined because of impressions these movies have given them and what they tried to bring to reality. But he says, "That will never happen to me as I'm a smart mouse." Very soon he, too, is caught in a trap because he frequents raunchy movie houses and tries to bring those movies to life.

As a superintendent, you will have these "three blind mice" children attending your school. It will be your duty to provide an environment that takes them away from the snares they have gotten trapped in. Many of these children do not have good role models in their parents. They come from dreadful homes, so you will have to be that role model to your principals, teachers, support people, and the community. Pray that the Lord will help you be the right example for your students and your staff.

Children, learn from your teacher and parents
To always obey your parents for this is right in God's sight.
Honor your father and mother is the first commandment
The school has a duty to make, to train student's right.

Shame on the educators who violate their sacred trust
and do not try to "open the eyes" of the "blind" mice.

Tough Decisions

Saying, Father, if thou be willing, remove this cup from me: nevertheless not my will, but thine, be done. **Luke 22:42**

We had a Bichon Frise named Samson. He was a good little dog, loyal to the end. We were given the dog when he was a year old because his owners were not able to care for him anymore. We had Samson for 7 years. In that time, he became like a child to us. He was so smart. For example, if he had to go outside to do his business, he would come and stand in front of you, open his eyes real wide, and wag his tail real fast.

He loved to go for walks. If you said the word "walk," he would become excited and start running in circles. He loved to go for rides. If you said "Samson, do you want to go for a ride," again, he would get excited, run in circles, go to the side of the car where his doggy bed was and spring into it.

He loved to sit beside you on the couch on his blanket. He'd snuggle right up to your leg, lay his head on your lap, and be content. When we had our devotionals, he'd go right behind my wife, where she was sitting, and lay down until the devotional was over. If I had to go on a trip to visit superintendent interns, he'd be in his doggy bed the whole way in the front seat of the car. He just loved to be with you and was extremely devoted.

If you put Samson outside or go inside while he was outside, he'd come to the door and wait for you. Samson loved my wife. He was always about two feet behind her wherever she was.

What does all this have to do with tough decisions? Samson got sick and we had to put him to sleep. That was an extremely tough decision and it was all I could do to hold back the tears, pay the bill, and talk to my wife without weeping. Then I thought about the *tough decision* the Lord made on our behalf when he offered up His only son to die on the cross for our sins. What love and what a sacrifice. Sometimes as a superintendent, you'll have to make a tough decision that will rip out your heart. Remember, the Lord is there to help you and sustain you.

> *After man's first fall, why the Lord of all in His majesty supreme,*
> *Fell upon a plan to redeem the man to His former high esteem,*
> *But a sacrifice was required to splice, every flaw we make today*
> *So the Lamb who died all our sins to hide, volunteered to softly say.*
> *Send me, send me, to set them freed.*
> –Otis L. McCoy

Making the tough decision for the right reason will always be the right decision.

Use It or Lose It

But continue thou in the things which thou hast learned and hast been assured of, knowing of whom thou has learned them; And that from a child thou hast known the holy scriptures, which are able to make thee wise unto salvation through faith which is in Christ Jesus. All scripture is given by inspiration of God, and is profitable for doctrine, for reproof, for correction, for instruction in righteousness: That the man of God may perfect, thoroughly furnished unto all good works. II Timothy 3:14-17

As we study scripture, we should think about the reasons we study. Do we read the Bible because it is has become a habit or routine? If so, then it isn't really studying the Bible. Perhaps you study the Bible to gain an understanding of the past. Do you study the Bible so you can find the significance of the Word with the application to our daily lives?

Once we try to examine scriptures for a guide to our lives, we will find other references helpful. I have a Bible dictionary and a Concordance that I use in my study. Studying the Bible becomes an in-depth search for more information, often leading to internet searches on topics and related Bible references. Close examination of others and their reactions to different experiences can help us understand how people have applied scripture and faith to their experiences. Sometimes different reactions to similar situations can be closely examined in an attempt to understand how people respond to God and how the Bible explains God's responses.

There is a saying about muscles and exercise: "Use it or lose it." This is why, after surgery, we are asked to get back to movement as quickly as possible. We study the Bible so we continue to learn and lose connection with God's word and our lives. The study of God is very personal, but can be strengthened by use. When it is combined with others' sharing of knowledge, it provides extra learning on the topic. Sharing of knowledge and experience brings a richer and deeper understanding of God's word. I find it exciting to hear different people's interpretations of verses and the different reasons people have connected with verses. It is important to keep our study of the Bible strong by doing it regularly and with an intensity and desire to be open to the Holy Spirit.

The study of the Bible is similar to our need to keep current in our professional life. Many leaders read journals and attend conferences to stay current in their profession. Additionally, leaders discuss situations to gain knowledge from others' experiences. Leaders also talk with each other to understand interpretations of rules and regulations. Leaders continue learning on a daily basis. Students forget lessons if they don't regularly study. You will forget God's word and truth if you don't read your Bible or have a daily devotional.

Therefore shall ye lay up these my words in your heart and in your soul, and bind them for a sign upon your hand, that they may be as frontlets between your eyes. And ye shall teach them to your children, speaking of them when thou sittest in thine house, and when thou walkest by the way, when thou liest down, and when thou risest up. Deuteronomy 11: 18-19

Willing to Give Testimony

And we have seen and do testify that the Father sent the Son to be the Saviour of the world. Whosoever shall confess that Jesus is the Son of God, God dwelleth in Him and he in God. And we have known and believed the love that God hath to us. God is love; and he that dwelleth in love dwelleth in God, and God in him. I John 4:14-16

As superintendents, we need to be ready to share our experiences and knowledge for others to learn about Jesus. The North American Mission in December 2008, at www.lifewayresearch.com, identified five ways people are most willing to get information about church. The largest percent of people, sixty-three percent, were most willing to get information about church from family members. Fifty-six percent were willing to receive information from a friend or neighbor. Forty-eight percent were willing to get information from newspapers, while forty-six percent were willing to get church information from outdoor signs and billboards. Also, forty-six percent of people were willing to get information about church from newspapers or magazine advertisements.

We may be considered the friend or, at least, an acquaintance of our employees. We should be prepared to share our testimony and experiences. It is important to share it confidently and through our lives so others may learn the truth about the Bible. This requires us to know the Bible, and how knowledge of the Bible affects our daily life.

When I am clear about my beliefs, it is easier for me to express them. Additionally, as we speak more about our beliefs, we become more comfortable telling others. We are to tell others kindly and gently without condemnation. The Holy Spirit guides us to people and provides opportunities to testify. The Holy Spirit has already laid the groundwork and will be the closer for our testimony. Our responsibility is to just testify and give information about the Word of God.

Thou art my portion, O Lord. I would keep they words. I entreated thy favour with my whole heart. Be merciful unto me according to thy word. I thought on my ways and turned my feet unto thy testimonies. I made haste and delayed not to keep thy commandments. Psalms 119:57-60

Giving our testimony is like learning how to ride a bike. At first, we may be shaky and off balance with no clear idea of how to stop. But after we have mastered it, we are able to see the opportunities, share our testimony with clear guidance and directions, know when to stop talking and allow the Holy Spirit to work. Even the disciple, Peter's brother, introduced Peter to Jesus. A family member gave the information to Peter about Jesus, sharing the knowledge of Jesus. Pray for courage so you can share the Good News.

Then Peter said unto them, Repent and be baptized every one of you in the name of Jesus Christ for the remission of sins, and ye shall receive the gift of the Holy Ghost. Acts 2:38

Witness

This Jesus hath God raised up, whereof we all are witnesses. Therefore being by the right hand of God exalted, and having received of the Father the promise of the Holy Ghost, he hath shed forth this, which ye now see and hear. **Acts 2:32**

Superintendents need to investigate things that supposedly occurred in their organization. It is both time consuming and necessary to interview several people to determine if there was any wrongdoing or neglectful acts. Their recollections need to be brought to the forefront with careful questioning. These questions can't guide their response or show bias but rather an attempt to find the truth. Some people may fear retribution. This also happens with students. Students may know something is wrong but fear how others will respond if they tell the truth.

There are even times when leaders must bring in experts to help them. The experts may specialize in risk management, energy savings, or curriculum. The experts may charge a fee for their knowledge, but their information may actually save the organization money in the long-term. The experts' knowledge and detailed reports provide guidance and recommendations to help an organization. However, it is the leaders who need to decide how to use the advice and recommendations.

Jesus' disciples were expected to go out and tell others about what they had witnessed when Jesus ascended. They were given comfort that they did not have to do this alone. They would receive the Holy Ghost to give them support. I am sure there were times they might have feared how others would respond. Yet they had witnessed Jesus' resurrection and were expected to be His witness. It was the long-term that they were to show others.

> *I love to tell the story of unseen things above,*
> *Of Jesus and His glory, Of Jesus and His love.*
> *I love to tell the story, because I know it's true;*
> *It satisfies my longings as nothing else can do.*
> —Katherine Hankey

But ye shall receive power, after that the Holy Ghost is come upon you; and ye shall be witness unto me both in Jerusalem, and in all Judea, and in Samaria, and unto the uttermost part of the earth. Acts 1:8

Rewarding Good for Evil

And he said to David, Thou are more righteous than I: for thou hast rewarded me good, whereas I have rewarded thee evil. **I Samuel 24:17**

David and his men were being pursued by King Saul as he sought to kill him. The king was tired and went and rested in a cave in the mountains. What he didn't know was David and his men were also hidden in the cave. David's men wanted him to kill King Saul, but he would not. David said, "He will not touch the Lord's anointed." David did, however, go and cut a piece of cloth off of King Saul's robe while he was sleeping.

When the king awoke, he left. When he was some ways away, David came out of the cave and called after him. King Saul was so convicted because he was not harmed he made the statement "thou has rewarded me good." At that time he stopped pursuing David. Later on, David came to Nabal and asked for some food and nourishment. Nabal was a rough and loud man who treated David's men very rudely. David came to exact vengeance on him when Abigail, Nabal's wife, quickly got some food together and took it to David and his men before they came to erase Nabal and his family. Abigail told her husband the next day what she did, and Nabal fell dead. The Lord avenged David.

Has anyone ever treated you poorly and maligned you when you didn't deserve it, causing thoughts to ran through your head about how you could get even? A superintendent was being brutally and maliciously attacked in the newspaper by a churlish reporter. He never fought back. In fact, as the saying goes, he "took the high road." When the superintendent came back to that district many years later, people were so impressed by his grace and professionalism he was welcomed very kindly. Remember, keep Jesus as your focus and let him fight your battles. He will see you through.

Tell it to Jesus, tell it to Jesus!
He is a friend that's well known;
You have no other such a friend or brother,
Tell it to Jesus alone.
                                                                –Unknown

The wicked can't harm or derail you when you let Jesus lead the way.

February 29

Serving God in Your Business

And a certain woman named Lydia, a seller of purple, in the city of Thyatira, which worshipped God, heard us: whose heart the Lord opened, and she attended unto the things which were spoken of Paul. **Acts 16:14**

Lydia was a successful business lady in Thyatira and was "seller of purple." She was in either the dry goods business or the apothecary business, selling either dyed cloth or the chemicals for dying clothing. Purple was the color of royalty, and undoubtedly would be a prized commodity. She was pretty well off and seemed to be the householder of her place.

Lydia did not let her business get between her and salvation. God didn't take her from her vocation but used her in her vocation for His work. God has a reason for placing us where we are. She was hungry for more of the power of God and humbly sought it. She became a champion for Christ while still working in her business. Today you will see superintendents and businessmen/women, athletes, and so forth who are sold out for the Lord and committed Christians who are still working in their "called" vocation.

Lydia took the advantage of hearing a great preacher and accepted the Lord as her personal savior. We must take advantage of this because we don't know when the Lord will move mightily again and bonds will be broken. The Lord opened her heart. When we seek God and reach towards Him, He will always open our hearts. That is His job!

When our mouth is open in prayer and our hearts are open to His service, then He will become very real to us. He will be as real to us as he was to Lydia.

Is your all on the altar of sacrifice laid?
Your heart, does the Spirit control?
You can only be blest and have peace and sweet rest,
As you yield Him your body and soul.
–Elisha Hoffman

When the Lord is number one in your life, He will be number one in your business.

MARCH

Upset

And it came to pass, that when all our enemies heard thereof, and all the heathen that were about us saw these things, they were much cast down in their own eyes: for they perceived that this work was wrought of our God. Nehemiah 6:16

Sanballat, Tobiah, and Geshem tried to stop the Israelites from rebuilding Jerusalem. They continually tried to upset the will of God by scaring the people but they were unsuccessful. I thought of this while I was watching the 2012 NCAA March Madness first rounds and saw a couple of major upsets. Missouri, a number two seed, was beaten by Norfolk State, a fifteen seed. Duke, a number two seed, was beaten by Lehigh, a fifteen seed. Needless to say, those were shockers. Seeing as I had chosen one of those number two seeds to play in the championship game, my brackets were broken.

I was looking at Coach K, the coach for Duke University; there was no joy on his face. In fact, the whole coaching staff was very downcast and solemn. The TV panned to Coach K's wife. She looked like she was almost ready to cry. The emotions you feel when you get upset by a team you should have handily beaten range from sickness, rage, crying, to being depressed as this is a real blow to your ego and team. Coach K kept his emotions in and was very professional and gracious about the loss. He shook hands with the opposing coach, was composed and complimented the other team in the interview with the reporters after the game.

How do you handle it when you are upset? Did a board vote against your recommendation which was devastating to you? Did you lose a bid on a piece of land you were trying to buy for your district? Did the teachers go on strike even after you offered the union a fair offer? Did your high school football coach, who was an icon in the district, just resign and take another position in another district? There are numerous ways you can get upset.

I knew of a person who was hired as an assistant superintendent in another district. When they gave him his contract, it was $10,000 less than the amount agreed upon. He could have acted angrily and unprofessional, but he was gracious and professional. About 4 months later, the board vice-president apologized and in six months, this person was named the superintendent. He behaved like Coach K did in his interview after the upset loss. He didn't let the Sanballats, Tobiahs, and Greshems of the world try to scare him as he knew that God was his source of strength and was on his side.

There is never a day so dreary,
There is never a night so long,
But the soul that is trusting Jesus,
Will somewhere find a song.
–Anna B. Russell

Being upset is not the end of the world, it is the start of a new beginning.

Call for Journal Authors

Blow ye the trumpet in Zion, and sound an alarm in my holy mountain: let all the inhabitants of the land tremble: for the day of the LORD cometh, for it is nigh at hand. Joel 2:1

In the world of academia, calls go out for manuscripts for journals and conference presentations. These are blind peer-reviewed. If you're fortunate, your manuscript will be selected for publication or your presentation will be selected for the conference. If your paper is not selected, there is a sense of alarm because in higher education you will not receive tenure or promotion without evidence of research on your vita.

In public education, the same, in essence, is true. The superintendent asks central office administrators or principals to be prepared to present information to the board, present current information on educational issues at administrative retreats, or lead a workshop for the district. This is when you "blow the trumpet" and sound the alarm.

The board will ask you, as superintendent, for an item or justification of an item, and this is when they "blow the trumpet." This is the call and it's very important because your contract and your administrators' contracts hinge on how well you respond to the "alarm."

The Lord calls for us. He wants journal authors for his harvest. I always pray I never lose the fire because the harvest is truly great but "the laborers are few" (Luke 10:2).

> *Lord of the Harvest, place your fire in me.*
> *Servant you need Lord, Servant I will be*
> *Give me the eyes of the spirit, and a heart of compassion to know*
> *Lord of the Harvest, show me where to go.*
> –Unknown

There is a crop of the Lord ready to be harvested, let us pray the Lord would send us out as His laborers, to help reap the harvest for Him.

God's Will

Abba, Father, he said, everything is possible for you. Take this cup from me. Yet not what I will, but what you will. **Mark 14:36**

I think it is in the nature of superintendents to want control over a situation. The position itself requires an individual with the ability to make tough decisions quickly. However, some problems seem to drag out over a long period of time, and this can be extremely frustrating and disheartening.

The leader inside of us is constantly looking for solutions and ways to solve the problem ourselves. Many times when we can't solve them, we begin to look for ways out. Perhaps we even question whether or not it is time to find a new school, new career, or retire. But often God uses these trials to teach us and help us grow closer to Him.

When we reason out our own deliverance from these problems we might not be following God's will at all. Just because you move the hands on a clock doesn't mean that you have changed the time; and prying open the pedals of a rose to open the flower will cause it to spoil. Always remember that it is better to walk through trials and tribulations with God, than to walk through prosperity without him. Matthew 16:26 reads, "What good will it be for someone to gain the whole world, yet forfeit their soul?"

Never try to solve problems in your own time. Allow it to happen in God's time and in His way. A time of trouble is meant to teach you lessons you desperately need. Hasty liberation from these problems may circumvent God's work of grace in your life.

Said the Robin to the Sparrow:
"I should really like to know
Why the anxious human beings
Rush about and worry so."
Said the Sparrow to the Robin:
"Friend, I think that it must be
That they have no Heavenly Father
Such as cares for you and me."

–Elizabeth Cheney

The will of God is not something you add to your life. It's a course you choose. You either line yourself up with the Son of God…or you capitulate to the principle which governs the rest of the world.

–Elisabeth Elliot

Asking for God's Advice

And David enquired of the LORD, saying, Shall I go up to the Philistines? Wilt thou deliver them into mine hand? And the LORD said unto David, Go up: for I will doubtless deliver the Philistines into thine hand. **II Samuel 5:19**

David inquired of God if he should go up and fight the Philistines again after previously defeating them. David used God's guidance to win the battles. Most people would have fought their battles without asking for God's advice. David, however, purposed in his heart to ask for God's advice before going into battle.

If you read about the Patriarchs in the Bible, they all inquired of the Lord when they went to battle. The Lord told Moses when to move and when not to move while he was leading them through the wilderness.

There was one time though, when Joshua forgot to inquire of the Lord and made a terrible mistake. In Joshua 9, the Gibeonites showed up with bags full of old moldy bread, worn-out sandals, cracked and old water skins, and old worn clothing. The Gibionites came after the Israelites entered the Promised Land and were gaining great victories. Joshua and the men did not inquire of the Lord, rather, they looked at the people's provisions and their outside appearance. It turns out they were the next door neighbors and Israel had been deceived. It caused a huge problem in Israel's future. Things are not always as they appear.

Learn from David. Do not take one step without God. Take God as your compass and let him lead you along life's path. Inquire of the Lord as you make decisions as a superintendent and He will guide your steps and make your way prosperous. Inquire of the Lord in everything, work and home!

> *O Lord, my best desire fulfill,*
> *And help me to resign*
> *Life, health, and comfort to thy will,*
> *And make thy pleasure mine.*
> *Why should I shrink at thy command,*
> *Whose love forbids my fears?*
> *Or tremble at the gracious hand*
> *That wipes away my tears?*
> *No; let me rather freely yield*
> *What most I prize to thee,*
> *Who never hast a good withheld,*
> *Or wilt withhold from me.*
>
> –Cowper

It pays to inquire of the Lord when you are going through difficult times because if you don't you will "open" the wrong door and not receive the prize.

Boasting

Let another praise thee, and not thine own mouth; a stranger, and not thine own lips. **Proverbs 27:2**

Do you ever find yourself bragging or boasting? Are you one who says, "I've done this," or "if it wasn't for me," or "I was able to do this," or "no one knows statistics better than me," or "I know school finance better than anyone else," or "no one knows how to pass a building bond issue better than me," or "I know policy and policy formation?" The list goes on and on, but you get my point. Braggarts make definitive statements about their abilities for all to hear. They desire to be praised and be put above others.

Luke 20:46 (NIV) says, "Beware of these teachers of religious law! For they like to parade around in flowing robes and love to receive respectful greetings as they walk in the marketplaces. And how they love the seats of honor in the synagogues and the head table at banquets." My nephew is a nurse, and he said when other nurses are loud and know everything, he leaves. He has found they are usually wrong and looks up the correct answer. Beware of braggarts!

It is easy to get into this mode of talking. When no one is praising us, we feel unimportant. We all have that inner desire to be praised and recognized. When we feel uncomfortable or incompetent, we don't want others to know, so we brag about ourselves. I worked for a lady that knew school leadership better than anyone else. She raised children better than anyone else; she understood the legislative process better than anyone else; and, in fact, there wasn't one thing she didn't know better than anyone else. How do I know this? Because she kept telling us so! When we examined her boasts, we found that she usually had very little experience about what she was bragging about.

It is easy to deceive people because most people aren't an expert in a certain field so they don't want to say something that isn't correct. The braggart doesn't care because he or she knows that it's the listener's responsibility to prove them wrong. Also, you don't want to get into a conflict with another superintendent or a colleague. If you have gotten into the habit of bragging or boasting about yourself, then ask the Lord to help you overcome this habit.

I boast not of works or tell of good deeds, for naught have I done to merit His grace
All glory and praise shall rest upon Him, so willing to die in my place
My trophies and crowns, my robe stained with sin
Twas all that I had to lay at His feet, unworthy to eat from the table of Life
Till Love made provision for me
I will glory in the cross in the cross, lest His suffering all be in vain
I will weep no more for the cross that He bore, I will glory in the cross.
–Dottie Rambo

If you want to boast, boast only about the Lord. I Corinthians 1:31 (NLT)

God's Favor on Your New Beginnings

The blessing of the Lord, it maketh rich, and he addeth no sorrow with it. **Proverbs 10:22**

My son is changing jobs. He worked for one law firm for eight years and is now going out on his own. As you can imagine, there is a feeling of excitement and also uncertainty. He has a very good reputation as a fair, honest, and hard-working attorney. He also had a good rapport with the people in his firm, which has caused him some undue worry because he didn't want them to think he was leaving because of them. This was his dream, and the opportunity arose so he could make this bold first step.

I gave him some fatherly advice when I called him. I told him to go to his new office space and pray over each room, asking God for His blessings. I also said that he needs to tell God that this is all for His glory. Finally, I told him that he should pray the prayer of Jabez.

The story of Jabez's prayer is found in 1 Chronicles 4:9, "Jabez cried to the God of Israel, saying, Oh, that You would bless me and enlarge my border, and that Your hand might be with me, and You would keep me from evil so it might not hurt me! And God granted his request." Later on in Jabez's life he became highly honored. He asked God for help and received it.

Israel offered sacrifices to the Lord asking for His blessings for all that they had and to give thanks to the Lord. Have you changed jobs or careers? Have you gone to your new office or home and asked the Lord to bless it for His service and glory? Have you turned everything that you do over to the Lord? Ask for his blessings and pray the following prayer:

O Lord, my God, Creator and Ruler of the universe,
May the work I do bring growth in my life and glorify Jesus
Draw all persons work that come in contact with me closer to you.
I unite all my work that it will be pleasing to You and give You glory.
Help me to do the work You have asked and come to the reward You have prepared.
In Christ name we pray, AMEN!

Jesus cares for you and His favor is ever upon you.
Let your praises be unto Him for the goodness
He is going to pour out in your new job!

Difficult Times

Truly my soul waiteth upon God: from him cometh my salvation. He only is my rock and my salvation; he is my defence; I shall not be greatly moved. How long will ye imagine mischief against a man? ye shall be slain all of you: as a bowing wall shall ye be, and as a tottering fence. They only consult to cast him down from his excellency: they delight in lies: they bless with their mouth, but they curse inwardly. Selah. My soul, wait thou only upon God; for my expectation is from him. He only is my rock and my salvation: he is my defence; I shall not be moved. In God is my salvation and my glory: the rock of my strength, and my refuge, is in God. Trust in him at all times; ye people, pour out your heart before him: God is a refuge for us. Selah. Surely men of low degree are vanity, and men of high degree are a lie: to be laid in the balance, they are altogether lighter than vanity. Trust not in oppression, and become not vain in robbery: if riches increase, set not your heart upon them. God hath spoken once; twice have I heard this; that power belongeth unto God. Also unto thee, O Lord, belongeth mercy: for thou renderest to every man according to his work. Psalm 62

How do we respond when times get hard? The nature of the difficulty, whether they be budget, personnel, outcomes, or facilities, is not as important as how we deal with them. It is always good to be proactive and plan ahead whenever possible. But there are also times when surprises happen, creating difficult times. How we respond to those difficulties determine our success at leadership.

During difficult times, I repeat to myself that God is with me. I know He is able to take care of everything. I just need to constantly remind myself that He is in control. He is my lifeline. He will not leave me or forsake me. Not only will God be with me during hard times, but he will remain with me after they are over. He provides safety. I am reminded of how mothers protect their children. In fact, most animal mothers are so very protective of their own children that they will sacrifice their own life in order to save their children. God provides that same security. He gives us strength when we need it. Often, I do not realize the strength God provides us.

I realize the strength He provided after the difficult times and I reflect on what God did for me. When times are difficult, I don't feel like I have strength. God provides the extra strength to continue and to lean on Him. I can cry out to the Lord as many times as I need and as long and loud as I need. I can talk to Him any time.

> *He hideth my soul in the cleft of the rock,*
> *That shadows a dry, thirsty land;*
> *He hideth my life in the depths of His love,*
> *And covers me there with His hand.*
>
> –Frances Crosby

What shall we then say to these things?
If God be for us, who can be against us? Romans 8:31

Entitlements

And he said unto her, What wilt thou? She saith unto him, Grant that these my two sons may sit, the one on thy right hand, and the other on the left, in thy kingdom.
Matthew 20:21

We are living in the age of the Entitlement Generation. Some believe they are owed certain rights and benefits without justification. They expect higher salaries, flexible work hours, and ample time off. Furthermore, they believe they should receive free college, free housing, free health insurance, and a host of other things free.

You are entitled only to the following things: the money you earn and the possessions you buy. The Bible talks about the benefits of being a ruler but a good ruler will be a servant. People who feel they are entitled to everything are spoiled and are a ME ONLY person.

Superintendents who feel they are entitled to everything make poor decisions and spend school money frivolously and for themselves. On top of that, they design contracts that totally benefit them. To be truly successful, as a leader, you need to follow the example of Jesus, the Prince of Peace, who humbled himself and washed his disciple's feet. This type of leadership is true servant leadership. Are you a servant leader? Do you put others above yourself? Do you have that peace that lives within? Then ask the Lord Jesus to give you this peace.

> *It is mine, mine, blessed be His Name!*
> *He has given peace, perfect peace to me;*
> *It is mine, mine, blessed be His Name!*
> *Mine for all eternity!*
> –Unknown

Humility is to make a right estimate of oneself.
–Charles Spurgeon

No one asked me to be an actor, so no one owed me. There was no entitlement.
–James Earl Jones

Exercise

For while bodily training is of some value, godliness is of value in every way, as it holds promise for the present life and also for the life to come. **I Timothy 4:8**

When I don't exercise, I don't feel right. My best day begins with cardiovascular exercises, strength exercises, and a walk. Exercise helps my body feel stronger since a good portion of my day is spent behind a desk. Research has found that if you stand at your desk or have a job where you stand, your health is better. Additionally, many medical experts state at least twenty minutes of sustained exercise such as walking helps a person stay healthy. Similarly, spiritual exercise also helps start my day. Prayer, studying the Bible, and having daily devotionals all help my spiritual exercise. The Word of God is available for us to read. The repetition of reading God's Word helps me remember and recall the word better.

If we stop exercising physically or spiritually, we quickly lose our strength. Both exercises need to be maintained in order to have a significant impact. These exercises help me model what I believe and say is important. There needs to be a relationship and an understanding to fulfill God's plan for us. This requires continual vigilance to a spiritual and physical developing to prevent loss of strength.

If people are just starting to build an exercise program, it is wise to start small and add on to the program. If a person wants to do more physical exercises, they shouldn't start with fifty pound weights or run a marathon. It is far better to start some aerobic and strength exercises and gradually increase distance to walking or running. It is also important to use warm up exercises as well as cool down exercises. This helps prevent injury. If a person wants to do more spiritual exercises, it may help to join a group bible study led by someone who has studied the Bible longer than us. That way, when we find parts of the Bible to be confusing, we can be guided through the understanding of God's Word.

Setting goals can also help us increase our exercising. Tangible and realistic goals along with benchmarks to check our progress are helpful. I may have goals of lifting ten pounds, decreasing my blood pressure, and walking for five miles. I also have goals of reading the entire Bible in one year, participating in a Bible study, and participating in two service activities each year. These are measurable goals that could be checked at benchmarks throughout the year. Spiritual exercise will help you reach your final destination – Heaven!

What? Know ye not that your body is the temple of the Holy Ghost which is in you, which ye have of God, and ye are not your own? For ye are bought with a price: therefore glorify God in your body, and in your spirit, which are God's.
I Corinthians 6:19-20

Exercise is labor without weariness.
–Samuel Johnson

God is Calling You

Now therefore, behold, the cry of the children of Israel is come unto me: and I have also seen the oppression wherewith the Egyptians oppress them. Come now therefore, and I will send thee unto Pharaoh, that thou mayest bring forth my people the children of Israel out of Egypt. **Exodus 3:9-10**

There are many opportunities for us to help others if we are open to them. God often presents us with opportunities we either have experience in or a talent for, but there are other times when God presents opportunities where we feel we have no talent. Yet, God always provides what we need if He asks us to do something. It doesn't matter your age because God can and will call you to tasks.

There are many examples in the Bible where God called people who would not be yours or my first choice. For example, Moses was old when God told him to free the slaves. David was young and small when he killed Goliath. Queen Esther could lose her life to help her own people. Jesus called fishermen to be his disciples.

I often think of my own children. When I have asked them to complete a task, sometimes they did it without question, while other times they asked why they had to do it. Occasionally, they refused. But overall, they usually did what had been asked. As these same children became adults, they did things for me when asked. Perhaps they felt I needed the help, or maybe they learned the importance of helping. They might have realized much had been given to them, and it was a small thing to help others in return.

Our Lord sent his own son to earth, to be humiliated and killed. He watched His son die for our sins, a son who had no blame and was innocent. How hard that must have been. I know anything He asks of me should be completed with a grateful and willing attitude. I do not have to understand the reasons why He asks me to do something, nor do I need to have experience or talents in the areas of His requests. God provides for those when He makes the request.

And he said, Certainly I will be with thee; and this shall be a token unto thee, that I have sent thee: When thou hast brought forth the people out of Egypt, ye shall serve God upon this mountain. Exodus 3:12

**Our response to God's request should be "yes".
No excuses, no second guessing, no uncertainty,
but just "yes".**

God's Mercy and Grace

Let us therefore come boldly unto the throne of grace; that we may obtain mercy and find grace to help in time of need. **Hebrews 4:16**

Our God is a God of mercy, and I can certainly attest to that. What does mercy mean? According to *Webster's Dictionary*, mercy is the compassion shown to an offender. God had mercy on me when I didn't deserve it. Grace is when God gives us unmerited favor and blessings. Now why do you think God would have mercy on us when we did not merit it? On top of that, why does God give us favor? I've contemplated that and I'm so humbled about this fact that it touches my inner being.

God loved us so much that he gave his all for us. He gave His only son for us! He would have saved Sodom and Gomorrah had there have been five righteous people in that evil city. The Bible tells us examples of God's mercy. In Exodus 34:6, you can see how mercy is part of God's DNA. In Deuteronomy 4:31, mercy is God's character in action. In the Psalms, David talks about God's great unchanging qualities and mercy among them. In II Corinthians, Paul speaks about God's mercy being available for our comfort when we're going through trials. In Ephesians 2:4, Paul says that God's mercy is abundant. The list and examples could go on and on.

God's grace is God's favor. Examples of His grace can be seen throughout the Old Testament, such as in Deuteronomy 4:5, when God showed Grace to Israel when giving his laws. Grace can't be earned. God is under no obligation, nor does he owe us anything. Grace is a gift with no strings attached. It is freely given from the giver to the recipient.

Thank the Lord daily for his mercy and grace towards you. As you work with people, remember to treat them as you'd like to be treated and have mercy and grace towards them as Christ has towards you.

Your grace and mercy brought me through
I'm living this moment because of You
I want to thank You, and praise You too
Your grace and mercy brought me through

There is grace for every need,
grace is full, grace is free,
saving grace yes, indeed,
flowing from the God's throne.

Holy

And he said, Draw not nigh hither; put off thy shoes from off thy feet, for the place hereon thou standest is holy ground. **Exodus 3:5**

Moses was in the presence of God when he was told not to place his shoes on that spot because it was holy ground. What does it mean to be holy? One source, *Nelson's Illustrated Bible Dictionary* (Lockyer, H. Ed, 1986, Thomas Nelson Publishers, Nashville, TN,), stated that holy means, "moral and ethical wholeness or perfection" (p. 485). This same source elaborated, "holiness is one of the essential elements of God's nature required of His people."

There are several other places throughout the Bible that describe God as holy. One of the commandments states "We are to remember the Sabbath Day and keep it holy." Holiness may also "be rendered sanctification of godliness. It denotes that which is set apart for divine service" (Lockyer, p. 485). The Bible uses the term holy as a purpose and a presence of God that sets us apart. God establishes holy. Sometimes we set aside certain things to be used at a later time or for a specific reason. God also sets apart. He is the only one who can make someone, someplace, or something holy. God shared that there was an expectation that His disciples and followers would be examples of showing righteousness. He called us to represent Him to others.

I Peter 1:14-16 clearly shows this expectation that we be holy. It reads, "As obedient children, not fashioning yourselves according to the former lusts in your ignorance. But as he which hath called you is holy, so be ye holy in all manner of conversation; because it is written, Be ye holy, for I am holy." How we act and respond to others should be in the fashion of God. This is everyday. When I think about everyday expectations of holiness, I am reminded of one of the school superintendent's standards that states the superintendent will act with integrity, ethically, and with fairness. These are attributes of showing holiness. It means leaders do not accept gifts that may jeopardize our decisions. It means treating all people with equal respect. It means correcting people who are using derogatory or slanderous language. It means standing up for the rights of children. From time to time, it may seem easier to not say something to correct a wrong, but that is not the route we are asked to go. It is clear that we are to be set apart and follow God's way.

> *I bowed my knees and cried Holy, Holy, Holy*
> *I clapped my hands and sang Glory,*
> *Glory to the Son of God.*
> –Nettie Washington and Dudley Cantwell

Who shall not fear thee, O Lord, and glorify thy name?
for thou only art holy; for all nations shall come and worship before thee;
for thy judgments are made manifest. Revelations 15:4

Jesus' Treatment of Women

And certain women, which had been healed of evil spirits and infirmities, Mary called Magdalene, out of whom went seven devils, And Joanna the wife of Chuza Herod's steward, and which ministered unto him of the substance. **Luke 8:2-3**

Women often were not respected or given admittance into organizations during the time of Jesus. Yet, the Bible mentions in several places that Jesus had women helping in the ministry. He pointed out that they supported the work through their finances, as well as their provisions.

Jesus also mentions women in his parables. This was during a time when women were not seen as important like the males in the society. Jesus healed and provided comfort to women during his ministry. "And when Jesus saw her, he called her to him, and said unto her, Woman, thou art loosed from thine infirmity" (Luke 13:12). He openly shared his concern for their welfare and their rights.

There are several verses that mention his concern for widows. Jesus even taught women, which was very uncommon during His time. "And she had a sister called Mary, which also sat at Jesus' feet, and heard his word" (Luke 10:39). Several of Jesus' examples for his treatment of women may not seem that large today. Yet it was an extremely different view of women during that time.

It must have been refreshing for women to be allowed to learn about God's word and to serve Jesus in a variety of ministry services. His disciples also showed great concern for the spiritual life of women. "And on the Sabbath we went out of the city by a river side, where prayer was wont to be made; and we sat down and spake unto the women which resorted thither" (Acts 16:13).

Since we should want to follow the ways of Jesus, we must also include women in our organizations. Jesus taught women were to be respected and there shown the same level of respect as He did. The Old Testament gave several examples of strong women used by God. Ruth, Lydia, Ester, and Lemuel's mother are just a few examples. King Lemuel describes the teaching of his mother in Proverbs. "She stretches out her hand to the poor; yea she reacheth forth her hands for the needy" (Proverbs 31:20).

God of the women who walked Jesus' Way,
Giving their resources, learning to pray,
Mary, Joanna, Susanna, and more;
May we give freely as they did before.
–Carolyn Gillette

No doubt, women of faith in the past, were reproached for His name's sake, and accounted mad women; but they had a faith which enabled them at that time to overcome the world, and by which they climbed up to heaven.
–George Whitefield.

Light a Candle

The spirit of man is the candle of the Lord, searching all the inward parts of the belly. **Proverbs 20:27**

Candles are lit for many reasons and purposes. They are lit in the front of some churches before the start of the service, in remembrance of deceased loved ones, to provide light when there has been a power outage, and to provide a romantic setting. Candles are also lit when we ask for forgiveness. In my home, I light candles because I enjoy the look as well as the beautiful aroma of the candles.

The Word of God mentions light in several places and is connected with good and helping others find their way to the Lord. We are to let God's light so that others desire His light. It has been my privilege to serve the Lord in a variety of volunteer jobs within the church. Some examples of letting my light shine included preparing children's sermons, teaching Sunday School, coordinating Vacation Bible School, visiting elderly church members in a local assisted living home, mentoring college youth, making quilts for boys in a children's home, making bags with supplies for women coming to a local women's shelter, collecting supplies for babies in third world countries, helping with our church kitchen group, and planning activities for evangelism. In all of these services, I felt a blessing from those around me. Many said they felt the light of God through those volunteer activities. These activities remind us that we are to let God's light shine and not hide our candles under a basket.

There are many people who walk through their lives in darkness, compromising themselves with activities that neither make them look good nor give glory to God. We are surrounded by things with bad language and bad visual images like magazines, television, and movies. There is a need for Christians to stand up against the darkness of this world so that God is not diminished. In order to stand up and share God's light, we need to repent of our own darknesses so that the Lord can use us. We want others to see Jesus and His light.

This little light of mine, I'm going to let it shine.
I won't let Satan blow it out, I'm going to let it shine.
I'll let it shine until Jesus comes, I'm going to let it shine.
Will I hide it under a bushel, No! I'll let it shine over the whole wide world.
–Unknown

For thou wilt light my candle; the Lord my God
will enlighten my darkness. Psalm 18:28

Paved Road

Prepare ye the way of the Lord, make straight in the desert a highway for our God. Every valley shall be exalted, and every mountain and hill shall be made low; and the crooked shall be made straight; and the rough places plain. And the glory of the Lord shall be revealed, and all flesh shall see it together, for the mouth of the Lord hath spoken it. **Isaiah 40: 3-5**

I have driven on some very rough roads. Ones that were bumpy and full of potholes and cracks. Some roads were in such poor condition, it required me to slow my driving so not to lose control of my car. This slowed down my time in getting to my destination and made the trip joyless. There was no time to look at the beautiful scenery, but rather I had to constantly watch out for the next obstacle in the road. Damages to the roads are often caused by the high volume of vehicles, especially heavy trucks. If routine maintenance had been done, the repair would not be as large and the life of the road would be longer. So when I find places where road repair has begun, I realize there is hope for smoother travel in the future.

Construction of new roads requires the removing of obstacles, such as rocks and trees. The ground needs to be leveled before the road crew can lay a surface base prior actually to paving the road. Roads are designed based on a purpose, the amount and type of traffic, and destinations. Designs are made to provide safety for drivers. For example, one safety precaution is the angle and length of curves. To prevent danger, roads are often designed to have more straight lines.

Leaders need to remove obstacles along the way so others can see the glory of God. If people are following crooked and rough ways, it takes them longer to find their way to the Lord. We all need help at times, and other times, we need to provide the help to others. Leaders can participate in Bible study, small groups in church, devotional study, and prayer life to ensure routine maintenance of their Christian life for a smooth road to their Lord. This helps provide a strong foundation with God's Word so we can know how to help others.

> *It's a Highway to Heaven,*
> *None can walk up there but the pure in heart.*
> *It's a Highway to Heaven,*
> *I'm walking up the Kings Highway.*
> –Unknown

Teach me thy way, O Lord, and lead me in a plain path, because of mine enemies. Deliver me not over unto the will of mine enemies; for false witnesses are risen up against me, and such as breather out cruelty. I had fainted, unless I had believed to see the goodness of the Lord in the land of the living. Wait on the Lord; be of good courage, and he shall strengthen thine heart: wait, I say, on the Lord. Psalm 27:11-14

Loyalty and Compassion by Ruth

And Ruth said, Entreat me not to leave thee, or to return from following after thee: for wither thou goest, I will go: and where thou lodgest, I will lodge: thy people shall be my people, and they God, my God. Where thou diest, will I die, and there will I be buried: the Lord do so to me, and more also, if aught but death part thee and me. Ruth 1:16-17

Superintendents must deal with economic issues, facility issues, personnel issues all during tough times. What do you do? Do you call to God for help? Do you rely on past answers? Do you ask others for help? Do you help others when the times are tough? Any of these might help you find your way through tough times, but you can also find help by studying other people's reactions, even tough times from the Old Testament.

Ruth lived during a time of great famine. Her husband died, and her sons married non-Israelites, then both died. It is difficult being a widow today, but it was even harder during the time of Ruth. Women did not have a way to support themselves. Ruth prepared to travel back to her home where she might find food and support. Though her daughter-in-laws started out with her, Ruth suggested they might want to remain in their homeland. It was at this point Ruth showed that she felt very upset, alone, and may have even felt God was punishing her and was not longer with her either.

When I learned Naomi openly expressed her bitterness, I realized that God is gracious enough to allow us to say how we feel. Ruth made a decision to stay with Naomi and go to her homeland. She must have felt a strong connection with her mother-in-law because she was willing to leave her home and travel to a place unknown to her. Times were tough for Ruth as well. Even though she was grieving, her relationship with Naomi was extremely strong. She wanted to stay with her and show loyalty and compassion. She wouldn't leave Naomi alone without support. She put Naomi's needs before her own.

There are many people around us who need support during tough times. When natural disasters strike, people reach out to help. It is most amazing when we hear stories about people who have been part of the natural disaster reach out to help others in the disaster. During their own struggles, they are willing to show compassion to others, as Christ showed compassion to them. Leaders must show that kind of compassion and willingness to act even during the tough times.

> *Intreat me not to leave you, or to return from following you;*
> *For where you go, I will go; and where you lodge I will lodge;*
> *Your people shall be my people, and your God my God.*
> *Your distress is my own; and never will I forsake you.*
> *May the Lord bless you henceforth, and more also.*
> –Saul Schechtman

Watch ye, stand fast in the faith, quit you like men, be strong. Let all your things be done with charity. I Corinthians 16:13-14

One More Night with the Frogs

Then Pharaoh called for Moses and Aaron and said, intreat the Lord, that he may take away the frogs from me and from my people; and I will let the people go, that they may do sacrifice unto the Lord. **Exodus 8:8**

Moses went to Pharaoh's Palace and asked that the children of Israel be allowed to leave Egypt. Pharaoh would have not allow this, so the Lord brought plagues upon Egypt. The second plague was frogs. There were frogs everywhere, in the bedroom, in the house, in the ovens, in the palace, on the beds, and in their food. Pharaoh was forced to grant permission for the Israelites to leave, so Moses would remove the frogs.

Frogs are cold, slimy creatures that start out as tadpoles, which resemble ugly little fish. As they mature, they learn to breathe, but still spend most of their life in the water. In early spring, their breeding season, they croak almost incessantly and are vile. Frogs in the Bible are associated with unclean spirits. These are the spirits of deception; they work miracles, and they are in the kings chambers. These evil spirits of deception live with rulers of people. Don't let that happen to you.

Don't let the frogs inhabit your life, professional or personal. How long are you going to let that persisting problem harass you? When are you going to get rid of the frogs in your life? Realize that they will stay around as long as you will let them. They will be there until you decide to go with the Word of God and tell them to leave. Clean your house! Don't live one more night with the frogs!

God promised to deliver and set us free,
And give us power over the enemy.
The Word of God will make the devil flee:
God's word is stronger than he'll ever be.

Say "Yes!" to Jesus and He will set you free by giving you power over the enemy.

Peace and Privilege

The grass withereth, the flower fadeth: because the spirit of the Lord bloweth upon it: Surely the people is grass. The grass withereth, the flower fadeth: but the Word of our God shall stand for ever. O Zion, that bringest good tidings, get thee up into the high mountain. O Jerusalem, that bringest good tidings, lift up thy voice with strength; lift it up, be not afraid; say unto the cities of Judah, Behold your God. Behold, the Lord God will come with a strong hand, and his arm shall rule. The privileges He gives to His believers for him: behold his reward is with him, and his work before him. **Isaiah 40:7-10**

I have a warm and fuzzy comforter that I love to use when it is cold outside. My little dog also loves it and will often jump up and lay on it beside me. God's forgiveness of sins provides me that same loving comfort. He provides comfort in order for us to gain strength. There are many places in the Bible that God reminds us that He will take care of His believers. He saved Noah and his family from the flood. He gave David the strength to kill Goliath. He provided food for Ruth and Naomi. He protected Daniel from the lions. He guided Moses through the wilderness.

Many of us have experienced obstacles in our lives when we looked ahead and felt hopeless. We feared the unknown. We also have experienced uncertainties when we might find help out of the hopeless and uncertain situation. The Old Testament illustrated many times when God fought the battle for His believers. God's Word provides me strength at difficult times. I only need to bring forth God's Word in my situations and I know He will bring me comfort through that strength. Any time life situations make us feel belittled or we can't see when there will be improvement, we just need to remember that we gain strength from our Lord and not to lose hope.

When I look back at the times in my life that seemed hopeless, I realize that if I could have seen the end I might have been more patient. The Lord often wanted me to learn how to lean on Him and not myself. As followers of Christ, we know His power and we should allow Him to guide us in our destiny of greatness for His glory. His comfort and peace are part of the privilege He gives to His believers. We just need to remember to accept it.

O spread the tidings around, wherever man is found,
Where human hearts and human woes abound;
Let every Christian tongue proclaim the joyful sound;
The Comforter has come!
–Frank Bottoms

But as many as received him, to them gave he power to become the sons of God, even to them that believed on his name. John 1:12

Prayer Benefits

Watch and pray, that ye enter not into temptation: the spirit indeed is willing, but the flesh is weak. **Matthew 26:41**

What is prayer? It is talking to God and listening to Him. It is two-way communication. In essence, it is communion with God. The benefits of prayer are many so we need to pray. Then, we can enjoy the riches and benefits of the Lord.

Prayer brings physical healing. Hezekiah became very sick and he prayed fervently to God. God answered his prayer and extended his life fifteen years.

Prayer heals you spiritually and is essential for forgiveness of sins. King David was terribly convicted in his soul after he committed adultery with Bathsheba and had her husband killed. Psalms 51 is his prayer and his petition. Prayer cleansed his heart and brought him back into fellowship with God.

Prayer helps you overcome temptation. Jesus was in the Garden of Gethsemane and found his disciples sleeping while he was praying. He told his disciples to watch prayer to avoid temptations. When we sin, we think how sin will satisfy our physical desires. But, when we pray, our desires are diverted away from sin and towards God. Prayer helps us defeat temptation!

Prayer brings peace to our country, to our jobs, and to our homes. In I Timothy 2:1, we are commanded to pray for all who are in authority that we may live a quiet and peaceful life. This pleases the Lord. Prayer causes the heavens to open, prepares one for the Holy Spirit to come, delivers you from danger, brings boldness, and builds you up spiritually.

The benefits are vast, so we then ask, what is the greatest benefit of prayer? I believe that the person who prays changes for the better. People who pray to God will show obedience and humility toward God. Humility will be shown toward other people.

Sweet hour of prayer that calls me from a world of care,
And bids me at my Father's throne, makes all my wants and wishes known;
In seasons of distress and grief, my soul has often found relief,
And oft escaped the tempter's snare by thy return, sweet hour of prayer.
                                                        –W. B. Bradbury

Communion with God can't take place without His presence touching us to become more like Jesus.

Press Towards the Mark

I press toward the mark for the prize of the high calling of God in Christ Jesus.
Philippians 3:14

I am what you would call a "duffer golfer." There are many times that my drives find the rough, hit the trees, find the water, or just get "plain lost." I then hit a "do over." In best-ball tournaments, you can buy mulligans, kicks, and throws so your score will look lower. I can remember one hole and I was driving off. I hit 5 straight drives over the fence and onto the airport, hitting a hangar. We were laughing so hard and each time I was hitting a "do-over."

In Christ, we are given the opportunity for a "do-over." Christ is giving us a mulligan to correct the mistakes we made. On the job, you don't get many "do-overs" so you have to take advantage of the one Christ gives us. If you are given another chance by your board of education to serve another year, thank the Lord for this. Do you have regrets for past performance? You need to take this "do-over" to improve. In your spiritual life, do you have regrets about the way you lived and your spiritual achievements? Then make the decision to allow Jesus to change you for the better.

Paul, in his letter to the Philippians, counted all that he was as nothing so that he might intimately know Jesus. He had the right attitude about life and it didn't matter what he had done or accomplished. The question to you is this: Are you more concerned that our savior Jesus Christ lives in you or what you can gain from this temporal life? Serving Jesus is a personal choice and no one is going to do that for you. When you press towards something, you follow after it with determination and this takes effort. It's not an easy road we are traveling on our way to Heaven, but Jesus will lighten every heavy load. When we reach the "mark," which is our goal, this is the end of the race and you are in Heaven praising God!

What is your ultimate goal in life? When everything is over; when everything is said and done, what do you hope to have achieved? What will be your legacy? Is your life aimless? As you press toward the mark in Christ, remember it's between you and the Lord. It will require effort, and a goal must be set to win the prize. The glory of this is that God allows us to press on in spite of our failures and flaws which is the ultimate honor. Remember, it is an honor and a privilege to live for, love, worship, and serve Jesus Christ.

> *The road may be dreary, the way may be bleak.*
> *The goal may seem impossible that God calls us to seek.*
> *The trials they may vary, The ignition less than a spark,*
> *But that should never keep us from pressing toward the mark.*

**Great will be our reward in Heaven if we press toward the mark
in Christ Jesus while passing through this world.**

Spring

But they that wait upon the Lord shall renew their strength; they shall mount up with wings as eagles; they shall run, and not be weary; and they shall walk, and not faint. **Isaiah 40:31**

I walked around the crowded aisles at a local home improvement store in the garden section. The aisles were crowded with shoppers wanting to buy new flowers, grass seed, fertilizer, shrubs, and fruit trees. The warm weather of spring had people out and ready to work on their yards after a long winter of browns and few growing things outside. People were smiling and patiently looking at the many choices on the tables.

As I purchased my selected flowers, I was ready to take them home. I knew I needed to prepare the ground and carefully remove the plants from the containers so I didn't damage the plants as I transferred them to my flower beds. I anticipated their growth and continued blooms for the rest of spring and summer.

Spring is a good time to renew our hope and recommit our lives to God. Spring is a beautiful time of year that gives us the hope of continued beauty for the rest of the season. Spring also finds many people wanting to clean their house as well.

We search to clean out clothes from our closets. It is time to sort out the unused and organize our papers so we can find things easier. We clean our windows to enjoy the new green and growth of the spring weather. This cleaning also means cleaning curtains, shades, and other things that don't get the weekly normal cleaning.

Our spirits may also need some spring cleaning. It may be time to reexamine things that are getting in the way of showing more service and love to God, family, and neighbors. Spring is a time to organize and prioritize the things that we need to release, which includes our past hurts and worries. Then, we can enjoy the freedom of God's forgiveness and care.

I don't know why Jesus loves me
I don't know why He cared
I don't know why He sacrificed His life
Oh, but I'm glad He did.
—Andrea Crouch

Therefore, if any man be in Christ,
he is a new creature;
old things are passed away;
behold, all things are become new.
II Corinthians 5:17

Stand Up For What Is Right

Plead my cause, O Lord with them that strive with me; fight against them that flight against me. **Psalm 35:1**

There are people who have very little political or social capital. Some of these include prisoners, children, and ill people. As leaders, we have a huge responsibility to ensure that people our treated equitably and fairly with respect. The Lord asks us to stand up and voice a concern when we see something that is wrong.

A popular television show asks what you would do when you see something wrong. The show has actors and actresses role play different scenarios that are obviously wrong in a public place. The program then shows how people respond to those situations. Sometimes the people ignore the wrongful situation. Other times, the people stand up and speak up for what is right. Then the host steps into the camera range and explains that this was not real but actors and actresses pretending to do the wrong. The people are then asked why they responded or did not respond. Some who did not respond often state that they did not want to get involved in other people's business. And yet other people, who did respond, said they did it because they felt it was the right thing to do. They would not let a wrong continue without speaking up.

Sins of omission are those that we commit when we fail to do something to correct a wrong. Sins of commission are those that we do when we know they are wrong. There are times when we may find it difficult to correct a wrong action. We have no excuse to not speak up and correct a wrong that we see. If others are hurting, we must step up and speak up for them. They may need gentle and kinds words to make them feel better after they have been hurt. Acts of kindness help those who have had injustices done to them. It helps them realize that others care about them. Compassion should not be slow to action for believers. We must give heartfelt counsel and try to right the wrongs we see in the world.

I am the true vine, and my Father is the husbandman. Every branch in me that beareth not fruit he taketh away; and every branch that beareth fruit, he purgeth it, that may bring forth more fruit. John 15:1-2

Stand up, stand up for Jesus, Stand in His strength alone,
The arm of flesh will fail you, Ye dare not trust your own;
Put on the gospel armor, each piece put on with prayer,
Where duty calls, or danger, be never wanting there.
–George Duffield

Don't try to be different but just be good.
Being good is different enough
and means that you are standing up
for principle and what is right.

Patience

Stand firm and you will see the deliverance the Lord will bring you today. Exodus 14:13

Sometimes one of the hardest things for us to do is to wait. In today's fast paced society we have become accustomed to getting answers and information quickly. In fact, having to wait in line at the bank, for internet service, or even for an application to load on our iPhone causes great frustration. Why is it that so often we permit emotion rather than reason to control our decisions?

As a superintendent, I have often been presented with challenges that I would like to resolve quickly. Dealing with complicated personnel matters or litigation can cause stress to mount in me if they are not resolved quickly. The truth is that most problems are not resolved quickly. Many times I have grown frustrated, even to the point of making myself sick, waiting for problems to be resolved. I often try different methods to solve the problems myself; when in reality I know that it will only cause me more grief. But this internal fire continues burning inside me; telling me to hurry up and resolve this issue. During these times of immense pressure, I often ask God, why is this happening to me?

The answer is simple. God allows these trials in our lives to help us grow closer to him. Have you ever noticed how much more time you spend in prayer when dealing with a personal trial or tragedy in your life? Often we grow frustrated waiting for God to work in our life during these difficult times. Psalm 119:42 says, "I trust in your word." All things take time; repeatedly we fail to give God the opportunity to work in our lives, not realizing that He will answer our prayers in His time. It takes time for great oak trees to grow; and for a flower to reach its fullest bloom. So we must have patience in our work, and know that by trusting in God's word, He will deliver us. As you deal with today's problems, trust that God has heard your prayers, and instead pray for the grace to deal with your situation until God presents a resolution.

> *Waiting on the Lord, for the promise given;*
> *Waiting on the Lord to send from heaven;*
> *Waiting on the Lord, by our faith receiving;*
> *Waiting for the answer from God.*
> —Charles Weigle

That is why, for Christ's sake,
I delight in weaknesses,
in insults, in hardships,
in persecutions, in difficulties.
For when I am weak,
then I am strong.
II Corinthians 12:10

Be Careful What You Say

Curse not the king, no not in thy thought; and curse not the rich in thy bedchamber: for a bird of the air shall carry the voice, and that which hath wings shall tell the matter. **Ecclesiastes 10:20**

I have been with people who have loose lips and maligned their boss and anyone else they could think of. This brings to my remembrance a Dean I once knew who worked in a mid-western university. She would talk very badly about the university president and other Deans. There was no one that was as good as she was in her eyes. When she spoke, word got around. She is now being diminished in the eyes of school districts in the area and the legislature, of which she a built quite a strong inroad.

In many countries, if you talk badly of the ruler, it is treasonous and you could forfeit your life or end up in prison. When you talk bad about the ruling class, you build yourself a pit to fall into. Sometimes people talk and they don't even think about the consequences of what they are saying or where they are. Remember, your voice does carry and you will be overheard by someone.

During World War II, there was a slogan that said, "Loose lips sink ships." An idle word from a military service man could lead to the enemy discovering their plans to counter it, resulting in, for example, a sunken ship.

In the same way, our lips can sink our own ship. Who has not been stung by the foolishness of their own words? But sometimes, in our pride, we feel as though our words can't harm us. Thinking that others won't find out will damage your reputation and career. You see, no one can control the course that words will take once they leave our lips or fingertips through modern social media. Emails can be forwarded, spoken words can be repeated, and as Solomon writes, they can come back to the very person we should not have spoken of. As this verse exhorts us, we are wise to leave these words unsaid. Colossians 4:6 tells us that our speech should be always with grace and seasoned with salt. If you've had loose lips, ask the Lord to be a lock on them.

May the words of my mouth
And the thoughts of my heart
Bless Your name, bless Your name, Jesus
And the deeds of the day and the truth in my ways
Speak of you, speak of you Jesus.
-Unknown

Lord, make my words as sweet as honey, for tomorrow I may have to eat them.
–Anonymous

Believe

And this is the will of him that sent me, that every one which seeth the Son, and believeth in him, may have everlasting life: and I will raise him up at the last day. John 6:40

We must believe and trust in Jesus to the point that we rely on Him to keep his promises. Our life will show that we are committed to obeying Him because we actively accepted Him as our Savior and He helped us from our self-centered ways. Are there times when you have questioned your belief in something? There are times when some pastors talk about having success and happiness if we just believe in God. I understand the ideas of contentment, but it feels that there is a stress that there will be no hardships in our life if we believe in God. This message is not stated in the Bible. In fact, quite the contrary is mentioned in the Bible.

Additionally, the Bible shows that we may have times of doubt, but God will show us His proof. He wants us to believe. Doubting Thomas had to see the wounds of Jesus in order to believe.

Then saith he to Thomas, Reach hither thy finger, and reach hither thy hand, and thrust it into my side: and be not faithless, but believing. And Thomas answered and said unto him, My Lord and my God. Jesus saith unto him, Thomas, because thou hast seen me, thou hast believed: blessed are they that have not seen, and yet have believed.
John 20:27-29

We are often the same way. He knew that others may also have doubts. Even those of us who have experienced the miracles of God may still have times of doubt.

I am so glad that Jesus assures me that He will help my disbelief. He appreciates the belief of those who have not seen. Those of us who have experienced His miracles must also remember and believe in God during our other times of uncertainty.

It is clear that we must believe in Jesus Christ as our Savior and that he is the only way to heaven. Is Jesus your personal Savior? If not, then ask Him to forgive you of your sins so you can have the inner peace to know that you will have a home in heaven.

Fear not, precious flock, He goeth ahead,
Your Shepherd selects the path you must tread.
Only believe, only believe
All things are possible, only believe.
–Unknown

The same came for a witness, to bear witness of the Light,
that all men through him might believe. John 1:7

A Strong Heart Equals Courage

Watch ye, stand fast in the faith, quit you like men, be strong. **I Corinthians 16:13**

On November 16th, Staff Sergeant Sal Giunta was awarded the Medal of Honor recognizing his exceptional bravery during combat in rescuing a comrade from Taliban fighters in Afghanistan. Giunta's incredible bravery in confronting enemy fire to rescue his comrade was exceptional. Giunta managed to pull his comrade to safety and looked after him until the MEDEVAC team arrived. Even through his comrade later died in surgery, Sergeant Giunta put his life on the line to save a fallen soldier.

Another example of courage is the story of Matthew, a brave refugee in Sudan, who escaped persecution in his own country. He suffered in prison, but managed to run away. He traveled thousands of miles, eventually finding peace and freedom in a land far from his own.

Odette Sansom worked as a British spy against Nazi Germany. She was imprisoned, tortured and sentenced to death. Despite these dreadful circumstances, she remained loyal to her country and her principles. Her brave actions saved thousands of people's lives.

If you lack courage and heart, pray that the Lord give you the needed quality to be a strong leader for your family, the students, the school, and the community.

The credit belongs to the man who is actually in the arena;
Whose face is marred by dust and sweat and blood;
Who strives valiantly; who errs and comes short again and again;
Who knows the great enthusiasm, the great devotion,
and spends himself in a worthy cause;
Who at the best knows in the end triumph of high achievement;
And who at the worst, if he fails, at least fails while daring greatly,
So that his place shall never be with those scared and timid souls
Who know neither victor nor defeat.
                                                    –Theodore Roosevelt.

Courage is resistance to fear, mastery of fear, not absence of fear.
                                                    -Mark Twain
Courage is contagious. When a brave man takes a stand,
the spines of others are often stiffened.
                                                    –Billy Graham

Fire from Heaven

Then the fire of the Lord fell, and consumed the burnt sacrifice and the wood, and the stones, and the dust, and licked up the water that was in the trench. And when all the people saw it, they fell on their faces: and they said, The Lord, he is the God; the Lord, he is the God. 1 Kings 18:38-39

Last year in Texas there were massive forest fires that swept through large areas. There had been drought conditions for most of the year prior to the fires and, thus, the majority of the timber areas were highly susceptible to the fires. The speed of the flames as well as the unpredictable nature of where the fires might turn due to winds made fighting the fires a challenge. It took many hours to keep the fires as controlled as possible. Even then, many homes and timber were lost to the fires.

As leaders, we often find that there are conditions that, if left unchecked, can also send us into the need to battle for survival. Leaders can't wait until the fires are upon them. If there are areas that need to be monitored, then it is the leaders' responsibility to keep a check on those areas. Just as Forest Rangers and Firemen watched for signs of potential fires, they also followed closely after a fire had been contained to make sure the hot spots did not flare up again.

Leaders must keep a vigilant watch on finances, outcomes, programs, and personnel. If there has been trouble in any areas of these in the past, the leaders need to have some careful checking mechanism in place to monitor those areas. Sometimes, people in an organization do not have a strong sense of direction. The leader must guide them when they can't make long lasting decisions rather are trying to follow the newest fad or promised way to success. It is hard for them to know which direction to turn. Leaders need to be the moral compass to guide their employees. There are many people who can help the leader, but ultimately the leader is hired to choose a correct path, and then monitor it and make changes when necessary.

Fire is mentioned many times in the Bible. Fire is often mentioned as a purifier. Fire is also connected to the power of God. God was seen in a burning bush and He was a pillar of fire for the Israelites escaping Egypt. God's fire is a purifier and a refiner with power. Our own actions will be tried by fire but with the help of God, we will make it through!

> *Thou Christ of burning, cleansing flame; send the fire,*
> *The fire will meet our every need; send the fire,*
> *For strength to ever do the right and grace to conquer in the fight;*
> *For power to walk the world in white; send the fire.*
> —William Booth

Every man's work shall be made manifest: for the day shall declare it, because it shall be revealed by fire; and the fire shall try every man's work of what sort it is. I Corinthians 3:13

True Friends

And as soon as the lad was gone, David arose out of a place toward the south, and fell on his face to the ground, and bowed three times: and they kissed one another, and wept one with another, until David exceeded. And Jonathan said to David, God in peace, forasmuch as we have sworn both of us in the name of the Lord, saying The Lord be between me and thee, and between my seed and their seed forever. And he arose and departed: And Jonathan went into the city.
I Samuel 20:41-42

A true friend is needed by everyone. Friends help us through many difficult situations. Friends are fun to be with as we share similar hobbies and enjoy talking with each other. Friends are loyal and honest. They are willing to tell us things to help us grow. Friends give up their own time to help us. They do the things that we are unable to do ourselves. In a reciprocal manner, we like to do things for our friends. Relationships take time to develop. The more we are together with friends, the closer we become with those friends.

Leaving a true friend is one of the hardest things to do especially when you are changing jobs or relocating to another place. New true friends need to be made. Work becomes a place where we often find our true friends. Other places where we make friends are our neighborhood and in church. Another place to develop true friends is in groups where we enjoy similar hobbies and interests. It is fun to be with others who share similar interests. Many of us are able to count only a few close true friends. An example of true friends, like Jonathan to David, is special. We know we are blessed when we have that type of friend.

Jonathan was the type of friend who went above what many people might consider possible. His bonding with David went above his own family and it even risked the future of himself becoming a king. Yet, Jonathan committed to being a true friend to David. Because Jonathan was a true friend, he was a dependable friend. Jonathan found a way to warn David when he knew his own father desired to kill David.

Who am I that you are mindful of me
That you hear me, when I call
How you love me, it's amazing
I am a friend of God, He calls me friend.
                                                              –Israel Houghton

Greater love hath no man than this,
that a man lay down his life for his friends.
Ye are my friends, if ye do whatsoever I command you.
Henceforth I call you not servants;
for the servant knoweth not what his lord doeth:
but I have called you friends;
for all things that I have heard of my Father
I have made known unto you. John 15:13-15

Getting Help from God

If my people, which are called by my name, shall humble themselves, and pray, and seek my face, and turn from their wicked ways; then will I hear from heaven, and will forgive their sin, and will heal their land. II Chronicles 7:14

The reasons why the Roman Empire fell was because of its moral decline, antagonism between the Senate and the Emperor, political corruption and the praetorian guard, fast expansion of the Empire, constant wars and heavy military spending, failing economy, unemployment of the working classes (the Plebs), the mob which led to rioting and the cost of the gladiator games, decline in ethics and values, natural disasters, barbarian invasions (terrorists strikes), and sexual perversion. Some feel America has lost its moral compass. Here are some things happening in America:

One out of four married men have had an affair.
47% of American families report pornography is a problem in their home.
70% of men between 18 and 34 visit at least one pornographic website monthly.
89% of pornography is created in America.
Researchers at University of Montreal could not find one man who
     has not looked at pornography.
Between U. S. and Canada, 665,000 are exchanging child pornography.
One in four teen girls in the U. S. now have an STD.
Over 90,000 sex offenders were identified and removed from MySpace.

Organizations have protected these souls under the guise of our First Amendment rights. Some courts have supported these arguments. To add to this, according to CNS News, "In 2009, Planned Parenthood preformed approximately one abortion every 95 seconds." Couple all of this with the assault on Christianity, the removal of prayer from pubic events, and the challenge of "one nation under God." It seems America has turned its back on God.

But if America turns back to God.
He will heal our land, and he will heal you.
Ask the Lord to forgive your sins
and start living a life in Christ Jesus
and you will be blessed!

Nearing Retirement

Now also when I am old and gray headed, O God, forsake me not; until I have shewed thy strength unto this generation, and thy power to everyone that is to come. **Psalm 71:18**

As I grow older and near retirement, I've observed the plans and actions of those who have retired before me and those new administrators who are beginning their career. God has a plan for you so you don't waste away and become depressed and lost. Those who kept living were a blessing and a help to their profession and to God. Those who quit and decided not to live, threw away many blessings and knowledge that others could have reaped from. So you have two choices, let God use you mightily for others or quit on life.

A Christian man became a widower when he was 76. Before he became a widower, he did not take the time to develop a network of friends or hobbies. After his wife died, he became depressed and negative. He faithfully attended church, but there was always a negative comment by someone or he was talking to someone so they would feel sorry for him. His sons were frustrated with him and it caused a rift between them which still isn't healed today. His comments were always "I don't know," or "I wish momma were here," or "I don't remember." He is squandering away his golden years.

I also know a Christian superintendent who retired in his late 60s and later became a widower in his early 80s. He let God use him in so many different ways. He told me that he's more busy today than when he was working, but he's doing what God is leading him to do. He's still active in community civic groups, sits on doctoral dissertation committees at Oral Roberts University, and gives workshops to Tulsa area school administrators.

Which one do you want to be like? The depressed or the living? Start planning for that day of retirement so you can be used to your fullest potential for God's glory. Don't allow yourself to become a "mall-walker" or a "rocking chair sitter." As one retired executive said, "I didn't plan for retirement and so I'm golfing everyday… not because I want to but I don't know what else to do and I'll get bored." This is because he didn't plan for retirement. Be a blessing to others and share your wisdom with them! King Solomon wrote in Proverbs 16:31 (NIV), "Gray hair is a crown of splendor; it is attained by a righteous life."

> *Over the hill but not yet old; I'm still spunky, so I am told.*
> *My life has been a bumpy ride; But, my inner-child smiles inside.*
> *As the winter of life slowly nears; It's time for me to switch some gears.*
> *While I'm waiting for that time; I'm alive for God and still thrive.*

As you walk through life, keep that walk strong right through the Pearly Gates into Heaven and don't slow down because of retirement.

Triumphing in the Cross

And having spoiled principalities and powers, he made a show of them openly, triumphing over them in it. **Colossians 2:15**

Palm Sunday, the Sunday before Easter, is when we start looking towards Easter. Between Palm Sunday and Easter a lot of events took place. Jesus triumphantly entered Jerusalem, on Friday he was crucified and three days later He rose from the grave. The crucifixion completed God's plan of salvation.

Jesus receives a hero's welcome from the crowd and later mingled with them at the temple. Matthew 21:46 said, "But when they sought to lay hands on Him, they feared the multitude, because they took Him for a prophet." Looking at this through human eyes, Jesus' coming into Jerusalem and the reception looked like a new level of acceptance but the cheering crowd and disciples did not understand Jesus' mission.

By the end of the week, Jesus was arrested by the Jewish leaders and convicted in a farce of a trial. These leaders then colluded with Pilate to execute Jesus. The Jewish leaders felt Jesus was a threat to their position of power. They lied to Pilate and said that Jesus would undermine Roman authority. What they didn't understand was that Jesus' rule of power was not of this world. When you as a superintendent have been lied to, whether in the press or in the gossip line, look to Jesus for your example. Jesus knew no sin and was crucified for our sins so that we might have eternal life.

The crucifixion was a victory even though it looked like a defeat. A glorious victory began at Calvary and ended when the stone was rolled away from the tomb. What everyone quickly saw was that Jesus was more than a prophet, He was the Son of God!

> *Up from the grave He arose,*
> *With a mighty triumph over His foes,*
> *He arose a Victor from the dark domain,*
> *And He lives forever, with His saints to reign.*
> *He arose! He arose! Hallelujah! Christ arose!*
> –Robert Lowery

I will weep no more for the cross that He bore. I will glory in the cross.
–Dottie Rambo

APRIL

April 1

The Fool

The fool hath said in his heart, There is no God. They are corrupt, they have done abominable works, there is none that doeth good. **Psalms 14:1**

In May of 2011, Stephen Hawking, the eminent British physicist, in an interview said, "I regard the brain as a computer which will stop working when its components fail. There is no heaven or afterlife for broken down computers; that is a fairy story for people afraid of the dark." Hawking is expected to die within a few years because of a degenerative motor neuron disease. Hawking gave the interview ahead of the Google Zeitgeist meeting in London where he will join others speakers addressing the question "Why are we here?" He will argue that tiny quantum fluctuations in the very early universe sowed the seeds of human life.

Robert Ingersoll, a noted atheist, made the statement in a speech that there is no God, "If there is a God, he will strike me dead in 15 minutes." The crowd gasped and waited. After 15 minutes Robert Ingersoll was still standing as said, "See, there is no God." A small lady in the crowd said, "Mr. Ingersoll, man deals in time, God deals in eternity." There was silence in the room.

Atheists try their hardest to argue a fact that is firmly established. God is real. You can't look on His creation and its ways and honestly deny it. I won't argue that 3+3=6 and I won't argue that God exists. An atheist once wrote, "3+3 is not necessarily 6". Well, write any other number on your math test and see if you get it right. The bottom line is that atheism is a false belief system composed of fools, and it is not new as the Bible tells us about atheism thousands of years ago.

When men refuse to have God in their knowledge, he gives them up to a "reprobate mind," (Romans 1:28). They are not "intellectuals," as they fantasize; they are fools. Court decisions have taken God out of the classroom and have emboldened atheists, the ACLU, and other anti-God groups. I had a board that said "We will honor God, no matter what." I admired the conviction of these board members. Do you have a conviction to serve God no matter what? Does your board have a strong Christian conviction? If not, then spend time on your knees in prayer and ask God to give you courage.

> *I serve a risen Savior, He's in the world today;*
> *I know that He is living whatever men may say;*
> *I see His hand of mercy, I hear His voice of cheer,*
> *And just the time I need Him, He's always near.*
> −A. H. Ackley

When men cease to believe in God,
they do not believe in nothing;
they believe in anything.

−G. K. Chesterton

Strong Leadership

Ye are witnesses, and God also, how holy and justly and unblameably we behaved ourselves among you that believe: As ye know how we exhorted and comforted and charged every one of you, as a father doth his children. I Thessalonians 2: 10-12

As superintendents and leaders, we should be role models and examples of what it means to be righteous people. There are times when superintendents fail as leaders because of their poor choices of actions and decisions to do foolhardy things. Those foolhardy decisions often embarrass the superintendent as well as their family and colleagues. It is times like these when I feel sad because this also sheds doubt on other superintendents.

The majority of superintendents are outstanding people who live with integrity and willingly share their expertise with others. These leaders work hard to ensure that their vision guides their organization to excellence. Exemplary leaders are willing to work hard in any part of the organization. They know that they are setting examples that are watched by others. But their actions are not based on others watching, rather their actions are based on a true caring for others and do what is right in order to honor God.

Strong leaders are like fathers who bring comfort to their children because they want to guide them to believe in God. It is important to build people up in an organization. Jesus shared many examples of finding the best in people and making them feel important. We want people in the organization to realize that they are important and that this organization includes people who care for each other. There will be times when corrections are necessary. But those corrections can be done in a caring manner. No one wants to work at a place where they fear their leader because that leader only sees the wrong in people. A strong leader knows when something is important enough to require no compromising of actions.

Additionally, good leaders don't compare themselves to other leaders as a way to determine their worth. Individual leaders have their own strengths and weaknesses. They compare themselves to the Lord's example when they want to improve themselves. Strong leaders strive to use Jesus as their example. Jesus imparted what leadership should look like and how leaders need to serve others. We must lead with that type of integrity and show the way.

> *When I come to the river at the ending of day*
> *When the last winds of sorrow have blown*
> *There'll be somebody waiting to show me the way*
> *I won't have to cross Jordan alone.*
> –Ramsey & Durham

Let a man so account of us; as of the ministers of Christ, and steward of the mysteries of God. Moreover it is required in stewards, that a man be found faithful. But with me it is a very small thing that I should be judged of you, or of man's judgment; yea, I judge not mine own self. For I know nothing by myself; yet am I not hereby justified: be that judgeth me is the Lord. I Corinthians 4:1-4

Change Makes us Grow

But Jesus beheld them, and said unto them, With men this is impossible; but with God all things are possible. **Matthew 19:26**

There are many times we hear about change when a new leader comes to an organization. Some people in the organization have seen many leaders come and go. And so many times they become skeptical of the changes advocated by a new leader. Some have even made comments about these new suggestions and just wait them out, believing "this too shall pass." But aren't there times when the suggestions advocated by the leader have validity and would actually improve the organization?

It may require time for the changes to be implemented and the results to come to fruition. Some leaders are better than others at explaining and/or selling their ideas for changes. But that does not mean the change is best for that organization at that time. Any recommended changes will have an impact on several people in the organization. Therefore, it is helpful to involve others in assessing the pros and cons of a significant change within an organization. Lower level changes may not need as much feedback prior to implementation.

I have listened to leaders who have advocated changes and discussed reasons to make changes. It is often helpful when they can provide concrete examples of how others helped with the implementation of the changes. I am a little skeptical when the leader claims that the change was successful because of his/her actions. There needs to be a realization that leaders can't make change happen in isolation if they want the actions to continue after the leader's departure from the organization.

God provides the outstanding example of a leader and change. He controls the change in our lives that is the most important for our growth. When we allow God to guide our life, then we are led to the changes that are needed in our life according to God's plan for us. It always amazes me when circumstances or people are placed in my life at a time when I need change. God makes sure that I see the need for change based on the presence of specific people. When we allow God to control the changes in our life, we will have a life that gives glory to God. Jesus accepted people as they were and then people wanted to find out more about Him and change to please Him because of this acceptance. When we allow God into our lives completely, we allow the changes to make life better.

The garden was bare and water was not found
Seed was sown and the sun heated the ground
Rain came and as the days passed by the plants began to rise
Good plants and weeds were sprouting in our Garden of Life
That is when we have to pull out the weeds and realize
Change can be good but if it's bad, it needs to be pulled out if we want to survive.

And Jesus answering said unto them, They that are whole need not a physician;
but they that are sick. I came not to call the righteous,
but sinners to repentance. Luke 5:31-32

God Leads Us

Now thanks be unto God, which always causeth us to triumph in Christ, and manifest the savour of his knowledge by us in every place. **II Corinthians 2:14**

I woke up thinking about the many places I have lived which included the places I thoroughly liked and those of which I detested. As I was thinking about that, the song "God Leads His Dear Children Along" came to my remembrance. I know that whether I am in a wonderful place or in a place of many trials, God is leading me. I've had to learn to put my trust in Him wherever I am and wherever I live. I found out that when everything was going great, there was a tendency to start to rely more on myself and not on God. What a mistake I made! Before David ever went to war, he inquired of the Lord and asked for His direction. I had to start doing the same thing.

One time, I was offered a job as a superintendent in a place I didn't really want to go. I knelt on my knees asked God for an answer. What came to me was the story about Moses and how he fled and went to the "back side of the desert." That is where God really positioned him to come back and lead the children of Israel out of bondage and Egypt. Going to this district was like going to the "back side of the desert." The Lord blessed me immensely for following His will.

From that experience, I learned to always trust in the Lord and in His leading. He grabs us by the hand and His eyes lead us through life. Always trust in the Lord and look to Him for your answers.

> *In shady, green pastures, so rich and so sweet,*
> *God leads His dear children along;*
> *Where the water's cool flow bathes the weary one's feet,*
> *God leads His dear children along.*
> *Some through the waters, some through the flood,*
> *Some through the fire, but all through the blood;*
> *Some through great sorrow, but God gives a song,*
> *In the night season and all the day long.*
> –George Young

God is leading you
and though sometimes the road is hard,
He is directing you to a better place.

Guard Your Mouth

He that keepeth his mouth keepeth his life: but he that openeth wide his lips shall have destruction. **Proverbs 13:3**

Football spring training is now upon us. The players are out there trying to win a starting spot. I noticed that there was not one player that did not have a mouth guard. In fact, in most sports today, players always wear a mouth guard. I began to think, if we go to this trouble to protect our physical mouth, how much more should we go to protect that which comes from our mouth.

Ecclesiastes 10:20 (NIV) came to my remembrance. "Never make light of the king, even in your thoughts. And don't make fun of the powerful, even in your own bedroom. For a little bird might deliver your message and tell them what you said." It is the safest to hold one's tongue and to discipline your speech. Tight lips over what you may say will prevent trouble. An Italian says, "The sheep that bleats is strangled by the wolf."

He who guards his lips guards his life. Two Hebrew words are translated in this verse. Both are commonly used to mean "protect", "keep a watch over", and "maintain". But he who speaks rashly will come to destruction. When you have an expressing, unexamined, and unconsidered speech of whatever comes into your mind, you will come to ruin. This ruin is the same as ashes in a fire. A free impetuous talker with offending lips is reduced to rubble and ashes.

The sins of the tongue include: arrogance, backbiting, boasting, bitter remarks, complaining, debate, despising others, disrespect to parents, extortion, false accusations, filthy language and sexual innuendos, flattery, foolish jesting and talking, hypocrisy, irreverence, nagging, name calling slander, speaking evil of dignitaries, speaking evil of a brother, speaking without study, swearing, tale-bearing, taking the Lord's name in vain, asking unlearned or quarrelsome questions, and whisperings. If you have a loose tongue and are always talking, pray that the Lord help you rein in your tongue and give you control over your thoughts and speech. If you talk with the Lord everything will be OK and you won't have to worry about saying the wrong things.

In this world below, there's one who loves me so,
and I'm talking, about my Lord.
I can feel his hands, and I know he understands
and I'm walking, with my Lord.
Every day is brighter, burdens get much lighter,
when He fills my heart with a song,
When my time runs out, in my heart there is no doubt,
I'll be walking, talking with my Lord.
Talk, talk, talk, talk, talk with the Lord.
                                        –J. D. Sumner

Least said, least mended.

God's Power

And do not lead us into temptation, But deliver us from the evil one. For Yours is the kingdom and the power and the glory forever. Amen. **Matthew 6:13**

Power is an interesting concept. Some people believe that there are different forms of power. Certain positions in organizations seem to have more power because of the position. Other types of power are earned by actions of someone. Other types of power are gained by being stronger and overtaking people. Leaders need to be careful on how they use their power. At times, they are able to make decisions and actions that will benefit many people when they use their power wisely. At other times, leaders use their power carelessly and become less effective. Or worse, they use their power corruptly and bring downfall to themselves and others.

Other examples of power are seen in nature. It is deafening to listen to waterfalls. It is frightening to watch floods tear up large trees and houses to be carried off. It is shocking to watch tornadoes and earthquakes destroy entire cities and bring down large buildings. These natural conditions are truly powerful.

Throughout the Bible we find amazing examples of God's power. God created the entire earth and heavens. He sent the plagues on Egypt in order to force the Pharaoh to release the Israelites from captivity. God divided the Red Sea so the Israelites could cross and then he returned it back to trap the Egyptians. He sent a flood to destroy all the earth except Noah and his family. God protected Shadrach, Meshach, and Abednego form the fiery furnace. God saved Daniel from the lions' den. He showed power of providing rain and withholding rain. God has power over death because His son died for our sins. He has power to heal and power to forgive sins.

I am always stunned by my own lack of faith at times when I know of all the examples of God's power and His control of everything. Numerous times He has shown his awesome power, even to me personally, and yet I still find myself going down the path of uncertainty. Then I stop and think about His power and almost scold myself for not just putting my trust and faith in Him. But He is powerful despite my own weaknesses.

The power, the power!
Gives victory over sin and purity within;
The power, the power!
The power they had at Pentecost.
–Charles Weigle

Now unto him that is able to do exceeding abundantly
above all that we ask or think, according to the power that worketh us,
Unto him be glory in the church by Christ Jesus
throughout all ages, world without end. Amen. Ephesians 3:20-21

Helping Your Neighbor Cross the Finish Line

And when they could not come nigh unto Him for the press, they uncovered the roof where He was: and when they had broken it up, they let down the bed wherein the sick of the palsy lay. Mark 2:4

This is a great story about neighbors helping their sick friend see Jesus so he would be healed. There are other accounts in the Bible where people helped others in need. A very good parable was the one about the Good Samaritan. A traveler is beaten and robbed and left for dead. A priest passes by, then a Levite comes along and both ignore him. Then a Samaritan comes along and helps the man. He takes him into town and pays for all his bills and health care as he heals.

A cross-country runner from Andover High School in Minnesota was making his way through the trail at the meet when he heard a loud scream during the first mile of a two-mile race. Most of the other runners didn't pay attention to the Lakeville South runner who was on the ground writhing in pain as the runners passed by.

The only runner who helped was the runner from the rival high school. This runner noticed his rival had a bloody ankle. Instead of calling for help, he carried the injured runner a half mile back to his coaches and family members. "I didn't think about my race, I knew I needed to stop and help him," he said. "It was something I would expect my other teammates to do." The Andover High School runner handed his rival off to one of his coaches. He was tired but he then turned around and proceeded to finish the race.

I work with a colleague who helped me over the finish line so I could receive tenure and promotion at the university. A superintendent with whom we work recently said to me, "Thanks for helping me over the finish line," in a project we were completing. Helping others in need is the mark of Christianity in action.

> *If I can help somebody as I pass along,*
> *If I can cheer somebody with a word or song,*
> *If I can show somebody he is traveling wrong,*
> *Then my living will not be in vain.*
> *If I can do my duty as a Christian ought,*
> *If I can bring back beauty to a world up-wrought,*
> *If I can spread love's message that the Master taught,*
> *Then my living shall not be in vain.*
> —A. B. Androzzo

The greatest leader isn't necessarily the one who does the greatest things. The greatest leader is the one who gets the people to do the greatest things and helps them over "the finish line."
—Ronald Reagan

How is Your Health?

I know, my God, that you test the heart and are pleased with integrity. All these things have I given willing and with honest intent. And now I have seen with joy how willingly your people who are here have given to you. **1 Chronicles 29:17**

Medical physicals are recommended in order to make sure our bodies and health are well. Many of the tests are basic such as cholesterol tests, blood pressure check, respiration rate, temperature, eyes, ears, nose, and stress tests. Additionally, doctors exam your lungs by asking you to take deep breaths while they listen with a stethoscope. The doctor will even look at your skin conditions for any potential irregular colors. There are also spiritual tests to determine our spiritual health.

We find out about our spiritual health when we know what is being examined by God. God wants us to know what a strong Christian feels and looks like. To become a strong Christian, we need to have action just like when we want our bodies to become stronger. There have been television shows that examine different situations for children with cheating. They found that when grades were emphasized over knowledge, cheating increased. Additionally, when one child stood up against the cheating, another student often would follow. Most of the children knew that cheating was wrong, yet they did not stand up against cheating in all situations.

Adults also have difficulty passing tests of situations in their daily actions that would show integrity. If a cashier gives you the wrong change, do you give back the extra money? If a company representative offers a free meal during a convention, do you accept knowing that you don't have to recommend using that company? A few years ago, some school personnel were caught changing test scores on state accountability tests. The testing had become so important that some were losing their jobs because of poor scores. Other teachers were receiving high monetary rewards for improved student achievement. Both scenarios pushed people's integrity. It was wrong to change the answers. God tests our integrity by examining our hearts. God knows our spiritual health.

> *Search me O God, and know my heart today;*
> *Try me, O Savior, know my thoughts, I pray;*
> *See if there be some wicked way in me:*
> *Cleanse me from every sin and set me free.*
> –J. Edwin Orr

Test me, O LORD, and try me, examine my heart and my mind. Psalm 26:2

Intercede

Likewise the Spirit also helpeth our infirmities: for we know not what we should pray for as we ought: but the Spirit itself maketh intercession for us with groaning which can't be uttered. And he that searcheth the hearts knoweth what is the mind of the Spirit, because he maketh intercession for the saints according to the will of God. **Romans 8:26-27**

I know there are times when others have interceded in prayer for me. When times were so difficult that I couldn't even find the words to pray, I was so glad that others stepped in on my behalf. It always amazed me when I would receive a phone call at a special time of need. It is also amazed me when someone would stop to visit just when I needed their company. The support of others interceded on helping me.

Another example of intercession is displayed by one of my friends. This special friend walks every day and stops by peoples' houses to say a prayer and intercede on their behalf. The prayers of intercession can follow the structure of the prayer taught by Jesus. First we praise God for what He has already done for us. We confess our sins, make our request to God, and give Him honor for his power. My special friend took the time to know the needs of the people in those houses. She made no judgments on their needs or causes of their needs. She listened to God for meeting His will and she interceded in prayer for them.

Praying always with all prayer and supplication in the Spirit, and watching thereunto with all perseverance and supplication for all saints. Ephesians 6:18

There are several examples in the Bible of people interceding on the behalf of others. Moses interceded for the Israelites when they complained about the food. Ezekiel interceded on behalf of Jerusalem. Peter interceded for a lame man. Jesus interceded for us. Esther interceded on behalf of her people. The Spirit intercedes for us.

God asks us to intercede on the behalf of others. He wants His people to confess their own sins. Then He wants to find people who are willing to prayer on behalf of others.

And He's ever interceding to the Father for His children;
Yes, He's ever interceding to the Father for His own;
Through Him you can reach the Father, So bring Him all your heavy burdens;
Yes, for you He's interceding, so, come boldly to the throne.
                                                              –Carolyn Gillman

Wherefore he is able to save them to the uttermost that come unto God by him, seeing he ever liveth to make intercession for them. Hebrews 7:25

Keep Looking Up

Keep yourselves in the love of God, looking for the mercy of our Lord Jesus Christ unto eternal life. Jude 1: 21

Jude wrote a letter to the early church telling them to contend for the faith, warning them about false teachers, and to keep looking for the "mercy of our Lord Jesus Christ." We should be aware of heresy lest it rob us of our eternal reward. Don't be surprised when "false teachers" arise because the Bible has already alerted us about this fact.

Jude exposes the workings of these false teachers who had infiltrated the church unnoticed and were leading God's people astray. Many of these false teachers had an appearance of holiness and spirituality, but they did not teach the same Gospel nor did they hold fast to the way of truth. These leaders were ungodly men who followed their own lusts and desires. By leading sensual and immoral lives, they took advantage of the grace of Jesus Christ. They claimed that the purpose of grace was to pardon their sins, thereby giving them an excuse to continue in the works of the flesh. These false teachers defied anyone who tried to correct their behaviors, and spoke evil about those in spiritual authority over them. They were complainers and flatterers, and caused much division among the believers.

Jude likened these false teachers to Cain, Balaam and Korah in that they began to covertly and forcefully take authority over the members of the church. They gained a following of their own, persuading them to leave behind the teachings of Jesus, and pursue their own selfish and evil desires. By doing this, these false teachers rallied around them an elite group of people who deceptively assumed themselves to be spiritually superior, and justified their evil actions by claiming to be guided by the Holy Spirit.

Today, one must be careful of false teachers or prophets. There once was a very successful minister in the Tulsa area that started to preach a false gospel. He lost his church, but has continued preaching this false doctrine. He currently is in Chicago spreading these false teachings and deceiving many. As a leader of children and teachers, you need to keep yourself pure before God and looking for His return. Living your beliefs is your Bible to the masses.

> *To him that overcometh, God giveth a crown*
> *Thru faith we will conquer, though often cast down*
> *He who is our Savior, our strength will renew*
> *Look ever to Jesus, He'll carry you thru.*
> –H. R. Palmer

Keeping your eyes on Heaven
as you travel this earthly journey
will always keep you on the right track.

Lending

If you lend money to one of my people among you who is needy, do not be like a moneylender, charge him no interest. If you take your neighbor's cloak as a pledge, return it to him by sunset. Exodus 22:25-26

It is interesting to look at different cultures and observe their customs. One of my friends lives near some Amish people. When the Amish people buy property, they get the money from their own people and not a bank and they do not charge interest. Additionally, they never sell the land again, unless to another Amish person. If one of their members is in need of money, they share the money. In this manner, they control their own financial interests.

The use of talents to increase money for the Lord is discussed in the New Testament. One man who hides the money and returns it with no increase is not praised for his hiding the money. He was admonished to have at least placed in a bank where it could have at least earned interest.

But he that had received one went and digged in the earth, and hid his lord's money.
Matthew 25:18. Then he which had received the one talent came and said, Lord,
I knew thee that thou art an hard man, reaping where thou hast not sown, and
gathering where thou hast not strawed: And I was afraid, and went and hid thy talent
in the earth: lo, there thou hast that is thine. His lord answered and said unto him,
Thou wicked and slothful servant, thou knewest that I reap where I sowed not, and
gather where I have not strawed: Thou oughtest therefore to have put my money to
the exchangers, and then at my coming I should have received mine own with usury.
Matthew 25: 24-27

Lending means that someone gives something, often money, with the expectation that it will be given back. The time that money or an item loaned is to be returned also impacts if someone will make a loan. Banks make the loans in order to make a profit so they charge interest. Banks often run credit checks in order to determine if the person wanting the loan looks like a good risk. Additionally, the size of the loan determines how much down payment may be required for the loan. Sometimes collateral is required in case a person defaults on their loan. Current lending, especially by banks, does not seem to have much connection to the words of the Bible.

The Bible gave guidance on loaning. But if the loaning was for basic needs such as a warm coat, it needed to be returned in the evening so the person would not have be cold without their coat. Also, if we loaned money, then we were not to make a profit from it when loaning to other believers.

God wants for us to be wise stewards of the resources He has provided for us. God will work on our behalf to help us get out of debt but we have to stop spending more than we have or we will always be in debt.

Living Above the Fly Line

If ye then be risen with Christ, seek those things which are above where Christ sitteth on the right hand of God. Colossians 3:1

A young lad from the mid-West was visiting New York City for the first time and noticed that some of the windows on the higher floors of a tall building were without screens. Innocently he asked, "Why do they not have screens on windows above certain floors?" The New Yorker said, "Because that's above the 'fly line.' You see there are no flies that high, and they all stay close to the ground."

This story made me think of how we could be saved from many troubles in life if we would fly high. We should seek with all of our hearts to let Jesus have His way with us. The more we live with Him leading us, the more we escape the problems and troubles of this life and know how to overcome them.

You say, "My problems are so big! How can I prevent my focus being drawn to them just as Peter's focus was drawn to the wind when he was walking on the water?" This is how to do it. Persistently replace every thought of the impossibility of your situation with the possibility that God's Word presents to you. Don't let yourself get down below the "fly line" level but live up above the problems standing on the promises of God. To keep yourself above the problems, read your Bible and pray every day. Have that daily communion with Jesus. When you do that, your problems won't be big because you'll be looking at them as victories.

> *Above the clouds the sun is always shining,*
> *Above the clouds all tears are wiped away,*
> *Our loving God will life you from sin's darkness,*
> *Above the clouds into eternal day.*
>
> –M. F. Rosell

For every look at your problems, take a hundred looks at the promises of God.

April 13

Loyalty, the Forgotten Character Trait

Peter said unto him, Though I should die with thee, yet will I not deny thee. Likewise also said all the disciples. **Matthew 26:35**

Loyalty is a character trait that is fast becoming extinct. We do have product loyalty or brand loyalty but they fall far short. Blind loyalty is inadequate because that is not what loyalty is all about. Then, what is loyalty? Loyalty is a sense of allegiance and an act of binding yourself to a person or course of action. Synonyms are trueness, faithfulness, fidelity, and devotion. People in yester-year were company and team loyal. You rarely saw professional players jumping from team to team. But, this is surface loyalty. To understand what true loyalty is you have to go to the heart. This is where true loyalty originates and gets its strength. Like many character flaws, our actions originate from within. Loyalty is the rudder on a ship and it's moved by the pilot, who follows the compass shaped by our Biblical moral core convictions. When faced with difficult decisions, our core convictions become the main factor in which direction we will take.

Life is a series of course corrections, but some decisions are permanent and even fatal. This is why loyalty is such an important character quality. Loyalty causes a mother to push her son out of the way of an oncoming car at the cost of her life. It causes a husband to shield his wife from the bullet of an armed robber. Loyalty to his ship causes a captain to stay on the sinking ship for the sake of his crew and passengers, as was the case of Captain Sullenberger when he put down his U.S. Airways Flight 1549 in the Hudson River, saving all 155 passengers.

Think of the people, organizations, teams, causes, etc. to which you are loyal. Which ones are deserving of your loyalty? Which ones are not? Have you been loyal to your Lord and Savior Jesus Christ? If not, you can turn that around by asking the Lord to forgive you. Peter went and wept bitterly when he failed in his loyalty to the Lord (Matthew 26:75). What does the Bible have to say about loyalty and being loyal?

Loyalty is unwavering in good times and bad. Proverbs 17:17
Loyalty is what you do, not what you say. Matthew 26:33-35 and 26:69-75
Loyalty is in your heart. It is willing and not reluctant. Psalm 78:8
Loyalty can be demanding. Exodus 17:8-13
Loyalty may involve sacrifice. II Chronicles 11:13-16
Loyalty to the Lord will be rewarded. Psalm 84:10-11

Anyone who thinks that the vice-president can take a position independent of the president of his administration simply has no knowledge of politics or government. You are his choice in a political marriage, and he expects your absolute loyalty.
–Hubert H. Humphrey

When we are debating an issue, loyalty means giving me your honest opinion, whether you think I'll like it or not. Disagreement, at this state, stimulates me. But once a decision is made, the debate ends. From that point on, loyalty means executing the decision as if it were your own.
–General Colin Powell

No Greater Love

Therefore will I divide him a portion with the great, and he shall divide the spoil with the strong; because he hath poured out his soul unto death: and he was numbered with the transgressors; and he bare the sin of many, and made intercession for the transgressors. **Isaiah 53:12**

A farmer in Kansas was driving two high-spirited horses into town. When he stopped in front of a store, the horses became excited. The farmer jumped in front of them and seized their reins. Panicked by the noises, the horses stampeded down the street dragging their owner with them. On they rushed, wild with frenzy, until the farmer could no longer hold onto the reins and fell to the ground under the horses' feet.

When the people rushed to the dying farmer, someone asked, "Why did you sacrifice your life for your horses and wagon?" He replied, "Go look in the wagon." They turned and there in the wagon was a little boy. The farmer had died for his boy.

Sometimes when we hear of Christ dying on the cross, we ask, "Why did He have to die on the cross?" And He will say, "Look at the people in this world, lost and in sin." Yes, Christ died for those people and for you and me.

I know of a superintendent who gave of his all for a community and was unjustly crucified by his enemies and the press. He left a broken man. People were asking him, "Why did you do that?" His reply was, "I care for the children and that they have the very best education possible." As he was leaving town, one community leader said to him, "You don't know how much we appreciate what you did. You took the high road."

As the dying farmer gave his life for his boy, this superintendent gave his career for the community children. The best model of God's love is when he gave his son for us, one who knew no sin but took the sins of the world, died on the cross in our place.

> *When hoary time shall pass away,*
> *And earthly thrones and kingdoms fall,*
> *When men who here refuse to pray,*
> *On rocks and hills and mountains call,*
> *God's love so sure, shall still endure,*
> *All measureless and strong;*
> *Redeeming grace to Adam's race—*
> *The saints' and angels' song.*
> –F. M. Lehman

God sacrificed for us so let us in turn sacrifice for Him.

Obedience

Behold, I set before you this day a blessing and a curse; A blessing, if ye obey the commandments of the Lord your God, which I command you this day: And a curse, if ye will not obey the commandments of the Lord your God, but turn aside out of the way which I command you this day, to go after other gods, which ye have not known. **Deuteronomy 11:26-28**

I can remember a time when I disappointed my father. It was so hard to see the hurt in his face. He didn't say very much, but I knew he was hurt because of what I had not done. If I had chosen a more obedient route, I would have showed more love for my father. That one experience stayed in my memory all my life. It made me want to do better in order to show my love for my father. I did not want to disappoint him again.

God also wants us to choose obedience. And we should want to do it in order to please God because He loves us. God wants to bless us and yet we must be obedient to his Word in order for those blessings. God has done so much for us that we should be grateful and do what He asks of us. We just need to listen to His word and obey it.

It is always makes us feel good when our children or even employees do the right things. It is wonderful when they express their gratefulness through their good actions. But sometimes my own children acted right because they feared the consequences. I always preferred that their actions were guided by internal understanding of the correct actions. But if that was not going to work, it was okay to have them fear the results of their wrong actions. If they were to be safe drivers when they first started driving, then we had a rule of no riders in the car with them. They feared losing the privilege of driving and did not have others in the car. Their obedience was based on fear at first.

Sometimes, people need to fear eternal life in hell without God in order to make sure they are in correct relationship with God. God provides many warnings that help keep us on the right track so we have eternal life.

Therefore shall ye lay up these my words in your heart and in your soul, and bind them for a sing upon your hand, that they may be as frontlets between your eyes. And ye shall teach them your children, speaking of them when thou sittest in thine house, and when thou walkest by the way, when thoud liest down, and when thou risest up. And thou shalt write them upon the door posts of thine house, and upon thy gates: That your days may be multiplied, and the days of your children, in the land which the Lord sware unto your fathers to give them, as the days of heaven upon the earth.
Deuteronomy 11:18-21

Until you have given up your self to Him you will not have a real self.
–C. S. Lewis

Offerings

And the Lord spake unto Moses, saying, Speak unto the children of Israel, saying, if a soul shall sin through ignorance against any of the commandments of the Lord concerning things which ought not to be done, and shall do against any of them: If the priest that is anointed, do sin according to the sin of the people; then let him bring for his sin, which he hath sinned, a young bullock without blemish unto the Lord for a sin offering. **Leviticus 4:2-4**

The Old Testament had a variety of different kinds of offerings that were required. There were meat offerings, peace offerings, sin offerings of ignorance, and trespass offerings. There were multiple laws for each of the offerings. Each of the offerings made a way for people to turn to their Holy God and find a way back to Him after they had sinned. The offerings required the best of what a person had and then the sin was symbolically moved to the animal as a sacrifice for the sin. Another offering was grain and yet another was a dove.

For Christ also hath once suffered for sins, the just for the unjust, that he might bring us to God, being put to death in the flesh, but quickened by the Spirit.
I Peter 3:18

After Jesus died for our sins, this changed the offerings. He gave His own life as an offering for our sins. He bore our sins on the cross. The requirement now is to ask for forgiveness from our sins and His offering cleanses us. We offer our best when we give to the Lord first and trust Him to provide for our needs.

I have tried to tithe to the church by giving my offering before my bills. Then I know I am giving my best to God. Jesus paid the ultimate price of our sins with His life. How little is it of us to return our thanks with giving our offerings and to immediately go to him in repentance when we have not done what He would expect of us? We need His sacrifice in order for us to have peace and joy on this earth while preparing for our eternal life with Jesus. Christians are to be holy and not of this world, but as humans this is not possible without a way to be saved from our failures. We must depend on God and He will provide us holiness.

Every man according as he purposeth in his heart, so let him give; not grudgingly, or of necessity: for God loveth a cheerful giver. II Corinthians 9:7

How much more shall the blood of Christ,
who through the Spirit offered himself without spot to God,
purge your conscience from dead works to serve the living God? Hebrews 9:14

Give according to your income, lest God make your income according to your giving. Spend and God will send.
–Unknown

Our Ladder to Heaven

And he lighted upon a certain place, and tarried there all night, because the sun was set; and he took of the stones of that place, and put them for his pillows, and lay down in that place to sleep. And he dreamed, and behold a ladder set up on the earth, and the top of it reached to heaven: and behold the angels of God ascending and descending on it. And, behold, the Lord stood above it, and said, I am the Lord God of Abraham thy father, and the God of Isaac: the land whereon thou liest, to thee will I give it, and to thy seed; And thy seed shall be as the dust of the earth, and thou shalt spread abroad to the west, and to the east, and to the north, and to the south: and in thee and in thy seed shall all the families of the earth be blessed. And, behold, I am with thee, and will keep thee I all places whither thou goest, and will bring thee again into this land; for I will not leave thee, until I have done that which I have spoken of. **Genesis 28: 11-15**

When I moved into a new house, the ceilings were 10 foot ceilings. Now the high ceilings made the rooms look bigger than they actually were, but I needed a ladder to do any painting. And the ladder could not be just a small step ladder that I usually would use, it had to be a very tall ladder. We also need a way to heaven. Jesus is our ladder to heaven. He came down to earth as a man to lead us to heaven. Heaven seems very high to me. Yet the only way to heaven was made easy because of Jesus' coming to earth to die for my sins.

Jacob saw the ladder in a dream and he saw angels go up and down that ladder. Jacob was not going up the ladder nor were other people going up the ladder. The angels were going up and down the ladder from heaven. God promised to be with Jacob and that he would protect him. Why did Jacob need protection? He was alone when he had the dream. He was alone as he ran because of his own actions to his own brother. Jacob was a man of many fears and yet God used him and promised to be with him and protect him wherever he went. God gave assurances to Jacob, a man whose actions were not considered honorable.

This earth seems a dangerous place and yet God says he will protect us. Jesus promises to be with us also so we do not need to fear the earthly things. It brings me great comfort to know that Jesus is with me wherever I go. He promised to be with me and to protect me. That does not mean I go into situations purposely knowing they are dangerous. Yet, I find comfort when I travel or when I have moved to new locations, knowing that Jesus is with me. I have comfort knowing that Jesus is my personal way to heaven. He is my ladder to the high heaven.

> *My heavenly home is bright and fair, yes I feel like traveling on;*
> *No pain or death can enter there, Oh I feel like traveling on;*
> *The Lord has been so good to me, I feel like traveling on;*
> *Until the blessed home I see, I feel like traveling on.*
> –James Vaughn

Keep looking up as you climb the ladder to Heaven.

Precious Memories

Who hath saved us, and called us with an holy calling, not according to our works, but according to his own purpose and grace, which was given us in Christ Jesus before the world began. **II Timothy 1:9**

Have you heard people say "How good the olden days were?" Sometimes it seems like we want to go back to those days because our mind always thinks of them as a very positive time in our life. Hollywood builds that feeling within us by making movies such as "Back to the Future" and TV shows such as "Happy Days." Bill Gaither, a southern gospel artist, starts out his program with the song "Precious Memories." That song gets you thinking about the past and missing your loved ones.

When my brother passed away, he had a video that showed him talking about his church. It was hard for me to watch because I missed him so much as we were the best of friends. Tears would come to my eyes. As time passed, I've overcome the feelings of "tears" but I still miss him.

When the children of Israel came out of Egypt, Moses kept reminding them where they came from so they would not want to go back to Egypt. If you've come from "Egypt," then you have to keep remembering those "precious memories" and how the Lord brought you out of that situation. It is those memories and traditions we pass on to our children so they have a heritage that is vibrant and rich in the Lord.

In the different districts I've worked, even though I experienced some bumps along the way, I choose to remember the good things. An example of this is when we drive through one town in which I was a superintendent, the memories are not pleasant to my wife but, gradually, those bad memories fade. We begin to realize there were only a few evil people in the town and we weren't going to let them dictate how we think and feel about others in the town.

The memories that I choose to have and feed upon are the ones the build me up and edifies my soul. If you didn't have Christ in your past, put him in the present and in the future. Your memories will then become precious.

> *Precious memories, how they linger,*
> *How they ever flood my soul,*
> *In the stillness, of the midnight,*
> *Precious, sacred scenes unfold*
>
> –J. B. F. Wright

The old days are great, but the future will be fantastic.

Royalty

So all the elders of Israel came to the king to Hebron; and king David made a league with them in Hebron before the Lord: and they anointed David king over Israel. David was thirty years old when he began to reign, and he reigned forty years. In Hebron he reigned over Judah seven years and six months: and in Jerusalem he reigned thirty and three years over all Israel and Judah. And the king and his men went to Jerusalem unto the Jebusites, the inhabitants of the land: which spake unto David, saying, Except thou take away the blind and the lame, thou shalt not come in hither; thinking, David can't come in hither. Nevertheless David took the strong hold of Zion: the same is the city of David. And David said on that day, Whosover getteth up to the gutter, and smiteth the Jebusites, and the lame and the blind that are hated of David's soul, he shall be chief and captain. Wherefore they said, The blind and the lame shall not come into the house. So David dwelt in the fort, and called it the city of David. And David built round about from Millo and inward. And David went on, and grew great, and the LORD God of hosts was with him. II Samuel 5: 3-10

Jesus calls us also to be His anointed priests when we are his followers. We are royalty. Do we act like we are God's royalty? If we have a strong faith that shows in our attitudes and beliefs, then we are God's royalty. But if you are like me, there are times when I falter and my faith is not strong. It is then that I need most of all to turn to the word of God and pray. Or even worse is when I think I am strong and that the strength is my own that I can also be in trouble. I must realize that the strength comes from God.

Even while David was appointed king, he lived in exile for a while because he was scared for his life. He was being threatened many times by King Saul. Yet, God expected him to show strength by obediently doing as he asked him. David was anointed three times. Once he was anointed by Samuel, once by the men of Judah, and then once by the elders. David did overcome the city and won the battle against those who had been very boastful against him. Why was David considered a man after God's heart when he often showed his own weaknesses? He realized that when he was king, that God was responsible and that his success was because of God.

David's victory reminds us that we are not to be boastful in own abilities, nor are we to think lightly of our enemies' strengths. It is wise to remember that God is with us and He provides the strength and protection.

I'm so glad I'm a part of the family of God,
I've been washed in the fountain, cleansed by His blood,
Joint heirs with Jesus as we travel this sod;
For I'm part of the family of God.
–William J. Gaither

And from Jesus Christ, who is the faithful witness, and the first begotten of the dead, and the prince of the kings of the earth. Unto him that loved us, and washed us from our sins in his own blood, And hath made us kings and priests unto God and his Father; to him be glory and dominion forever and ever. Amen.
Revelation 1:5-6

Scouting Spies Saved

And Joshua the son of Nun sent out of Shittim two men to spy secretly, saying, Go view the land, even Jericho. And they went and came into an harlot's house named Rahab, and lodged there. And it was told the king of Jericho, saying, Behold, there came men in hither to night of the children of Israel to search out the country. And the king of Jericho sent unto Rahab, saying, Bring forth the men that are come to thee, which are entered into thine house: for they be come to search out all the country. And the woman took the two men, and hid them, and said thus, There came men unto me, but I wist not whence they were. Joshua 2: 1-4

Scouts often go out to look at potential athletes that they might want to include with their team. Other times, scouts go out to watch an opposing team to try and determine their strengths and weaknesses. Coaches watch game films for a similar purpose. They want to get their best plan of action by looking to the opposing side.

Rahab also may have decided to look to the opposing side because of their wins. These scouts or spies she helped had been sent out to see what might confront them in this city. Rahab must have heard about the Israelites because of what had happened to previous places that were conquered by them. As an opposing group, she may have decided that if she helped them, her odds of survival might be increased.

God is amazing. Again, He chooses to use a person of not the highest morals. Rahab was a prostitute and yet she helped the men of God. She decided to put her faith in God when she protected the spies. If she had been found out by her own people, she would probably have lost her life. She put all her trust in God. She placed her hope on this God and these spies to save herself but also to save her family members. She had heard the conquests of the Israelites but had not seen those, so she must have believed in the words about God saving these people. This faith led her to action of protecting the spies.

> *There was a girl God used for good and Rahab was her name.*
> *She hid the spies that came from God with flax upon her roof.*
> *The walls of Jericho fell down because of God and faith*
> *Rahab's house was saved and because of faith she was in Jesus' family line.*
> —Sharon Broome

Jesus saith unto him, Thomas, because thou hast seen me, thou hast believed: blessed are they that have not seen, and yet have believed. John 20:29

God will Fight Our Battle

And the Lord said unto Gideon, The people that are with you there are too many for me to give the Midianites into their hands, lest Israel vault themselves against me, saying, Mine own hand hath saved me. **Judges 7:2**

Gideon may have started out with the right attitude coming from a farming background and not wanting to be a king, while, at the same time, being willing to do battle according to God's directions. But then he acted like he was an earthly king. Gideon wanted proof of God's direction. He asked that God make a piece of wool wet while the rest of the floor was dry, then he would know that God would save Israel through him. And God did this for Gideon. God told Gideon that he had too many people willing to fight and they might take pride and think they had accomplished a victory. The final number to stay with Gideon was 300 people. God then told Gideon that he would have victory with those 300 people.

We must be careful not to take too much credit for successes. Oftentimes, there are many people who have been involved in making any project or assignment a success. And any of our own talents and abilities are a gift from God, so we should not let pride say we have accomplished something that others may not have done.

Our attitude needs to always be checked. It is very easy to find that people are very impressed with certain wins and yet these wins must be done in a righteous manner and without taking credit by ourselves. We also must realize that when times are difficult and we don't have success, that we can go to God in prayer. He is willing and able to fight our battles. He doesn't need certain circumstances to be in place to make a victory. He doesn't need a certain number of people to surround and follow us in order to make a victory. He just needs us to follow His directions and then to give the credit where the credit is due.

> *A mighty fortress is our God,*
> *A bulwark never failing;*
> *Our helper He, amid the flood,*
> *Of mortal ills prevailing*
> *The right Man is on our side.*
> —Martin Luther

Likewise, ye younger, submit yourselves unto the elder. Yea, all of you be subject one to another, and be clothed with humility; for God resisteth the proud, and giveth grace to the humble. Humble yourselves therefore under the mighty hand of God, that he may exalt you in due time. I Peter 5:5-6

Stopping for People

And Jesus stood still, and called them, and said, What will ye that I shall do unto you. **Matthew 20:32**

Jesus had a bad habit—he stopped for people. He had compassion on them even though the crowd wanted him to go on. Two blind men heard that Jesus was passing their way and began to shout "Son of David! Have mercy on us!" The crowd scolded them and told them to be quiet, but they shouted all the louder. When Jesus stopped and asked them what they wanted, they said, "Sir, we want you to give us our sight" (Matthew 20:33, GNT). Jesus had pity on them and touched their eyes and healed them and they followed him (Matthew 20:34, GNT).

There is another story in the bible when Jairus, a synagogue leader, pleaded to Jesus to come and heal his only daughter who was extremely sick. On the way, Jesus stopped and healed a woman who had been sick for 12 years. While he was there, people from Jairus came to him and told Jairus his daughter was dead. Jesus overhead this and said, "Don't be afraid; just believe" (Mark 5:36). When Jesus finally came to Jairus' house, he told them the child is just asleep. All laughed him to scorn so he put them out of the house, went into the young girl and he brought her back from the dead. "At this they were completely astonished" (Mark 5:42 NIV).

The two stories are just two quick examples to show where Jesus stopped to help and heal people. He had compassion on them. As a superintendent, do you stop and listen to your people and have compassion on them? I was watching a program on TV call "Undercover Boss." When the boss of the company goes out, in disguise, to their company they hear from the employees and that they are giving their all for the company. When the boss gets back to headquarters, he or she calls in the employee and helps them through their struggles because they have compassion for them. If you don't have that compassion and stop for your employees, ask the Lord to give you a servant heart that is one of compassion. Remember, Jesus stopped for you because he cares and has compassion!

> *Hear the blessed Savior calling the oppressed,*
> *O he heavy laden, come to Me and rest;*
> *Come no longer tarry, I your load will bear,*
> *Bring Me every burden, bring Me every care.*
> –Charles Jones.

Do all the good you can, by all the means you can, in all the ways you can, in all the places you can, at all the times you can, to all the people you can, as long as ever you can.
–John Wesley

Two are Better Than One

Again, if two lie together, then they have heat: but how can one be warm alone?
Ecclesiastes 4:11

I was helping my wife make the bed and I said to her, "You sure like this help, don't you?" She said, "Yes. I could do it myself as I did many years ago but it would take a lot longer." King Solomon recognized the need for help when he said that "Plans fail for lack of counsel, but with many advisers they succeed" (Proverbs 15:22 NIV). "Jesus sent his disciples out two-by-two with authority over evil spirits" (Mark 6:7, NIV). In Ecclesiastes 4 (NIV), King Solomon lists the additional advantages of two people:

> They have a good return for their labor.
> When one fails the other can help the other up.
> They can defend themselves more easily.

In our departments, when two work together on a service project or research project, the output is much greater and more robust. I will work on a research project, have another professor read it and make corrections, and then send it in to be published with both names. This is a way we can help each other increase our research production. The additional benefit is that there is very good morale in the department.

The same can be in the public schools. If people work together, then the intended outcome comes much more rapidly and the morale has drastically increased. I've been out in the public schools and I've heard people say, "When did that happen? Or who did that? Or when was that decision made? And so forth." The morale has drastically decreased, and the decision that was handed down is met with silent resistance. The superintendent is then frustrated and if this continues to happen, there is superintendent turnover. The superintendent would have been much wiser if s/he would have "not gone it alone." Some will say, "We didn't go it alone because we had central office administrators help us." If that is all that helped you, in the eyes of the building teachers and administrators, you went alone.

It gets hard and lonely doing things alone. There is only one that went alone and that was Jesus because He bore our sins on His way to Calvary. That was required because He bore my sins and yours as a sacrifice which was required.

> *Up the Calvary way, walked my Savior one day,*
> *With a heart that was breaking into;*
> *Crown of thorns that He wore, lowly cross that He bore,*
> *it was all for me and for you.*
> *Lonely road, up Calvary's way was a lonely road, to Jesus that day.*
> *Lonely road, He bore my sins on that lonely road, up Calvary's way.*
> –Elmor Mercer

To go it alone means that you will
have to "cut your arm off to save your life"
when you get into a life and death situation.

What About Me?

For we are his workmanship, created in Christ Jesus unto good works, which God hath before ordained that we should walk in them. **Ephesians 2:10**

Everyone has been given special gifts from God. And yet this does not mean that we are to be boastful of our gifts or success. It also means we are not to think highly of ourselves. The gifts were freely given with nothing done on our part. We are also admonished to not think too highly of others' gifts. There is a sense that the individual gifts need to be brought together in unity for the church. There is also a sense that the gifts are given so they can be used in service to God and others. The ultimate service is to take care of other Christians and bring others to a faith in God.

The gifts God gives as well as our work using God's gifts do not mean we get special wealth or health on this earth. It is the relationship that sustains us for eternal life with Christ. No one is perfect except Jesus. Even with all the gifts He has granted us, we still fall short of His glory. We are still sinners needing to be saved. The following of Jesus and realization that He has given us gifts, means Jesus will always be with us and take care of us. God wants us to use the gifts we have been given to serve God and put God first in our decisions.

This is not how the world answers "What about me?" The world might say that you worked hard, used your talents wisely, saved consistently and so you should be rewarded. Often the world would see the rewards as physical and financial well-being. But it means nothing if it does not have eternal significance.

Our reward will often be an eternal reward in heaven. We should be excited to serve God each day with the gifts He allows us to use on His behalf. What an honor to be able to use God's gifts as a service to Him. God could certainly take care of these needs, but He lets us have the joy of being a part of the service and there's joy in serving Jesus.

> *There is joy in serving Jesus,*
> *Joy amid the darkest night*
> *For I've learned the wondrous secret,*
> *And I'm walking in the light.*
>
> –Oswald J. Smith

Let your light so shine before men, that they may see your good works, and glorify your Father which is in heaven. Matthew 5:16

What are Your Reasons for Serving God?

But Jehu took no heed to walk in the law of the Lord God of Israel with all his heart: for he departed not from the sins of Jeroboam, which made Israel to sin. In those days the LORD began to cut Israel short: and Hazael smote them in all the coasts of Israel. II Kings 10:31-32

We always need to take a look at the motives behind actions, even our own actions. Some people do actions because they want to look good. Others want to show off their talents. Still others may want to do good actions as a way to get to heaven. Even though the Bible is clear that the only way to heaven is through Jesus, God does examine our own motives. The reasons we do things are as important as the actions. We may not understand someone's motives for their action the first time, but usually the motives can be determined with subsequent actions.

Churches and preachers have not been immune from wrong motives. If a preacher wants to have a large church because that makes him feel important, then the motives are wrong. If a person wants to complete many hard tasks in order to gain recognition, then the motives are wrong. If a person volunteers for charity activities so others will think better of them, then the motives are wrong.

Leaders are also not immune from wrong motives. There may be times when decisions appear in gray areas with no clear black and white response. Yet we usually know very well if some decisions are the correct ones. And if we do not know, that is when we need to go to the Lord in prayer. Our motives must always be to give God the glory.

When Jehu's actions were not done with the correct motives, the country suffered. God did not let them prosper; in fact God removed their area. Earlier, Jehu had removed idol worshipping but his motive evidently did not follow through to all his actions.

Is your all on the altar of sacrifice laid?
Your heart, does the Spirit control?
You can only be blessed and have peace and sweet rest,
As you yield Him your body and soul.
–Elisha Hoffman

People may be pure in their own eyes,
but the LORD examines their motives. Proverbs 16:2

What is in a Name?

Thou shalt say unto the children of Israel, I AM THAT I AM. **Exodus 3:14**

Many expecting parents put time and thought to a name for their new baby. They might look at several family names or they might look at books that give the meaning of names. Often, they will try combinations of first and middle names to make sure the names sound good together. It is a big decision to name a baby because the name identifies that person all through his/her life.

The names of God show the many attributes of God as well as how people know him. When Moses was told by God to free the Israelites from the Pharaoh and slavery, he was asked questions by Moses. One of the questions was about the name of God.

And Moses said unto God, Behold, when I come unto the children of Israel, and shall say unto them, The God of your fathers hath sent me unto you, and they shall say to me, What is his name? what shall I say unto them? Exodus 3:13. And God said unto Moses, I AM THAT I AM: and he said, Thus shalt thou say unto the children of Israel, I AM hath sent me unto you. Exodus 3:14. Then God went on in Exodus to give his other names. And God said moreover unto Moses, Thus shalt thou say unto the children of Israel, The Lord God of your fathers, the God of Abraham , the God of Isaac, and the God of Jacob, hath sent me unto you; this is my name for ever, and this is my memorial unto all generation. Exodus 3:15

Additionally, there are many other names given for God in the Bible. The following are some of those names:

Creator (Genesis 1:1) In the beginning God created the heavens and the earth
Prince of Peace (Isaiah 9:6) For unto us a child is born, unto us a son is given: and the government shall be upon hi shoulder and his name shall be called Wonderful, Counselor, The mighty God, The everlasting Father, The Prince of Peace.
Christ (Mark 8: 29)And he saith unto them, But who say ye that I am? And Peter answereth and saith unto him, Thou art the Christ.
Immanuel (Isaiah 7:14) Therefore the Lord himself shall give you a sign; Behold a virgin shall conceive, and bear a son, and shall call his name Immanuel
Awesome God (Nehemiah 9:32) Now therefore, our God, the great, the mighty, and the terrible God, who keepest covenant and mercy, let not all the trouble seem little before thee, that hath come upon us, on our kings, on our priests, and on our prophets, and on our fathers, and on all they people, since the time of the kings of Assyria unto this day.
The Most High (Genesis 14:20) And blessed be the most high God, which hath delivered thine enemies into thy hand. And he gave him tithes of all.
The One God (Malachi 2:10) Have we not all one father? Hath not one God created us? Why do we deal treacherously every man against his brother, by profaning the covenant our fathers
Almighty God (Genesis 17:1) And when Abram was ninety years old and

nine, the Lord appeared to Abram, and said unto him, I am the Almighty God; walk before me, and be thou perfect

Everlasting God (Genesis 21:33) And Abraham planted a grove in Beersheba and called there on the name of the Lord, the everlasting God.

God of Knowledge (1 Sam 2:3) There is none holy as the Lord for there is none beside thee; neither is there any rock like our God. Talk no more so exceeding proudly; let not arrogancy come out of your mouth; for the Lord is a God of knowledge, and by him actions are weighed.

True God (Jeremiah 10:10) But the Lord is the true God, he is the living God, and an everlasting king: at his wrath the earth shall tremble, and the nations shall not be able to abide his indignation.

The One and only God (Isaiah 45:5-6) I am the Lord, and there is no other; apart from me there is no God. I will strengthen you, though you have not acknowledged me, so that from the rising of the sun to the place of its setting men may know there is none besides me. I am the Lord, and there is no other.

Gracious God (Jonah 4:2) And he prayed unto the Lord, and said, I pray thee, O Lord, was not this my saying, when I was yet in my country? Therefore I fled before unto Tarshish: for I knew that thou art a gracious God, and merciful, slow to anger, and of great kindness, and repentest thee of the evil.

God, my Rock (Deuteronomy 32:15) But Jeshurun waxed fat, and kicked: thou art waxen fat, thou art grown thick, thou art covered with fatness; then he forsook God which made him, and lightly esteemed the Rock of his salvation.

God of Israel (Psalm 68:35) O God, thou art terrible out of thy holy places: the God of Israel is he that giveth strength and power unto his people. Blessed be God.

God, name above all names, reigns in power.

Where You Are Not Allowed

And the Lord spake unto Moses, saying, Take the rod, and gather thou the assembly together, thou, and Aaron thy brother, and speak ye unto the rock before their eyes; and it shall give forth water, and thou shalt bring forth to them water out of the rock; so thou shalt give the congregation and their beasts drink. And Moses took the rod from before the Lord, as he commanded him. And Moses and Aaron gathered the congregation together before the rock, and he said unto them, Hear now, ye rebels, must we fetch you water out of this rock? And Moses lifted up his hand, and with his rod he smote the rock, twice; and the water came out abundantly, and the congregation drank, and their beasts also. And the Lord spake unto Moses and Aaron, Because ye believed me not, to sanctify me in the eyes of the children of Israel, therefore, ye shall not bring this congregation into the land which I have given them. **Numbers 20:7-12**

Are there places into which you are not allowed to go? There are places you may choose not to go, but, for the most part, we can go to most places. As superintendents, we tell our employees that they must think about places they go and how that might affect what others think. If employees go to a local bar every night, parents may question their ability to teach their children. If they go to a gambling establishment, people may worry about their ability to manage money.

Other places you may not be able to go may be because of other circumstances. Perhaps you had planned a family trip for your family only to find out that the cost had become too prohibitive for your budget, or the place you had planned to visit was no longer a safe place. These are just a couple of reasons you no longer can go to certain places.

Another reason someone may not be allowed to go somewhere, is because of their actions. When my children were teenagers, they sometimes lost the privilege of attending some event because of their actions. Either they had not completed their chores or had not completed their homework.

Moses and Aaron both were not allowed to go to the promised land because they did not follow God's directions for getting water to the people. The Israelites were in the wilderness after being released from slavery in Egypt and had no water. They had complained about no water so Moses and Aaron prayed to God for the water. God gave Moses specific directions and yet Moses did not follow those directions. He was the leader of the people and should have provided an example to follow God's word explicitly. Moses was to use God's Word to get the water and yet he struck the rock, making it look like his own actions made the water. We are to respect God's Word and follow the directions so we know and others know that God is in charge and not us.

> *I'll follow Jesus here, I'll never ever fear,*
> *Though Satan's temptin powers assail;*
> *And though I'm tempted sore, I'll trust Him evermore*
> *For through His grace I shall prevail.*
> –William Henry

Do you want to reach the promised land? Then always obey the Lord.

Roadblock: Lack of Confidence

So that we may boldly say, The Lord is my helper, and I will not fear what man shall do unto me. **Hebrews 13:6**

Have you ever lost your confidence? I have and it really makes you feel inferior and inadequate. When that has happened to me, I've had to ask the Lord to help me through and put this "totally negative thought" out of my head.

When do you lose your confidence? If you're a baseball player and in a slump, you can lose your confidence in your hitting. If you've interviewed for jobs and have not been offered a job yet have been strongly considered, you can lose confidence in your ability to do the job. If you've made a bad business decisions, you can lose your confidence to try again. Losing confidence happens when we've been hit with an adversity when we're in a vulnerable state.

Look at all of the people who have failed in history, did they lose their confidence? They might have, but not for long, because they kept on trying. I was fortunate to have been raised in a home where my father and mother said that "I was always good enough to do the job." They believed in me and so I believed in myself. We all have a heavenly father who believes in us and has confidence in us.

Remember, you are made in the image of God and the Lord will open the doors that he wants you to walk through and close the ones He doesn't want you to walk through. Jesus knows what is best for you. So have confidence in yourself and say "The Lord is my helper."

> *Some people wonder how I smile, even though I'm going to trial*
> *How can I have a song, everything is going wrong,*
> *I don't worry and I don't fret, God has never failed me yet*
> *Trouble's come from time to time, that's all right, I'm not the worrying kind.*
> *Because, I've got confidence, God is going to see me through*
> *No matter what the case may be, I know He's going to fix it for me.*
> –Andrea Crouch

It may sound strange, but many champions are made champions by setbacks.
–Bob Richards.

Serving God Out of a Pure Heart

Behold, the days come, that all that is in thine house, and that which thy fathers have laid up in store until this day, shall be carried to Babylon: nothing shall be left, saith the LORD. **Isaiah 29:6**

When King Hezekiah's actions were done with the correct motives, the country prospered, but when he let pride come into his heart, the country was destroyed. God did not let Israel prosper. In fact, God removed them to Babylon and King Hezekiah's sons were made eunuchs in a foreign land. Earlier, Hezekiah had prayed to be healed and his life was extended 15 years, but pride came along which was demonstrated by the fact he showed off all of the wealth of Israel to the travelers from Babylon. King Hezekiah had let pride come in and tarnish his soul.

A clean, pure heart is essential to having a right relationship with God. Your heart includes your mind, will, and emotions. The enemy wants you to become distrusting, prideful, offended, disillusioned, and hurt, so it will tarnish your soul. If you desire genuine fellowship with God, you must present yourself properly to Him.

A pure heart is required to be pleasing to God.

He that hath clean hands, and a pure heart;
who hath not lifted up his soul unto vanity. Psalm 24:4

Truly God is good to Israel, even to such as are of a clean heart. Psalms 73:1

Now the end of the commandment is charity out of a pure heart,
and of a good conscience, and of faith unfeigned. I Timothy 1:5

Flee also youthful lusts: but follow righteousness, faith, charity, peace,
with them that call on the Lord out of a pure heart. II Timothy 2:22

To serve God out of a pure heart, you have to get rid of pride. Serving God out of a pure heart will lead you home to Heaven. It will also help you in your professional life and personal life. You will be known as a real Christian and not as a phony.

There is one vice (pride) of which no man in the world is free; which every
one in the world loathes when he sees it in someone else;
and of which hardly any people, except Christians,
ever imagine they are guilty themselves.
–C. S. Lewis

Great thoughts and a pure heart, that is what we should ask from God.
–Johann Wolfgang Von Goethe

Faith and Prayer

Everyone who calls on the name of the Lord will be saved. **Joel 2:32**

Somewhere around the middle of my fourth year as a superintendent, I started a new morning ritual. Like many school administrators, the daily grind of balancing my personal life with my job began to wreak havoc on me. I decided that each morning, as soon as I entered my office, I would do three things: (1) I would pray. I would thank God for the many blessings in my life, ask for His grace as I dealt with the day's problems, and finally pray for the students and staff in my district. (2) Secondly, I began reading one full chapter out of the Bible. Once I finished making my way through the book, I would just start again. It was amazing how I learned something new each time I read. (3) Finally, I would read a short morning devotional (much like the one you are reading today). It brought me great comfort and joy to understand how similarly God works in my life and in the lives of others.

Early in my Christian walk, I would pray for more faith. However, as I went through more and more trials I began to realize that it was not faith that I was asking for, but rather my faith be turned into sight. I did not want to walk in faith; I wanted God to show me what I was praying for. Finally, I realized, faith does not say, "I see this is good for me because God has sent it." Instead, faith declares, "God sent this, therefore it must be good for me." This simple understanding of faith and prayer has helped me deal with issues and problems too numerous to count. When we are in difficult situations, all God asks is that we hold Him more tightly for He has the power to carry us through any situation.

I encourage you to start your own morning ritual. A ritual that allows you to spend some alone time with God is reflecting on the things that are happening in your life. For "We know that the Lord causes everything to work together for the good of those who love God and are called according to His purpose for them" (Romans 8:28).

> *Pray is the key to Heaven,*
> *But faith unlocks the door*
> *Words are so easily spoken*
> *Prayer without faith is like a boat without oars.*
> –Samuel T. Scott

My own Christian faith has given me great strength. I believe those of faith-and not just my faith- have something powerful they can draw on.
–John Wooden

MAY

May 1

Inquire of God

And when David inquired of the Lord, he said, Thou shalt not go up; but fetch a compass behind them, and come upon them over against the mulberry trees. II Samuel 5:23

Millions of decisions are made every day by teachers, administrators, superintendents, board members, executives, families, and so forth. Some decisions made are very important, like buying a home, and some are very insignificant, like choosing to eat a hamburger.

King David had just come in from a mighty victory over the Philistines and the Philistines were getting ready to attack Israel again. Most people would have said, "This is going to be an easy victory, let us go whip them again." But David did differently, as he "inquired of the Lord." The Lord told him if you go to battle with them, you'll lose, but do this and wait until you hear the rustling in the "mulberry trees" as that means I have gone on before you and the battle will be won.

I've seen several superintendents get into trouble because they have made poor decisions. The board lost faith in them and the community no longer trusted them. These superintendents made decisions as though they were invincible. They didn't wait for the right time and just "plowed ahead." Now, they are fighting for their career and job. Has that happened to you?

How can you make certain that you will make the right decision in your job as superintendent? You've done all your paper work, collected the data, studied the current research, talked with colleagues and mentors, and visited with the state department. But your decision now has you in hot water. Did you inquire of God? Did you ask Him for His guidance? Did you ask Him to give you wisdom in this matter? Did you ask Him to guide your steps? Don't forget to inquire of the Lord in all of your decisions because then you will have great success. The most important decision you can make is to accept Jesus Christ as your Lord and Savior.

God hold the future in His hands,
And every heart He understands;
On Him depend, He is your Friend;
He holds the future in His hand.
—James D. Vaughan

It's not hard to make decisions when you know what your values are.
—Roy Disney

We shall steer safely through every storm, so long as our heart is right, our intention fervent, our courage steadfast, and our trust fixed on God.
—St. Francis De Sales

A Wise Person

Who is wise, and he shall understand these things? Prudent, and he shall know them? For the ways of the Lord are right, and the just shall walk in them; but the transgressors shall fall therein. **Hosea 14:9**

When you hear the phrase "a wise person," you may think of it as a sarcastic comment about a person. Sometimes it is used for someone who spouts off many times as if they are knowledgeable on many topics. Or the phrase, "a wise person" could be a positive comment about a person who has a lot of knowledge on a specific topic.

Television reporters will often give some information on a story and a current event, then follow that with an expert on that topic. The experts are considered wise people who have a lot of knowledge about the topic being reported. Another place we see the use of experts is during courtroom trials. Experts will be asked to give their knowledge on topics that relate to the trial.

Many times, people want to rely on other humans for a knowledge base as experts who can help them. But, ultimately, people will not have all the answers and they can even provide inaccurate advice. When we look at experts in the field of approving medicine, we can see experts that have not always made the right decisions. Either drugs were approved too quickly and the side effects were devastating to patients, or drugs were tested for a long time and people died without treatment. Another area where experts have not had the best advice may have been in the ways to teach certain skills such as reading and mathematics. Time and research later may have shown other methods more successful. Human experts will never be accurate all of the time because they are human. "Who is a wise man and endured with knowledge among you? Let him shew out of a good conversation his works with meekness of wisdom" (James 3:13).

God is the only wise one who has all of the knowledge on everything. He showed what it meant to be wise as well as knowing and showing that in the actions.

All of us need the wisdom from God to run our lives well.
We may get knowledge from different places
but nothing works as well as God's wisdom.
It's because, God is the One who created us
And all that we see in this universe.
–Unknown

For it is written, I will destroy the wisdom of the wise,
and will bring to nothing the understanding of the prudent.
Where is the wise? Where is the scribe?
Where is the disputer of this world?
Hath not God made foolish the wisdom of this world?
For after that in the wisdom of God the world by wisdom knew not God,
it pleased God by the foolishness of preaching to save them that believe.
I Corinthians 1:19-21

Making the Right Choice

The Lord has established his throne in heaven, and his kingdom rules over all. Psalm 103:19

I had an incredible job offer today. I was asked to become the superintendent of a large district located on the outskirts of the Dallas/Fort Worth area. The pay is incredible, and I would be working for a good school. With a little work, it could be a great school. My problem is that I currently work in a wonderful district with many people that I care about deeply. My wife and kids both love our current situation, and any move would be difficult on them. I know that eventually, I will move on to another school district. But is now the time? I want to make sure that I make the right choice. I don't want to leave a place where I am happy and risk putting my family in a difficult situation, simply to advance my own career and make more money.

Psalm 32:8 reads, "I will instruct you and teach you the way you should go; I will counsel you with my eye upon you." For three days, I prayed that God give me a sign. I prayed, "Lord, please guide me down the path that is best for my family. Give me the grace to hear your voice, and the courage to follow your will." I wasn't asking for a huge sign. I didn't need to be swallowed up by a whale like Jonah. I just wanted to hear that soft voice in my heart; you know like the one we sing about in the hymnals on Sunday mornings: "Softly and tenderly Jesus is calling..." But after three days of prayer; I got nothing. No billboard with letters saying, "TAKE THE JOB," not even a small whisper in my ear. Why did God not hear my prayer?

In the book, *Quiet Strength*, by Tony Dungy, he talks about how he would pray for God's guidance during career choices. God never spoke to Tony either. But Tony trusted that as long as he was doing God's will, then he would be blessed by God. Most people that are faced with tough career choices find themselves in similar situations. They want to follow God's will, but they don't really know what that will is.

The simple truth that I have learned is that God allows things to happen. He opens and closes doors for us, not just in our careers, but also in life. We make the right choice every time we ask him into our hearts and follow his word. Just because God does not answer your questions with a loud thunderous voice, does not mean that he isn't working for you. Proverbs 3:5-6 says, "Trust in the Lord with all your heart, and do not lean on your own understanding. In all your ways acknowledge him, and he will make straight your paths. By trusting in God, we always make the right choice and anchor our soul in Him."

> *I've anchored my soul in the Haven of Rest,*
> *I'll sail the wide seas no more;*
> *The tempest may sweep o'er the wild, stormy deep,*
> *In Jesus I'm safe ever more.*
> –Henry Lake Gilmour

Keep your face to the sunshine and you can't see the shadows.
–Helen Keller

A Queen's Role

So it came to pass, when the king's commandment and his decree was heard, and when many maidens were gathered together unto Shushan the palace, to the custody of Hegai, that Esther was brought also unto the king's house, to the custody of Hegai, keeper of the women. And the maiden pleased him, and she obtained kindness of him; and he speedily gave her things for purification, with such things as belonged to her, and seven maidens, which were meet to be given her, out of the king's house; and he preferred her and her maids unto the best place of the house of the women. And the king loved Ester above all the women, and she obtained grace and favour in his sight more than all the virgins; so that he set the royal crown upon her head, and made her queen instead of Vashti.
Esther 2:8-9, 17

A modern day queen is often the head of a monarchy. Her roles vary depending on the country. Queen Elizabeth II has been the queen for 60 years. She became queen because she was the oldest daughter of the family holding the throne. She was twenty five years old when her father died and she became queen in 1953, and thus began her career with several visits to other countries. Her role continued as she made many ceremonial visits as well as appointing subjects to political positions. But to our knowledge, Queen Elizabeth has not had to make a choice in her role that could cost her life.

Other women have become queen because of their marriage to a king. Esther was such a woman who became queen when she married a king. She had found favor with her beauty and grace. Esther's role, like other queens, was a very visible role. But, her role took a more dramatic turn when she found out about plans to kill her own people. She had to decide whether sharing about her own family background would give the king reason to kill her also. If she did not attempt to protect her own people, then she would lose her family and her life. Esther had to decide if her own life or her people's lives was more important. Queen Esther chose to go to the king and plead for her people. She and her people were saved. She had fulfilled a major role in saving lives.

As leaders, we also have the ability to save people when we clearly understand how our policies and practices affect the lives of our employees. Some companies have come under attack because they have used child labor or have deplorable working conditions. Some leaders of these companies have even suggested that they knew nothing about those conditions when confronted with the truth. The leaders' responsibility is to know their own practices and to ensure that their employees' rights are kept in the forefront of their decisions.

> *A queen's role is defined as a woman of beauty, a woman of grace*
> *A woman of excellence beholding God's face.*
> *She walks with the Lord with integrity, knowing her purpose and destiny*
> *In everything she walks in God's love, reflecting the beauty of her Father above.*
> –M. S. Lowndes

For the commandment is a lamp; and the law is light; and reproofs of instruction are a way of life. Proverbs 6:21

Ashamed of the Gospel

For I am not ashamed of the gospel of Christ: for it is the power of God unto salvation to everyone that believeth; to the Jew first, and also to the Greek. **Romans 1:16**

The gospel is the good news of Jesus who was born of a virgin, lived a sinless life, had a shameful death, was resurrected on the third day, and ascended to heaven to be with the Father sitting on His right hand side.

Many people today do not believe in the virgin birth. *I believe in the virgin birth!* With man, it's impossible, but not with God. Many people today do not believe that Jesus lived a sinless life. *I believe Jesus lived a sinless life!* He took on our sins and ransomed us from death, hell, and the grave. Many people today do not believe that Jesus died on the cross. *I believe Jesus died on the cross and that death bought our salvation!* He redeemed us by sacrificing Himself on the cross. He willingly laid down His life for us. Many people today do not believe that Jesus rose from the dead. *I believe Jesus rose from the dead*! These are not fables. Many people today do not believe that Jesus ascended up to heaven. *I believe that Jesus ascended to heaven and sits on the right-hand side of God!* Many people will challenge you for being a Christian. They will shame you for carrying your bible. They will shame you for praying over your food. They will try to make you look foolish. They will call you a fanatic. But remember Romans 8:12 (NIV), "As the scripture says, anyone who trusts in him will never be put to shame."

In II Timothy 1:8, 12 (NIV) it says, "So do not be ashamed of the testimony about our lord of me his prisoner. Rather, join with me in suffering for the gospel, by the power of God. That is why I am suffering as I am. Yet this is not cause for shame, because I know I have believed, and am convinced that he is able to guard what I have entrusted to him until that day."

Jesus says, "If anyone is ashamed of me and my words in this adulterous and sinful generation, the Son of Man will be ashamed of them when he comes in his Father's glory with the holy angel" (Mark 8:38, NIV).

But, what is about the Bible that shakes people up? They know that it is the way to eternal life but Satan has blinded their eyes. Pray for them! Stand up for Jesus and be strong in the Lord. As a superintendent, live your real life and stand up for what is right.

> *Stand up, stand up for Jesus! Stand in His strength alone,*
> *The arm of flesh will fail you, ye dare not trust your own;*
> *Put on the gospel armor, and watching unto prayer,*
> *Where calls the voice of duty, be never wanting there.*
> –George Duffield, Jr.

Don't ever step back from anyone talking bad about your savior.

Building Leaders

Now when Ezra had prayed, and when he had confessed, weeping and casting himself down before the house of God, there assembled unto him out of Israel a very great congregation of men and women and children: for the people wept very sore. Then arose Ezra, and made the chief priests, the Levites, and all Israel, to swear that they should do according to this word. And they sware. Then Ezra rose up from before the house of God, and went into the chamber of Johanan the son of Eilashib: and when he came thither, he did eat no bread, nor drink water: for he mourned because of the transgression of them that had been carried away. **Ezra 10:1, 5 -6**

When we train leaders, we can find no better example than the Bible. God trained Ezra to be a leader. He wanted Ezra to have knowledge about His word. God trained Ezra to give up on his own abilities and trust in God. Ezra knew he needed to pray and then share with others what God's vision was for his actions and theirs. He got the people's attention and their willingness to do whatever he asked of them. Ezra told the people that God wanted their repentance. Further, Ezra showed great emotion over the people's sins. He realized how far they had removed themselves from the will of God.

In the New Testament, Jesus trained his disciples to be leaders. He taught them through modeling the behaviors that were important. He confronted them with what they would face. He also taught them through examples in ordinary life. His first miracle showed that he cared for the well-being of his people. Jesus prayed in times of need. Jesus showed that ordinary people were often willing participants in His will because He showed his acceptance of them first. He prayed all night in the garden of Gethsemane.

As a superintendent, you will have many people that need to be helped into leadership roles. Show them the behaviors that are most successful. Additionally, you need to guide them in learning knowledge that will help them understand the role of the superintendent. They may need new knowledge in areas of finance, program development, human resources, communication, community outreach, facilities, and management. Further, they may need support with dispositions. Again, modeling may be the best way for an emerging leader to develop dispositions of a superintendent. When we act with integrity and take all our concerns to God in prayer, we have His word to know what are actions should be. His word is our continual guide.

Godly leadership is about knowing your limitations,
It is growing in wisdom and seeking to understand rather than be understood.
It is caring for people and in being brave
It is seeing the future and helping each person lead the band in praise to God!

But we will give ourselves continually to prayer,
and to the ministry of the word. Acts 6:4

Dedicated to Worshipping God in a Church

Now then, O LORD God of Israel, let thy word be verified, which thou hast spoken unto thy servant David. But will God in very deed dwell with men on the earth? Behold, heaven and the heaven of heavens can't contain thee; how much less this house which I have built! Have respect therefore to the prayer of thy servant, and to his supplication, O LORD my God, to hearken unto the cry and the prayer which thy servant prayeth before thee: That thine eyes may be open upon this house day and night, upon the place whereof thou hast said that thou wouldest put thy name there; to hearken unto the prayer which thy servant prayeth toward this place. Hearken therefore unto the supplications of thy servant, and of thy people Israel, which they shall make toward this place: hear thou from thy dwelling place, even from heave; and when thou hearest, forgive. Now, my God, let, I beseech thee, thine eyes be open, and let thine ears be attentive unto the prayer that is made in this place. Now therefore arise, O LORD God, into thy resting place, thou, and the ark of thy strength: let thy priests, O LORD God, be clothed with salvation, and let thy saints rejoice in goodness. And when all the children of Israel saw how the fire came down, and the glory of the LORD upon the house, they bowed themselves with their faces to the ground upon the pavement, and worshipped, and praised the LORD, saying, For he is good; for his mercy endureth forever. II Chronicles 6:17-21, 40-41; II Chronicles 7:3

I am always sad when I hear that churches are no longer needed. People can meet in each other's homes or they can even virtually and not leave their homes. It is very difficult for me to see how that form of church will be a place to worship God. The major reason to have a church is to come together and worship God. This would be difficult for me to do in a virtual setting. Although there may be a greater feeling of connectedness, I am not sure that would be giving God His holy day. There are times when I am in church that I forget I am there to praise God. I let my mind wander or I think about myself. Or even worse, I think about something I am doing that afternoon. But, I know my purpose is to worship God.

The Bible mentions Christians coming together because there is power in bringing all of the gifts God gave each other. Solomon dedicated the temple that his father wanted to build, but was directed by God that it would be built by his son instead. Solomon immediately honored God in the dedication by giving a listing of all the things God had done for His people as well as the promise made to His people. Solomon also talked about their need for repentance as well as the consequences of their sin. There is joy in worshipping together. This is true for a superintendent because when people collaborate there is great camaraderie and sense of accomplishment which brings joy to you and your staff.

The body of Christ is a unit, though made up of many parts.
Its segments are many, forming one body and one heart.
All must be built up in their spirits, in line with the Word of God.
Having all parts fitted and doing their task of love to impart.

For wherever two or three are gathered together in my name, there am I in the midst of them. Matthew 18:20

Giving All of Yourself

For scarcely for a righteous man will one die: yet peradventure for a good man some would even dare to die. **Romans 5:7**

A roofing company employee in New Jersey jumped into a vat of nitric acid to save a co-worker who had fallen 40 feet when the roof collapsed. When the co-worker saw this, without hesitation, he jumped into the vat to help get his co-worker out. He said, "I had to get him out of there." The ambulance came and took the roofer who had fallen into the vat to the hospital where he was in critical condition. The co-worker who saved him suffered burns on his legs and abdomen and was taken to the hospital where he was treated and released.

Another news item involves a pit bull which pulled her owner off of the tracks from an oncoming train. The owner had passed out while crossing the tracks and the dog pulled and pushed the woman to safety before the train arrived. In the process, the dog lost her leg when it was ran over by the train.

Another news item is about a dog that saved a woman and her child from robbery. A robber had pulled a knife on the lady and this dog came out of nowhere to save them. If people and animals will give their all for us and be willing to lay down their lives, imagine how much more willing we should be to give our all. Jesus went to the cross and gave Himself for us. He prayed that this trial would pass and said, "Father, if you are willing, take this cup from me; yet not my will, but yours be done" (Luke 22:42, NIV). Do you give your all to God? Do you give your all to your family? Do you give your all for your job? Do you work as unto the Lord? Are you willing to go the last mile for your employees, your family, and your neighbor? If not, pray that the Lord help you to give yourself for His glory and learn to put others first.

> *All to Jesus I surrender,*
> *All to Him I freely give;*
> *I will ever love and trust Him,*
> *In His presence daily live*
> –J. W. VanDeventer

Winning is everything, to win is all there is. Only those poor souls buried beneath the battlefield understand this.
–Navy SEALS

God Will Make A Way

Wherefore, sirs, be of good cheer: for I believe God, that it shall be even as it was told me. **Acts: 27:25**

Paul was a prisoner on the way to Rome. The ship was caught in a violent storm and the captain of the ship started to unload the cargo so the ship wouldn't be lost. The storm continued for many days and they gave up all hope of being saved. When it seemed like all was lost, an angel of the Lord came to Paul and told him that the lives of the people on board would be saved if they stayed on board. They were all saved, but the ship was destroyed. God made a way!

I know that sometimes superintendents will get into predicaments or situations and it looks like every storm that is imaginable is thrown at them. But if they trust in God, He will make a way of escape. In the county where I work, last year there were a couple of superintendents that were in storms, but God made a way to escape. When you are trying to find a job and there is nothing out there or you are not getting the offers or interviews, remember: God will make a way!

There was a time when I had trouble finding a job and I was getting depressed. I could have let the devil sit on my shoulder and whisper in my ear, "God doesn't care for me." But the devil is the father of all liars and I put my situation in the hands of the Lord and He made a way and opened up a job for me. Also, how many times have you looked to your left and right crying out to God for help because you could not find it wherever you looked? That also has happened to me. But, again, I knew that I served a God who is able to make a way out of nothing. God brought me out to a "wealthy place" because I trusted in Him.

As Paul said, "be of good cheer because God will deliver you" (Acts 27:25).

God will make a way
Where there seems to be no way
He works in ways we can't see
He will make a way for me
He will be my guide
Hold me closely to His side
With love and strength for each new day
He will make a way.

–Don Moen

Through the clouds of midnight, this bright promise shone,
I will never leave thee and will never leave thee alone.

–Anonymous

Blow the Trumpet

Therefore also now, saith the LORD, turn ye even to me with all your heart, and with fasting, and with weeping, and with mourning: And rend your heart, and not your garments, and turn unto the LORD your God: for he is gracious and merciful, slow to anger, and of great kindness, and repenteth him of the evil. Who knoweth if he will return and repent, and leave a blessing behind him; even a meat offering and a drink offering unto the LORD your God? Blow the trumpet in Zion, sanctify a fast, call a solemn assembly. Joel 2:12-15

A sounding trumpet has a variety of uses. My church has a praise team that includes some wonderful musicians. Their singing in harmony, accompanied by piano, guitars, drums and even a trumpet, gives beautiful praise to God. The trumpet player is careful not to overpower the vocalists. Trumpets are also used in many other places besides the church and music. Trumpets may be used at the funeral of military personnel, calls to war, or to announce events. There are 104 verses in the Bible that mention trumpets. The trumpet is one of the oldest musical instruments.

The trumpet is also used as a call to prepare for battle. A Christian's preparation means prayer, study of the Bible, quickly repenting of sin, working with other Christians and worshipping God. The trumpet is a call to listen and know the signs. We are not to be surprised by the signs sent by God. The trumpet is sounded as an alarm and a warning. Bill Gaither wrote a song that says, *"Blow the trumpet in Zion, Zion, sound the alarm in my Holy mountain..."*

Superintendents also must identify ways to communicate warnings to their employees and students in case of emergencies. Schools must have well designed, articulated, and practiced emergency plans for different disasters. Additionally, everyone needs to clearly understand the warning signals in order to correctly react. If a warning sign is confusing then the consequences could be disastrous. For example, if the warning sign for a tornado is confused with the warning sign for a fire, then wrong actions will be taken. If a tornado is close to the school and students with teachers go outside, this would be a wrong action that could cause death. Or if the warning sign was for a fire, and the hearers thought it was for a tornado, they would go to an interior small room and crouch down close to the floor. This would also cause death from smoke and the fire. Superintendents' trumpet warnings must be clearly understood.

When the Lord returns, he will sound the trumpet and all Christians will be caught up to live with Christ forever! I Thessalonians 4:16

When the trumpet of the Lord shall sound, and time shall be no more,
And the morning breaks, eternal, bright and fair;
When the saved of earth shall gather over on the other shore,
And the roll is called up yonder, I'll be there!
–James Black

And he shall send his angels with a great sound of a trumpet,
and they shall gather together his elect from the four winds, f
rom one end of heaven to the other. Matthew 24:31

God Will Take Care of Vengeance

Rejoice not when thine enemy falleth, and let not thine heart be glad when he stumbleth: Lest the LORD see it, and it displease him, and he turn away his wrath from him. Fret not thyself because of evil men, neither be thou envious at the wicked: For there shall be no reward to the evil man; the candle of the wicked shall be put out. **Proverbs 24: 17-20**

The Old Testament talked about an eye for an eye. Yet, the New Testament does not advocate for our retaliation. In fact, in the New Testament, Jesus said, *revenge is mine.* Yet, we are also told to yield to the authority of government that is there to protect people. But, if the nation doesn't protect its people, then that is when others need to stand up and do what is right.

There are times to be obedient and there are also times to make a stand to change laws or things that are offensive to our Christian heritage and the well-being of our fellow man. It may not be easy to stand up for what is right, but we are to do it when others need that support in a major way.

There was a time that Jesus also showed his anger and stood up for the house of God. That was when church people had created the act of making a profit from the sales of animals and birds for the atonement of sins. This created a burden that Jesus had not required of his people and turned the house of God into a mockery. In essence, it was not showing a respect for the house of God.

Jesus wants us to be very careful of our motives when we stand up for something. Whatever we make a stand for must be in alignment with the Bible. Our first response is to show love to our neighbors and allow God to take control.

You shall not take vengeance, nor bear any grudge against the children of your people,
but you shall love your neighbor as yourself: I am the LORD.
Leviticus 19:18

As I drive on one highway, there is a small town with a small building that has a sign that takes up one entire side of the building. The building is a private business and the sign is the *Ten Commandments.* I am so impressed that someone is willing to place their beliefs clearly on their own property. This business owner has the courage to stand for his beliefs. He does it in a very respectful way. It is not done out of vengeance but rather as a stand in a way to honor God.

Revenge is like a rolling stone,
Which, when a man hath forced up a hill,
Will return upon him with a greater violence,
And break those bones whose sinews gave it motion.
–Albert Schweitzer

Vengeance is Mine, and recompense;
their foot shall slip in due time;
For the day of their calamity is at hand,
and the things to come hasten upon them. Deuteronomy 32:35

God's Constant Word

Hath a nation changed their gods, which are yet no gods? But my people have changed their glory for that which doth not profit. Jeremiah 2:11

At what instant I shall speak concerning a nation, and concerning a kingdom, to pluck up, and to pull down, and to destroy it; If that nation, against whom I have pronounces, turn from their evil, I will repent of the evil that I thought to do unto them. And at what instant I shall speak concerning a nation, and concerning a kingdom, to build and to plant it; If it do evil in my sight, that it obey not my voice, then I will repent of the good, wherewith I said I would benefit them. Jeremiah 18:7-10

The Word of God is constant. It is so amazing that after so many years the Bible still reaches and guides people. I am also amazed to read a section in the Bible that I know I had read earlier, and yet it has a new meaning for me. Then I wonder if I missed something when I read it the first time or if it is clearer upon reading it again. As leaders, it is important that our message is also constant. We must communicate the same thing to various groups. If we say one thing to a certain group and a different thing on that same topic to another group, then there will be confusion. People will not trust our word.

It also worries me when I find my country seeming to lean away from the ways of God. When God's name is removed from our coins, it sends a message that God is no longer important. Hopefully, the removal of God's name will only make people realize how important it is for them to stand up and express their desire to keep God in their lives as well as part of the country including on the coins.

We no longer allow prayer in school and even the moment of silence has come into question. Tolerance for the rights of people has led to the lost rights of Christians. The Old Testament had some similar problems. Jeremiah was sent to point out the sins of the people and pleaded that they return to the Word of God. It seems that the same message could be preached today. Jeremiah simply told them the truth from the Word of God and that they would be destroyed because of their actions against the Word of God.

As superintendent, you have the Word of God to help you know what God's expectations are for you. The only way to understand the Word of God is to allow God to help you and be obedient to His will. There is no way for you to correct the wrong actions on our own; you just have to remember that Jesus is constantly with you and has taken care of everything!

> *Constantly abiding Jesus is mine*
> *Constantly abiding, rapture divine;*
> *He never leaves me lonely, whispers, oh, so kind:*
> *"I will never leave thee"—Jesus is mine.*
> –Anne Murphy

We are of God: he that knoweth God heareth us; he that is not of God heareth not us. Hereby know we the spirit of truth, and the spirit of error. I John 4:6

Hardship

Lay down now, put me in a surety with thee; who is he that will strike hands with me? Job 17:3

Job needed to have God with him. Bad things happen even to good people. Job had suffered some very bad things. All his earthly possessions were destroyed. His body was full of disease. Job pleaded to God not to forsake him. He turned to his friends for their support, understanding, and comfort and they didn't support him. They thought that he had done something wrong to have this slate of hardships fall against him. At the point he called out for God not to leave him, he was at a very hopeless frame of mind. He had lost possessions and family. His friends came to him but gave him no support.

"Bear ye one another's burdens, and so fulfil the law of Christ" (Galatians 6:2). When we feel lost and discouraged because of the hardships in our lives, we often go to our friends to get their support. But, if friends treat us the way Job's friends treated him, we will find little support. This is also an area we need to examine of ourselves. When our friends need support, do we give them help or do we question what they had done to get into such a bad state?

I have watched many superintendents struggle in some school districts and yet be very successful in other districts. It seems that there is not an identifiable point that shows their demise in those certain districts. As others question the leader's decisions, it becomes obvious that some seem like Job's friends. They assume the leader has done something wrong; otherwise they would not be struggling. If the superintendent had more supporters, that superintendent might be able to work more successfully in a more caring and supportive environment. This kind of support would have the majority of people assuming there are at least two sides to every story. They would be willing to withhold their judgments until they had all the information rather than presuming the leader was wrong because some were opposing that leader.

"Who comforteth us in all our tribulation, that we may be able to comfort them which are in any trouble, by the comfort wherewith we ourselves are comforted of God" (II Corinthians 1:4). This verse showed that because of our experiences in needing comfort, we should be able to help comfort others. We need to turn to God when our times are hard. Everyone will have hardship. It is what they do when hardship arrives that often determines their attachment to God. Allow God to carry the burdens. When my husband died suddenly, I would cry out to God each night. He carried me through the hardship.

Bring all your needs to the alter
Bring all your needs to the Lord.
He is so willing and able to help you,
Bring all your needs to the Lord!
–Dottie Rambo

Cast thy burden upon the LORD, and he shall sustain thee; he shall never suffer the righteous to be moved. Psalm 55:22

Money Never Satisfies

He that loveth silver shall not be satisfied with silver; nor he that loveth abundance with increase: this is also vanity. Every man also to whom God hath given riches and wealth, and hath given him power to eat thereof, and to take his portion , and to rejoice in his labour, this is the gift of God. Ecclesiastes 5: 10-11, 19

I can remember, in my youth, thinking of all the things I could purchase if I only had a million dollars. I knew beyond a shadow of a doubt that this would make me happy. It took me many years before I realized that happiness and contentment had nothing to do with money. The things that really made me happy were not even things, not material things, but non-material things. I enjoyed my family and spending time with them. The time spent with family did not have to be an expensive vacation either. It was just as much fun going to a neighborhood park or to the public swimming pool as going on any vacation.

I also enjoy designing and planting flower gardens. But I am always amazed when I look in nature and see all of the beautiful work of God. My own designs always pale in comparison to God's designs in nature. There are no other materials greater than in God's nature. The other night, the full moon was so bright that it looked like day time outside. And yet the few clouds were scattered across the sky in a beautiful dark blue seemed to shine like diamonds. Those colors would seem impossible to recreate.

The happiness I find is surrounded by enjoying the work of God in nature. I can try to replicate it, but it never has the same majesty. God's work always is beautiful and it is a gift, just like money is a gift. How we use money and think about it is what is important. God wants us to remember that He is the source and owner of everything. It is all His. Our possessions are not for showing off to others.

This is important in superintendency as well. How we conduct business is more important than how great our buildings look. We do not need beautiful structures to make sure we have success. I am not advocating that we don't take care of our buildings. But a new structure by itself will not bring success. The success is by the people inside and how they treat each other and the integrity of their work. Money and possessions can't be the ultimate goal. How others are served should be important in order to give God glory with the correct use of our materials. Possessions and money are to be shared for others' benefit.

> *Only Jesus can satisfy your soul.*
> *Only He can change your heart and make you whole.*
> *He'll give you peace you never knew, sweet joy and love and Heaven, too.*
> *For only Jesus can satisfy your soul.*
> –Lanny Wolfe

Thine, O LORD, is the greatness, and the power, and the glory, and the victory, and the majesty: for all that is in the heaven and in the earth is thine; thine is the kingdom, O LORD, and thou art exalted as head above all. 1 Chronicles 29:11

Nevertheless

Nevertheless the foundation of God standeth sure, having this seal, The Lord knoweth them that are his. And, let every one that nameth the name of Christ depart from iniquity. **ll Timothy 2:19**

Dr. Mark Rutland, president of Oral Roberts University, in 2001, wrote a book titled, *Nevertheless.* It was an excellent book about when you want to confuse your enemy, you say, "nevertheless". According to Webster's Dictionary, "nevertheless" is defined as "in spite of that, however, notwithstanding." "Nevertheless" is a word that means you will listen, but will always do what is right. You've listened to everyone and after the words have passed, this is when you say, "Nevertheless, it will be like this or this is what is going to happen," or "this is how it works because it is right and built on a solid foundation." This gives comfort to your employees and your family or to those in your circle of influence.

Peter writes in 2 Peter 3:13 (KJV), "Nevertheless, we according to His promise, look for a new heaven and a new earth, wherein dwelleth righteousness." Peter was telling us that everything around us was going to be destroyed, but then said "nevertheless" there will be a new heaven and earth. He was stating a truth and giving comfort. The same is true of Paul when he was telling about Hymenaeus and Philetus, who had departed from the faith and were preaching falsely. (II Timothy 2:17, NIV). He goes on to say, "nevertheless" Gods foundation stands firm. "Nevertheless" gives us comfort.

The word "nevertheless" keeps our foot, as a superintendent, on the solid rock. We may not always understand the paths the Lord is taking us, but we can certainly trust Him. I can remember when I was going through trials or having to do a certain thing that I didn't understand, but I could say "Nevertheless" I can trust God. Rev. Charles Spurgeon wrote, "I am continually in Thy favor, continually with thee. Here is comfort for the afflicted soul; vexed with the tempest within. Say in thy heart, nevertheless, and take the peace it gives. Nevertheless, I am continually with thee."

My hope is built on nothing less
Than Jesus' blood and righteousness;
I dare not trust the sweetest frame,
But wholly lean on Jesus' name.
On Christ, the solid Rock, I stand;
All other ground is sinking sand.

–Edward Mote

Jesus is why there is a "nevertheless."

Recipient of Vicious Gossip

Let not then your good be evil spoken of. **Romans 14:16**

How many times have you done something with very good intentions and you found out that you were the object of ridicule, derision, scorn, and envy? You thought, how in the world did that happen? What did I do that caused people to think that way about me or my actions?

Lydia was a principal who seemed to lack common sense. At the end of the school year, she hosted a "teacher appreciation" luncheon for her teachers by having a very nice lunch catered in. Instead of eating with her teachers, she, her assistant principal, and the secretary left the building at noon, for almost two hours, to treat a teacher to lunch who was leaving to take another position. Lydia's intentions were good, but her timing was very bad. Not only did she not eat with her teachers but she left her building unattended without an administrator for almost two hours.

Dr. Lee was a superintendent who worked hard for his teachers. One year, the teacher's union submitted a laundry list of 21 items to be negotiated. These items, if they became part of the negotiated agreement, would have been very detrimental to the school district. Through the negotiation process, not one of the union's items made it to the final agreed upon negotiated agreement. Dr. Lee felt that he had done a very good job in negotiating the new teacher agreement. The union leadership did not think that way and ran a full page ad the next day in the newspaper stating, "Vote of No Confidence for Superintendent Dr. Lee." That was devastating and it hurt Dr. Lee to the very core.

You have heard the saying, "perception is reality" and this becomes true because people, in general, are too indifferent to find out the truth. You will have envious, evil people accuse you of the most ridiculous things just because of your position. For example, a parent got up at a board meeting and accused a superintendent of cheating because her son was not named valedictorian. The superintendent was devastated because she worked her heart out for that school and every child in it.

To help you through these times like this, pray, "Dear Lord, guide my actions so that they are always seen as good for the school district. Give me the wisdom to always do what is right. Help me to communicate in a timely fashion to my employees and to be that servant leader for them so my intentions are always seen correctly. Finally, Lord, please keep me humble before you. For your glory, I pray. AMEN."

When I'm low in spirit I cry, "Lord lift me up. I want to go higher with thee!"
But the Lord knows I can't live on the mountain, so he picked out a valley for me
He leads me beside still waters, somewhere in the valley below.
He draws me aside to be tested and tried, but in the valley He restoreth my soul.
                                                              –Dottie Rambo

Your motto should be, "If it's illegal, unethical, or immoral, I will not do it as long as the world turns and in addition, even if it is ok, if it causes my teachers to stumble, I will not do it."

Praise the Lord

Praise the Lord with gladness: Come before His presence with singing. Enter into His gates with thanksgiving, and into His courts with praise; be thankful unto Him, and bless His name. **Psalms 100:2, 4**

The Lord made us to praise him! He is a holy God and we are made in His likeness and created in His image. Praise brings us closer to the Lord. Praise also has the benefits of helping remove mountains, overcome difficulties, and destroy obstructions. Praise turns conflict into conquest.

Praise multiplies our faith in God. It is faith in action. It takes our eyes off our situation and focuses them on God. God is the creator of everything and causes everything to work together. Praise is the highest form of worship, the best type of medicine, and most effective type of therapy.

Praise drives out distractions, brings heaven down to earth and causes glory to fill our souls. It's time to stop worrying, fretting, and fearing. It's time to start praising God. There is no faster way to defeat the Satan than to enter His courts with thanksgiving and praise. Praise turns fear into delight and sorrow into song. Praise puts a royal crown on prayer.

Have you lost the power of praise in your life? If so, you can discover it again by just praising the Lord and telling Him how much you love and adore Him. Rediscovering praise in your life will help you through your daily life, both personal and professional. The person who knows the joy of praise rarely knows the grief of failure.

Join the hosts in heaven in singing, "Alleluia: for the Lord God omnipotent reigneth" (Revelations 19:6). "Praise is comely for the upright" (Psalms 33:1). If you want a new fountain of joy and to be the superintendent you desire to be, then start shouting the high praises of God.

> *Praise Him! praise Him! Jesus, our blessed Redeemer,*
> *Heavenly portals, loud with hosannahs ring!*
> *Jesus, Savior, reigneth for ever and ever;*
> *Crown Him! crown Him! Prophet and Priest and King!*
> *Death is vanquished! Tell it with joy, ye faithful,*
> *Where is now thy victory, boasting grave?*
> *Jesus lives! No longer thy portals are cheerless;*
> *Jesus lives, the mighty and strong to save.*
> —Fanny Crosby

Praise is melody in God's ears.

The End Times

Let no man deceive you by any means: for that day shall not come except there come a falling away first, and that man of sin be revealed, the son of perdition.
II Thessalonians 2:3

We are living in perilous times. Everything is changing at rapid speed and people are frantically rushing to and fro trying to find happiness and satisfaction. The cultural war is at full pace and is being pushed on the school. These sons of Belial know that if they changed the minds of the children they could change the culture (Proverbs 22:6). This cultural war didn't start all at once but it was put in place by people many years ago, by people bent on destroying the American way of life and the world. This technique of changing the children was done by Hitler when he took over Germany. He indoctrinated the children through false education.

This cultural war started when the Bible was taken out of the school. Then, the courts said abortion was ok under the guise of a "woman's right." Next, people with alternative lifestyles and their supporters are lobbying congress to pass "hate" and "bullying" laws that would make it a crime if you didn't accept the changes or if you spoke out against them. The appointment of liberal judges coupled with the gradual takeover of the media, the movie industry, and higher education would quickly hasten these changes. Finally, the education of our students, by twisting the real meanings of words like diversity, bullying, and tolerance, will cause them to accept any changes that come. People who speak out for the truth will be ridiculed with their character assassinated.

As a school superintendent, you will be faced with pressure from groups to have the same standing to use the school building as churches, to silence your opinion, to recognize demands of alternative life-style adults, and so forth. In the last days, men will be lovers of themselves and call evil good (II Timothy 3:2). As a superintendent, you will have to be strong and courageous to stand against the onslaught of the enemy. Your country and your children's future are at stake. Pray that the Lord give you wisdom and the power to stand up for what is right.

> *Troublesome times are here, filling men's hearts with fear,*
> *Freedom we all hold dear now is at stake*
> *Humbling your hearts to God saves from the chastening rod*
> *Seek the way pilgrims trod, Christians awake.*
> –Oak Ridge Boys

Stand up for what is right even if you are standing alone.

Rebuilding

Then I told them of the hand of my God which was good upon me; as also the king's words that he had spoken unto me. And they said, Let us rise up and build. So they strengthened their hands for this good work. **Nehemiah 2:18**

The rebuilding of Jerusalem's walls was a well-organized project with leaders and several people. The sheep gate was built by Eliashib, a high priest, and his men. The fish gate was built by sons of Hasseniah and the old gate was repaired by Jehiada. Malchijah repaired the tower of the furnaces. The valley gate was repaired by Hanun. The dung gate was repaired by Malciah. The gate of the fountain was repaired by Shallun. The horse gate was repaired by the priests. The goldsmiths and the merchants repaired the corner to the sheep gate. The lists of the different groups that helped in the rebuilding showed what a large project had been undertaken.

Chapter three of Nehemiah also mentions some that did not help in the work: "And next unto them the Tekoites repaired, but their nobles put not their necks to the work of their Lord" (Nehemiah 3:5).

The remodeling or building of new buildings requires someone to oversee the work and make sure that things are done in a timely manner while some things, such as site preparation, need to be completed prior to others. Additionally, the leader or contractor orders the materials and supplies needed while trying to stay on a budget. Contractors must guide different subcontractors at times in order to get the specialty work completed. The contractor reports to the leader whom hired him or her. This process helps keep everyone informed and also helps employees complete the work by following rules and regulations. Along the process of building, different inspection agencies visit the job site to ensure that the building meets the expectations of codes.

Christ is busy at rebuilding us as well as His church. He is our leader who has many leaders to guide our spiritual walk and to learn more about His word. Jesus also sent us the Holy Spirit to help us on our rebuilding of ourselves so we may be used by God to rebuild others. Sadly, there are still people who refuse this encouragement and don't seem to want anything to do with rebuilding of themselves or a church. My desire is to always be a rebuilder for Christ, because Jesus asked me to tend and feed His sheep.

If I was a teacher, I'd tell you what to do
I'd keep on teaching and working on the building for my Lord
If I was a superintendent, I'd tell you what to do,
I'd keep on leading and working on the building for my Lord.
                                        –Var. Oak Ridge Boys

O house of Israel, can't I do with you as this potter? Saith the LORD.
Behold, as the clay is in the potter's had, so are ye in mine hand,
O house of Israel. Jeremiah 18:6

Graduation Day

In a moment, in the twinkling of an eye, at the last trump: for the trumpet shall sound and the dead shall be raised incorruptible, and we shall be changed. **I Corinthians 15:52**

Graduation day—what a joyous event for the graduate and the parents! I've watched and sat through many graduations, as a student, a graduate student, a parent, superintendent, and as a professor. As the music plays, the faculty, administration, and board file into the auditorium with their long gowns, then come the graduates. Once all are seated, the ceremony begins. The emotions are all the same and the people are ecstatic! When the graduate's name is called and she or he walks across the stage, whistles sound, horns are blown, and cheers come from the graduate's family and friends. After the ceremony, a graduation party is given in honor of the graduate with the most delicious food.

What is the prelude to this graduation? The graduate has to make certain they meet all school requirements or at higher education, university requirements. One young teacher in the master's program was frantic that he would not be able to "walk" because he forgot to take his prelim exams. The chair of the program accommodated him so he could quickly come in and take them. He passed, and he walked.

You see, you can't graduate unless you meet certain standards. The same is with the graduation of earth to heaven. The Bible in Galatians 5:19-20 (NIV) lists those who will not inherit the kingdom of God. This list is summarized again in Revelations 21:8 (NIV).

Those who are victorious will graduate to Heaven to live forever with the God! Praise the Lord! These are people who have asked the Lord to forgive them of their sins and believe on the Lord Jesus Christ (John 3:16). When we ask the Lord to forgive us of our sins, He is faithful and just to forgive us (I John 1:9), throws our sins away as far as the east is from the west (Psalms 103:12), and our names are written in the Lamb's Book of Life (Revelations 20:12).

Some glad morning we shall see, Jesus in the air
Coming after you and me, joy is ours to share
What rejoicing there will be, when the saints shall rise
Headed for that jubilee, yonder in the skies

Our Lord has written the promise of resurrection, not in books alone,
but in every leaf in springtime.
–Martin Luther

Rejuvenating Sleep

It is vain for you to rise up early, to sit up late, to eat the bread of sorrows: for so he giveth his beloved sleep. **Psalm 127:2**

I was so tired that I fell asleep sitting on the sofa while watching television. I started to contemplate sleep and why we need it. To rejuvenate yourself, you need to sleep. Your whole body functions better when it is rested. I know that I found that a 15 minute "power nap" at noon, instead of lunch, helped me function drastically better. I was more alert and ready to face the afternoon. As I pondered the benefits of sleep, it befuddles me that many administrators, and even pastors, don't get their necessary sleep. Even God rested on the seventh day.

Matthew Walker, an assistant professor, from the University of California at Berkley, found that napping an hour can dramatically restore and boost brain power. Think of that: a nap makes you smarter. On the other hand, the more hours we're awake the more sluggish our minds become. Staying up all night cramming for finals by college students decreases their ability to learn by almost 40 percent. Finally, a sleepy driver is as dangerous on the road as a drunk driver. Your bodily functions are impaired and you don't react as quickly as a non-sleepy driver. Sleep awakens your senses.

To fall asleep at night, many people take sleeping pills or melatonin. Being unable to fall asleep can be due to stress, being over-tired, having caffeine in your body, and so forth. As your body gets behind on sleep, a "sleep debt" builds up and then you need to build it up by a deep refreshing sleep.

As a superintendent, many situations will face you during the day. A micromanaging board member, a complaining parent, the teacher's union, deciding when to run a bond issue, and a host of other school decisions will weigh heavily on your mind, causing you to lose sleep. Turning all these situations and problems over to God relaxes you so you can sleep at night. There were times I fretted and worried about the day, and then tossed and turned all night. The next day I was extremely tired and worthless at work. I had to learn to turn it all over to the Lord. If this is you, ask the Lord to give you peace and rest.

I am resting tonight in this wonderful peace,
Resting sweetly in Jesus' control;
For I'm kept from all danger by night and by day,
And His glory is flooding my soul!
–Warren Cornell

If God is bigger than any problem that you can or can't see,
then he's big enough to give you restful sleep.

The Classes Didn't Make

For where two or three are gathered together in my name, there am I in the midst of them. Matthew 18:20

Every year curriculum coordinators, department chairs, and principals will be scrambling to make certain classes "are large enough" to have the class. At the university, the policy says that you can't have a class unless five students have enrolled in the class. Currently, because of the budget crisis, the number has been raised to 10. In the K-12 schools, unless it's a core class, you will be forced to close a class if enough students have not signed up for it. Again, it's all tied to the budget. It's not important enough to have the class unless there are enough students.

When you're a student, teacher, or faculty member and you hear the dreaded words, *"the class didn't make,"* you start wondering what you're going to do. The student might need the class to graduate, the faculty member needs to teach the class to supplement their income, and the parents wonder if their child is going to make it through school on time. You began to wonder how important your needs are to the decisions being made.

You, as a superintendent, will have to keep on top of your building administrators to make certain that a class has more than the minimum number because you are responsible for making certain that the tax dollars are spent wisely. I'm thankful that the Lord did not say, "Sorry, the class didn't make, so you are not worthy." The prodigal son came home and his father welcomed him back. He didn't have to worry about "not making the class" with his father as he knew his father was waiting for him. In the parable of "The lost sheep," the shepherd searched until he found that one lost sheep. You are important in the eyes of the God. He's never too busy for you and class always "makes" for you.

> *Central's never busy, always on the line,*
> *You may hear from heaven, almost any time;*
> *It's a royal service, free for one and all,*
> *When you get in trouble, give the Lord a call.*
> –F. M Lehman

You are always relevant and important to the Lord.

Oppression and Judgment

Hear this, O ye that swallow up the needy, even to make the poor of the land to fail, Saying, When will the new moon be gone, that we may sell corn? And the Sabbath, that we may set forth wheat, making the ephah small and the shekel great, and falsifying the balances by deceit? That we may buy the poor for silver, and the needy for a pair of shoes, yea, and sell the refuse of the wheat? The Lord hath sworn by the excellency of Jacob, Surely I will never forget any of their works. Shall not the land tremble for this, and every one mourn that dwelleth therein? And it shall rise up wholly as a flood; and it shall be cast out and drowned, as by the flood of Egypt. **Amos 8:4-8**

The Lord is very clear on our purpose as Christians. Three times he told his disciples that they were to tend and feed His sheep. The sheep are the fellow Christians. In Amos, God made it clear that those who oppressed the poor would be judged. Amos felt strongly that in his time, the wrongs that were committed against the poor and needy were perpetuated within the business system as legal and that it was against God.

Some actions today may be legal, but that does not make them right in God's eyes. Nor should these acts be seen as right in our eyes. It is wrong to pass the blame because we do not feel we are a part of the wrong. If we are aware of an injustice and someone being demeaned, then we are called to speak up. It is not acceptable to say that, "It is just the way things are done here." The way things are done are not okay when others are belittled or wronged.

The quick loan places seem to flourish because of the needy. Many of these businesses charge high interest rates for repayment. Some even hold car titles for repayment of loans. Now if a needy person loses his car, he won't be able to get to work and then he can't pay off his loan. It seems like a vicious cycle of wrong actions. There are many areas of our political and business system that need to be examined for the fairness of their treatment of people.

As superintendents, we must ensure that our practices not only follow the law but also do not wrong other people. Our reputation as an honest business will be judged by our actions. If we allow any forms of injustice at the work place, we have created an environment of distrust. It is our responsibility to examine our policies and always evaluate areas of our organization that have struggled with fairness. This fairness could be in areas of promotion, salary, benefits, or job duties. Any of these areas can be handled legally, but not always ethically. A strong leader knows the organization's strengths and also the weaknesses that need to be fixed for no oppression to exist in it. If you have problems of being partial to people and looking out for the downtrodden, then pray that the Lord give you a servant heart and that He take away your heart of stone.

He saith unto him the third time, Simon, son of Jonas, lovest thou me? Peter was grieved because he said unto him the third time, Lovest thou me? And he said unto him, Lord, thou knowest all things; thou knowest that I love thee. Jesus said unto him, Feed my sheep. John 21:17

The Façade

Beware of false prophets, which come to you in sheep's clothing, but inwardly they are ravening wolves. **Matthew 7:15**

Some people are extremely clever about deceiving others. Jesus warned about this that in the last days false teachers would be out deceiving many people. Paul frequently expressed dismay on how often we are so easily misled by "wolves" that prey upon the flocks. He warned about doctrines that sound good but are not good if they contradict God's Word. The devil is a smooth talker.

These smooth talkers put on a façade which is a false front and portray a person they are not. As a superintendent you really have to be careful and alert as you interview people for administrative positions. These smooth talkers will do their best to "snow" you so that you will hire them. If you do hire them, you will have an administrator who's not in education for children—someone you'll have to be firing in a very short time.

Margaret, an elementary principal, was fired after two years. She had been let go from a principal's position at her previous district in which she was employed. Margaret was a nice looking woman and presented a very good first impression by portraying a caring administrator. Margaret was always successful in getting hired by superintendents who desired a minority administrator. I feel sorry for the teachers and students at her new middle school. This type of leader creates a toxic non-learning environment.

Another example is of the time my wife was cooking a beautiful-looking zucchini casserole dinner. It was nice and large, no flaws, and it looked luscious. She cut it in half, put herbs on it, and then layered it with cheese. This mouth-watering dish was baked and the aroma filled the air. When it was done we cut a piece out of it. The first bite took our tongues and twisted them. It tasted so bad and was so bitter that you could not eat it. The dog wouldn't even eat the cheese that we scraped off of it. This beautiful zucchini put on a façade.

As a superintendent, pray that the Lord opens your eyes so that you are aware of the façade that administrators might be portraying to you. Also pray that the Lord opens your eyes to the "false prophets" in the world that are trying to turn you away from the truth.

Open my eyes, that I may see
Glimpses of truth Thou hast for me;
Open my eyes, illumine me,
Spirit divine

No man, for any considerable period, can wear one face to himself and another to the multitude, without finally getting bewildered as to which may be the true.
–Nathaniel Hawthorne

The Rejected Cornerstone

The stone which the builders refused is become the head stone of the corner.

Psalms 118:22

Jesus saith unto them, Did ye never read in the scriptures, The stone which the builders rejected, the same is become the head of the corner: this is the Lord's doing, and it is marvelous in our eyes? Matthew 21:42

And are built upon the foundation of the apostles and prophets, Jesus Christ himself being the chief corner stone. Ephesians 2:20

Unto you therefore which believe he is precious: but unto them which be disobedient, the stone which the builders disallowed, the same is made the head of the corner. I Peter 2:7

This is the stone which was set at nought of you builders, which is become the head of the corner. Acts 4:11

And he beheld them, and said, What is this then that is written, The stone which the builders rejected, the same is become the head of the corner? Luke 20:17

A corner stone of a building can have two definitions. One is a memorial set near the corner. It can be a special stone, a stone which has some inscription that commemorates the building or builders, or even a stone with a time capsule placed within it. Another definition of the cornerstone is true corner foundation where all other parts of the wall will be laid. If the corner stone is not level and true then the rest of the building will not be straight.

Christ is the corner stone and yet, while on this earth, the majority of the religious sect refused him. The disciples did not even fully understand Christ's role. Many wanted a Savior that came to be a king and set up a kingdom as an earthly king might do. Even though some initially followed Jesus with praising during Palm Sunday, this would change soon. The people wanted that form of earthly king that could show them earthly prizes immediately. Many did not see Christ as the Savior for all those who accepted Him. He is the true and only way to the eternal kingdom of heaven. Christ as our foundation, when we believe in him, gives us the strength as well as the grounding of a level life committed to Him.

Many superintendents will supervise the construction of new buildings. One part of this building might be a memorial time capsule placed in a stone in the corner of the building. Certain special items will be placed in the container for others to examine later in years. One school placed a Bible in its capsule as a sign that Jesus is their district's cornerstone. While others may open the container many years later, it may not be clear why something placed in the container was important. The word of God made it clear that Christ is the cornerstone of life for those who accept Him. It should appear very clear that Christ is the only way to eternal life. May we show physically and emotionally that Christ is our foundation.

Jesus is our Rock of Ages and we can hide in him.

Editing

I pray not that thou shouldest take them out of the world, but that thou shouldest keep them from the evil. **John 17:15**

As we were sitting in the work room editing this devotional, we came across many mistakes. These mistakes ranged from misspelled words, words that were wrong but the spell-checker did not pick them up (i.e., their or there), extra spaces, double devotionals, words that were left out, and grammatical errors. It was a tedious job but before this devotional is published, we had to make certain that we found and cleaned up as many mistakes as possible.

The same is true in our spiritual life here on earth. The Lord continually edits us to make certain that all impurities are purged before the final trumpet sound. It is essential that we clean ourselves from all impurities because Hebrews 12:14 it reads, "Follow peace with all men and holiness, without which no man shall see the Lord." We are required to present ourselves a living and holy sacrifice to the Lord.

Ways the Lord brings these impurities to our attention are: our conscious (it starts to bother us), bringing Bible verses to our remembrance, and being chastised. The Bible says, "For whom the Lord loveth he chasteneth, and scourgeth every son whom he receiveth" Hebrews 12:6. Jesus is the "author and finisher of our faith" (Hebrews 12:2). He is therefore our authorship and we, as Christians, are products of His editing of our lives.

John Bunyan said it best in his book *Pilgrim's Progress.* Christian is a character than makes his way to the Celestial City. Along the way, he faces and, with the help of the Lord, overcomes many obstacles. His final reward is entrance into the Celestial City.

> *Search me, O God, and know my heart today;*
> *Try me, O Saviour, know my thoughts, I pray;*
> *See if there be some wicked way in me:*
> *Cleanse me from every sin and set me free.*
> –J. Edwin Orr

We are the products of God's editing, rather than of our authorship.

Preparation for the Storm

The great day of the LORD is near, it is near, and hasteth greatly, even the voice of the day of the LORD, the mighty man shall cry there bitterly. That day is a day of wrath, a day of trouble and distress, a day of wasteness and desolation, a day of darkness and gloominess, a day of clouds and thick darkness, A day of the trumpet and alarm against the fenced cities, and against the high towers. **Zephaniah 1:14-16**

When blizzards are forecasted, many people head to the grocery stores to buy bread, water, and milk. Additionally, people might check the batteries in the flashlights. The people with fireplaces often stock more wood in case the electricity goes out, leaving the fireplace as the only source of heat. Many people have experienced blizzards and know how long it can take to recover from the storm. Businesses will close because of the blizzards as no one is able to shop or even travel during the blizzard. Schools close because of blizzards.

There are signs of warning on this earth also that forecast the end of times. Some people will heed these warnings and prepare themselves. Other people will hear the warnings and choose not to believe them and continue with their lives. Other people will hear the warnings and believe the warnings, yet not prepare for the forecasted wrath. The reason is that many people are not concerned about the warnings and the signs.

The signs include the collapse of businesses and the financial system. The United States has a large deficit and owes money to other countries. The collapse of the financial system also is seen in correlation with the downfall of the housing business as homes lose value and people owe more on their homes than the homes' values. The unemployment rate is at a high enough rate that it affects people's ability to purchase things or feel secure about their jobs. It would seem that God is trying to warn us that we should be repenting and changing our ways.

Additional signs are riots and national unrest. Many of us saw the unrest in Egypt on television which led to the removal of its top leader. Yet, we are told not to be afraid because we have the protection of God. We can prepare because we know that our refuge from the blizzard will be close to God. God has told us that He will come quickly and those who have accepted the Lord as their savior will be caught up to be ever with the Lord.

In times like these you need a Saviour
In times like these you need an anchor
Be very sure, Be very sure
Your anchor holds and grips the Solid Rock.
–Ruth Jones

Behold I come quickly; blessed is he that keepeth the sayings of the prophecy of this book. And behold, I come quickly; and my reward is with me, to give every man according as his work shall be. I am Alpha and Omega, the beginning and the end, the first and the last. Blessed are they that do his commandments, that they may have a right to the tree of life, and may enter in through the gates into the city. Revelations 22:7,12-14

The Value of Memorials

Verily I say unto you, wheresoever this gospel shall be preached throughout the whole world, this also that she hath done shall be spoken of for a memorial of her. **Mark 14:9**

Memorial Day is a very special day in the United States. It is a time that Americans honor all of the soldiers who have fought for America's freedom. Since the beginning of the United States, we have fought in over 11 wars. The number of men and women soldiers who gave their lives, to protect us and our freedom, from these wars total over 1,350,000.

In the Revolutionary War, we lost 5,000 patriots. A few years later in the War of 1812, the United States lost over 2,000 men. The Mexican War fought in the middle 1800s took the lives of 13,000 men in battle. The Civil War toll of lives lost was almost 700,000 men. In the Spanish-American War in 1898, America lost another 2,000 men. In World War I, 116,000 soldiers were killed. World War II took the lives of 400,000 men. Along came the Korean War and America lost another 36,000 soldiers. In the Vietnam War, almost 60,000 soldiers were killed. The Gulf War cost us another 382 lives. The Iraqi War, Afghanistan, Grenada, Panama, Mogadishu, and the Balkans all took American lives.

The Israelites crossed over the Jordan River into the Promised Land. After they finished crossing, the Lord said to Joshua to choose 12 men, one from each tribe, to take up a stone from the middle of the river to serve as a sign among you so in the future when the children ask what these stones mean, you will tell them that the Lord stopped the flow of the river before the ark of the covenant of the Lord and the rivers were stopped. These stones are to be a memorial to the people of Israel forever (Joshua 4:1-10).

The simple act of love this woman had for the Lord (Mark 14) would be a memorial for ever. Her act of worship is still a memorial wherever the Gospel is preached. In Luke 22, the Lord's Supper followed the Passover Meal. Jesus instituted this sacred memorial so that believers down the centuries would remember Him in His death. The broken bread reminds us of Christ's body, given for us, and the cup reminds us of His shed blood.

Memorials are made so that we never forget. Humans have a great propensity to quickly forget the price paid, the victories won, and the goodness of the Lord. That is why you have to continually remind people what happened and build memorials. As a superintendent, make certain that you hold the memorials in your school of your nation, community, and district.

> *A memorial is to keep in memory some person, action, or event,*
> *That contributed to others in some positive way.*
> *It also can keep in memory some terrible event,*
> *In an effort to help people remember that event.*

It is wonderful to remember our men who gave their all for our freedom.
But for the child of God it is far better to remember our God's great work
and what our Lord did for us on the cross.

New Day, New Hope

And I said, My strength and my hope is perished from the LORD: Remembering my affliction and my misery, the wormwood and the gall. My soul hath them still in remembrance, and is humbled in me. This I recall to my mind, therefore, have I hope. It is of the Lord's mercies that we are not consumed, because his compassions fail not. They are new every morning: great is they faithfulness. The Lord is my portion, saith my soul; therefore will I hope in him. The LORD is good unto them that wait for him, to the soul that seeketh him. It is good that a man should both hope and quietly wait for the salvation of the LORD. **Lamentations 3:18-26**

Have you ever had one of those days when you think perhaps you should just have stayed home? This morning I went to a meeting, only to find out no one else was there. I would have thought I had the wrong day or time, but the secretary for the leader of the meeting had it on his schedule. After waiting awhile, the secretary apologized and I left for my office. On the way to the office, sitting at a red light, a large SUV does not stop in time and runs in to the back of my car. As I wait for the police officer, many of my Sunday school colleagues drove by and asked if I was okay. Once in the office, there were numerous calls to insurance companies, and repair shops. I was glad that no one seemed to be hurt. And the vehicles did not look too bad. However, the replacement of an entire auto bumper can be very expensive. And it will be time- consuming for the car to stay in the repair shop.

Perhaps tomorrow will be a better day. I look at a Bible reference on my list to check and it is Lamentations. I felt like lamenting today. But my hurt over a vehicle was nothing compared to how Jeremiah must have felt on the destruction of Jerusalem. As superintendent, your life will have challenges and you will have days that present challenges. The challenges may even seem extremely difficult to handle. Yet our Lord promises to be with us. Our Lord is there to help us every day. Each day provides the hope to be better than the previous day.

Every day is a good day to give thanks unto the Lord
To give thanks unto the Lord for all He's done for us.
For He has done great things for us
Oh, how we love Him for what He's done.
–Vickie Winans

I will lift up mine eyes unto the hills, from whence cometh my help. My help cometh from the Lord, which made heaven and earth. He will not suffer thy foot to be moved: he that keepeth thee will not slumber. Behold, he that keepeth Israel shall neither slumber nor sleep. The Lord is thy keeper: the Lord is thy shade upon thy right hand. The sun shall not smite thee by day, nor the moon by night. The Lord shall preserve thee from all evil: he shall preserve thy soul. The Lord shall preserve thy going out and thy coming in from this time forth, and even for ever more. Psalm 121:1-8

Pride Sends Us to the Ground

The king spake, and said, Is not this great Babylon, that I have built for the house of the kingdom by the might of my power, and for the honour of my majesty? While the word was in the king's mouth, there fell a voice from heaven, saying, O king Nebuchadnezzar, to thee it is spoken; The kingdom is departed from thee. And they shall drive thee from men, and thy dwelling shall be with the beasts of the field: they shall make thee to eat grass as an oxen, and seven times shall pass over thee, until thou shall pass over thee, until thou know that the most High ruleth in the kingdom of men, and giveth it to whomsoever he will. **Daniel 4:30-32**

It should not be difficult to realize that God is not fond of prideful people. And we should take care not to be proud ourselves, either. We have our success based only on what God has given us. In a nation that prizes independence and hard work to get ahead, many people feel they have the right to be proud of their accomplishments. People who are not proud of their own works may be very proud of their children's accomplishments or especially proud of their grandchildren's accomplishments. It is our family members in which we see the best. It is okay to see the great things in our offspring. But, again, we must remember where they gained their skills. God gives those gifts. Many have worked also to increase skills, but we must give God the credit because He gave us those skills for us to develop.

It is hard to be around very proud leaders who are arrogant and think very highly of themselves. They see that they have power and strength. Additionally, they may flaunt all of their accomplishments without giving credit to other people who have helped them or to God.

Any time I want to feel pride in something I have completed, I am compelled to think about King Nebuchadnezzar. He was a king who controlled a large empire and was very proud of his accomplishments. His empire, like so many others, failed. And he personally suffered and became a wild and crazy person, eating grass like an animal. His failure came when things appeared very secure. Our own lives may seem very secure and yet, if we don't trust in the Lord, He will get our attention so we understand and give Him the glory. Sometimes our success leads us to believe we have control of situations. I don't want pride so large that God has to send me out like a wild animal to get my attention. I want to control my own pride and give all the glory to God.

> *When I survey the wondrous cross*
> *On which the Prince of glory died,*
> *My richest gain I count but loss,*
> *And pour contempt on all my pride.*
> —Isaac Watts

Pride goes before destruction, and a haughty spirit before a fall. Proverbs 16:18

The Joys of Righteous Rulers

When the righteous are in authority, the people rejoice: but when the wicked beareth rule, the people mourn. **Proverbs 29:2**

There have been many despotic rulers throughout the ages. Timur (1336-1405) spent his life gaining control over Asia. He was a ruthless leader who massacred huge populations without showing mercy. Ivan the Terrible was a cruel ruler who tried to expand Russia. He employed evil means to attain his goals. He killed many of his wives and murdered his son in an act of fury. Maximillien turned France into a police state masterminding the Reign of Terror. People were beheaded on the guillotine without trial. Over 300,000 people were imprisoned and 40,000 died in prison. Stalin (1929-1953) crushed the people of Soviet Russia. He sent thousands of people to labor camps because they didn't accept his communist policies. Many people died by execution, starvations, and entry into labor camps. Hitler was one of history's most chillingly despotic tyrants. He suppressed people of non-Germanic origin and tortured them horrendouly. He slaughtered the gypsies, communists, and 6 million Jews. His ambition was to rule the world. Mao Tse-tung controlled China from 1949-1976. His economic plan cost the lives of 30 million people. In the name of cultural revolution, he gave vent to his cruel nature by imprisoning and torturing the bourgeoisie community. Idi Amin ruled Uganda from 1971-1979. He destroyed the economy by driving away ethnic Asians and by persecuting tribes. He ransacked the country's wealth and called himself the conqueror of the British Empire. Finally, Pol Pot was a radical Marxist leader of Cambodia from 1975-79. Over 2 million people were massacred in Cambodia or were forced to death through hard labor.

"When the righteous are in power the people rejoice" (Proverbs 29:2). The same is true with superintendents. If you have a superintendent that is selfish, vindictive, and mean, you will have a school district that is in turmoil, students who are not learning, and high teacher turnover. Superintendents who are ethical, practice servant leadership, have high human relations, and do things right will have a district that is stable, have lower teacher turnover, and increased student learning. What are you? Pray that the Lord gives you a caring humble heart that will always do what is right for the district and community and that you will be an advocate for what is right.

I am only one, but I am one. I can't do everything, but I can do something.
And what I can do, I ought to do, and what I ought to do,
by the grace of God, I will do.
I will do more than belong, I will participate. I will do more than care, I will help.
I will do more than believe, I will practice. I will do more than be fair, I will be kind.
I will do more than dream, I will work. I will do more than teach, I will inspire.
I will do more than earn, I will enrich. I will do more than give, I will serve.
I will do more than talk, I will act. I will be more than good,
I will be good for something.

What is liberty without virtue? It is madness, without restraint.
–Edmund Burke

JUNE

Nothings is too Hard for God

Behold, I am the LORD, the God of all flesh: is there anything too hard for me? Jeremiah 32:27

I had read over this verse many times and today it just seemed to jump out at me. My son is having a difficult time finding a job, another son is in the midst of building a new law practice, and I have had problems that seemed overwhelming. It seemed like I will never be able to make it out and there is nothing anyone can do to help me. Then, I sit and listen to the troubles and struggles that people in the church are going through and it seems like "why us, Lord?" That is what the devil likes to tell us but then God said, "Is anything too hard for me?"

The devil is the great deceiver and will cause you to forget how big and great your God is. That is why you have to keep your eyes on the Lord. God created the heaven, the earth, all mankind, all animals, all plants, the air and water, the universe and stars. So, why worry and fret about what God will do for you? If your name is in God's Book, then you know that you are a child of the King. Harriet Buell in 1877 wrote the song, "I'm a Child of the King" and a verse goes like this: *My Father is rich in houses and lands, He holdeth the wealth of the world in His hands! Of rubies and diamonds, of silver and gold, His coffers are full, He has riches untold. I'm a child of the King, A child of the King: With Jesus my Savior, I'm a child of the King.*

Since we are a child of the King, therefore, I ask again, is anything too hard for God? If you are discouraged and feel like there is no hope and God isn't listening, then ask Him for the faith you need and trust in Him. The creator of all creation has never failed us. We in our finite minds can't comprehend that but that is the truth.

> *God is bigger than all the giants of pain and unbelief;*
> *God is bigger than any mountain that I can or can't see.*
> *God is bigger than any discouragement, bigger than anything;*
> *My God is bigger than any mountain that I can or can't see.*
> –Unknown

Remember God will help you through everything you will ever go through.

Praising God Makes You Triumphant

By Him therefore let us offer the sacrifice of praise to God continually, that is, the fruit of our lips giving thanks to his name. **Hebrews 13:15**

Praise and prayer should never be separated. Praise and prayer are the two steps by which you move forward in the Lord. As soldiers march "left, right, left, right," so you must keep praising and praying daily. Your prayer meeting or secret place of prayer will come to life if you praise the Lord. If there is anything that is a better gauge of the spiritual life than the prayer life, it is the praise life. Satan fears prayer, but he fears praise even more.

God loves to hear the voices of His children and it is music to His ears. He really delights in our voices of praise and adoration to Him. Prayer adds a sweet aroma to our life, but praise is even more fragrant. It is not a question between choosing prayer or praise because we must keep the two together. Praise makes the soul beautiful as a life filled with praise becomes most angelic. Praise, thanks-giving, love, and adoration are qualities that make life glow. The Holy Spirit shines through our life when it is saturated with praise.

Praise God every time you feel tempted to doubt, fear, worry, criticize, or yield to any kind of temptation. Praise fills you with faith and power. Praise has so many benefits and will help us in every way of our life while drawing us closer to God.

Praise adds sweetness to the voice and loveliness to the soul.
Praise fills the life with song, the heart with joy, and adds graciousness to all of life.
Praise clothes you with heaven's beauty.
Praise opens the gates to blessings.
Praise opens the way to answered prayer
Praise opens the way to the very heart of God
Praise multiples the presence and power of the Lord
Praise fills the life with the atmosphere of heaven
Praise turns sorrow into joy.
Praise causes grumbling and criticism to wither at its roots.
Praise is the breath of Heaven that blows the clouds away.
Praising God opens your heart to God and to All His heavenly influences
Praising God gives you the eagle's vision as you see the victory ahead.
Praising God multiplies your faith.
Praising God brings to you all the resources of Heaven.
Praising God turns the battle into a rout of the enemy.

Praising God gives the Holy Spirit welcome and right of way in your life.
Praising God lifts you above the trivial accusations of Satan
and God reduces your problem mountains into hills of blessings.

Advice

Hear, for I will speak of excellent things, and the opening of my lips shall be right things. For my mouth shall speak truth and wickedness is an abomination to my lips. All the words of my mouth are in righteousness; there is nothing forward or perverse in them. They are all plain to him that understandeth, and right to them that find knowledge. **Proverbs 8:6-9**

Why do people read advice columns? Or why do people write to advice columnists for advice? People may feel isolated or find that their problems are unique and they feel embarrassed to ask advice from people they know. Or they may feel that advice columnists have access to experts who can help with their problems. Many people read the columns to get a sense of how people are dealing with current demands in society. Or they read the columns because they have found help with situations or learn how to help others with similar problems.

It may be the same reason people buy self-help books. It takes great courage to share your inner hurts with other people. So people who are hurting may find it easier to share those hurts with someone distant, like an advice columnist.

The book of Proverbs is the advice book of the Bible. It has the answer to many relationship problems. It helps us understand that our problems and situations are not unique. It also gives us answers to what we should do during the difficult times.

God provides the advice we need. He is the expert we need to turn to with our questions. We can go to God with our inner hurts. He already knows our hurts because He knows us. Our difficult situations are nothing compared to the crimes done to Jesus when he was a man on this earth. Jesus was a king who was treated as a criminal. He was a healer who was condemned for helping others. He was accepting of people and, yet, belittled because of his kindness to people. He was a teacher who brought understanding of eternal salvation and strong relationships while on this earth as well as for eternity. His advice was and is the expert advice we need.

**Hear, ye children, the instruction of a father,
and attend to know understanding. Proverbs 4:1**

**A soft answer turneth away wrath:
but grievous words stir up anger. Proverbs 15:1**

**Better is a dry morsel, and quietness, therewith, than an house full of sacrifices
with strife. Proverbs 17:1**

**Better is the poor that walketh in his integrity,
than he that is perverse in his lips, and is a fool. Proverbs 18:1**

**Be not thou envious against evil men,
neither desire to be with them. Proverbs 24:1**

**Boast not thyself of tomorrow; for thou knowest not what a day may bring forth.
Let another man praise thee, and not thine own mouth;
a stranger, and not thine own lips. Proverbs 27:1-2**

Old Age

Cast me not off in the time of old age; forsake me not when my strength faileth. But I will hope continually, and will yet praise thee more and more. Now also, when I am old and grayheaded, O God, forsake me not; until I have shewed thy strength unto this generation, and thy power to everyone that is to come. **Psalm 71: 9, 14, 18**

I am over 50 and some days my body certainly feels old. If I work outside in the garden too long, I find my back aching. Or if I exercise too long, I will definitely have some aches the next morning. Overall, I am blessed with good health. As I get older and think about opportunities at church, I sometimes don't volunteer immediately because I think someone else will do it. Or I tell myself that I already did that when my children were young and parent volunteers were needed. But as we get older, perhaps that is when we need to step up and volunteer more in church and in our communities, and exercise our spiritual workout.

Throughout the Bible, we have examples of elderly people still serving God. In fact, some were not asked until they were much older. Abraham and Sarah, Joseph, Joshua, Aaron, Caleb, and Moses were all examples of elderly people who served the Lord. They continued in their faith despite their age.

We also have many examples of people who have started new careers in their older age or have continued their service in their older age. Queen Elizabeth continues her reign at 86. Colonel Sanders started his franchise at age 65. Laura Ingalls Wilder published her first book at age 65. Grandma Moses did her first painting at age 76 and continued to paint when she was 100. President Ronald Reagan started in politics at the age of 55. Clara Peller did the "Where's the Beef" commercials at age 81. Leo Tolstoy wrote a book at 82. Pablo Picasso did drawings at age 90. Coco Chanel was the CEO of a fashion firm at age 85.

We should also think about ways we can continue our service to God no matter what. There are ways we can continue our service despite our age. Some elderly people who might have been very active in their younger years may find they can still serve God, just in a different format. Their words may help build up others. Or their experiences may be helpful to help others organize work in the church. Their experiences are invaluable when provided as suggestions for how to improve things. Keep always giving and working for the Lord until you pass through those Pearly Gates.

The elderly years are a gift from the Father
A gift on display to be shared with all others
This time of life can be your best
A time to receive blessing and a time to bless.
–Joyce Guy

And thou shalt go to thy fathers in peace;
thou shalt be buried in a good old age. Genesis 15:15

Benefits of Work

He that tilleth his land shall be satisfied with bread: but he that followeth vain persons is void of understanding. **Proverbs 12:11**

I know a man who dreamed continually of being a par golfer, but all he did was dream. In fact, he did buy Ping golf clubs, golf shoes, and the best golf balls, but he never practiced. He would play in best ball tournaments and was the worst player in the tournament and in his group. He couldn't drive or chip. If you were golfing with him and thought you were doing terrible, his play made you feel better because he was that awful. Why was he so horrendous? He never practiced so he could enjoy the benefits of the work it takes to be a good golfer. He just sat on the couch, watching golf tournaments, and dreamed.

When I was a boy, my father would tell us to go out and weed the garden. But, along came Bobby and he enticed us to go swimming with him. We were not too smart because the consequences of not weeding the garden resulted in "seat warming" from our father. The next day when Bobby came by, we tended to our duties and weeded the garden. In the end, we were thankful for the bountiful fruit and vegetables the garden produced.

If you work hard, you will enjoy the fruits of your labor. This is true in the superintendency. If you work hard to become a learned master of curriculum, finance, facilities, school law, food service, transportation, and developing human relation skills, then you will enjoy the "fruits of your labor" and will be a superintendent who is revered and loved. Become a student of the superintendency and wrap it in a servant attitude for your district. All will benefit!

Let's think of work in terms of hope
And speak of it with words of praise,
And tell the joy it is to grope
Along the new, untrodden ways!
Let's break this habit of despair
And cheerfully our task regard;
The road to happiness lies there:
Why think or speak of it as hard?
–Edgar Best

I'm a great believer in luck and find the harder I work, the more of it I have.
–Thomas Jefferson

Controlling Your Words

He that keepeth his mouth keepeth his life: but he that openeth wide his lips shall have destruction. **Proverbs 13:3**

People have lost their jobs, their lives, and have started fights because they could not keep their mouth shut. In James 3, it says that quarrels and wars were caused by people not being able to tame their tongue.

I was watching an NBA game the other night. One of the players started to "trash talk" another player and really got in his face. Pretty, soon, punches were thrown and the benches emptied. It took several minutes for the refs to get the game under control. Both players were given a technical foul and the player that started the melee was ejected from the game.

This also goes on in our daily lives. I've seen students get into fights because someone says something to them or "disrespects them." I've also seen friendships dissolved because of harsh words spoken to each other. Marriages have fallen apart because neither partner could control their tongue and spoke mean, harsh words to each other.

There is another way people open their mouth and cause destruction and that is by whispering, backbiting, tale-bearing, and rumor-mongering. These people like to keep the pot stirred, but in the end it all comes back to them and they are seen as outcasts. The braggart is also like this. They boast and soon their acquaintances shun them. The braggart and the tale-bearer both come to a swift destruction.

As superintendent, you need to be able to control your speech. "The tongue of the wise commends knowledge, but the mouth of fool gushes folly" (Proverbs 15:2). Once we learn not to act upon how we feel, we will learn not to speak about how we feel. Remember, our moods should not dictate how we act or speak. The word tells us if we can control our speech we can control our entire nature: "We all stumble in many ways."

Let the Lord dictate your speech. Let Him be glorified through you. He chooses the unqualified and makes them qualified! We need to slow down at times to hear Him. God doesn't yell at us; He whispers. Let God speak through you today!

> *Love through me, Holy Spirit, love through me,*
> *I will be my brother's keeper, love through me;*
> *Hearts are bleeding deep inside, love can dry the weeping eye,*
> *Love through me, Holy Spirit, love through me.*
> –Barbara Tubbs

Watch your thoughts, for they become words. Watch your words, for they become actions. Watch your actions, for they become habits. Watch your habits, for they become character. Watch your character, for it becomes your destiny.
–Anonymous

Glory in God, Not in Yourself

Thus saith the Lord, Let not the wise man glory in his wisdom, neither let the mighty man glory in his might, let not the rich man glory in his riches: But let him that glorieth glory in this, that he understandeth and knoweth me, that I am the Lord which exercise lovingkindness, judgment, and righteousness, in the earth: for in these things I delight, saith the Lord. **Jeremiah 9:23-24**

I was a superintendent in a district and had a young assistant principal in the high school. One day, when I was visiting the school, he said to me, "I've arrived. I own a house on the golf course and I'm an administrator in the district." I thought to myself, you arrogant person! He gave himself all of the glory.

You have read of people who put all of their trust in riches and how they gained their great wealth. Bill Gates, Mark Zuckerberg, George Buffet, and Donald Trump extol their wealth and glory in it. They don't realize that the Lord is the one that gives and he is the one that deserves all of the glory.

Have you been around superintendents who are extremely proud of their positions and think that they are the smartest and wisest superintendent? A fellow superintendent in the Tulsa area was like this. Getting away from his arrogant personality was like a breath of fresh air. The Bible says that you should give God all of the glory for everything. Do you find yourself saying, "Look what I've done and look what I've accomplished?" If so, ask the Lord to forgive you and give you a humble heart. Remember to always give God all the glory for your success!

I boast not of works or tell of good deeds
For naught have I done to merit His grace
All glory and praise shall rest upon Him
So willing to die in my place
I will glory in the cross
Lest His suffering all be in vain
I will weep no more for the cross that He bore
I will glory in the cross
—Dottie Rambo

I will glory in my Redeemer, whose priceless blood has ransomed me.
—Steve & Vicki Cook

June 8

Eight Blessings from the Lord

Blessed are the poor in spirit: for theirs is the kingdom of heaven. Blessed are they that mourn; for they shall be comforted. Blessed are the meek: for they shall inherit the earth. Blessed are they which do hunger and thirst after righteousness: for they shall be filled. Blessed are the merciful: for they shall obtain mercy. Blessed are the pure in heart: for they shall see God. Blessed are the peacemakers: for they shall be called the children of God. Blessed are they which are persecuted for righteousness' sake: for theirs is the kingdom of heaven. Blessed are ye when men shall revile you, and persecute you, and shall say all manner of evil against you falsely, for my sake. Matthew 5:3-11

When Jesus Christ was preaching on the Mount he gave to us the eight Beatitudes. These truths are simple, but unique and innovative. The message of Jesus is one of humility, charity, and brotherly love. He teaches transformation of the inner person. Love becomes the motivations for the Christian. While the Beatitudes of Jesus provide a way of life that promises salvation, they also provide peace in the midst of our trials and tribulations on this earth.

The Devil's beatitudes are the opposite of the Lord's eight Beatitudes. The Devil's beatitudes would go like this: Blessed are those who are too tired, too busy, too distracted to spend an hour once a week with their fellow Christians in church they are my best workers. Blessed are those Christians who wait to be asked and expect to be thanked I can use them. Blessed are the touchy; with a bit of luck they may stop going to church they are my missionaries. Blessed are those who are very religious but get on everyone's nerves they are mine forever. Blessed are the troublemakers they shall be called my children. Blessed are those who have no time to pray they are easy prey for me. Blessed are the gossips, for they are my secret agents. Blessed are those critical of church leadership, for they shall inherit a place with me in my fate. Blessed are the complainers I'm all ears for them. Blessed are you when you read this and think it is about other people and not yourself I've got you.

Pray this prayer if you are following the devil's beatitudes: "Lord, never let us unwittingly become one of the Devil's emissaries, by forsaking the love Christ commanded us to have for one another. In His name we pray. Amen."

St. Gregory of Nyssa who lived in Asia Minor around 380 AD described the Beatitudes this way:

Beatitude is a possession of all things held to be good,
from which nothing is absent that a good desire may want.
Perhaps the meaning of beatitude may become clearer to us
if it is compared with its opposite.
Now the opposite of beatitude is misery.
Misery means being afflicted unwillingly with painful sufferings.

The Beatitudes are the ideal for every Christian life.
–St. Augustine

Our Pets

Knowing that a man is not justified by the works of one law, but by the faith of Jesus Christ, even we have believed in Jesus Christ, that we might be justified by the faith of Christ, and not by the works of the law: for by the works of the law shall no flesh be justified. **Galatians 2:16**

Many of us have pets or have had pets. I certainly love my little dog. But, she does require some care. She needs to be fed every day, provided water, and taken outside for walks and bathroom. In return for a little care, she always greets me when I come home. She runs to me, wagging her tail, and it seems as if she is smiling at me.

There are times when she upsets me. She will bark at thunderstorms and even pee on my bathroom rug. Some people take their dogs to obedience school to help their dogs behave better. The training helps the owners learn how to teach their dogs how to act. It seems that the emphasis is on the consistent responses by the owner with simple commands and rewards. It requires the owner to change their behaviors in order to lead their pet. When my son-in-law is present, my dog acts better. It seems that she has a fear of him because one time he raised his voice at her. I don't think she has any fear of me. There are times that I am better at my consistency with my pet. Even if my dog doesn't always obey me, overall her companionship and good qualities far outweigh her bad behaviors. I want her with me!

Jesus loves me and also wants my obedience. He also realizes that I will not always obey and has provided a way for me to come back to a right relationship with him by admitting my wrong actions. I know that I am not able to live the perfect life and that I also will not act in the way that God wants. He is consistent in His love and forgiveness. He cares for me and provides me with everything I need. God created us because He loves us. He chose us!

Jesus' teachings help me understand with simple commands and stories that are easy to follow so I know His expectations. The rewards are provided during my earthly life. But the rewards will also be given in heaven as all my actions while on earth will be judged. I am so glad that God wants me with Him and that His companionship is important to me.

> *When I'm sad, He loves me*
> *Even when I'm bad, He loves me*
> *When it seems no one cares for me*
> *I talk to Jesus, He loves me!*
> –George Webster

Having therefore these promises,
dearly beloved, let us cleanse ourselves
from all filthiness of the flesh and spirit,
perfecting holiness in the fear of God.
II Corinthians 7:1

Exercise

For bodily exercise profiteth little; but godliness is profitable, unto all things, having promise of the life that now is, and of that which is to come. I Timothy 4:8

I love to wake up and do my devotional reading and then exercise to start my day. The exercise of walking, bike riding, and other quality exercise helps me feel more energized and ready for the day. The reading of the devotional is also a way to be ready for the day. Both help me get a great start. One helps my body and one helps my soul. Although, both the physical exercise and the spiritual exercise really help my body and soul. Oral Roberts, the founder of Oral Roberts University, recognized this when he designed his curriculum to benefit mind, spirit, and body.

The physical exercise does help my muscles, heart, and weight. But it also helps my mind as it releases endorphins that are so important for my mental state. I notice a difference in my mood and attitude on the days I don't have time for the physical exercise. Additionally, I also notice a difference in my body and attitude when I don't have my daily spiritual exercise. It is rare that I don't read my devotional each morning. But some mornings, I don't give the reading my full attention. Nor do I listen to what the Word of God is saying to me that day. I did not pay attention to what the Lord was trying to speak to me.

There was a television commercial that showed inanimate objects from a store speaking to the customer. The store was trying to get buyers to purchase what spoke to them. It was a catchy way to get people's attention. I often wonder if I don't require some of those catchy ways for God to speak to me. He reminds us in Timothy that bodily exercise will profit us little if we don't take care of our souls. My exercise that helps my body compares nothing to that of spiritual exercise. The starting of any exercise program often reminds us to have a check-up by our doctor. The spiritual exercise program should also start with a request of our Savior to save us. This will then give us the Holy Spirit and His power and strength. We should also continue in our prayer life and Bible reading to build us up. Our spiritual exercise increases our spiritual strength.

We may live to an old age, but if we don't take care of ourselves, we may not have a quality of life. In many schools, there has been a cut back on the amount of recess and physical education time. This has been done in order to have more time for academic subjects. It may not serve someone well to have more knowledge but yet have a shorter life because they did not take care of their physical needs. We need to be careful on what we prioritize and keep in our schedules. If we examine our schedules we will find what has priority in our lives. We need to give our first priority to God in the morning to take care of our spiritual lives.

With my soul have I desired thee in the night;
yea within my spirit within me will I seek thee early:
for when thy judgments are in the earth,
the inhabitants of the world will learn righteousness. Isaiah 26:9

God's Blessing to Those Who Fear Him

Then they that feared the LORD spake often one to another; and the LORD hearkened, and heard it, and a book of remembrance was written before him for them that feared the LORD, and that thought upon his name. And they shall be mine, saith the LORD of host, in that day when I make up my jewels; and I will spare them, as a man spareth his own son that serveth him. Then shall ye return, and discern between the righteous and the wicked, between him that serveth God and him that serveth him not. **Malachi 3:16-18**

Malachi is the last book of the Old Testament. It is a short book, but Malachi was a prophet who warned that priests had not been offering God their best offering, rather they had offered blemished offerings. He further warned that they had not listened to God and had not given God glory. Because of their actions, God would curse them and corrupt their seed. He reminded them that Lord wanted to give life and peace.

The priests were to use their knowledge about God so they could be the Lord's messenger. Malachi went further to say that their actions had wearied the Lord. I don't know about you, but it scares me to think that any of my word would weary the Lord. I don't want God sending me curses. And worse than that is the curse would be visited upon my children and grandchildren. Now, that is serious when my actions would impact my family. My children and grandchildren are very special to me. And I want them to be a blessing to God. I certainly don't want harm to come their way because of me. Any departure from what we know is God's way has serious consequences. And those serious consequences harm not only us, but also those around us.

As superintendent remember your model in life can be a stumbling block for others. Further, it is a disappointment to our Lord when we err. I can remember when I disappointed my earthly father and it hurt to see the sadness I had caused him. How much more it must hurt my heavenly Father when I do wrong! I should always value what God thinks of me. I hope that I live in ways that are true to God because I know that is important to Him and our relationship. God deserves to be first in all of our lives. When our actions are led by God being first, then we have a promise of peace. People should be able to see that God is first in our lives. They should be able to see that we have something special and should want that also.

> *When upon life's billows you are tempest-tossed,*
> *When you are discouraged, thinking all is lost,*
> *Count your many blessings, name them one by one,*
> *And it will surprise you what the Lord hath done.*
> –Johnson Oatman, Jr.

But sanctify the Lord God in your hearts:
and be ready always to give an answer to every man
that asketh you a reason of the hope that is in you
with meekness and fear.
I Peter 3:15

Repent for Restoration

The LORD hath been sore displeased with your fathers, therefore say thou unto them, Thus saith the LORD of hosts; Turn ye unto me, saith the LORD of hosts, and I will turn unto you, saith the LORD of hosts. Be ye not as your fathers, unto whom the former prophets have cried, saying, Thus saith the LORD of hosts; Turn ye now from your evil ways, and from your evil doings; but they did not hear, nor hearken unto me, saith the LORD. Zechariah 1:2-4

Our Lord makes it very clear that we are to repent for any evil first and then turn to Him so He can turn to us. I know there are times that I turn to the Lord and wonder why I still feel alone. It appears that I often forget to repent of any of my wrong actions and thoughts. Overall, I do not see myself as an evil person and you probably do not see yourself that way either. But yet, if we are to truly examine ourselves, we would find that many of our thoughts are not as honorable as they should be.

I find myself judging others when I really may not have all the information. Or I may judge others and not say anything, but still my thoughts were not kind or right. Other times, I wanted to take actions to fix things that may not have been for me to fix.

We all should remember that Moses grew weary of his people and their complaining as well as their actions. He threw down the first stone tablets written with the Lord's hand. And later, he struck a rock to make the water flow. But God had not told him to hit the rock. God had told him to speak to the rock. It may seem small, but God's instructions are to be followed if we want peace with God. Our unkind thoughts may seem small, but God wants our acknowledgement of our wrong thoughts and actions first. We want God to turn to us, so we must turn from our evil.

Many have seen images of the aftermath of a tornado. There is utter destruction with entire buildings demolished. It was this look of destruction that was described in Zechariah because of the evil ways of people and God's anger at them for their evil. I do not ever want to find that kind of anger against me. God provides us a way of escape from that. We need to turn to Him and He will turn to us.

It is the simple and clear that the Word of God guides us. God makes it abundantly clear that we must repent before there can be a restoring of our relationship with Him. For me, it is a daily need to repent. My comfort is given when I realize I need to repent and then my actions will follow a changed inside.

Create in me a clean heart, oh God
And renew a right spirit within me
Cast me not away from Thy presence,
And take not Thy holy spirit from me.
                              –Keith Green

Draw nigh to God, and he will draw nigh to you.
Cleanse your hands, ye sinners;
and purify your hearts, ye double minded. James 4:8

Counting Sand

How precious also are the thoughts unto me, O god! How great is the sum of them! If I should count them, they are more in number than the sand: when I awake, I am still with thee. **Psalm 139:17-18**

Recently, I sat staring at my sand-covered hand on a beach in Melbourne, FL, and marveled at the tiny grains peppering the ridges of my fingerprint. After focusing my attention on a single grain, I then lifted my eyes and looked down the beach as far as I could see. It was easy to see how it would be humanly impossible to count the sands on that beach alone, much less on the hundreds of thousands miles of shoreline on the planet. Making a few conservative assumptions, one could estimate that the shores of the earth might contain several quintillions (a billion billions) of grains of sand. Expanding grossly on that thought, Archimedes once estimated that it would take, perhaps, vigintillions (a billion billion billion billion billion billion billion) of grains of sand to fill the known universe. That's a lot of sand!

I was reminded of Psalm 139:17-18, "How precious to me are your thoughts, God! How vast the sum of them! Were I to count them, they would outnumber the grains of sand." This was the psalmist's way of visualizing the infinite amount of God's concern for us, and what is even more remarkable is that He not only has an accurate count of the sand grains, but he also knows the varied characteristics of each one and how they change over time and are subject to nature's erosive forces. Can you imagine trying to keep track of that?

How does this apply? As a superintendent, you will face new problems daily, whether it is with your staff, peers, customers, allies, or competitors. Your individual challenges may seem daunting, but you can rest in the fact that you serve an infinitely wise God. In times when you lack confidence, you can take peace in the fact that God thinks highly of you, believes in you, and presents you with opportunities to grow as a leader. Though you might fear failure, it is almost too easy to believe that the best strategy is, in fact, to trust in God to handle those challenges for you. Isn't it ironic that something as small as a grain of sand can serve as big reminder of how infinite God is in His wisdom and love towards us?

> *When hoary time shall pass away,*
> *And earthly thrones and kingdoms fall,*
> *When men who here refuse to pray,*
> *On rocks and hills and mountains call,*
> *God's love so sure, shall still endure,*
> *All measureless and strong;*
> *Redeeming grace to Adam's race—*
> *The saints' and angels' song.*
> –Frederick Lehman

Cast all your cares on Him because he cares for you. I Peter 5:7

Bed Rock

He is like a man which built an house, and digged deep, and laid the foundation on a rock: and when the flood arose, the stream beat vehemently upon that house, and could not shake it: for it was founded upon a rock. Luke 6:48

When the Brooklyn Bridge was being built, the bridge builders had to dig down deep into the ground. They were trying to find solid rock on which to build the bridge. While they were digging the chief engineer said to one of the diggers, "Have we reached the bed rock?" The digger replied, "No, sir, this is just soapstone." The engineer said, "Well, keep on digging."

After a while the digger shouted, "Stop the engines; we've reached the bed rock!" "How can you tell so quickly?" asked the engineer. The digger replied, "We go right through soapstone like a hot knife through butter, but when we come to bed rock the sparks just fly."

I have first-hand experience of this law in action when I built a small shed. I did not attach it to a firm foundation and when the first little wind came along, it blew the shed down. I was too lazy to do the extra work and, in the end, it cost me more work and money than if I had done it correctly the first time.

This same principle holds true for a superintendent when leading a district towards greatness. When you develop curriculum and make recommendations to the board, it must be true and built on solid research—not on your likes. Then it will stand the test of time and do for your district what you said it would do.

Someday, Jesus will come again. You want to be sure your life is built on the solid foundation of salvation in Jesus Christ. It must be fixed upon His grace and not on our own works.

> *My hope is built on nothing less*
> *Than Jesus' blood and righteousness;*
> *I dare not trust the sweetest frame,*
> *But wholly lean on Jesus' name.*
> *On Christ, the solid Rock, I stand;*
> *All other ground is sinking sand.*
> –Edward Mote

I personally developed the Academy training program. All our training is based on solid educational principles. We present the material in four training formats: lecture, demonstration, drill, and implementation.
–Jim Evans

Cleansing Spirit

And ye shall know that I am in the midst of Israel, and that I am the LORD your God, and none else; and my people shall never be ashamed. And it shall come to pass afterward that I will pour out my sprit upon all flesh, and your sons and your daughters shall prophesy, your old men shall dream dreams, your young men shall see visions. And also upon the servants and upon the handmaids in those days will I pour out my spirit. And I shall shew wonders in the heavens and in the earth, blood and fire and pillars of smoke. **Joel 2:27-30**

It brings great joy when I hear about kind and great deeds done by my children and grandchildren. It is those times that help me as I think of other times when I have not done enough for my family members or my family members have done things that would not make anyone proud. I also enjoy hearing the glorious parts of the Bible that provide me hope. It is often preceded by a warning and a command by God for those to turn back to Him. It is not easy to hear about the need for repentance or when I know I have displeased God. There is a need to repent.

There are children who immediately say they are sorry after they do something wrong, only to do the same things again. And again, they say sorry, but do not change any of their actions. They have made the confession of their wrong action, but they truly have not changed their ways or repented of their ways. Is it because they believe it is okay to do wrong actions or do they believe there are not consequences for their sins? Joel talks about the chance to return to God and give Him priority in our lives. He is a gracious and merciful God who is slow to anger. But the book of Joel makes it clear that He is not indifferent to the wrongs. Even though Joel pointed out that God is gracious and merciful, it did not mean that God would not have consequences or was proud of his families' wrong actions.

And rend your heart, and not your garments, and turn unto the LORD your God; for he is gracious and merciful, slow to anger, and of great kindness, and repenteth him of the evil. Joel 2:13

Many of Joel's contemporaries showcased their religious look, but still continued their wrong actions. They would tear their clothes as if to show repentance. Yet, they were like the child who always said sorry but still did not change his or her actions. This is not what God required. God wants people to examine their inner heart. He wants us to turn to Him with an inner cleanliness and not just outward appearances.

The cleansing stream I see, I see,
I plunge and O, it cleanseth me!
O praise the Lord! It cleanseth me!
With heart made pure and garments white.
–Mrs. J. F. Knapp

Have mercy upon me, O God, according to thy lovingkindness: according unto the multitude of thy tender mercies blot out my transgressions. Wash me thoroughly from mine iniquity, and cleanse me from my sin. For I acknowledge my transgressions: and my sin is ever before me. Psalm 51:1-3

June 16

Don't Fear, Trust God

Fear thou not; for I am with thee: be not dismayed; for I am thy God: I will strengthen thee; yea, I will help thee; yea, I will uphold thee with the right hand of my righteousness. **Isaiah 41:10**

What catapults fear into your life? The doctor gives you bad news. The boss tells you that you no longer have a job. Your spouse tells you he or she is leaving. The board of education votes not to renew your contract. The media runs a false and slanderous story about you. News comes of a loved one in a terrible accident. A family member has escaped the jaws of death. There could be many examples of what brings that dreaded fear into your life.

My pastor told of a time when he was jet-skiing in the Gulf of Mexico with his family. A terrible storm came in and they were making haste to get back to the shore. When he arrived at the shore, he found out that his son had been knocked from his jet-ski by a giant wave. He said that fear drenched his body and he quickly went out to look for his son. He found the jet-ski but his son was not to be found. After frantically looking for him for 10 minutes, he found him and got him back to shore safely.

As a superintendent you will face obstacles that put fear into life, but remember that Jesus is with you. He's always with you! Jesus is saying to you, "Fear not, I'm with you and that will make the difference." "Whatever the enemy intended, I will not allow it to happen." "Your best days are ahead of you, not behind you." "Don't worry, I've got this." "Do not be afraid of this current day as I'm with you." "Be encouraged because I'm with you." "Don't be confused into thinking that I've forsaken you because we're going through this together."

> *The sea of life is raging, the storms clouds round me roll.*
> *I'm tossed about in turmoil and it's growing very cold.*
> *By myself I'll never make it, but this one thing I know*
> *When I speak the name of Jesus the storms clouds have to go*
> *When I say "Master," my sorrows disappear;*
> *When I say "Father," He drives away my fears;*
> *When I say "Saviour," my blinded eyes can see,*
> *When I say "Jesus," He speaks peace to me!*
> —J. Swaggart

Whatever is coming against you, Jesus is walking on the water to you.

G.O.L.F.

But God, who is rich in mercy, for his great love wherewith he loved us. **Ephesians 2:4**

Golf had its beginning in Scotland and an old wives' tale said it meant, "gents only ladies forbidden." Further research fount that the word "Golf" was derived from the Dutch word Kolf, which is a generic word for club or mallet.

Golf is a game that takes you through 18 holes and a score of par is the expected norm. It's the stokes counted from the time you tee off until you putt the ball in the hole. Each hole has numerous snares, such as sand traps, water hazards, short rough, high rough, and trees. When you hit an errant shot, you can end up in one of these hazards which will usually cost you many strokes. Some errant shots are downright dangerous and you end up losing your ball or possibly hitting another person or player.

Like the game of life, there are many opportunities for us to fall or fail. When we make a wrong decision or become rebellious, that will lead us on a path away from God. As we traverse this road of life we have to be ever so vigilant and alert because there are traps and snares along the way that are designed to make us fail or give up. They are put there by the enemy of our soul, but God our heavily father is there to help us get out of every hazard.

To make certain that we make "par on every hole," we have to continue to read our Bible and pray. It is that communion with God that helps us withstand the lures of sin. I went golfing the other day and I had not swung a club in 3 years. I was so terrible and rusty that I couldn't drive a ball off of the tee, chip or even putt and, to top it off, I lost a dozen balls. I was thinking that "it is time for me to hang up my clubs." That is what happens when we don't read our Bible and pray every day. We get out of sync with God, but you can't give up. My partners were forgiving and they didn't even laugh but I didn't give up or hang up my clubs.

As a superintendent, you will face many challenges. To be that successful superintendent, you have to keep alert and aware of the changes in education and latest research. You have to be that servant leader and "be the administrator you'd like to work under as a teacher or principal." Thank the Lord daily that your loving Father helps you through each day and guides your steps.

Our God is an awesome God
He reigns from heaven above
With wisdom power and love
Our God is an awesome God.
–Michael W. Smith

God, Our Loving Father = G.O.L.F.

Good Fruit Comes from Good Trees

For every tree is known by his own fruit. For of thorns men do not gather figs, nor of a bramble bush gather they grapes. **Luke 6:44**

One day my father took my brother and me into the woods when we lived in the panhandle of Idaho. We dug up a crab apple tree sprout, took it home and planted it in the garden. We cultivated, weeded, and fertilized the ground around the tree. We made certain that it got plenty of water. In the winter the tree was not sheltered from the snow and icy cold temperatures. After several years, with careful care of the tree, it began to yield crab apples but they were very bitter crab apples.

"Sons," my father said, "you haven't cultivated it sufficiently or it would have brought forth better tasting crab apples." So, the next year, my brother and I worked harder than ever in caring for that tree. But, again, the fruit was bitter. Then father said, "Sons, we shall have to try another plan." He sawed a twig from a good apple tree and drafted it to the crab apple tree. The next year we had luscious tasting apples.

In the same way, our lives are filled with the bitterness of sin. The only fruit we bear is of the flesh. NO work will help. Only Jesus can change our sinful natures and enable us to lead lives of good works which will please God.

This same principle holds for school teachers and principals. If we let a poor teacher or principal continue as they are, they will continue to yield "bad fruit" and the students will be the ones who suffer. Providing them with mentor master teachers, mentor master principals, and professional development that is specific to their area and need will change these poor teachers into good teachers who yield "good fruit." They will be a "new teacher" and take on the character of the master teacher.

This the secret nature hideth,
Harvest grows from buried grain;
A poor tree with better grafted,
Richer, sweeter life doth gain.
Oh! It's so sweet to die with Christ,
To the world, and self, and sin'
Oh! It's so sweet to live with Christ,
As He lives and reigns within.

A sinner saved by grace and grafted into Christ will lose his natural character and take on the character of Jesus Christ.

Hold to God's Unchanging Hand

Heaven and earth shall pass away, but my words shall not pass away.
Matthew 24:35

There is a cultural war being waged today in America and in the world. It is being fueled by activists who want to see a change in our moral code and the definition of "what is right and wrong." Confusion abounds and many people who use to have strong moral beliefs are changing their opinions. In political terms, it used to be called "flip-flopping" but now it is called "evolving."

Colorado and Washington voters recently approved same-sex marriage and legalized the usage of marijuana. The Supreme Court is now deciding the definition of "marriage." Some states, such as California in HB 1172 are trying to outlaw Gay Counseling by making it a crime to counsel gay young people about changing their sexual orientation. The Bible speaks about this in Isaiah 5:20 (Today's NIV), "Woe to those who call evil good and good evil, who put darkness for light and light for darkness, who put bitter for sweet and sweet for bitter."

The Gallup Poll listed the moral issues that Americans are facing such as doctor assisted euthanasia, gay/lesbian relationships, abortion, having children out of wedlock, adultery, animal rights, gambling, cloning of animals, banning the death penalty, and divorce. This war has made its way into the public schools of America. For example, many children are coming to school today with two mommies or two daddies. Some states are holding their ground, but most are caving to the demands and are changing the curriculum. The activists are pushing hard against traditional Christian values who see moral issues as the sanctity of life, religious liberty, human rights, marriage, terrorism, judiciary roles, faith-based solutions, marginalized citizens, education, and the media as significant moral issues facing America today.

This is all coupled with the issues that children are facing such as single-parent households, drug and alcohol abuse, violence in schools, materialism, obesity, disparity in education quality, shifting economy, poverty, and erosion of national pride. As you can see, it is a very confused and mixed up world. People are panicking and can't decide which way to believe. As a superintendent, it is your job to lead your district is what is right, moral, and ethical. Ask the Lord to give you wisdom during these quickly changing times. Remember to hold to God's unchanging hand!

> *Time is filled with swift transition,*
> *Naught of earth unmoved can stand,*
> *Build your hopes on things eternal,*
> *Hold to God's unchanging hand.*
> –Jennie Wilson

What God has promised, He will accomplish—if, with His help, we are willing to set aside our fears, trust Him, and by faith have courage.

Miracles

Jesus saith unto them, Fill the waterpots with water, And they filled them up to the brim. And he saith unto them, Draw out now, and bear unto the governor of the feast. And they bare it. When the rule of the feast had tasted the water that was made wine, and knew not when it was; (but the servants which drew the water knew) the governor of the feast called the bridegroom. And saith unto him, Every man at the beginning doth set forth good wine; and when men have well drunk, then that which is worse; but thou hast kept the good wine until now. This beginning of miracles did Jesus in Cana of Galilee, and manifested forth his glory; and his disciples believed on him. John 2:7-11

Jesus performed many miracles that showed His power over everything on earth as well as His power over sovereign things. His miracles showed His compassion for people hurting as well as for those in need both physically and emotionally.

Miracles have the purpose of showing God's glory through supernatural events that can't be explained in any earthly fashion. Miracles are connected with power. The miracles showed that God does exist and does have power. God's miracles provided protection while providing also for the needs of His people. The parting of the Red Sea so the Israelites could escape the Egyptians and then feeding them manna were examples of God's miracles. Miracles were seen in the New Testament as well. Jesus's first miracle was turning water to wine at a wedding. This was during a joyous event and showed Jesus's desire for humans to have happiness as He blessed marriages. It also helped the disciples believe in His glory. Another miracle showed Jesus's ability to forgive sins when he forgave the sins of a paralyzed man and also healed his body. Yet other miracles showed His power over sickness and death. He raised Lazarus and the widow's son from the dead. As we look to the examples of miracles in the Bible, we learn about God's glory. We learn about the character of Jesus and have hope and belief because of the miracles.

There are times in people's lives when they need a miracle. For me, it was after my husband's sudden death from an accident. I could not sleep one night and I could not stop the tears. As I sat in the middle of my bedroom floor, I heard the angels singing praise to God. That miracle lifted my hopes and gave me an understanding that God was with me and cared for me. The miracles showed me that God had compassion and I needed to remember to trust in Him.

> *My Father is omnipotent, and that you can't deny*
> *A God of might and miracles, it's written in the sky.*
> *It took a miracle to put the stars in place;*
> *It took a miracle to hang the world in space,*
> *But when he saved my soul, cleansed and made me whole,*
> *It took a miracle of love and grace.*
> —John Peterson

The same came to Jesus by night, and said unto him, Rabbi, we know that thou art a teacher come from God: for no man can do these miracles that thou doest, except God be with Him. John 3-2

The Name of Jesus

That at the name of Jesus every knee should bow, of things in heaven, and things in earth, and things under the earth, and that every tongue should confess that Jesus Christ is Lord, to the glory of God the Father. **Philippians 2:10-11**

Who is Jesus? He came from heaven and was the son of God. He was born contrary to the laws of nature, lived in poverty, reared in obscurity, and crossed the boundary of the land once in childhood. He did not have wealth or influence, and had neither training nor formal education. His relatives were average people and were not influential. He startled a king, puzzled wise men, walked upon the sea, calmed the waves, healed multitudes, healed the broken hearts, and never wrote a book or song.

He is the Star of Astronomy, the Rock of Geology, the Lion and the Lamb of Zoology, the Harmonizer of all discords, and the Healer of all diseases. Great men have come and gone, yet He lives on. Herod could not kill Him, Satan could not seduce Him, Death could not destroy Him, the grave could not hold Him. He is wonderful and merciful, and He is your Savior! He Is The Incomparable Christ!

Gloria Gaither, a Christian artist, wrote, "Jesus: the mere mention of his name can calm the storm, heal the broken, and raise the dead. At the name of Jesus I've seen sin harden men melted, derelicts transformed, and lights of hope put into the eyes of a hopeless child. At the name of Jesus hatred and bitterness turned to love and forgiveness, and arguments ceased. I've heard a mother softly breathe his name at the bedside of her child delirious from fever and watched as that little body grew quiet and the fever grew cold. I've sat beside a dying saint and her body racked with pain when in those final fleeting seconds she summoned her last ounce of ebbing strength to whisper her sweetest name Jesus, Jesus! Emperors have tried to destroy it, philosophies have tried to stamp it out, tyrants have tried to wash it from the face of the earth by the very blood of those who claimed it and yet it still stands. And there shall be that final day when every voice that has uttered a sound, every voice of Adam's race shall rise in one mighty chorus to proclaim the name Jesus for in that day every knee shall bow. For you see it was not mere chance that caused an Angel to say to a virgin maiden his name shall be called Jesus. Sweet Jesus, there is something about that name."

Jesus, Jesus, Jesus
There's just something about that name
Master, Savior, Jesus
Like the fragrance after the rain
Jesus, Jesus, Jesus
Let all heaven and earth proclaim
Kings and kingdoms shall all pass away
But there's something about that name.
–Gloria Gaither

Have you accepted Jesus as your Saviour? You can! You can accept Him now!

Priorities

Now therefore thus saith the LORD of hosts; Consider your ways. Ye have sown much, and bring in little; ye eat, but ye have not enough; ye drink but ye are not filled with drink; ye clothe you, but there is none warm; and he that earneth wages earneth wages to put it into a bag with holes. Thus saith the LORD of hosts; Consider your ways. Go up to the mountain, and bring wood, and build the house; and I will take pleasure in it, and I will be glorified, saith the LORD. Ye looked for much, and lo, it came to little; and when ye brought it home, I did blow upon it. Why? Saith the LORD of hosts. Because of mine house that is waste, and ye run every man unto his own house. Therefore the heaven over you is stayed from dew, and the earth is stayed from her fruit. Haggai 1:5-10

Many times we have large tasks as well as many tasks. It is at these times when we may lose sight of what is most important. I often have to make a list of the priorities for what needs to be done immediately as well as the list of the order of things to be done for each task. In this way, I make the task more manageable and it does not overwhelm me as easily. But, there are other priorities that we often abuse besides tasks at work or in our lives.

When we let things in our lives overtake us such as work over family, then we have lost the balance in our lives. Or if we spend all our time focused on our family, then our work may suffer. But overall, if we put all earthly things above God, then our focus and priorities will always be out of line with no balance possible. When we worry about things or let things bother us, then we must take time to step back and consider if we have allowed God to control our lives. Or have we tried to set our own priorities without God's guidance?

Our spiritual well-being must be strong so the rest of our lives have balance. We strengthen our spiritual well-being by taking the time to read God's Word. My morning starts with a devotional time. A chance to reflect on what God wants from me in this day. It helps ground my day and hopefully also shows my priority to God. I should make time to give God the praise. I often wallow in my own worries, when I should be thinking of all God's blessings. At times, I remember to count all of those blessings and name each of them individually. The things that I do should bring God glory. As we put the priorities of God in our lives in order, then we find that our service and actions will follow after our praise to God.

> *So amid the conflict whether great or small,*
> *Do not be discouraged, God is over all;*
> *Count your many blessings, angels will attend,*
> *Help and comfort give you to your journey's end.*
> —Johnson Oatman, Jr

That ye might walk worthy of the Lord unto all pleasing, being fruitful in every good work, and increasing in the knowledge of God; Strengthening with all might, according to his glorious power, unto all patience and longsuffering with joyfulness; Giving thanks unto the Father, which hath made us meet to be partakers of the inheritance of the saints in light. Colossians 1:10-12

Satisfied With The Contract

But he answered one of them, and said, Friend, I do thee no wrong: didst not thou agree with me for a penny? Matthew 20:13

Jesus tells a parable about a landowner who hired people to work in his fields. In the morning, he asked laborers if they would work for a certain wage and they said, "Yes." In the afternoon, he asked laborers if they would work for the same wage and they said, "Yes." In the late afternoon he asked the same question and the answer was, "Yes." When all three groups came to collect their wages there was discontent and grumbling because some worked longer than others. What they failed to remember was that they all agreed to their wages. The workers became envious of the workers who were hired at the end of the day.

Working with labor unions can bring the same discontent. A contract can be agreed upon but next year, contract negotiations start again because the current contract isn't the same or equivalent to a teacher's contract in another district. The union spokesperson will pull out many different contracts to prove their point. The same is true when a superintendent gets hired by a district. They agree to a contract and are satisfied until they find out other superintendents in the state of similar sized districts are receiving more money. They will become disgruntled and try to negotiate with the board a better contract.

No one is satisfied and envy or jealousy takes root. Our want for more is never satisfied. We want more, more, more! Proverbs 14:30 (KJV) reads, "A sound heart is the life of the flesh: but envy the rottenness of the bones." In James 3:16, it says that confusion and evil work abide where there is envy. When we envy others and we continue to want more, we become like the grave, the barren womb, dry land, and fire, which never says, "Enough" (Proverbs 30:16). The eyes of man are never satisfied (Proverbs 27:20). If you find yourself in that position, be thankful what the Lord has provided for you and ask him to forgive you for having an unthankful and envious spirit. Your only desire should be to want to learn more about Jesus and to be like Him!

More about Jesus let me learn,
More of His holy will discern;
Spirit of God my teacher be,
Showing the things of Christ to me.
                                        –J. R. Sweeney

When talking about contracts you should be like Paul Getty when he said "I always believed in sticking to an agreement."

Our Stronghold

The LORD is good, a strong hold in the day of trouble, and he knoweth them that trust in him. **Nahum 1:7**

It is always reassuring to know that God is our protection and our comfort in times of trouble and that He knows us. A stronghold makes me think of forts in the old days that gave a protection by having people inside the walls and also having a watchtower to ensure that they could fend off attacks. Strongholds today seem to be places like church and our homes. They are places where we feel safe. As I walk around my neighborhood, I feel comfortable and safe. But still I am observant of things around me. I am watchful of things that look strange or out of place. I do not walk blindly without understanding that there could be dangers. It is one of the reasons I walk in known areas that have a good amount of traffic and visibility. I do not walk at night in the dark or alone in unknown areas. Protection does not mean I am unaware of potential dangers.

God is jealous, and the LORD revengeth; the LORD revengeth, and is furious; the LORD will take vengeance on his adversaries, and he reserveth wrath for his enemies. The LORD is slow to anger, and great in power, and will not at all acquit the wicked; the LORD hath his way in the whirlwind and in the storm, and the clouds are the dust of his feet. He rebuketh the sea, and maketh it dry, and drieth up all the rivers: Bashan languisheth, and Carmel, and the flower of Lebanon languisheth. The mountains quake at him, and the hills melt, and the earth is burned at his presence, yes the world and all that dwell therein. Who can stand before his indignation? And who can abide in the fierceness of his anger? His fury is poured out like fire, and the rocks are thrown down by him. Nahum 1:2-6

Nahum was led to warn those in that nation that God would have revenge if they continued in their wicked ways. As a nation, I pray that our leaders and our people will stand up for what if right and not try God's patience. Over and over in the Bible, it is made clear that nations have been destroyed that did not follow God's ways. I also believe that any nation that does not support Israel, God's chosen nation, is on the edge of God's destruction. As a democracy, the people must be strong advocates for their voice counting in elections as well as in their freedom of speech. It requires Christians to be the voice of the nation, if the nation is to stay strong. Prayer for our nation is our hope.

You are my strong tower, a shelter over me,
Beautiful and mighty everlasting King,
You are my strong tower, fortress when I'm weak,
Your name is true and whole and Your face is all I see.
                                                                        –Kutless

If my people, which are called by my name, shall humble themselves and pray, and seek my face, and turn from their wicked ways; then will I hear from heaven, and will forgive their sin, and will heal their land. II Chronicles 7:14

Running Away is Not the Right Attitude

Arise, go to Nineveh, that great city, and cry against it; for their wickedness is come up before me. But Jonah rose up to flee unto Tarshish from the presence of the LORD, and went down to Joppa and he found a ship going to Tarshish, so he paid the fare thereof, and went down into it, to go with them unto Tarshish from the presence of the LORD. Jonah 1:2-3

Many times we need an attitude adjustment. There are times we try to escape our job, our duties, and any of our responsibilities. Near the end of each school year there seem to be a million things to do. Textbooks have to be checked, summer facility requests need to be updated, inventory needs to be completed, student reports need to be finished. The students are restless and ready for summer, also. Most of their assignments are complete. All of the state tests have been completed. So it is hard to keep the students' attention on learning any new concepts.

Educators have all of these responsibilities, but they also have their own families. Educators still have their own laundry to do. They still have to prepare meals and clean their houses. Their cars still need to have gas and maintenance. Their lawns need to be mowed. So it should not surprise us when at times, we might want to just escape. Jonah wanted to escape his responsibilities. He did not believe in the assigned task so he did not want to complete the task. He went the opposite direction and ran from the assignment. This led him into more trouble and also jeopardized others because of his running away. His attitude was not right and needed an adjustment.

God wants us to trust him. We are to follow his directions and He will guide us to the best comfort zone. Our attitude at all times should be grateful for all God has done for us. When we remember that He is in control, we can know that things will get done on His schedule. Our attitude of gratefulness should be the first order. We should be willing to complete God's directions. He will give us everything we need to in order to accomplish anything He asks of us.

> *I've taken off the weights, I've laid down the sins*
> *I've made up my mind that I'm gonna win*
> *The shackles have fallen, the chains now are gone*
> *I'm running with Jesus, I'm going on!*
> —The Crabb Family

For though we walk in the flesh, we do not war after the flesh: For the weapons of our warfare are not carnal, but mighty through God to the pulling down of strong holds; Casting down imaginations, and every high thing that exalteth itself against the knowledge of God, and bringing into captivity every thought to the obedience of Christ. And having in a readiness to revenge all disobedience, when your obedience is fulfilled. II Corinthians 10: 3-6

The Lord's Requirement

Wherewith shall I come before the LORD, and bow myself before the high God? Shall I come before him with burnt offerings, with calves of a year old? Will the LORD be pleased with thousands of rams, or with ten thousands of rivers of oil? Shall I give my firstborn for my transgression, the fruit of my body for the sin of my soul? He hath shewed thee, O man, what is good; and what doth the LORD require of thee, but to do justly, and to love mercy, and to walk humbly with thy God? **Micah 6:6-8**

Today, when I read the Bible verse for my devotional, it reminded me of a song about coming in front of the Lord and whether I would be able to even stand in front of Him or if I would fall to my knees in awe. I think the feeling would be overwhelming. Here stands my Lord who knows everything about me, the inside and the outside.

I have watched the crowds of people waiting in lines to see the Queen of England. They show reverence by appropriate dress and manners. How much more will we show reverence to our Lord! He has accepted us even knowing all about our faults. There are no offerings we can give that would be worthy of Him or could cover all our sins. There is no work or way we can have salvation except by accepting God's gift of His own Son.

When we accept God's gift, we want to please God. God wants us to love mercy, act justly, and walk humbly. Loving mercy means that we should help others. As leaders, we have many chances to show acceptance of others without prejudice. Sometimes showing mercy means giving someone a second chance. Other times, showing mercy means we assume the best in people instead of assuming the worst.

Acting justly means we are superintendents with strong ethics who work hard to examine any practices and policies in our organizations that treat others unfairly. It is our responsibility to speak up for the rights of others. There are sins of omission and sins of commission. When we know something is wrong and don't speak up we have committed sins of omission. Walking humbly means we understand that we have been granted much in life and therefore much is required of us. I am reminded of the saying, "There except by the grace of God go I". In other circumstances, I might also have a similar experience that would drop me to my knees.

> *Mercy there was great, and grace was free;*
> *Pardon there was multiplied to me;*
> *There my burdened soul found liberty,*
> *At Calvary.*
> –William R. Newell

Grace be with you, mercy, and peace, from God the Father, and from the Lord Jesus Christ, the Son of the Father, in truth and love. 2 John 1:3

Talking with God

I will stand upon my watch, and set me upon the tower, and will watch to see what he will say unto me, and what I shall answer when I am reproved. And the Lord answered me, and said, Write the vision, and make it plain upon tables, that he may run that readeth it. For the vision is yet for an appointed time, but at the end it shall speak, and not lie though it tarry, wait for it, because it will surely come, it will not tarry. Behold, his soul which is lifted up is not upright to him; but the just shall live by faith. **Habakkuk 2:1-4**

Do you ever wonder what God wants you to do? Do you ask God for advice on major decisions? God clearly wants us to ask Him. We need to write down what He tells us to do. God told Habakkuk that he should write down what God told him clearly so that others would be able to read it and wait. That is where I get myself in trouble. I go to God with my requests and many times I try to be very specific in my requests. But I want the answers immediately. I don't want to wait.

God told Habakkuk to live by faith. So, while I am waiting, I continue to live by faith. I am to expect that God will answer me. If we live by the example Jesus showed while on this earth, we would find the time to be by ourselves to pray. We need to make time for the quiet prayer. Then, we need to focus on the way to pray.

Jesus clearly showed in the example of the Lord's Prayer, that the prayer starts with praise and worship to God. We are to acknowledge that God deserves our worship and that He is in control. My requests come after I've first turned toward God in worship. I then have a realization that God has all power and He wants me to come to Him with my requests. Nothing is too small or too large for God to handle.

Habakkuk said that he would watch to see what God would say to him. How interesting to not say that he would listen to what God would say to him, but that he would watch. There are times that I have seen many of God's wonders and have never thought of this being a way that He spoke to me. The visions God gives can be tested to align with His Word so we are assured that it is not just our own self answers or even a deception of answers from the devil. God's answers will align with His word. God wants us to know Him, to sit and talk with Him. He cares for our questions and wants to give us answers. The last part of the Lord's Prayer is an acknowledgement that God has the power and control over all things.

Keep walking and talking with the Lord all the way;
Keep trusting in His Word every day.
Keep looking for the Son, watch and pray;
Keep walking, talking, trusting all the way,
Looking, watching praying every day.
                                        –Frank Garlock

The eyes of your understanding being enlightened;
that ye may know what is the hope of his calling,
and what the riches of the glory of his inheritance in the saints.
And what is the exceeding greatness of his power to us-ward who believe,
according to the working of his might power,
which he wrought in Christ, when he raised him from the dead,
and set him at his own right hand in the heavenly places. Ephesians 1:18-20

June 28

Please Say "You Love Me."

But whoso shall offend one of these little ones which believe in me, it were better for him that a millstone were hanged about his neck, and that he were drowned in the depth of the sea. **Matthew 18:6**

Rodney Berget was on death row in South Dakota for bludgeoning a prison guard to death with a pipe in a failed attempt to escape. He died by lethal injection in September of 2012. His older brother, Roger Berget, was convicted of killing a man for his car and was sentenced to death in Oklahoma. He lived on death row at Big Mac until his execution in 2000 at the age of 39.

The siblings, who lived in South Dakota, came from a poverty-laden, stormy family. Their crime-ridden adult lives show the effects of a damaged upbringing and the years of havoc wrought by two men who developed, what the courts called, a wanton disregard for human life. The two boys were born into a family that already had four kids. A former prison principal described Rodney as a "throwaway kid" who never had a chance at a productive life. His lawyer said he was an "ugly duckling" with little family support.

The boys were born after the family moved to the city when the farm failed in rural South Dakota. With the loss of his farm, the patriarch Berget went to work for the state highway department and the mother took a job as a bar manager at the local Holiday Inn. The loss of the farm and new city life strained the family and the couple's marriage. When the family moved to town, "things kind of fell apart." The elder Berget was rarely around and always away on business. When he was home, he drank and became physically abusive. In the 1970s, the couple divorced and Roger and Rodney started getting into trouble. Roger skipped school and Rodney started stealing. Soon, they were taking cars. Both went to prison for the first time as teens. There is no light at the end of this type of upbringing and what usually happens at the end is execution.

Life is so precious and how our children are raised and their need for acceptance will dictate their outcomes. King Solomon recognized this when he wrote, "train up a child in the way he should go and when he is old he will not turn from it" Proverbs 22:6. Raising and training a child is the most important duty a parent has and when they fail to do so properly, they, in essence, cause that child to sin and they themselves are guilty. When a child comes from a dysfunctional family, their chances of making it into society are only 20%. As a superintendent, you will meet many irresponsible parents and you must pray to have a positive impact on their child's life. Pray, "Dear Lord, give me the wisdom to lead these children and to help them break this chain of bondage they are in and make me a blessing in their lives."

Jesus loves the little children; all the children of the world
Red, brown, yellow, black and white
They are precious in His sight.
Jesus loves the little children of the world.

On the inside we all yearn for intimacy and affection. This yearning is especially true in our relationships with our parents.
–Gary Smalley

Work of Righteousness

Until the spirit be poured upon us from on high, and the wilderness be a fruitful field, and the fruitful field be counted for a forest. Then judgment shall dwell in the wilderness, and righteousness remain in the fruitful field. And the work of righteousness shall be peace; and the effect of righteousness quietness and assurance for ever. **Isaiah 32:15-17**

Righteousness is not possible without God. When we work at righteousness, then we are able to live a life that is pleasing to God. It is not possible for us to work on righteousness on our own because we will always fail. Yet, our focus can't be on our sinful nature and all the wrongs we do. We must keep our focus on Jesus, knowing that He is righteous. When we believe in Jesus, we receive His work of righteousness. The righteousness leads to peace with the effect of quietness and assurance.

I like the idea of being calm and having assurance that God is in control. There are times when my life does not seem calm, so it is extremely helpful to know that I just have to remember that God is in control. There is a reason for his timing and my need to wait on His time. His timing is for my own growth. It is often later that I realize what I was to learn from waiting on God. And there are other times when I don't understand His timing. But I stay focused that He is in control and He knows what is best for me.

As a superintendent of a school, we have the opportunity to see many people work extremely hard and dedicate their time and talents to help others. Teachers buy supplies when their classroom budgets run out of money. They stay late and help individual students catch up on work. Additionally, they spend their evenings planning lessons in order to reach students and help them learn new concepts. Often, they don't see the results of their teaching until much later in their students' lives. Their work is based on a code of teaching, for doing what is right. But even this higher calling, is not at the same level of God's work of righteousness. God's sending of His son who was righteous gave us righteousness.

Jesus, thy blood and righteousness
My beauty are, my glorious dress;
Midst flaming worlds, in these arrayed,
With joy shall I lift up my head.
                    –Nikolaus L. von Zinzendorf

Then Peter opened his mouth, and said, Of a truth I perceive that God is no respecter of persons: But in every nation he that feareth him, and worketh righteousness, is accepted with him. Acts 10:34-35

The Good Shepherd

I am the good shepherd: the good shepherd giveth his life for the sheep. John 10:11

One night, a Wyoming shepherd was counting his sheep and found that there were two missing. Outside of the sheepfold it was storming fiercely, a tornado producing a thunderstorm with no equal. He went to the dog kennel where his Australian Shepherd was lying, pointed out into the stormy night and said, "Two sheep are missing; go." The dog obediently arose and ran off into the night. When she found one sheep that was lost, she brought it back.

The storm grew fiercer and the night still longer. But once more the shepherd came to his dog and pointing out into the fierce storm, again said, "One sheep is missing; go." When the dog looked out into the storm she obediently rose, looked at her master's face and then hurried away.

Several hours passed and the shepherd heard a scratching at the door. The dog had returned and brought with her the second sheep that was lost. Then the dog staggered back toward the kennel and just outside the door, she fell dead. She had saved the sheep, but had lost her own life.

Jesus, our Good Shepherd, did this same thing for us. He came to this world and gave His life. He died on the Calvary's cross for mankind in sin. Jesus is the good and faithful shepherd. The reason we can know that Jesus is truly the good shepherd and the right door is that he laid down his life for us and that He has the power to take it back up.

The Good Shepherd loves His sheep so much that He stops at no sacrifice in protecting them and saving them. "The good shepherd giveth his life for the sheep." The Eastern shepherd often had to fight battles for his flock. David tells of killing a lion and a bear in defense of his sheep. Sometimes, the shepherd, in defending his flock against wild animals, is wounded or even loses his life. Our Good Shepherd has wounds upon Him, and if we ask when He received them, His answer is, "In defending My own."

Out in the desert hear their cry,
Out on the mountain, wild and high;
Hark! 'tis the Master, speaks to thee,'
Go, find My sheep where'er they be.
Bring them in, bring them in,
Bring the wandering ones to Jesus.
–William Ogden

A good superintendent cares for and protects the staff and students just like a good shepherd cares for and protects the flock.

JULY

Being an Example

And, ye fathers, provoke your children to wrath: but bring them up in the nurture and admonition of the Lord. **Ephesians 6:4**

I always wondered if my children were following my example. I knew there were times that I would stumble, but I always asked the Lord to forgive me as I tried to live that Christian life. I knew that I had to keep them in church, Sunday school, and Wednesday services, which I coupled with daily devotions. Bringing them up in the "nurture and admonition of the Lord" is tough today because of time pressures and daily stresses. I knew it was important for my children to have a solid foundation so they could withstand today's peer pressure and temptations.

My fears were put aside when I received a letter from my oldest son. He had just graduated from college and entered the Air Force. He wrote: "Dad, I wanted to send you this because I thought it was good. Lead the way Dad, I'm following. Thanks for choosing the good path. Love, Marc." Then he taped a small article to the letter that read: "A man and his young son were climbing a mountain. They came to a place where the climbing was difficult and even dangerous. That father stopped to consider which way he should go. He heard the boy behind him say, 'Choose the good path, Dad; I'm coming right behind you!'"

Tears came to my eyes as I read this because I knew that my son saw my example. As an ex-superintendent of schools, I tried to "choose the good path" and live a good Christian life. I wanted the parents, teachers, and students to know that not only did I desire the best education for them, but I also lived by my strong Christian convictions. Being a superintendent, I've learned the importance of effective leading, and setting a good example is effective leading. As Albert Einstein said, "Example isn't another way to teach. It's the only way to teach."

Lives of great men all remind us
We can make our lives sublime,
And, departing, leave us behind
Footprints on the sands of time.
–Henry Wadsworth Longfellow

Preach the gospel at all times and when necessary use words.
–St. Francis of Assisi

Forgiveness

For if you forgive men when they sin against you, your heavenly Father will also forgive you. But if you do not forgive men their sins, your Father will not forgive your sins. Matthew 6:14-15

This is a very important truism. We have to forgive those who trespass against us. Almost every day, a person will trespass against a school superintendent or a school administrator. That is the nature of the job. The benefits of forgiveness are enormous. According to the Mayo Clinic, this includes: healthier relationships, greater spiritual well-being, less stress and hostility, lower blood pressure, fewer symptoms of depression and chronic pain, and lower risk of alcohol and drug abuse.

According to the Mayo Clinic, it's easy to hold a grudge because once you allow negative feelings to crowd out positive feelings, you find yourself swallowed by your own bitterness. The effect of holding a grudge is that you become depressed, and anxious and lose enriching connectedness with others. You can reach a state of forgiveness by choosing to forgive the person who's offended you and moving away from your role as a victim. As you let go of your grudges, you no longer look at how you've been hurt but view situations with compassion and understanding.

I remember when I was working in a school district in Oklahoma and we were in the midst of teacher negotiations. It was getting heated, and the teachers' chief negotiator, who was a teacher in the district, was quite agitated. As we caucused, she yelled down the hallway, "You pinko commies!" We shrugged off her comments as we arrived into the caucus room. We came back to the table and finished the negotiation session successfully. If we had held a grudge, the negotiations would have stalled. A few years later, when I became a superintendent in a neighboring district, the teacher negotiator's sister applied for a job in my district, and I hired her. She did superbly. If I had held a grudge, I would have lost an excellent teacher. As Christians, we have to learn to forgive so our Father in heaven will also forgive us.

Forgiving is the power
That sets my spirit free!
Forgiveness is God's wondrous gift
That sets my spirit free!
–Brenda Terrell

Forgiveness is a funny thing. It warms the heart and cools the sting.
–William A. Ward

The Responsibility of Administration

Do not withhold good from those to whom it is due, when it is in your power to do it. Do not say to your neighbor, "Go, and come again, tomorrow I will give it" when you have it with you. **Proverbs 3:27-28**

This quote from Proverbs is a voice, which states that compassion is actually what life is all about. In order for an organization to live and grow, there must be compassion. Today in education, we are beginning to realize that what has been done in the past is not going to meet the needs of students in the future.

When I entered education ten years ago, I was a naive young teacher on a quest to change the world one student at a time. Fortunately, I was blessed with quality administrators to guide me during my first few years. They understood the value of an advanced education. Their encouragement and support led me in the pursuit of graduate studies almost immediately. For three years, I was mentored and encouraged by some of the best educators in the area. They were more than my teachers; they were my friends. I learned the theories of Constructivism, Behaviorism, and Postmodernism. Names like Dewey, Vygotsky, Wheatly, and Schlechty became meaningful. I quickly began to grasp some of the complex ideas surrounding a rapidly changing system. Only through the support and encouragement of these mentors was I able to become a building principal at the age of twenty-five and superintendent at age twenty-seven.

With many more years in the public school system ahead of me, I now have a new goal: to tear down some of the old stereotypes surrounding educational leaders today. School administrators are no longer the pencil-pushers and tyrannical dictators of the past. They are not an invisible voice that calls out from behind a desk, ordering teachers to keep their rooms quiet and their students busy completing meaningless, routine tasks.

Administrators are the heart and soul of a district. Dr. C. Everett Koop, former U.S. Surgeon General, once wrote, "Life affords no greater responsibility, no greater privilege, than the raising of the next generation." As educators, we have the opportunity to touch the lives around us each and every day. Don't let today be the day that you "withhold good from those whom it is due."

Jesus, use me
Dear Lord, don't refuse me
There is a work that I must do
Though the cost be great I'll work for you.
                                    –Anonymous

Today you can make a difference.

Integrity

Judge me, O Lord; for I have walked in mine integrity: I have trusted also in the Lord; therefore I shall not slide. **Psalms 26:1**

Most people make integrity synonymous with honesty, but integrity has a finer point. The root word for integrity is "integer," which implies singleness, unity, something not divided, consistency, and by extension, reliability and trustworthiness – in everything.

A superintendent of integrity is an honest person. They do not lie, steal, cheat, or treat employees unfairly. The true follower of Christ has little problem with these major issues. Even the best superintendent, however, can sometimes be careless about integrity in little things. It is important they maintain their integrity at every level. It is the "little foxes that spoil the vines" (Song of Solomon 2:15).

The superintendent of integrity presents the same *face* every time and in every situation. In contrast, a hypocrite presents a different *face* to different people. Even a little two-facedness violates scriptural principles and undermines our integrity. Those who observe this behavior lose the ability to trust our "face" and believe us.

Offhand promises that superintendents fail to fulfill can also damage their integrity. They should allow for unanticipated circumstances when they make promises. Furthermore, the superintendent of integrity will explain the new circumstance and revise the promise at the earliest possible moment. Promises are contracts, and the superintendent of integrity honors his contracts.

The concept of the contract extends top appointments and is on time. To do otherwise violates our word. To have integrity means that our word is totally trustworthy and our actions are completely consistent. The superintendent of integrity shares God's lack of variation and shadow of turning (James 1:17).

> *I walk a road less traveled, to a vision few men see*
> *The road is straight and narrow but leads to integrity*
> *The journey is quite easy when all eyes are focused on me*
> *But it's what I do when I'm alone which defines integrity.*
> –Unknown

Image is what people think we are; integrity is what we really are.
–John Maxwell

Positive Thinking

"...whatsoever things are true, whatsoever things are honest, whatsoever things are pure, whatsoever things are lovely, whatsoever things are of good report; if there be any virtue, and if there be any praise, think on these things." **Philippians 4:8**

The superintendency can be exhilarating, as well as exhausting, and it can exact a toll on our well-being. In an environment of accountability and expectations for high performers, everyone expects superhuman feats from the superintendent. Rohland (2002) summarized that, today, superintendents must guide challenging, dynamic educational systems while appropriately responding to social and political pressure. He goes on to say that he thinks that the high standards and people-intensive nature of school districts are primary reasons the job is so demanding. The higher up the career ladder, the more exposure to criticism. Whenever you are the boss, there will always be employee dissatisfaction in regards to your performance.

One key stressor that strongly affects the superintendent is time management. Every interest group is competing for their time. Other stressors affecting the superintendency are role overload, board politics, role conflict, and lack of fiscal resources. Harvey (2003) said that success for the superintendent lies in gleaning wisdom from attacks and criticism without being defeated in the process.

One strategy in overcoming these stressors, so you won't be defeated, is to have a positive attitude and positive thinking. Positive thinking does the following: reduces stress, helps you enjoy life more, keeps you healthier, and helps you develop better coping skills during hard times. *Business Review* (2004) reports a board member's comments about his superintendent, Dr. Robinson, when he said, "He always has a positive slant on everything...he finds the positive in the negative and he's never really negative about anything. Even if we think it's bad, he turns it into something good." This attitude and thinking affects the environment of the school which supports ISLLC standard two: "A school administrator is an educational leader who promotes the success of all students by advocating, nurturing, and sustaining a school culture...conducive to student learning and professional growth."

A songwriter captured this verse when he wrote:

Think about the good things God has done
Think about the victories my Lord has won
Don't think about the time when you were down and out
But think about a God who brought you out.

The positive thinker sees the invisible,
feels the intangible,
and achieves the impossible.

Close Enough to Make a Difference

And when I saw him, I fell at his feet as dead. And he laid his right hand upon me, saying unto me, Fear not: I am the first and the last. **Revelations 1:17**

John was banished to the isle of Patmos, which was a harsh, barren prison colony for the Romans. The king did not want to hear him and wanted to shut him up. While on the isle of Patmos, lonely and waiting to die, Jesus shows up and says, "Fear not!"

John was with Jesus for three years. The last time John saw Jesus, his feet were bruised, but this time they were made of brass. His voice was in fervent prayer, and now it is as the sound of many waters. His eyes were filled with tears, and now they are like flames of fire. His hair was bloodied and brown, and now it's as white as snow. His countenance was broken on the cross, and now it's as the sun shineth in his strength. John last saw Jesus as a man, and now sees him in splendor and majesty. He saw Jesus after the battle and exalted.

Sometimes, Jesus seems so far away, and we think he doesn't see the harsh trial we are going through. Have courage and hold on to what you have. Be faithful, as the victory is worth the fight. He knows what you're going through and the battle you're fighting. He cares about you and is with you. As a school superintendent, the Lord knows and sees the battles, challenges, and obstacles you're facing. He sees your fears, tears, and anguish.

Jesus is very near to you and is close enough to make a difference. Jesus overcame and is sitting on the right hand side of the Father and interceding for you night and day. A mansion is being prepared for all who overcome. There is only one God (Isa. 46:9) and only one way to heaven (Acts 4:12). There is no other name in Heaven by which man can be saved.

> *Tho' others would be lonely when all their friends are gone.*
> *My Lord is ever standing by my side,*
> *There is a heavy load upon me and yet I'm pressing on,*
> *Because I've found a Savior, Friend, and Guide.*
> –V.P. Ellis

It is the duty of every Christian to be Christ to his neighbor.
–Martin Luther

Vision

And he said unto the king, Let the king live forever: Why should not my countenance be sad, for the city where my ancestors are buried is in ruins, and the gates have been destroyed by fire. **Nehemiah 2:3**

During the night I went out with a few men without telling anyone what my God had inspired me to do for Jerusalem. The only animal I had was the one I was riding. **Nehemiah 2:12**

The book of Nehemiah is important because it provides a clear example of Christian leadership. Nehemiah provides us with an example of vision, vision sharing, vision implementation, and how to handle those opposed to God's vision. In Nehemiah 2:3, the state of Jerusalem is in disarray and this troubles Nehemiah.

As Nehemiah learns of the state of Jerusalem and of what remains of the Jewish people living there, it clearly has a profound effect, moving him to a period of fasting and prayer. Out of this prayer Nehemiah senses a clear calling and vision, identifying with the Jewish people and confessing their failure to follow God's guidance. Nehemiah 2:12 indicates that Nehemiah understands God's vision. Nehemiah then begins to share God's vision with others and, with God's help, develops a plan of action to implement that vision. However, Nehemiah is not without his adversity. During Chapter 4, there is opposition and threats to the vision from those outside of the city. Nehemiah responds by strengthening the confidence of the builders by stationing guards behind the least exposed areas. In Chapter 5, the threat is coming internally, in the face of distractions over the culture and accepted norms of the society. Nehemiah demonstrates openness by calling a meeting. He shows integrity in not demanding the rights of his predecessors and once again demonstrates his commitment to God. In Chapter 6, the threat is personal. Nehemiah discerns the motives of his opponents and refuses to play into their hands. Again he turns to the Lord in prayer and is given the discernment necessary to avoid the traps laid for him.

As a superintendent, it can be difficult to implement a vision. School districts support a wide variety of stakeholders that have their own motives and agendas. Many times, superintendents find that the agenda they deem best for students might draw strong opposition from certain segments of the community. Like in the story of Nehemiah, these "threats" can come from outside of the school, internally, or from within your own heart. As a Christian leader it is important for you to remain in prayer when tackling tough decisions. Nehemiah is a good example of a leader who showed restraint by not implementing his will, but by implementing instead the Will of God. As leaders in our field we must remain vigilant in prayer as we begin the process of implementing a new vision; this will insure that the vision is divinely inspired and that it will have a positive impact in our schools.

Where there is no vision, there is no hope.
–George Washington Carver

Give to us clear vision that we may know where to stand and what to stand for because unless we stand for something, we shall fall for anything.
–Peter Marshall

Greatness

Let us not become weary in doing good for at the proper time we will reap a harvest if we do not give up. Galatians 6:9

The superintendency is one of the most demanding positions in the public school system. While there are other administrative positions in a school district, none possess as much influence and authority as the superintendent. The uniqueness of the position is substantiated by the multi-year contract, higher salary, and state mandates located in school board policy. Legal statutes and accountability measures also provide superintendents with an incredible amount of power. Unfortunately, many superintendents never reach their full potential. The demands and accountability that come with such authority become a burden, and it entrenches administrators into a state of complacency. It is much easier to become "weary" and stagnate than it is to wait for the harvest that God has promised.

In the book *Good to Great*, Jim Collins writes, "We don't have great schools principally because we have good schools. We don't have great government, principally because we have good government. Few people attain great lives, in large part because it is just so easy to settle for a good life. The vast majority of companies never become great, precisely because the vast majority become quite good – and that is their main problem."

Though the daily struggles of life might tear us down, we must never forget that we are part of a greater plan. There is integrity in working hard and doing what is right. Do not settle for having a "good school" or "good students" or for being a "good educator." Decide today that you will be great, and be ready to reap the harvest God has in store for your life. Finally, to be great you have to be humble, as when Jesus said there was none greater than John the Baptist yet even the least in the Kingdom of Heaven is greater than he.

A sunbeam, a sunbeam,
Jesus wants me for a sunbeam;
A sunbeam, a sunbeam,
I'll be a sunbeam for Him.

I want it said of me by those who knew me best, that I always plucked a thistle and planted a flower where I thought a flower would grow.
–Abraham Lincoln

Servant Leadership

Then Jesus poured water into a basin and began to wash the disciples' feet and to wipe them with the towel that was wrapped around him. **John 13:5**

I was 27 years old when I was named interim superintendent of Oakwood Independent School District. Even though there were less than 300 students in the entire district, I remember feeling overwhelmed by the job. To this day, the small community of Oakwood holds a special place in my heart because of the invaluable lessons I learned while serving that community.

Specifically, I remember one frosty morning in March. Robert, the head of our maintenance department (actually he was the only maintenance worker), came into my office upset over a break in the sewer line. The line had broken overnight, and the front lawn of the school had become a muddy, stinking mess. Robert was in a panic because he couldn't find the break in the line. After I got him calm, I grabbed some rubber boots out of my truck and walked out to help him find the leak. Now keep in mind, here I am, a first time superintendent wearing a sport coat, tie, dress pants, and rubber boots, stomping around in sewage, looking for a broken line. About ten minutes into our task, the school board president comes driving up to see me, and he yells from the road, "Hey, I don't think the superintendent is supposed to be walking around in all that sewage mess!" I replied back to him, "If I don't get down here in it, how can I find out what's wrong."

In John, 13:5, Jesus knew that his time on earth was short, and this would be the last time he would be with his disciples. He had an opportunity to teach them one last lesson: humility. Jesus said the second greatest commandment is to "love your neighbor as yourself," so it is not surprising that he taught humility and service to others, which is evidence of love. Jesus said, "I tell you the truth, slaves are not greater than their master. Nor is the messenger more important than the one who sends the message" (John 13:16).

For school administrators, this is an important lesson. People line up to do work that is thrilling, respected, and exciting. However, Jesus showed humility by doing the job nobody wanted to do. As a school superintendent, it is a good rule of thumb never to ask anyone to complete a task that you would not be willing to do yourself. And on some occasions, particularly those frosty mornings in March, it might be necessary to step down into the "junk" to find out what is wrong.

A servant leader, I will be
Letting people see Jesus through me
I will work for my staff
And let them see love in the administration craft.

Servant leadership is intentional action that seeks the best for others.
–Tony Baron

Strength in Christ

For I can do all things through Christ, who gives me strength. **Philippians 4:13**

I once heard a story of a time when Dr. Martin Luther King, Jr. was leading a nonviolent protest in Alabama. Dr. King was a pacifist; however, many of his marches, particularly those in the South, would draw large, extremely hostile crowds. These crowds despised Dr. King and his agenda. On this particular day, the police officers were on high alert and were having to force the crowds away from Dr. King and his supporters. At one point a man broke through the barricade, ran directly up to Dr. King, and spat in his face. The men behind Dr. King were ready to fight, but he held them back, pulled out a handkerchief, wiped the spit from his face, and kept walking. Later that day, a reporter asked Dr. King why he did not fight back. King replied, "I chose who I was going to be this morning when I woke up. I am a pacifist, and I will not let a little spit change who I am."

As school administrators, we are often faced with conflicts. How we handle those conflicts speaks volumes to who we are as individuals and how others view us. Philippians 4:3 affirms our need to rely on God, for whom nothing is impossible. It is our relationship with Christ, expressed by beholding His word and depending upon Him in prayer, which allows us to draw the power necessary to lead a godly life.

We do not know the power of God or what he has in store for us. Think of the donkey's jawbone lying on the ground. What power does it hold? The answer is none, until the moment when Samson picks it up. At that moment, we begin to wonder what can that bone not do? In a way, we are like that jawbone. We often find ourselves in situations where we ask, "What can I do?" The answer is clear. When the spirit of Christ grasps us, there is nothing we can't accomplish. Unfortunately, Dr. Martin Luther King, Jr. was assassinated long before I had the opportunity to meet him, but I think if he were here today he would tell us that it was the strength of Jesus Christ which allowed him to "turn the other cheek" that day in the streets of Alabama. Fortunately for us, we have the opportunity to draw from that same strength today.

Whom have I in heaven but You?
And there is none upon earth that I desire besides You
My flesh and my heart fail;
But God is the strength of my heart and my portion forever. Psalm 73:25-26

In Christ alone, I place my trust.

There is a God

The fool hath said in his heart. There is no God. Corrupt are they, and have done abominable iniquity: there is none that doeth good. **Psalms 53:1**

The greatest conversion story in the Bible is the story of Saul on the road to Damascus to continue the persecutions of the Christians. A bright light came from heaven and blinded him. After this dramatic conversion, Saul became Paul, and he became the most prolific writer of the New Testament.

There is a list of former atheists who became Christians. Some of these are Mortimer Adler, Kirk Cameron, Dawn Eden, Francis Collins, Simon Greenleaf, C. S. Lewis, William Murray, Lee Strobel, and a host of others. Each of these were noted experts in their fields and came to acknowledge Jesus Christ as their Lord and Savior.

Upon his return from war, a young veteran enrolled in a philosophy course in college. The professor, an acknowledged atheist, started to berate God and say, "There is no God." He went on to say, "If there is a God, he will knock me off this stage." The room was quiet, and several minutes went by. He kept challenging God and saying, "Where are you if you are there?" This young veteran got up from his seat and walked to the stage. He knocked the professor off the stage. The professor staggered, got up from the floor and said, "Why did you do that?" The young veteran said, "God is busy, and so he asked me to do his work."

Another story is told about the noted atheist Robert Ingersoll, who challenged God to strike him dead within a certain length of time. After that time came and went, Robert Ingersoll was still alive and made the proclamation that "this proved there was no God." An older lady in the crowd spoke up and said, "Mr. Ingersoll, man deals in time, God deals in eternity," at which he was left speechless.

As a superintendent, you will face the forces that want Christianity out of society. There is a God, and he has everything under control.

There is a God, Almighty God
Creator of heaven and earth and all there is
He is the beginning, He is the ending,
He's the unseen destiny of man.
                                        –J. D. Sumner

Without the assistance of that Divine Being...I can't succeed.
With that assistance, I can't fail.
                                        –Abraham Lincoln

Coming Through Trials

Beloved, think it not strange concerning the fiery trial which is to try you, as though some strange thing happened unto you. **I Peter 4:12**

Have you ever faced a trial or been through a trial and wondered, 'where is God?' That has happened to me, and I wondered how much more I could bear. I had to remember that God is there and cares about every aspect of my life.

I know of a superintendent who was viciously libeled in the local newspaper. A technology director, who was harassing a female employee, was demoted by the board at the recommendation of the superintendent and school attorney. This angry ex-director quit and went to the newspaper with fabricated "bold-faced" lies about the superintendent. The newspaper was all too eager to print the story, and the lies were headlined. The superintendent's fiery trial began and was so severe that he thought it would never end as the newspaper daily attacked his integrity. To make matters worse, the superintendent was just recovering from a life-threatening surgery that did not turn out well. To heal physically and mentally, the superintendent left the district. An attorney offered to file a libel suit against the newspaper pro-bono, but the ex-superintendent declined because he cared about kids and did not want that type of publicity to take away from their education. He was brave enough to run away. Several years later, the athletic director of that district ran into the ex-superintendent and told him how he and others admired his character as he went through that trial. As a superintendent, you will face fiery trials, and it will be your character and faith in God that will see you through. The trial makes you stronger so you can be a lighthouse to others going through trials.

When we consider the early church and their success, we may forget that what they gained, they gained out of the furnace of trial and affliction. Watching them as they faced a difficult and dark day can help us when we, too, have to face trying times. However, when these times come, we must handle them, correctly, or they will handle us! Peter said that we're to "rejoice." It is the trials you go through that make you strong enough to come through other trials.

Bigger than all of our trials
Bigger than all of our fears
God is bigger than any mountain
That you can or can't see.
                                    –Unknown

Only if you've been in the deepest valley
can you ever know how magnificent it is to be on the highest mountain.
                                    –Richard Nixon

Contentment

Now godliness with contentment is great gain. For we brought nothing into this world, and it is certain we can carry nothing out. **I Timothy 6:6-7**

Contentment almost seems like a myth sometimes in my life. Am I ever really content with where I am at this point in my life? I think not; there is always something:

> Desire for more money.
> Desire for a better job.
> Desire for success.
> Desire to be liked by people.

I know I could go on with the list. I think the one that I struggle with most often at this point in life is that desire for a bigger and better job. Not a bad desire in and of itself, but it can definitely cause issues and problems when I over-emphasize that desire – when I am not content with my current position. This has caused me to compromise at times and hold on too tight at other times.

But very recently, it hit me that I am just flat out not content with what the sovereign ruler of the universe has for me, and I try to fight Him on the issue! Instead of looking at the truth of my situation, I magnify my own desires and, quite frankly, am a "big baby" about wanting my desires met.

So what is the truth? The truth is that God is for me and not against me! He has plans for me! You and I both were created for His purposes, not our own. My own recognition of this on a consistent basis will indeed help in my contentment with what God has for me.

A colleague once encouraged me to work to be content and to pray for contentment in all things except for my relationship with Christ...he said to never be satisfied in my walk because we can always improve in that area. Good words to live by.

What is it that you are not content with? Do you struggle with your marriage? Do you struggle with thinking you need more money or things? Whatever it is, I challenge you to pray today that God would give you a content heart. I am not saying that you should stop working to achieve goals, or earn money, or quit looking for that better job. I am saying to seek contentment and to honor Him fully right where you are in life! All those things we chase will take care of themselves (or I should say, He will take care of them as He sees fit).

You say, 'If I had a little more,
I should be very satisfied.'
You make a mistake.
If you are not content with what you have,
you would not be satisfied if it were doubled.

–Charles H. Spurgeon

Spinning

Woe unto them that call evil good, and good evil; that put darkness for light, and light for darkness; that put bitter for sweet, and sweet for bitter. Isaiah 5:20

There are people who vigorously claim the Holocaust never existed and is a lie. The Lord gave General Eisenhower the wisdom to anticipate that some would attempt to turn the truth into a lie because he knew there were people out there like the Russian dictator Lenin, who said, "A lie told often enough becomes the truth."

General Eisenhower said, "The same day I saw my first horror camp, it was the town of Gotha. I have never been able to describe my emotional reactions when I first came face to face with indisputable evidence of Nazi brutality and ruthless disregard of every shred of decency…I felt that the evidence should be immediately placed before the American and the British publics in a fashion that would leave no room for cynical doubt." Eisenhower, upon finding the victims of the death camps, ordered all possible photographs to be taken to prove to future generations what truly did happen. He knew that, as the years passed, liars and spinners would come in denying the very existence of this terrible deed.

Have you ever had someone tell you a "bald-faced" lie or misrepresent the truth to you? I've been in executive sessions and heard board members say one thing and then say the exact opposite when they come back to open session. You have to be prepared like General Eisenhower was so you aren't caught off guard.

Today, there is a word that is used in politics, and the word is "spin," which is just another word for lying, deceiving, and twisting the truth. As a superintendent, the Lord will bless you if you are always honest and never spin the truth.

> *Keep our faith strong so our hearts can mend*
> *And please Lord be with me till the very end*
> *Then answer in judgment and the right to defend*
> *For one day in YOUR House, we will all attend.*
> –Daniel Cunningham

A dog barks when his master is attacked. I would be a coward if I saw that God's truth is attacked and yet would remain silent.
–Pearl Buck

Mercy and Truth

Let not mercy and truth forsake thee, bind them about thy neck, write them upon the table of thine heart. So shalt thou find favour and good understanding in the sight of God and man. **Proverbs 3:4**

Mercy means to show kindness and compassion that eases pain. So how does an administrator show mercy and truth? The axiom, "praise publically and reprimand privately" might apply here when used in a truthful manner. This correction should be presented in a way that is representative of Jesus' way. Remember in the Bible when Jesus quietly stopped the men from stoning a woman who had been caught in an adulterous act? Jesus' word showed mercy and truth. He didn't say she was accused wrongly, for that would not have been the truth. But he quietly told the men that he who was without sin could continue the stoning. Jesus showed the woman mercy.

Superintendents have to also respond to employees when they have not performed correctly. It may not be a serious act of disobedience that is illegal, but it could be an act that does not follow procedures of the district. It is best to deal with the person before problems escalate and more damage is done because you did not correct it.

It is huge comfort knowing that Christ continues to show us mercy. As Christians, we know how often we need to have Christ's mercy. We must repent of our sins. I don't want to stand before Jesus and account for some of my actions. I am grateful for His mercy and forgiveness. I rely on His mercy. The truth is that God hates the sin, not the sinner. His mercy is compassion. He wants us to show compassion to others who need it in a hurting world.

> *For years I traveled a road all wrong*
> *My heart had lost its joy and its song*
> *Till grace placed me right where I belong*
> *When mercy rewrote my life.*
> –J. Swaggart

A good leader knows the way, shows the way, and goes the way.

Honor the Lord

Honor the Lord with thy substance and with the first fruits of all thine increase. So shall thy barns be filled with plenty and thy presses shall burst out with new wine. Proverbs 3:9-10

Honor means to display high ethical character. The ultimate honor is to give God glory by using our personal integrity so that we will please our Lord.

Daniel and his friends lived their lives giving God honor. They were courageous and would not compromise how they lived. Even when they would not follow the rule of bowing to other gods, they refused in a respectful way. Our obedience demonstrates to others our testimony to God. When we face temptations, we also must choose respectful ways to not compromise our beliefs in order to honor God.

We honor God with a realization that our trust must be with Him in times of plenty as well as times of suffering. Paul was able to state he was content whether in jail or in time of plenty. He praised God at all times. It is easier to praise God when things are going well. But we often search for Him desperately when we are in need. God deserves our honor at all times. He desires for us to have a satisfying life.

I often think of honor when I think of children who obey their parents. Honor is shown more when children do what they should and show empathy with compassion even when their parents are not present. As parents and administrators, we are honored when our children, students, and employees perform in a manner that shows respect and empathy.

Socrates stated that the shortest and surest way to live with honor in the world is to be in reality what we would appear to be; all human virtues increase and strengthen themselves by the practice and experience of them.

> *To live you must be living right*
> *No different in the dark than light.*
> *And though life's path be full of pain*
> *It's through that path that Honor's gained.*
> –W. McGehee

I am not bound to win, but I am bound to be true. I am not bound to succeed, but I am bound to live up to what light I have.
–Abraham Lincoln

Right Thing, Right Time, for the Right Reason

To everything there is a season and a time to every purpose under the heaven.
Ecclesiastes 3:1

It is not our good works that will get us into heaven, and yet Jesus told His disciples to "tend my sheep." We are called to help others, and we are told to follow God's will. This means that when we do something, it should be at the time needed by others and for the right reason in order to give God glory.

There are different forms of using our talents given by God. One is to use our gifts on a regular basis. For example, if God gave you the gift of organization, you might help organize meetings, or materials, or office procedures. If God gave you the gift to teach, you might regularly teach Sunday school. Or if God gave you the gift of caring, you might regularly visit church members who are homebound. Another form of helping is possible in the opportune times that arise quickly, in which you find yourself able to help immediately. These types of help might be answering a request for a needed piece of equipment for the church when you have the resources to supply it. Or it might be answering a request to provide meals to someone who has just returned from the hospital. These opportunities are often short-term and need a quick response.

There are ways we can also use this same philosophy as superintendents. There are times that arise as excellent opportunities to give to others in our districts; these times may be very short-term but will show that you understand and can help with others' needs. You also show your talents over time through the things you do consistently for the district's employees, students, and families.

There's a time to laugh and a time to cry
A time to live and a time to die
The reason I know the Bible told me so
The good Lord watches over everyone
Morning, noon, and night so everything will be right.

All that is necessary for the triumph of evil is that good men do nothing.
–Edmund Burke

Armor of God

Finally, my brethren, be strong in the Lord and in the power of His might. Put on the whole armor of God, that you may be able to stand against the wiles of the devil. For we do not wrestle against flesh and blood, but against principalities, against powers, against the ruler of the darkness of this age, against spiritual hosts of wickedness in the heavenly places. Therefore take up the whole armor of God that you may be able to withstand in the evil day, and having done all, to stand.
Ephesians 6:10-14

One of Satan's oldest tricks is not to convince people that there is no God, but that there is no Satan. Before we get into girding ourselves with the armor, there is a reminder here by Paul that we need the armor because what we fight is not of this world. As any soldier knows, we are stronger when fighting with the armor.

1. We are first told to "gird our waist with Truth." What a great analogy, since the belt is what ties everything together.
2. Next, we are to "put on the breastplate of righteousness." This can be seen as taking on the righteous character of Christ – walking in obedience.
3. Then we are to "shod our feet with the preparation of the gospel of peace." When I think of peace, I see a calm sea and not one tossed to and fro. The peace that comes from the gospel and surpasses all understanding. This allows us to stand firm, ready for battle.
4. Next, we "take the shield of faith." Faith can be abstract in my mind at times. How does it work? Looking at Hebrews 11:1-3, Paul writes, "Now faith is the assurance of things hoped for the conviction of things not seen. For by it the men of old received divine approval. By faith we understand that the world was created by the word of God, so that what is seen was made out of things which do not appear."
5. Then we put on "the helmet of salvation." Interesting again that this protects the part of our body where doubts attack us! Don't let the evil one have his way, but instead be thankful daily of your sure salvation.
6. Finally, your offensive weapon: "the sword of the Spirit, which is the word of God." The attacks on us will come, that is a guarantee! Write God's word on your heart. Memorize His word so that, when the time comes, you will be able to fend off the attacks.

Finally, a bit of encouragement: we are not called to win the battle but just to fight. Christ has already won it for us. He is the victor, and to Him be the Praise!

> *Tell me what did you put on this morning*
> *I put on the armour of God*
> *I put on the breastplate of Righteousness*
> *And the helmet of Salvation*
> *I'm a soldier in the Army of the Lord*

Clothe yourself with truth and cover your feet with His peace.

Ten Reasons to Take A Stand

Whosoever therefore shall be ashamed of me and of my words in this adulterous and sinful generation; of him also shall the Son of man be ashamed, when he cometh in the glory of his Father with the holy angels. **Mark 8:38**

As a superintendent, you will need to take a stand. Do you have the courage and the ability to do what is always right, correct, and proper and thereby TAKE A STAND? There are ten reasons to take a stand for Jesus. These are:

1. Stand up for Him. (*Matthew* 10:32)
2. Stand out among the crowd. Be like Jesus and don't be like the world. (*Matthew* 23:11 & *II Corinthians* 6:17)
3. Stand with the people of God. (*Acts* 2:13-14)
4. Stand by for God's best and wait for God. (*Psalms* 27:14)
5. Stand aside and let God take care of it. (*Romans* 12:19 & *Psalms* 23:5)
6. Stand against the enemy for he has no good plan for you. (*Ephesians* 6:11)
7. Stand in the gap. Be the intercessor for people in peril and who need the help to withstand the devil. (*Isaiah* 59:16 & *Ezekiel* 22:30)
8. Stand still and know that I am God. (*Psalms* 46:10)
9. Stand guard! Be alert! (*1Peter* 5:8)
10. Stand on the devil's head. You have the power to stand on the devils head. (*Genesis* 3:14- 15)

Don't be ashamed of Jesus and what is right. If you have troubles in standing for the truth, ask the Lord to give you the strength and courage to stand for Christ.

Stand
When you find your appropriate spot,
Challengers will dare to knock you off.
Rivals will test you to see what you got,
Taunt, tempt to entrap you with scoff.
Should they be unable to irk your nerve,
Rest assured the struggle is not done.
The blitz will intensify with more verve.
Evil acts may be masked as harmless fun.
The whole intent is to bring you down,
To draw you into their misguided band.
No matter what, don't you breakdown.
Brace yourself and maintain your stand.

–Rev. L D Reed, Sr

Overcoming daily with the Spirit's sword by standing on the promises of God.
–Russell Carter

Perseverance

Know ye not that they which run in a race run all, but one receiveth the prize? So run, that ye may obtain. **I Corinthians 9:24**

As you face the struggles of life (whether personal, spiritual, or career), you will be defeated if you only look inward at your current situation. You have to have the attitude that you can make it and be like the Little Engine That Could when it was going up the long hill and kept saying, "I think I can, I think I can, …" and when it reached the top and went down the other side saying, "I knew I could, I knew I could…"

As a school superintendent, you will have obstacles, setbacks, trials, and temptations, but perseverance and an optimistic attitude will get you through. Abraham Lincoln was like the Little Engine That Could in that he had many struggles and defeats in his lifetime but kept an optimistic attitude and continually persevered. The value of courage, persistence and perseverance has never been illustrated more convincingly than in the life story of this man. He persevered and became one of America's greatest and most beloved presidents. It was through his perseverance that slavery ended in the United States.

Trials Abraham Lincoln faced:	His age:
Failed in business	22
Ran for Legislature - defeated	23
Again failed in business	24
Elected to Legislature	25
Sweetheart died	26
Had a nervous breakdown	27
Defeated for Speaker	29
Defeated for Elector	31
Defeated for Congress	34
Elected to Congress	37
Defeated for Congress	39
Defeated for Senate	46
Defeated for Vice-Pres.	47
Defeated for Senate	49
Elected President of USA	51

When things go wrong as they sometimes will;
When the road you're trudging seems all uphill;
When the funds are low, and the debts are high;
And you want to smile, but you want to cry;
Stick to the fight when you're hardest hit -
It's when things go wrong that you mustn't quit.

–Anonymous

The greatest oak was once a little nut who held its ground.

–Unknown

Heaven

He that hath an ear, let him hear what the Spirit saith unto the churches; To him that overcometh will I give to eat of the tree of life, which is in the midst of the paradise of God. **Revelations 2:7**

Heaven is God's dwelling place, and only the righteous will live in Heaven with God. The wicked will not be allowed to enter and will forever be banished from God and his presence.

Heaven will be a beautiful place of continual praise and worship. It'll be a place of great joy and satisfaction because there we shall see God and live with him eternally. Heaven will not be a place for one race of people, but people of all races and tongues from every nation will be represented. Other facts about Heaven are: there will be no marriages; time will be no more; it's an endless place; it's a place of no sin; and it's a place of rewards. The redeemed are there – "a great multitude which no one could number" (Rev. 7-9) – as well as angels (Matt. 18:10), and there will be "thousands upon thousands" of them (Heb. 12:22).

What will not be in Heaven? There will be no sickness or pain; no sorrow or crying or mourning, as God will wipe away all tears. There will be no violence or wars, but only perfect peace and rest. There will also be no more death and no more hunger or thirst.

The promise of Heaven should be a great source of joy and hope to us, as Jesus longs for us to join him there. This promise keeps our eyes on the prize.

Just imagine Heaven, what God's kingdom will be like,
Where we will live forever, no more tears or sin or strife
Some call it Canaan land, some call it Beulah land
It's peace beyond that old river, a place not made with hands
It's that great celestial city with mansions round God's throne
But for all who know my Lord, they call it Home.
–Anonymous

No it's not the jasper walls and the pearly gates that are going to make heaven attractive. It is the being with God.
–Dwight L. Moody

Hard Work

Whatever your task, work heartily, as serving the Lord and not men. **Colossians 3:23**

As superintendents, God constantly presents us with opportunities to serve those around us. We in turn make decisions about how much effort we are willing to put forth when given those opportunities. During my last year as a high school basketball coach, I had the opportunity to work with a senior athlete named Eric. As a high school junior, Eric was the starting point guard for our team. He was not the biggest or fastest athlete, but Eric worked hard and contributed to our team's success. However, in Eric's senior year, there was a freshman point guard who was an incredible basketball player. This freshman would win the starting point guard position, moving Eric to the bench.

At this point, Eric had a choice to make. First, he could quit. He was a senior and had given three years of his life to the program. No one would blame him for not wanting to play "second fiddle" to a freshman. Eric's second choice was to accept his new role on the team and contribute when needed. Eric decided to accept his back-up role, and he continued to work hard throughout the season. Eric played limited minutes that year, but never once did he express anger about not starting at point guard. In the last game of the year, our team found itself down by two points with less than a minute to go.

Our freshman point guard stole the ball at half court, but as he cut around a defender, he twisted his ankle and had to be pulled from the game. We were now down to the final seven seconds of the game and had time for one more offensive play. With our best player out, I looked down the bench and decided to put Eric in the game. My plan was simple. The opposing team had been playing a tight "man-to-man" defense all night. I told Eric to feed our post the ball; we would score the quick two points and regroup in overtime. As we broke the huddle, Eric put his hand on my shoulder and asked, "Coach, do you want me to shoot the three?" I remember thinking to myself, "Eric, if I thought you could shoot, I wouldn't have had you sitting on the bench." However, I slapped him on the back and told him, "Only if you're open." We passed the ball in to Eric, and without hesitation Eric threw up a three-pointer. He shot it with such a high arch that it seemed like it would never come down. But when it finally did, it hit nothing but the bottom of the net. Eric's three-point shot won us the game, and the crowd stormed the court to pile on top of him.

Eric had every reason to give up, to quit. However, Eric remained faithful, and when presented with an opportunity, he was able to take advantage. In thinking of Eric's story, whatever you are called to do, even if it's to be a street-sweeper, do it to the best of your ability and as "unto the Lord."

What is the Lord calling you to do today? Whatever it is, remember that you are serving Him, and through your work, you can bring Him glory.

Teaching

Train up a child in the way he should go, and when he is old he will not depart from it. **Proverbs 22:6**

Superintendents often find themselves in the thick of student discipline problems. It is very difficult for parents to hear that their child is misbehaving or struggling in school. Like many superintendents, I have listened to parents who insist on complaining about the school system and how the school is responsible for their child's problems. The one thing many parents can't understand is that, if their discipline system worked at home, there would be no need for a discipline program at the school.

I remember one particular mother making a huge scene in front of my administrative team. She was upset that her 16-year-old son was being suspended, and she blamed the school for all of the young man's problems. After a few minutes of listening to her belittle our school and staff, I told her that I had the answer she was looking for. Sarcastically, I stated, "Since you know everything, you can immediately upgrade your child's education by withdrawing him to home school." The only problem with my suggestion was that it could have been construed as "cruel and unusual punishment" to make that boy stay at home with her 24/7. Of course, in the end she didn't withdraw the boy. They rarely do, and when they do, they always come back. The truth is that teaching a child is difficult, and parents need our help as much as we need theirs.

Which brings us to our verse, Proverbs 22:6; as superintendents, we have a great responsibility to educate the whole student. While academics are important, we often overlook character traits, such as honesty, responsibility, respect, kindness, fairness, and citizenship. Not only do these qualities represent the U.S. Department of Education's *Six Pillars of Character*, but, more importantly, they are basic principles found throughout the Bible. In Matthew 19:14, Jesus says, "Let the children come to me. Don't stop them! For the Kingdom of Heaven belongs to those who are like these children." Jesus wanted to emphasize the importance of mentoring young children and "training them in the way they should go."

As educators, we must be cautious not to isolate ourselves from parents, but rather to partner with them in providing their child with a good education. Teaching is a difficult job and is often looked down upon in our society for the long hours and low pay. However, even when people come into my office upset with our educational system, I continue to take pride in the career I have chosen. You are doing the work the Lord has chosen for you.

Our critics are our biggest friends because they tell us our faults.
–Benjamin Franklin

Gracious Speech

Let your speech be always with grace, seasoned with salt, that ye may know how ye ought to answer every man. **Colossians 4:6**

Being a superintendent means that you communicate with people continually, whether by the spoken word or written word. Even your body language speaks to people. There are situations we face, and because of the heat of the moment, we say something that is not beneficial to our professional career, to our personal life, or to God. We just "spout off," and we later regret it, but it's too late.

As a superintendent, you will face an irate parent, community member, unbearable board member, or employee. What you say and how you handle yourself will speak volumes. There are times to defend yourself, and you can even be angry. Remember, you can be angry, but do not do yourself any harm. Even Paul taught us in Ephesians 4:26, when he wrote, "be ye angry, and sin not." Control the anger by controlling the tongue.

In my first superintendency, I was in executive session, and the president of the board started to really come down hard on me, which I felt was very unjust. The president of the board was the "pipe-line leak" of executive sessions to my high school principal, as they were very close friends. During his tirade in that session, I had all I could take and angrily retorted back to him. Oh, I did not swear or curse, but my speech was not seasoned with salt and with grace. I walked out of that session knowing that I did not do the right thing, as I didn't control my tongue. Needless to say, I never again received a yes vote on my contract extension from that board member. I should have remembered the example our Lord and Savior gave us when he was reviled against: he said not a word. I should have graciously kept my mouth shut. So when the temptation arises to angrily lash out, remember, DON'T DO THAT! As my grandma Schmautz would say, "Least said, least mended."

> *An eye for an eye, a tooth for a tooth ...So they say.*
> *I tell you, don't stand against an evil person today.*
> *If someone slaps you in the right cheek - don't yell,*
> *Just turn, right to them, the other cheek as well.*
> —Rachael Koszalinski

Grant me greater stewardship of my words.
Jesus as you speak to me,
please speak through me.

Making God-Driven Decisions

And be not conformed to this world; but be ye transformed by the renewing of your mind, that ye may prove what is that good, and acceptable, and perfect will of God. **Romans 12:2**

How do we discern what God wants us to do? God leads us through His word, through the Holy Spirit, through circumstances and events He places in front of us, and by other Christians. There must be an alignment and agreement between the above if we want to be assured of our understanding of God's will for us.

When you are traveling, you may check a road map or an online direction map to determine which way to proceed to your destination. You may even ask others who have traveled to that destination. If the directions do not align or are not in agreement, you would be confused and want to recheck the directions.

The decisions we make as superintendents impacts our lives and the lives of others. We want to be at peace with God, and this comes by searching and asking for God's help in our decisions. Solomon asked for wisdom over other possible gifts from God. It was this desire to make wise decisions to follow God's will that gave Solomon favor in God's eyes. As we look to God's will for guidance and answers in order to perform His will in our lives, we become more able to discern His will as we align our understanding of His word and His examples. He provided many examples in the Bible to guide us in completing His will. He will direct our ways for what we are to do as well as how and when we are to complete something according to His will.

Trust in the Lord with all thine heart; and lean not unto thine own understanding. In all thy ways acknowledge him and he shall direct thy paths. Proverbs 3:5-6

Choose ye today whom you will serve, will it be God or man?
Well now the choice is yours
But you must choose this day whom you will serve,
Without a moment to lose you must choose.
–The Winans

If you have arrived at your decision
with the sincere intention of pleasing the heart of God,
you can proceed with confidence
knowing that God will work out his purposes through your decision.

Surround Yourself With Good People

Enter not into the path of the wicked and go not in the way of evil men. Avoid it, pass not by it, turn from it, and pass away. **Proverbs 4:14-15**

When we look around us, it is important that we know we have good people who are trustworthy and confidential people. My administrative assistants helped me understand the daily trials of those around me as well as reactions to my decisions. They helped me keep a pulse on how well I was doing and where I needed to make improvements.

Also, when we look for advice from other leaders, it is wise to know their values before we take their advice. Otherwise, the advice at best is worthless and may even get you in trouble. As you stay in a district or an organization, you will be able to hire other employees who exemplify your own values.

The Lord reminded His followers not to assimilate with the current cultures that were not based on the values of the scripture. However, the followers were told to share God's word amongst those who didn't believe. Jesus said, "I came not to call the righteous, but sinners to repentance", Luke 5:32. He did go to the sinner's place of work or home. It is a balance to not conform to the ways of the world while showing the world God's way.

As the superintendent, you will want good people working with you. The work is hard, and a good team of people can help make the work possible. A good team almost makes it look effortless because they bring out each other's strengths. This surrounding ourselves with good people helps ensure success for ourselves and our organization.

But the path of the just is as the shining light, that shineth more and more unto the perfect day. Proverbs 4:18

When good people are part of your team,
You'll receive counsel that will make your district dream
Winning is accomplished by all doing what is right
While losing is just the opposite and will bring your district blight

Do not be misled: "Bad company corrupts good character."
I Corinthians 15:33, NIV

Look Forward

Remember ye not the former things, neither consider the things of old. Behold I will do a new thing, now it shall spring forth; shall ye not know it? I will even make a way in the wilderness and rivers in the desert. **Isaiah 43:18-19**

The Lord told the Israelites the above passage when they were being led from Egypt. He wanted them to understand that He would take care of His people. They may have considered some of the things they enjoyed in the past and forgotten the harsh life. Yet the Lord wanted them to look ahead, and He would lead them to a far better place.

Our Lord doesn't want us to miss out on His plans for us either. We can't dwell on past things, past hurts, or past mistakes. He wants to shows us His plan for us and to understand that he can make beauty arise where we least expect it. This is true in our personal lives as well as our professional lives.

As superintendents, we lead others as part of changes to improve our schools and organizations. It is our opportunity to help others envision new possibilities without dwelling on past actions that may not have been successful. Reform efforts require the involvement and commitment of time by those wanting to make it a success. We need to encourage those people that there can be a better place and way of doing things that will help the students as well as the adults working with them.

People have experienced many changes and reform efforts in their workplace. Not all of those efforts were successful, and even those that were successful may not have been attributed to all the people involved in the effort. So many employees may feel that any new change effort is just part of the new leader's agenda. However, there will always be room for improvements in an organization. It is everyone's responsibility to help shape those improvements and reforms. It is our role as the leaders to help the employees see beyond the past efforts, whether mistakes were made or not. If there were mistakes, the leader can help them not dwell on repeating the mistakes. There is the possibility that the efforts were not mistakes, but rather just were not made at the right time. Either way, the leader must establish the timing and pacing of a reform in order to lead the successful plans to actions while encouraging and inspiring others to see the beauty in the midst of the uncertainty of changes.

Looking forward requires vision. Ask the Lord for guidance and wisdom to lead the district into the future.

Lord, be Thou my constant Guide,
Lead me all the way,
Till I reach Thy home at last,
Nevermore to stray. Amen

Where there is no vision, there is no hope.
–George Washington Carver

Power

For God hath not given us the spirit of fear: but of power and of love, and of a sound mind. II Timothy 1:7

Many people are uncomfortable with power and see power as a negative. Actually, power is a gift from God. God's presence helps assure us, so we don't need to be fearful. It helps keep us in check of our power and realize that it is a gift from God. There are people who are very comfortable with power and actually may abuse it. As a leader, decisions need to be made on a daily basis. If we are not careful, we may put too much faith in our own power. Or we may fear who we might hurt or offend, thus leaving us powerless in our decisions. It may be helpful to have a clearer understanding of power.

There are several different types and definitions to power. A couple of types are legitimate power and earned power. Legitimate power is based on your position in the organization. As the leader or superintendent, you have legitimate power because you were hired to be the chief leader. This legitimate power is further established as you complete your role successfully. However, the legitimate power can be reduced if you do not fulfill your responsibilities or if others perceive you are not fulfilling your responsibilities. The earned power is the type of power you gain when you have had success because of your performance.

Problems in organizations often don't have absolute answers. Superintendents can't be strangled by their fear in their decisions. After examination and prayer, leaders can boldly make decisions that are best for the children and their organization. Pilate didn't want to make a decision regarding the acquittal of a man. So instead of using his legitimate power, he handed the decision to the people. Do we delegate decisions because we don't want to make the difficult choices and stand by our decisions? Jesus also had difficult decisions. He prayed in the garden before his death. He did not pass on the decision that had to be made. There was no one else who could perform the task. He was the only man with no blemish, no sin.

Surely the presence of the Lord is in this place.
I can feel His mighty power and His grace.
I can hear the brush of angels wings.
I see glory on each face.
Surely the presence of the Lord is in this place.
    –Lanny Wolfe

As the leaders of organizations, we need to prayerfully make our decisions and use our power for the good of others.

Confidence

Cast not away therefore your confidence, which hath great recompense of reward. Hebrews 10:35

I was reading an article about body language, and it struck me how people can read our body language and determine how confidant we feel. If our employees feel that we don't have confidence in ourselves, then they will be like a ship without a rudder, and chaos will ensue because they will "do their own thing." So the moral of this is don't act like you don't know what you're doing.

There is a difference between humility, confidence, and cockiness. Confidence is that happy medium between the two extremes. I was visiting with a retired superintendent in Oklahoma, who was an icon in the state. He said that when he was in, the district was growing and he was buying land for future school sites. He wondered if he was doing the right thing. I have felt that way when I wondered if I even knew what I was doing. My wife would validate me, but I felt her opinion was skewed. It was when other ex-employees or current employees would come up to me and say, "Thank you for making that decision" or, "Thank you for doing that," that I would feel assured in my decisions.

This reminds me about the time I took over a coaching job in the state of Washington. I was just hired as the boys basketball coach, and the team the year before went 0-20. The outgoing coach said to me, "You know how to coach, but when the going gets rough, don't sway from what you know. You just don't have the talent." I thought to myself, "Yeah, he just didn't know how to coach." Well, he was right, I didn't have the talent. I started to lose, and the temptation was to start changing, but I remembered his words and stayed the course. By the way, he went to another school as a coach, and his only loss was in the state championship game.

Dr. Tom Leding, founder of Leding Ministries says, "When disappointment strikes, simply hold tight to your confidence. Do not petulantly toss it away. Instead, affirm, 'I am confident. I believe I have confidence.' It will require some mental and spiritual effort to maintain confidence."

> *I've got confidence*
> *God is going to see me through*
> *No matter what the case may be,*
> *I know he's going to fix it for me.*
> —Andrae Crouch

Do not let what you can't do interfere with what you can do.
—John Wooden

Successful Plans

Commit thy works unto the Lord and thy thoughts shall be established. **Proverbs 16:3**

The Lord wants us to succeed as superintendents, and if we put Him first, we will be able to focus our plans and work so that we can show a passion to work. Then we work for God's glory and not our glory. He wants us to work with conviction and passion. Further, if the Lord is in the forefront of our plans, we will also act with integrity. Successful plans require checkpoints along the way to determine if we are meeting the targets toward the goals of our plans. Again, we must be careful that our plans are following God's directions. Any of our works will be tried by fire. If the works were for God's success and glory and not our own, they will pass the test of fire.

Anytime we sense doubts in the plans, we need to turn to the word of God and to prayer. It is easy to forget that God's plans are not the same as the world's. The way to determine success with God is that we do things that are pleasing to him, that we have a faith and a trust in Him to guide us.

Many successful plans are those that are determined by individual groups in each organization. Every organization has unique components that require a needs assessment particular to it. The process of developing the plan while building relationships is as important as the components of the plan. Yet we must not get stuck in planning. There must be carefully chosen actions with a strong evaluation component in a successful plan.

Rick Warren, in *A Purpose-Driven Life,* stated that people find their purpose through their gifts from God as well as from opportunities or events that happen to an individual. Our gifts may be areas that allow us to find our place in any organization's plans. If we are the leaders, we try to place people where they have the talent. For example, if we need someone who is highly organized, they may be able to design a way to collect and organize the data for our plans. Or if we have someone who is able to communicate well, then we may place them with a portion of marketing the plan. It is our responsibility as the leaders to make sure that everyone understands their role in the plan.

Commit they way unto the Lord; and he shall give thee the desires of thine heart.
Psalms 37:5

Bite off more than you can chew
Then chew it.
Successfully plan with the help of the Lord
To do more than you can
Then plan successfully to do it.
–Unknown

You got to be careful if you don't know where you're going because you might not get there.
–Yogi Berra

Sunburned or Son-Burned?

And it came to pass, when the sun did arise, that God prepared a vehement east wind; and the sun beat upon the head of Jonah, that he fainted, and wished in himself to die, and said, It is better for me to die than to live. **Jonah 4:8**

Jonah was told by God to go to the people of Nineveh and preach to them that they might be saved. He did that, the people repented, and God did not destroy the people of Nineveh. Because God did not destroy the evil city of Nineveh, Jonah became so angry with God that he left the city and went out to "pout." He was sitting under a giant plant for shade, but because of his disobedience, God sent a worm to destroy the plant. He became so burned and hot that he wished that he would die.

This reminds me of the time I went to a college graduation held at the football stadium. The sun was so hot that I received a really nasty sunburn. Thank the Lord, my wife brought some sun-lotion to stop the sunburning and to soothe the already burnt skin. Jonah was getting burned because he was disobeying God, and I was getting sunburned because I forgot to get sun-lotion.

There is another type of sunburn, and that is the son-burn. That is the type of burn we want to receive, son-burn. Doing the will of God so that he guides every moral fiber of our body is truly being son-burned. We don't need sunburn lotion because being son-burned means being totally comforted by God and in His care. As a superintendent, you can get into some very hot circumstances, but remember, if you are son-burned, then you are safe in God's arms. God cares for you because He loves you!

The son of God shines on me
I can feel Him and He's so warm
Oh what a comfort it is to be
Safe in the shelter of His arms.

The sun in our lives is so important and enjoyable.
The son of God in our lives is priceless.

AUGUST

Winners Persevere

Seest thou a man diligent in his business? He shall stand before kings; he shall not stand before mean men. **Proverbs 22:29**

Have you ever known someone who was successful at something and it surprised you? Maybe that person wasn't the smartest or quickest and yet, they found success. They showed a relentless drive or desire for something to the point of success. They forced themselves to continue despite setbacks. It was their resolve that helped them stay the course to completion. They didn't spend time with self-pity or a dwelling on their mistakes. Rather, they strove to push forward with the end goal in mind.

As superintendents, we hope that others will want to win also. It is exciting to help people in our organization grow in their own leadership skills. This is best accomplished by determining the current strengths of our faculty and administrators, then providing training on specific needed leadership skills, giving opportunities for practicing newly learned skills in a safe environment, and encouraging them to use those skills independently. It is a compliment when our leaders grow and even advance to new positions. Our gift to them is the empowerment to grow in their leadership.

I want to hear Jesus tell me, "Well done, faithful servant". I want Him to see me as a diligent worker who strove to do his best in order to give Him glory. I can remember a pastor talking about his dad who was dying. His dad used the phrase, "just one more for Jesus". He felt he was to continue living so one more person could be brought to a faith in Jesus and have eternal life. His dad wanted the winning of heaven for more people.

Our goal is heaven and eternal life to give glory to God. The way to heaven is by a faith in Jesus Christ as our Savior, it is a gift from God. So we win eternal life by accepting the gift.

Marching on through the hosts of sin,
Marching on, I am marching on.
Victory's mine, while I've Christ within.
Marching, marching on.
–Captain Johnson

Gardens are not made by singing 'Oh, how beautiful!' and sitting in the shade.
–Rudyard Kipling

Path Direction

***In all thy ways acknowledge him and he shall direct thy paths.* Proverbs 3:6**

As a superintendent, sometimes we just do not know what to do. We have exhausted all of our earthly resources and we are still befuddled. Are we to make this recommendation to the board? Should we put our application in for a job here? Should we buy a home in the community? The questions keep coming. I have found out that if I pray and ask God to direct my paths, then I will have a peace about the decision I will make.

I took over a superintendency in Minnesota in a district that was in the "red." In some states, they will say that district is in "fiscal distress." I had never faced this type of situation before because, in the state from which I was coming, school districts could not operate in the "red." In visiting with the previous superintendent, who did an excellent job, he told me that the district was in trouble financially and some tough decisions had to be made. I just didn't realize the extent of the trouble. After visiting with the state department of education, I found out that I had to develop a three year or five year plan on how the district would get out of their financial "hole." The state was very helpful as we worked through this process.

One strategy we came up with was that an outlying elementary school had to be closed. To close the school, the state required a hearing. I was nervous, to say the least, as I knew that gym would be filled with angry parents. I prayed, "Dear Lord, guide my paths and give me wisdom on how to handle this." I had originally thought the board would sit in the front with the hearing officer, but right before the meeting started, the school district attorney came to me and said, "Would you like for the board to sit in the audience?" That turned out to be an excellent idea and a brilliant move. When the patrons got up to speak, they had no one to vent their anger on except the hearing officer and since they didn't know him, there, in essence, was very little outrage. When the meeting adjourned, the people just quietly filed out and I said, "Thank you, Lord." My board president came up to me and thanked me for having them sit in the audience.

The Lord directed my path!
He does not lead me year by year
Not even day by day
But step by step my path unfolds
My Lord directs my way.
                                        –Unknown.

God is not in need of anything but all things are in need of him.
                                        –Marcus Aristides

Trusting Jesus for the Impossible

But Jesus said unto them, "They need not depart; give ye them to eat." **Matthew 14:16**

Reverend Whitehead, in studying this verse, had the following comments: "It is interesting to note that when Jesus was about to feed the multitudes he commissioned his disciples with the task. He knew that they did not have the resources and they knew it, too. Yet, following Jesus will lead us into situations where we do not have the means to meet a need, yet Jesus tells us to do so anyway. Do you feel overwhelmed with your current circumstances? Take the resources you have and bring them to Jesus in prayer. Humility and prayer can do amazing things. It can provide for many in ways that you would never have imagined."

Sometimes, as a superintendent, we are asked to do the impossible and we have to humbly petition the Lord for an answer. I can remember when I had three new board members elected to the board and they were bent on making certain early elementary class sizes were at a certain student-teacher ratio. I knew that the teachers' union, which was controlled by the elementary teachers, was clamoring for smaller class sizes. To get elected, these new board members had made promises to the union and were anxious to deliver on their promises. They would not be deterred from their mission.

I quickly started in-servicing them on the nuances of school finance and bringing them up-to-speed on the district's financial picture. I needed help from the Lord as I knew they had the votes to do what they desired and I could not stand by and let them destroy a district out of ignorance. The Lord worked a miracle. By studying the staff of the district, we were able to lower elementary class sizes by reassigning teachers and hiring only two additional teachers. We stayed within budget, the board was satisfied as they saved face with the union, and the teachers were satisfied. The Lord answered my prayer. He took the "five loaves and two fishes, blessed them and fed the multitude, while picking up 12 full baskets afterwards."

> *Nothing is impossible when you put your trust in God;*
> *Nothing is impossible when you're trusting in His Word.*
> *Hearken to the voice of God to thee;*
> *"Is there anything too hard for Me?"*
> *Then put your trust in God alone and rest upon His Word;*
> *For everything, yes everything is possible with God.*
> –Eugene Clark

Nothing is impossible with the Lord in our lives.

Attitude

So if there is any encouragement in Christ, any comfort from love, any participation in the Spirit, any affection and sympathy, complete my joy by being of the same mind, having the same love, being in full accord and of one mind. Do nothing from rivalry or conceit, but in humility count others more significant than yourselves. Let each of you look not only to his own interests, but also to the interests of others. Have this mind among yourselves, which is yours in Christ Jesus. Philippians 2:1-5

I once heard that when Bill Gates, the founder of Microsoft, was in high school, he and his friends would go to football games. During the course of the game if a player was to fumble, throw an interception, or make any type of mistake, Gates and his friends would chant, "That's alright, That's okay, You can work for us one day!" Even at a young age, Bill Gates possessed an ambitious attitude and was determined to be successful.

On the other end of the spectrum is a man named Johnny Paycheck. He is most famous for his hit song, "Take this job and shove it!" As superintendents, sometimes we might want to tell our constituents this very thing. However, Paycheck's song represents a negative attitude, and let's not forget that Paycheck suffered from drug and alcohol addiction and was sent to prison for attempted murder. While we sometimes think being negative is appropriate, it can certainly lead us down a dark road.

Our attitude is the only thing we have absolute control over. Dr. Martin Luther King Jr. once said, "The ultimate measure of a man is not where he stands in moments of comfort and convenience, but where he stands at times of challenge and controversy. " Where is your attitude today? Do not be afraid to seek encouragement through Christ. Look beyond your own interests and seek to serve those around you. Let those around you who do not know Christ, but know you, come to know Christ because of your attitude.

I believe the single most significant decision I can make on a day-to-day basis
is my choice of attitude.
It is more important than my past, my education, my bankroll,
my successes or failures,
fame or pain, what other people think of me or say about me,
my circumstances, or my position.
Attitude keeps me going to cripple my progress.
It alone fuels my fire or assaults my hope.
When my attitudes are right there is no barrier too high, no valley too deep,
no dream too extreme, no challenge too great for me.
–Charles Swindoll

Ability may get you to the top, but it takes character to keep you there.
–John Wooden

Working in Unity

Behold, how good and how pleasant it is for brethren to dwell together in unity.
Psalms 133:1

When people are in unity and working together, it is a blessed feeling and great things happen. The psalmist said it is "like the dew on Hermon." I can certainly say a hearty "Amen" to that. When people work together, stress, anxiety, and rivalries disappear. When that happens, then you can get quality work done and your school will excel.

I had the opportunity to work with a very dysfunctional board and a board working in harmony and unity. To say the least, it was not fun working for the dysfunctional board and I did not look forward to it. My goal was to get the dysfunctional board working together again so the students in the district would be the beneficiaries. I had a board member tell me she would never again buy furniture from the board president (he owned a furniture store). On this board, I also had board members who had used to be friends, now enemies. My goal was to bring this board back together so they would work like clockwork. To accomplish this, I had to make certain that each board member was treated fairly, respectfully, and equally. I also tried to find a little humor at every board meeting. In January, the lady board member said at the beginning of a board meeting that this was the very best board she had ever worked on. How did that turn around happen? When the board started working together and in unity, the tenor of the meetings changed and morale increased. This started producing very positive results.

Unity is a key principle that can be applied both to people and to technological systems in business. Unity between workers and unity between systems can lead to higher production and good morale. Good morale is a symptom of unity in business teams. By good morale I mean esprit de corps—a fellowship that's created by working together in a common enterprise. Ask the Lord daily to give you wisdom in creating harmony and unity in your life and school.

> *Unity! For this, Lord we pray!*
> *Harmony! Let all strife fade away!*
> *Let us stand in Your presence until we are one in Thee*
> *Let us all seek Your face until we are one in Thee.*
> –Unknown

Talent wins games, but teamwork and intelligence wins championships.
–Michael Jordan

Quiet

And that ye study to be quiet, and to do your own business, and to work with your own hands, as He commanded you. That you may walk honestly toward them that are without and that you may have lack of nothing. I Thessalonians 4:11-12

It is difficult to find a time for quietness at work. Many superintendents go to work early in the morning so they have the opportunity to plan their day, set their goals, and organize their work. Once other employees arrive at work, there are often many interruptions during the day. Many decisions need to be made quickly and effectively. Some decisions can wait for further explorations. Other decisions may require extensive research.

Superintendents need to listen carefully to many people. Some interactions need to be turned back respectfully to those closest to the solution. Other interactions require immediate solutions. And still other interactions don't require any solution, but just our listening.

If we could discern the times to listen with no action, time to listen and solve, and time to listen and guide that person to others for help, then we would lead more effectively and efficiently. There may even be times that our office door needs to close as we spend time on reflection.

If everyone in the organization clearly understands their role, then the work is completed more smoothly. It is also helpful to have procedures in place when there are differences in opinions. People do prefer to work in peaceful environments where work is accomplished in a business-like fashion. This requires careful attention to the climate in an organization. Often, the administrative assistants and receptionists have the clearest view of the climate in an organization on a daily basis. It takes the leader checking on this climate frequently and then making actions based on the personal needs of the employees.

And the work of righteousness shall be peace; and the effect of righteousness quietness and assurance forever. And my people shall dwell in a peaceable habitation, and in sure dwellings, and in quiet resting places. Isaiah 32:17

A quiet time in prayer will heap great rewards.

Finding Joy

Having many things to write unto you, I would not write with paper and ink,
but I trust to come unto you, and speak face to face that our joy may be full.
II John: 1:2

What brings you joy? Is it things or people? I enjoy spending time with my grandchildren. We make special memories when we do simple and fun activities together. They wonder and awe at the little things in nature. Those are special moments of joy as we share each other's company. Other family joys were when my children came home from college. It was fun to plan and prepare the meals that they enjoyed. And it was fun to watch them enjoy their favorite memories of home again.

Other memories that bring me immense joy are seeing a friend whom I have not seen for a long time. It does not take any time to get back to the conversations we once enjoyed together. Those times spent with family and friends bring more joy to me than any material objects.

I also find joy in doing hobbies. For me, the hobbies are gardening and quilting. For some, it is fishing or golfing. Those are times that do not seem like work. But there is pure joy in accomplishing something or finding relaxation for ourselves.

I am sure everyone has different people and activities that bring them joy. Giving gifts that others want or need is another area of great joy. The excitement of watching someone open a present that brings them happiness, always brings me joy.

Another joy for me is to watch those around me do well. Superintendents who build the capacity of their employees are able to share of themselves and take pride in the major accomplishments of others. It brings great joy to mentor another leader and be a small part of their success. Find your joy in relationships with other people.

> *You may have the joy-bells ringing in your heart,*
> *And a peace that from you never will depart;*
> *Walk the straight and narrow way,*
> *Live for Jesus every day,*
> *He will keep the joy-bells ringing in your heart.*
> –J. E. Ruark

The joy of the Lord is our strength.
–Nehemiah 8:10

Grace

Therefore, brethren, stand fast, and hold the traditions which ye have been taught, whether by word or our epistle. Now our Lord Jesus Christ himself, and God, even our Father, which hath loved us, and hath given us everlasting consolation and good hope through grace. II Thessalonians 2:15-16

When I think of grace, I think of God's gift of salvation for us. We did not and can't earn that salvation. It is only given by the grace of God for us to accept. We understand the teachings of right and wrong and the Golden Rule. How do these and the Ten Commandments fit with grace? We realize that we can never measure up to the fulfillment of all commandments without God's grace first. The Ten Commandments were given as laws to guide us. Further, there is an expansion on the Ten Commandments beyond just actions and include the intentions. Remember Cain and Abel. Both offered their sacrifices and yet one was not accepted by God. God wants and deserves our first fruit, the best of our offerings. The teachings of right and wrong are not to be dismissed as unimportant. We will make mistakes and then we need to quickly repent and correct our actions. God's grace gives us hope to conquer.

Superintendents set the rules and regulations in order to provide a safe and secure place for students and employees. The rules have consequences that need to be enforced fairly in order to for districts to remain out of the court system. But the true measure of the fair enforcement is a component of social justice. Our consequences must be used the same for every student. There can't be one set of rules and consequences for star athletes and then another set of consequences for the same infractions by other students. The community needs to see that there are clear expectations that will help guide everyone.

> *Love sought me, mercy found me*
> *But it was grace that set me free,*
> *Love saw my teardrops, mercy had compassion*
> *But it was marvelous grace that set me free.*
> –Unknown

**Wherefore we receiving a kingdom which can't be moved,
let us have grace, whereby we may serve God
acceptably with reverence and godly fear. Hebrews 12:28**

Unworthy

For all have sinned and come short of the glory of God. **Romans 3:23**

Webster's Dictionary defines unworthy as "not deserving; lack of merit or value; not warranted; beneath the level considered befitting to." We are unworthy of God's love and unmerited mercy. There is nothing we could have ever done to deserve this love.

I was watching the television program, "I Shouldn't Be Alive." In this one episode, a young runner was training in the back country of Utah. Running along the side of a cliff, it gave away and she fell 30 feet suffering a broken pelvis and internal bleeding. No one knew she was out there, critically injured. All she had with her was her dog. After she had been absent for a couple of days, her friends went to the police and turned in a missing person's report. On the start of the third day and no help in sight, she told her dog to leave her and go find help. The dog found its way out of the canyon and ran into the rescuers. The dog led the rescuers back to its injured owner. The runner was air-lifted out of the canyon and to the hospital. She was told she would never walk again, but, today, she is running.

Why was she found worthy to live? Why were we found worthy to live? We should not be alive, but Jesus came and took our place on the cross, taking the sin of the world upon himself. He came and rescued us from death and eternal separation from Him. There is nothing we have done or could have done to merit the great love of God. As the song writer wrote, "The love of God is greater far than tongue or pen could ever tell."

> *Unworthy am I of the glory to come,*
> *Unworthy with angels to sing,*
> *I thrill just to know that he loved me so much*
> *A pauper, I walk with the king.*
>
> –Ira Stanphill

I do not know any way to explain
why God's grace touches a man who seems unworthy of it.
–Whittaker Chambers

Teachable Moments

And Jesus said to him, 'I am the way, and the truth, and the life. No one comes to the father except through me.' John 14:6

My wife and I believe strongly in what we call "teachable moments" when working with our kids. For example, if we see one of our children acting out we immediately stop the action, explain to the child why it was wrong, and discuss better choices they could have made.

One afternoon, my wife was in the kitchen making grilled cheese sandwiches. My oldest daughter, Katie and my youngest son, Jayce, were at the table fighting over who was going to get the first sandwich. The argument was becoming extremely heated; so much so, that my wife stopped cooking and walked over to the two and asked, "Is this the way Jesus would treat his brother or sister? Would he yell at them and fight to get the first sandwich, or would he insist that his family be served first?" Both kids thought for a second and said they understood what she was trying to explain. My wife then went back into the kitchen, put a grilled cheese sandwich on a plate and asked the kids, "Alright, who gets the first sandwich?" My daughter quickly replied, "I am going to let Jayce be Jesus today!" Obviously, she had missed the point.

As parents, sometimes it can be difficult trying to get our point across to our children. As a school administrator, that difficulty is magnified by the numerous people we manage. In John 14:6, Jesus begins to reveal that which belongs to us through His death, and he teaches who He is on earth and who He was before time began. Jesus said that He is the way, the truth, and the life, and only through Him can we enter heaven. In Christ's final days, he explained that He was going to prepare a place for us in heaven. Broken down into its simplest form, Jesus' time on earth was a sequence of "teachable moments." His disciples referred to him as "teacher" and often He used parables to explain the word of God to people.

As superintendents, we can better serve those around us by taking advantage of "teachable moments." Whether it means taking the time to work with a first year principal, or reviewing lesson plans with a veteran teacher, if we watch closely, we can seize opportunities to help and guide those around us.

Teachable moments need three ingredients
The first is open relationship and is expedient
The second is the catalyst which is patience
The final ingredient is biblical truth which is the sealant.
–Unknown

When you put faith, hope, and love together,
you can raise positive kids in a negative world.
–Zig Ziglar

Accomplish Your Purpose

And I will make of thee a great nation, and I will bless thee, and make thy name great; and thou shalt be a blessing. **Genesis 12:2**

When the word prosperity is mentioned, most people think of money, but it means to accomplish your God-given purpose. It doesn't exclude money, but it means more than just financial security. Prosperity is the ability to do more with the gifts and talents God has endowed upon you.

God wants to bless his people and for that to happen we must move from a poverty mentality to a prosperous mentality. Poverty expectations need to be broken. It's time to break negative mind-sets. Thoughts like: *I could never have that kind of amazing relationship with the board of education; I could never have that kind of high-profiled and paying superintendent position; I could never have that kind of good things happen in my life and career; I could never have that doctorate or any other prestigious award; I could never be a respected sought after educator in my state;* or *I could never pass that bond election to build a new school,* should not belong in you as a believer.

God has given you the ability to be successful and fulfilled. Who you listen to is who you will become. Superintendents need to set their hearts to hear the voice of the Lord. Prosperity has a purpose. God blessed Abraham so that He could then bless nations. Abraham's covenant with God continues to bless us today. God wants to bless you so that you can be a blessing to others. He wants you to prosper in every area of your life so you can be a blessing to children, teachers, and a community. God blesses you with wisdom so you can share it with others. He gives you a gift to share with others.

Accomplish your God-given purpose. Begin to see yourself as God sees you. Begin to say the things that God has said in His Word about you.

There shall be showers of blessing:
This is the promise of love;
There shall be seasons refreshing,
Sent from the Savior above.
–Daniel Whittle

God has a purpose and plan for your life.

The Rain Will Stop

So shall they fear the name of the Lord from the west, and his glory from the rising of the sun. When the enemy comes in like a flood, the Spirit of the Lord shall lift up a standard against him. **Isaiah 59:1**

We just received a call from our daughter who just started to go through a major trial. Since she's my only daughter, my heart broke because I wanted to make the pain go away. After she hung up, I started to think and pray about her situation. I needed an answer because, being her father, I was aching and tears were in my eyes.

During the time of meditation, I turned on the TV and as I was scrolling through the channels, I happened to stop on a channel featured southern gospel singers sponsored by Bill Gaither. Janet Paschal, a beautiful singer, was singing the song "It Won't Rain Always". That song hit me right between the eyes, and the tears really started to flow. I knew then, that the sun will start to shine again and the Lord will "lift up a standard" against the enemy of our soul.

Are there times in life when you feel that you are never going to make it through a trial or you wondered why you are facing this trial? As a superintendent of schools, situations and trials will come that will make you think that God is hiding. You will feel like the loneliest person on earth. Just remember, "It won't rain always and the sun will shine through."

Someone said that in this life, something is bound to fall
And each one sheds his share of tears and trouble troubles us all
But the hurt won't hurt forever
And the tears are bound to dry
And it won't rain always the clouds will soon be gone
The sun that's been hiding, has been there all along
And it won't rain always Gods promises are true
The sun's going to shine in His own good time
And he will see you through.
                                                    –Janet Pascal

The One who made you, holds you close to His heart today and always.

Worthy is the Lord

Thou art worthy, O Lord, to receive glory and honour and power: for thou hast created all things, and for thy pleasure they are and were created. **Revelations 4:11**

Superintendents giving praise and adoration is a common occurrence in the school setting. We recognize the athlete of the year, student of the year, teacher of the year, principal of the year, superintendent of the year, and so forth. This glory and honor is bestowed upon them because of their great accomplishments and feats. They are worthy of it!

Why do we praise others? 1) It draws people together through an exchange of appreciation. 2) It motivates people to greater achievement. 3) It tells people they have performed well. 4) It observes examples of excellence that others may follow. If we praise other human beings, isn't our Lord and Savior so much more worthy of our praise as he created all things and came to earth for the redemption of our sins?

Praising God is important because God deserves to be praised. If we don't give praise, the rocks will cry out (Luke 19:40). Praising God reminds us of God's greatness. Praise strengthens our faith which allows God to move on our behalf. God inhabits the environment of praise. Everyone is to praise the Lord (Psalm 150:6). God is worthy of our praise!

We were lacking value or merit and undeserving of God's great love. We were wretched and poor, yet he took us in and laid down his life for us. Because of his unlimited love and what God has done for us, He demands that we praise him. I know when I have been helped in a situation that was too daunting for me. I was humbled and overwhelmed with thankfulness towards the person that helped me as I know I was not worthy of their favor. That person receives my praise. God deserves and is worthy of our praise!

> *Worthy is the Lamb, seated on the throne.*
> *We crown You now with many crowns*
> *You reign victorious!*
> *High and lifted up, Jesus, Son of God.*
> *Worthy is the Lamb.*
>
> –Steve Green

I bowed on my knees and cried "Holy, Holy, Holy,"
then I clapped my hands and sang "Glory, Glory, Glory,"
to the Son of God.

–Jimmie Davis

Taking Care of Yourself

Or do you not know that your body is a temple of the Holy Spirit within you, whom you have from God? You are not your own, for you were bought with a price. So glorify God in your body." I Corinthians 6:19-20

School superintendents often become so absorbed in taking care of their school that they forget to take care of themselves. The Bible teaches that "our body is a temple," but I have watched as many of my colleagues have been placed on medical leave because they failed to take care of their health.

There is no other position in a district that comes with the pressure and responsibility of the superintendency. It is often a job that can be overwhelming. Early in my superintendent's career, I was placed on blood pressure medication, and later, at the age of 32, diagnosed with stomach ulcers. By failing to take care of my body, I had begun to fail those around me because I was not performing at a high level.

In order to better serve those around us and fully glorify God, it is imperative that we maintain our health. Here are 10 quick tips to help you in your quest to be a better superintendent:

1. Get plenty of rest to restore your energy.
2. Schedule physical activity into every day.
3. Eat a healthful diet that includes plenty of fruits and vegetables.
4. Learn healthful ways to manage stress.
5. Set realistic goals for what you can get done each day.
6. Drink plenty of water.
7. Keep a positive outlook.
8. Have regular health exams and screenings.
9. Maintain a healthy weight.
10. Make time to enjoy family and friends.

I have never really considered myself a person who throws around a lot of mottos. However, as superintendent, I have always stressed to my staff that: "The people we serve deserve our very best." As you go forward this week, be sure that you are able to give those around you your very best.

My body is the temple of the Holy Spirit
My body is the temple of the Living God
I will take care of it in part of God's great plan
What I do and what I eat will make me what I am

Take care of your body. It's the only place you have to live.

–Jim Rohn

Synergy

You will seek me and find me; when you seek me with all your heart. **Jeremiah 29:13**

I have often been asked the question, "What is synergy?" The easiest way for me to describe synergy is through a metaphor about horses. Research shows that the average horse can pull about 400 pounds of dead weight. However, if you tie two horses together the amount of dead weight they can pull increases to around 1,200 pounds. Now, logic would lead us to believe that if one horse can pull 400 pounds then two horses should pull no more than 800 pounds. So how are two horses working together able to pull that additional 400 pounds? The answer is synergy. The more individuals you have working toward a common goal, the more you can accomplish.

As a superintendent I had the opportunity to see how God uses synergy in our everyday lives. My wife and I were at the County Fair and decided to stop by and see the animal sale. It was late in the evening and many of the championship animals had already sold. As we walked into the sale barn, I saw one of my students. He was a 5th grader with Down's Syndrome named Lane. I was surprised to see Lane at the show, because he had been extremely ill and missed a lot of school. Lane came from a poor, but hardworking family, and on that night his father was there to help take his hog into the sale arena. I remember watching in amazement as the bids started coming in $1,000… $1,500… $3,000! The hog final sold for just over $10,000. This was amazing considering the grand champion hog sold for only $6,000. However, that is not what made this story synergistic. It was what happened next.

The gentlemen who bought the hog jumped up and yelled, "Re-sell!" So, they sold it again, this time for $11,000. And once again, the buyer jumped up and screamed, "Re-sell!" So, once again they resold the hog. That night Lane's hog was resold seven times and when he finally left the arena buyers had spent over $30,000 on his animal. Lane's father, as well as, many of us in that arena were in tears as Lane passed through the crowd hugging everyone he came across. That night God stirred the hearts of many individuals, who had come together to help a young man and his family who were dealing with struggles that many of us will never understand. Let us never underestimate the awesome power of our God and how through Him we can have a great influence on those around us.

People and relationships in our family are more important than things (people on their death bed never talk about spending more time at the office – they talk about relationships). We are responsible for our own attitudes and behaviors, and we can choose our responses to circumstance.

–Stephen R. Covey

God Forgets Our Drops

The LORD is merciful and gracious, slow to anger, and plenteous in mercy. **Psalms 103:8**

Ken Horn wrote about the impossible catch and the unforgettable drop. In 1941, Texas A&M was playing the University of Texas. Late in a 0-0 tie contest, a long high pass was thrown to Noble Doss of the University of Texas. Somehow, he made an "impossible catch" that day in 1941. Because of that catch, Texas scored the only touchdown in a legendary 7-0 upset of Texas A&M. But it was another pass, the following year in 1942, that Doss has dwelt on throughout his life. One he did not catch. Doss dropped a pass against Baylor, a team the No. 1 Longhorns were favored to beat, and Baylor eked out a 7-7 tie.

"That cost us the national championship," Doss told ABC. "We almost got there, but I didn't make the big play." Tears came to Doss's eyes as he recounted the disappointment. The wound was still fresh 63 years later. Until his death in 2009, he remembered the drop. "Not a day goes by I don't think about that," he said.

Doss was a standout athlete who served in the Navy during World War II and was a member of the Philadelphia Eagles that won the NFL title in 1948. He was inducted into the Longhorn Hall of Fame along with other life accomplishments.

Why do the "drops" in life haunt our memories often over-shadowing the good or "catches" in our lives? The desire for perfection continually drives us and we don't want to be remembered as the "cause" of a lost "championship." A "drop" is a haunt that you should not meditate on but rather learn from. Remember, even as a superintendent, you'll have "drops," so learn from them and move on. As the songwriter wrote, "Don't think about the time you were down and out, but think about a God that brought you out."

> *Amazing grace shall always be my song of praise,*
> *For it was grace that brought my liberty;*
> *I do not know just why He came to love me so,*
> *He looked beyond my fault and saw my need.*
> –Dottie Rambo

Whether a failure or a forgiven sin,
God forgets our drops, we should do the same.
–Ken Horn

A Time Such As This

For if thou altogether holdest thy peace at this time, then shall there enlargement and deliverance arise to the Jews from another place; but thou and thy father's house shall be destroyed: and who knoweth whether thou are come to the kingdom for such a time as this? Esther 4:14

Esther was given the unique role of being the queen of Babylon when the king had given an order to eliminate the Jewish people. Her uncle, Mordecai, reminded her that she was placed there for purposes that they could not have fathomed until now.

In the same way, superintendents have been placed in positions for "such a time as this." Whether employed or unemployed, demoted or promoted, God has placed us where we are for a unique purpose. If we hold our peace and fail to do what is right, we will be harmed just like all of the other people. Could it be that everything up until now in our career has been pointing toward this one purpose? Superintendents are placed in positions to guide the course of that district's education. The education of the district's children is on the line. There will be political insurgents who will rise up against you as you try to do what is right for that community and its children. Will you have the courage to do what is right?

I know of a superintendent who was hired in a district and because of his willingness to be open with the people, a servant leader, he was able to pass a bond issue for a new build (which was sorely needed). He was placed in that district for a "time such as this." Another superintendent had to fire a politically strong high school principal who was harming the high school and district by his actions. Though it cost the superintendent his position, he was put in that district for a "time such as this." People came by to thank the superintendent for having the courage to do what was right and correct.

As God's child, He's placed you here today,
To be a light of hope, in a world that's gone astray.
Will you embrace your destiny, or His calling will you miss?
Let's have no doubt He's chose you, for such a time as this!
–Unknown

Lord, make us world changers for You
by choosing others' needs over our own desires.
–Rev. Ed Rea

Teammates Matter

Iron sharpens iron, and one man sharpens another. **Proverbs 27:17**

In 2006, after The University of Texas had just upset USC to win the college football National Championship game, their head coach Mac Brown was at a table fielding questions from reporters. One reporter asked Coach Brown, "What did you tell your players after you won the game?" Mac Brown replied, "I told them two things: First, I reminded them that they had just beat an incredible football team, and I expected them to show respect to the USC players. Secondly, I told them they had just accomplished an incredible task, but I did not want them to look back on this day and for it to be the best day of their life. I reminded them they were all young men in their early twenties, and that football was just a small part of their lives. I told them to go out into the world and be good husbands, good fathers, and good men in their communities. Today was certainly a good day; but if it becomes their best day then I have failed them as a coach."

Research shows that much of our temperament and disposition is formed during the first six to seven years of life. It is true that, during those developmental years, many children are learning habits and character, rather than knowledge. Our mannerisms begin to develop at a very young age. The character and principles that guide us our entire life are largely developed during our first few years of life. God has constructed us that way. This does not mean we can't change, because one can change when we find new life in Jesus Christ. As a school superintendent, we need the support of our district's stakeholders as much as they need our leadership. Ultimately, our success rides on the shoulders of those around us. "Iron sharpens iron," meaning we grow stronger when helping others grow stronger through our actions. Therefore, it is in our best interest to build up those around us. It is in our best interest to be a good teammate.

Lying on his death bed at Baylor University Medical Center in 1995, Mickey Mantle was asked by some of his former Yankee teammates what he wanted placed on his statue at Yankee Stadium. Now keep in mind, many people consider Mickey Mantle to be one of the greatest baseball players of all time. No one would have second guessed him had he asked for "the greatest player ever" or "a true leader" to be placed on the statue. Mickey was probably deserving of both of those titles. However, that is not what Mantle asked for. Mickey asked for only one thing to be put next to his name, the phrase: "A Great Teammate." Do those you serve consider you to be a great teammate? If not, ask God to help you be that great teammate.

> *We all do extol Thee, thou Leader in battle,*
> *And pray that Thou still our Defender wilt be;*
> *Let Thy congregation escape tribulation:*
> *Thy name be ever praised! O Lord make us free!*
> –Theodore Baker

**Don't measure yourself by what you have accomplished,
but by what you should have accomplished with your ability.**
–John Wooden

Learning to Trust Your Friends

Faithful are the wounds of a friend, but the kisses of an enemy are deceitful. **Proverbs 27:6**

I was reading my e-mails when a friend sent me one about the *Fable of the Porcupine.*

> "It was the coldest winter ever. Many animals died because of the cold. The porcupines, realizing the situation, decided to group together. This way, they covered and protected themselves, but the quills of each one wounded their closest companions even though they gave off heat to each other. After awhile, they decided to distance themselves one from the other and they began to die, alone and frozen. So they had to make a choice: either accept the quills of their companions or disappear from the Earth. Wisely, they decided to go back to being together. This way they learned to live with the little wounds that were caused by the close relationship with their companion, but the most important part of it, was the heat that came from the others. This way they were able to survive."

As a superintendent, we will hear advice that we don't want to hear. I had a director who was not afraid to give me advice, even if it hurt. I remember one incident when he came into my office and, in no uncertain words, let me know where I was going wrong. He quickly turned and went back to his office. Needless to say, I was fuming. After calming down, I went to his office with the intent of reprimanding him.

When I went into his office, he gave me a hug and with a tear in his eye said he was so sorry. That caught me off guard and it was there I realized that he desired the best for me and the district. As time went on, I learned to trust and accept his advice. His advice and willingness to give it saved me and others from "freezing to death." He learned to live with my imperfections and I learned to live with his imperfections.

> *For united we stand*
> *Divided we fall*
> *And if our backs should ever be against the wall*
> *We'll be together, you and I.*
> —Tony Hiller/Peter Simon

The best relationship is not the one that brings together perfect people, but the best is when each individual learns to live with the imperfections of others and can admire the other person's good qualities.

Seeing God's Beauty

And God saw everything that He had made, and behold it was very good. **Genesis 1:3**

There are many forms of nature that almost take my breath away because of their beauty. There is the Grand Canyon, sunsets, rainbows, flowers, and beaches, just to name a few. How wonderful it will be when the Lord refines this earth and renews everything for the new heaven and earth! It excites me to think about having the time to see all His wonders and creations, especially unspoiled by a cursed earth. The Lord describes Heaven with streets of gold, a river running from the throne, walls of jewels, and gates of a large pearl.

As I think about the current and future beauty of God's creation, I wonder what it was like for the disciples to walk with Jesus from town to town. Were they amazed by the sights of a new town? When I travel, I like to see the unique things that are specific to that city or area. It is clear that each city holds unique and beautiful parts of their city. Some of the things were created by men while others were directly provided by God. The beauty of the Rocky Mountains, Niagra Falls, the rolling pastures of Wisconsin, the caves and Black Hills of South Dakota, the Loess Hills of Iowa, the pine trees of East Texas are all marvels of God's creation.

These are the huge awe inspiring creations, but there are also creations that I enjoy on my early morning walks. There are beautiful colors all around me. Wild flowers growing in the ditches need only to be left alone to return each year. It is peaceful to watch the birds and butterflies.

> So where do you see the wonders and beauty of God's creation?
> Fair are the meadows, fairer still the woodlands,
> Robed in the blooming garb of spring, Jesus is fairer,
> Jesus is purer, who makes the woeful heart to sing!
> –Munster Gesangbuch

**One thing have I desired of the Lord, that will I seek after,
that I may dwell in the house of the Lord all the days of my life,
to behold the beauty of the Lord
and to inquire in His temple. Psalm 27:4**

Comfort

I will not leave you comfortless. I will come to you. John 14:18

There are many times in people's lives where they need comfort. Relationships between people are not always easy and feelings may be hurt. Or worse, relationships are ended and people feel rejected, or a relationship ended because of death. Jesus constantly provides us comfort. I often wonder why we seem to realize Jesus' comfort only at our low parts of our life. Perhaps it is then when we realize how desperately we need Him. We should realize His comfort at all times.

Jesus is always there to provide us comfort. It is comforting when our children are home and safe in their own beds. It is comforting when we see our children do well at things. It is comforting to get back to familiar surroundings after a trip. It is comforting to know when you ask for someone's help, they will provide it. And it is comforting to know Jesus stays with us.

There is comfort in familiar things and places. Many of us have our favorite chair, favorite pillow, or favorite blanket. I even have a favorite comfortable pair of jeans. When we know Jesus and are familiar with Him and His word, then our relationship is strong. We find his comfort as a familiar and safe place. He brings this comfort no matter what happens in our life. It is the study of His word that helps when we don't have the strength to search His word because we are feeling lost. The familiar words need to be ingrained in our mind so that we can call forth those words from the Bible to help us during the times we need comfort.

I know it brings me great comfort to know that Jesus promised to never leave me. As a widow, it was Jesus' comfort during that lowest part of my life. Others had gone through similar loss and yet it is such a personal loss, that it dropped me to my knees. My prayers to Jesus give me the strength and comfort to continue each day.

Safe in the arms of Jesus, safe from corroding care,
Safe from the world's temptations; sin can't harm me there.
Free from the blight of sorrow, free from my doubts and fears;
Only a few more trials, only a few more tears!
–Fanny Crosby

For whatsoever things were written aforetime
were written for our learning,
that we through patience and comfort of the scriptures
might have hope.
Romans 15:4

Adversity

Trust in the Lord with all your heart, and do not lean on your own understanding. In all your ways acknowledge him, and he will make straight your paths. **Proverbs 3:5-6**

Jimmy Johnson, two-time Super Bowl Championship Coach with the Dallas Cowboys, once told a group of Fortune 500 CEO's that leadership entailed four things: (1) A good leader knows how to identify talent, (2) Leaders know how to recruit quality talent, (3) Leaders assign those talented individuals to positions that will make them successful, and (4) Good leaders know how to motivate the talent around them.

Being a good leader is not always easy when so many problems surround you. For example, the CEO of a large cooperation is expected to answer to a Board of Directors which is educated in that particular field. However, school superintendents often find themselves answering to School Board members who lack college degrees and have no understanding of the educational process. This often causes adversity.

What makes the superintendency even more problematic is the fact that we deal with people's two most precious commodities: their children and their money. No CEO holds a greater responsibility, and it is our job to insure each child is given an equal chance at life. The Bible tells us that we will encounter adversity in our lives, but we are also given grace through Jesus Christ.

God has given us grace to guide us in our everyday lives. He has instilled the instinct in the birds to fly to warmer weather, and for the fish to spawn upstream. Our God has also instilled in us a sense of confidence that allows us to overcome difficult situations. He who helps the birds and the fish will bring hope into our hearts and not fail us as we press forward. No one ever said that being a superintendent would be easy, but when we lean on Christ there is nothing we can't overcome.

Walk with God through adversity by acknowledging God's sovereignty;
By affirming God's righteousness; by keeping on in following in God's ways;
By going to God with your pain; by asking God to intervene;
By trusting God with all your heart;
And by letting your joy in God transcend your own desires.

Therefore I tell you, do not be anxious about your life,
what you shall eat or what you shall drink,
nor about your body,
what shall you put on.
Is not life more than food and the body more than clothing?
Look at the birds of the air:
they neither reap nor gather into barns,
yet your heavenly Father feeds them.
Are you not more valuable than they? Matthew 6:25-26

Regaining Hope

Who against hope believed in hope, that he might become the father of many nations; according to that which was spoken, So shall thy seed be. **Romans 4:18**

Terrorism, a regressing economy, and spiritual decline are some of the themes we hear today from the media. You would think terrorism would abate, but it has not. The bad economy is affecting banks, the auto industry, the stock market, and the like. You would think things would improve, but they have not. The unemployment rate is staying close to 10% and people are losing their homes through foreclosure like never before. Sin and perverseness abound. People have lost faith in the government to fix things. Things will not be better for our children. We have lost our hope.

It seems like we have faith, but have lost hope for the future. Statements like, "I don't see it getting any better," or "It doesn't matter who I vote for. They are all liars," or, "It doesn't matter how hard I try," or "That'll never work, we've tried that before," or "We've always done it this way"…are all statements from hopeless people. Hope is diminished in us when the following happens:

When we look at only what we can see.
When what we see is what we believe.
When we begin to question God's provinces.
Statements such as "we are not able…" or "yes, but" increases doubt in us.
When we want everything right now.
When we've forgotten how to wait on the Lord and be of good courage.

Now the good news, hope can be regained by remembering: 1) God is the source of all hope. Hope produces joy and fills you with peace. 2) Believe what God says. Today is a great day. 3) Hope comes from the Holy Spirit (Romans 15:13). The minute God's spirit filled our being, our relationship was healed and we started saying and believe there is a "light at the end of the tunnel."

Be not dismayed what ere be betide, God will take care of you!
Beneath His wings of love abide; God will take care of you!
God will take care of you, through every day o'er all the way;
He will take care of you; God will take care of you!

–Unknown

Once you choose Hope, anything is possible.
–Christopher Reeves

An Excellent Spirit

Then this Daniel was preferred above the presidents and princes, because an excellent spirit was in him; and the king thought to set him over the whole realm. Daniel 6:3

In looking at Daniel's life, he was captured when King Nebuchadnezzar of Babylon besieged Jerusalem. As he did with all of his conquests, King Nebuchadnezzar relocated the leaders and nobles of Judah to Babylon. One of those was Daniel. The King would train these captured leaders to help in the administration of his government since they knew the culture, custom, and language of the people captured.

Daniel could have been a bitter person, but he had an excellent spirit. *First,* Daniel didn't compromise. He kept his faith. We need to stand as firm as Daniel did when we are faced with the opportunity to compromise our position or faith. *Second,* Daniel surrounded himself with companions of like faith. Loyalty and like-mindedness is essential to the success of a superintendent. When Daniel made the decision not to eat the King's food, his companions stood with him. *Third,* Daniel allowed God to use him. He had direct access to kings and rulers,yet he did not try to use it for his advantage. He used it for God's advantage. *Fourth,* Daniel was not afraid to tell the truth. He was a man of integrity. It was this honesty and integrity that impressed the kings the most. They could always count on him to tell the truth and do the right thing. *Fifth,* Daniel always gave God the glory. He did not try to steal the glory for himself nor hide his faith. He used the opportunity of his life and position to glorify God. People with excellent spirits always give God the glory. *Finally,* Daniel was an excellent employee. Daniel's test of excellency was that his enemies could not find any fault in him.

Superintendents need to lead students to success in school. We need school superintendents with the capacity and foresight to effectively lead schools forward. An excellent spirit will lead them successfully through any trial and help them avoid potential problems. Superintendents with an excellent spirit exhibit the 4H's of Leadership: Hustle, Heart, Humor, and Humility. They, in essence, are dependable leaders and have the disposition to be an outstanding superintendent.

Give of your best to the Master
Give Him first place in your heart;
Give Him first place in your service;
Consecrate every part.
–Howard Grose

The quality of a man's life is in direct proportion to his commitment to excellence, regardless of his chosen field of endeavor.
–Vince Lombardi

Anger

For the anger of man does not produce the righteousness of God. James 1:20

Have you ever thought about what causes anger? When people are calm they are able to think reasonably, but, when angered, they often become irrational. Psychologists tell us that all anger is derived from one of three sources: fear, frustration, or pain. As educators, it is important for us to understand the source of anger.

I have worked with many teachers in order to help them understand why people get angry, and why we should not take seriously statements said in anger. There is no wisdom in letting an angry parent or student get the best of you. Seek first to understand why the person is angry, and then begin to work toward solutions.

Christian research shows that 50% of individuals who come in for counseling have issues dealing with anger. Anger is divisive and can tear relationships apart. Unfortunately, many people tend to justify their anger rather than taking responsibility for it. But, fortunately, God's Word reveals to us appropriate ways to handle our anger in a Christian manner. We can control our anger, the bible says, by not returning evil with evil (Romans 12:22, Mark 12:31). When our actions come from our heart, we can change our feelings toward others by choosing how we act toward others.

There is a Native American proverb about an old man and his grandson. The old man told his grandson that inside all of us there are two wolves. The first wolf is all that is good and pure. This wolf conducts himself with honor and integrity. The second wolf is all that is evil. This wolf feeds on hate and destruction. The old man goes on to tell the boy that these two wolves battle everyday inside each of us. The boy then asked the old man, "Which wolf wins?" The old man replied, "The one you feed." Which wolf will you feed today?

> *Would you live for Jesus, and be always pure and good?*
> *Would you walk with Him within the narrow road?*
> *Would you have Him bear your burden, carry all your load?*
> *Let Him have His way with thee.*
> –Cyrus Nusbaum

Children have never been very good at listening to their elders,
but they have never failed to imitate them.
–James Arthur Baldwin

Dirty Cups

Woe unto you scribes and Pharisees, hypocrites! For you make clean the outside of the cup and of the platter, but within they are full of extortion and excess. Thou blind Pharisee cleanse first that which is within the cup and platter, that the outside of them may be clean also. Matthew 23:25-26

When you have been working outside in the heat, you often need to stop and get a drink of water. If you only have two cups available, one that is dirty on the outside and one that is dirty on the inside, you may want to drink from the cup that has dirt on the outside. If our hearts are full of dirt, others will not want to be around us. Again, if I had to choose a friend from one who is well dressed and evil or one that is dirty on the outside but a clean heart, then I would choose the latter. Our Lord provided the perfect example of a clean and pure person. To many people, Jesus did not look like a king. He may even have been dirty outside because of his long walks on dusty roads. He had the perfect inside, full of grace and purity. Jesus was the only true and clean vessel.

As I look at my sink full of dirty dishes, I am reminded of my own pile of mistakes. I am so overwhelmed at times because of my own unclean motives or at the very minimum, selfish motives. Even when I want to do good things, I find that I also would like others to know how much I have done. I know I should be grateful for how much I have received from the Lord. Yet, I still struggle with having a pure and clean motive behind all my actions. This is when I need to ask for guidance from the Holy Spirit.

I think we also need to be careful when we examine ourselves. We also need to be careful when we consider our own actions. It is not just our actions but also the motives behind our actions that are important to the Lord. As individuals and superintendents are we presenting a cup that is clean only on the outside or a cup that is foremost clean on the inside?

Search me, O God, and know my heart today,
Try me, O Savior, know my thoughts, I pray.
See if there be some wicked way in me,
Cleanse me from every sin and set me free.
–J. Edwin Orr

When thou doest alms, let not thy left hand know what thy right had doeth.
That thine alms may be in secret
and thy Father shall reward thee openly. Matthew 6:1

Words: The Tongue Is A Deadly Weapon

A soft answer turneth away wrath, but grievous words stir up anger. The tongue of the wise useth knowledge aright; but the mouth of fools poureth out foolishness. **Proverbs 15:1-2**

Many organizations, sadly even the church as an organization of people, may have times of severe dissension. The dissension can build to the point of people saying hurtful things. My grandmother use to say, "If you don't have anything nice to say, don't say anything at all." These words might be wise for all of us during times of disagreements. Major decisions are needed in all organizations, but never should be made at the expense of the people within the organization. There is no place for harmful and rude comments in a healthy organization. If we allow this, then we are allowing adult bullying.

Whoso keepeth his mouth and his tongue keepeth his soul from troubles.
Proverbs 21:23

Also, be watchful of times when you know there will be major decisions that have differing opinions. These are the times for a superintendent to set the stage, openly affirm that there are differing opinions, and establish the ground rules for respectful discussions. Then, when the discussions start to dissolve, the leader needs to step forward and stop hurtful words. Hurtful words can't be retracted. And even if someone, maybe yourself, is sorry for the hurtful words, the hurt has occurred and it is difficult to repair relationships. Guard your own words and protect others from harmful words.

Death and life are in the power of the tongue;
and they that love it shall eat the fruit thereof. Proverbs 18:21

Angry words, O let them never
From the tongue, unbridled slip.
With the soul's best impulse
Ever check them, ere they soil the lips.
Angry words are quickly spoken,
Bitter thoughts are rashly stirred.
Fondest links of life are broken.
By a single angry word.
–Unknown

The tongue should always bring wonderful words of life and healing.

Maximizing Your Leadership Potential

Is this not the carpenter, the son of Mary, the brother of James, and Joses, and of Juda, and Simon? And are not his sisters here with us? And they were offended at him. **Mark 6:3**

Your leadership style will bring out the good and the bad in people. An effective superintendent will recognize this and emphasize the good and minimize the bad.

Your motives will always be questioned by some and they will take offense with you. I have had some teachers, especially those who were union leaders, come up with the most elaborate schemes, believing that I was allegedly plotting to harm them. Those thoughts were the farthest from my mind and I could not have done what I have been accused of doing even if I had wanted to. The accusations were ludicrous. Sometimes those closest to me, other administrators, would believe those conjured up plots.

But, just as the people of Nazareth refused to see Jesus other than just a person from their community, in spite of His teachings and miracles, some would never recognize His leadership talent. A classic example: a boyhood friend of Mark Twain, who was jealous of the writer's fame, said, "I know just as many stories as Mark Twain. All he did was write them down."

When I received my doctorate, my immediate family and friends were happy for me and celebrating my achievement. But my grandmother made a remark that, in essence, was *this was no big deal and anyone could achieve it.* Some celebrate with you and some do not. I realized that to maximize my career and leadership I had to leave home. This is the reality of leadership.

Jesus could do no mighty work in Nazareth because of their unbelief. A lot of leadership ability has been wasted because of a person's refusal to leave their home town or state. As Briner and Pritchard said, "Although it is good to have a strong appreciation for home, returning periodically to visit as Jesus did, maximized leadership usually occurs away from home." Remember, Peter, James, and John did not become leaders by staying in Capernaum, but by traveling to Jerusalem.

> *He leadeth me: O blessed thought!*
> *O words with heavenly comfort fraught!*
> *Whate'er I do, where'er I be,*
> *Still 'tis God's hand that leadeth me.*
> –Gilmore

For most of us, leaving home is a part of God's plan for our leadership.
–Briner and Pritchard

Remember the Poor

Only they would that we should remember the poor; the same which I also was forward to do. **Galatians 2:10**

Poverty is abundant and we will always have the poor with us. Today, there are more than 3 billion people who live on less than $2.50 per day. Some 1.1 billion people in developing countries have inadequate access to water while 2.6 billion lack basic sanitation. About 1.6 billion people live without electricity. In the United States, almost 20 million children receive free or reduced-price lunch, which is an all-time high. Children from low income families tend to do poorer academically, have lower attendance, and have lower vocabulary skills.

Paul appeared before Peter, James, and John (the three church leaders) to defend his ministry to the Gentiles. Their only instruction was to "remember the poor." The poor are easy to forget and, when we are used to the comforts of life, we can easily forget them. In today's economy when we are faced with struggles, it's easy to forget that millions of people are in worse shape than we are. An oddity is this, it's easy to forget the poor and put them out of our mind, no matter what our condition is.

Although the poor are easy to forget, they are all known and loved by our Heavenly Father. Jesus said, "Are not two sparrows sold for a farthing? and one of them shall not fall on the ground without your Father knowing." (Matthew 10:29). God, who sees each sparrow fall, values every person on earth and has called us to value and care for them also.

We have poor children in our school and we can't comprehend the environment they come from. Many of them lack proper nourishment, clothing, shelter, and the necessities of life. I remember one student in a district in which I was a superintendent who lived on his own and in a shack with no utilities. Because my athletic director cared for him, he was able to keep the student in school, help him stay active in athletics, and help him graduate. We can get short-tempered with poor children and not even "listen to them" because we do not take time to understand the environment from which they came.

> *No one ever cared for me like Jesus;*
> *There's no other friend so kind as He.*
> *No one else could take the sin and darkness from me.*
> *O how much He cared for me.*
> –Weigle

When we remember the poor, we can make a difference in their lives— not only now, but for eternity.
–Randy Hurst

The Siren of Flattery

Jesus said unto him, Why callest thou me good? There is none good but one, that is, God. **Mark 10:18**

Most every superintendent will hear flattery at sometime in their career and it will be like "sweet music" to their ears, but it will be "bitter to the belly." A superintendent new to a position will usually hear the sirens of the flatterer. This is because vain and base people will want to make a good impression on the superintendent telling him/her how great he/she is. Psalms 5:9 says, "there is no faithfulness in them and their throat is an open sepulcher." I learned to take those vain complements with a "grain of salt." A superintendent has a lot of friends due to the position they hold. These "fair-weather" friends are just flattering the superintendent because of the position.

The rich young ruler called Jesus "good." He saw Jesus as a gifted, Spirit-filled rabbi who had unusual understanding into the ways of God. Jesus said this was flattery and refused comments from people who hardly knew him. The young ruler was trusting on his own goodness to get into heaven just like a young flattering administrator is trusting in their goodness to move up in the district. He was "clueless" about who he was.

Jesus never varied from His mission. He always gave God glory and credit. In the same vein, you must never vary from your mission of educating children and always give God the glory.

Being a superintendent, by its very nature, generates positive comments. The better you do your job, the more praise you receive—and the greater the possibility of being misunderstood and having flattery turn your head. Superintendents need to have some charm for the district to succeed and because of this, you have to be vigilant to flattery's seductive nature. Do not get sucked in! You are not above the law or criticism. Jesus said, "Woe to you when all men speak well of you." (Luke 6:26). Remembering that Jesus humbled himself to wash the feet of the disciples will help you combat arrogance.

> *Words spoken with purpose of gaining favor,*
> *Never accept or permit to savor,*
> *By unearned praise influence gained,*
> *Leaves the victims heart and honor chained.*
> –N. Hessler

Be aware that flattery is a weapon of the enemy.
It can lead to arrogance and arrogance is deadly.
–Briner and Pritchard

Loyalty from Others

Peter said to him, 'Even if I must die with you, I will not deny you!' And all the disciples said the same. **Matthew 26:35**

In the 26th Chapter of Matthew, we see Peter and other disciples pledge their loyalty to Jesus. Yet, Jesus responds to Peter by saying, "Truly, I say to you this very night, before the cock crows, you will deny me three times." Later, just as Jesus predicted Peter and the other disciples would deny Him.

As a superintendent, sometimes we find ourselves in situations where we question the loyalty of those around us. During my first superintendent's job, I had a secretary named Patti. She had been with the district over twenty years and had worked for three other superintendents. One day, I asked her which superintendent she thought was the best. She refused to tell me. I continued to pester her about where I ranked among the four, until finally she told me that I was number two. I felt pretty good considering I was a first time superintendent and the other three superintendents had more experience. A couple of weeks later, I asked her who was number one, and with hesitation she informed me that the other three were tied for 1st. *Ouch!* The lesson here is that sometimes it is just better not to ask.

That was a blow to my ego, but I really liked Patti. I distinctly remember giving her good pay raises, birthday and Christmas gifts. I even remember carrying her belongings to her car for a three month period when she had hip surgery. I felt like we had a good working relationship. In my final year with that district, budgetary concerns forced me to lay off a number of teachers and staff members. A lady named Sally that worked in Central Office with Patti and me was one of the cuts. A farewell card was passed around the office that everyone signed for Carla, and it ended up on my desk. I was shocked when I read what Patti had put in the card. In bold black letters, she wrote, "I am sorry that we work for such a JERK!" *Big Ouch!* That was pretty hard to take. Out of everyone in that office, I honestly thought Vicki was my most loyal employee.

In Corinthians 3:6, Paul writes, *"I planted the seed, Apollo watered it, but God made it grow."* The importance of Paul's message is that whether it is in church, home, or at school, no one gets results alone. Everything we do is a team effort, and we must treat our coworkers as a part of the team in order to maximize efficiency. Obviously, from Patti's perspective, I had failed in that area. Proverbs 18:8 reads, "The words of a gossip are like choice morsels; they go down to a man's inmost parts." The Bible says a lot about gossip and none of it is good. As a superintendent, it is difficult when you find out that you do not have the support of those around you. However, when you honor God in your work and have the best interests of students at heart, you can rest well at night knowing you are doing a good job. Remember, that being a superintendent is not a popularity contest. You are a servant, and as a servant you are expected to work the hardest while receiving the least amount of recognition. In doing this, we give God the glory and show our loyalty to Him. In the end, that is what matters most.

When you come to the end of your rope, tie a knot and hang on.
                                                          –Franklin D. Roosevelt

SEPTEMBER

Ego

I can do nothing on my own. As I hear, I judge, and my judgment is just, because I seek not my own will but the will on Him who sent me. John 5:30

There is an old saying that "absolute power corrupts absolutely." As CEO of the school district, no one can argue that the superintendency comes with a lot of power. This increased sense of power can also lead to a bigger ego. A simple definition for ego is *an increased sense of self-significance*. As a superintendent, I often find it difficult to keep my ego in check. There are several things you can do to avoid letting your ego get the best of you:

1) Show humility: Even as superintendent, you are only a small part of a greater plan. Service and patience should always take precedence.
2) Learn from others: Nobody knows everything, so focus on things that can make you a better leader. Do not ever forget that much of your knowledge and success came from the hard work of others.
3) Show appreciation: Take pride in the accomplishments of those you work with, and be sure and let them know how much you need their contributions. Everyone needs encouragement, especially from their supervisors.
4) Be a good listener: Really listen to what people are telling you. Don't be afraid to ask clarification questions, and take time to reflect on what they told you before speaking.
5) Loosen up: Release the need to always win. You do not always have to be right!

I remember speaking at a High School Baptist Baccalaureate service as a principal. I was one of two speakers chosen to address the graduates. I worked for nearly a month on my speech, and when the time came I delivered it with remarkable flair. I have to admit that my chest was "puffed out" pretty far when I finished. After the event, the mayor's wife came up to me and went on and on about what a great job I had done. If memory serves me well, her exact words were, "I have heard many speakers in my time, but that was by far the best speech I have ever heard." She then asked me to remind her of my name, and I told her that I was the local high school principal. She immediately said, "Oh, I am so sorry. I was looking for the other guy who spoke tonight." At the time, I remember being crushed by her comment, but now I look back and laugh at how my own overinflated ego got the best of me.

As Christians, we are called to be humble. We are called to set aside our own ego and to serve others. It is easy to get wrapped up in our own accomplishments. However, it is impossible to reach your full potential when your own ego supersedes your charity for others. As you move forward this week, take time to listen and learn from others. Show those around you that you appreciate all they do for the students in your district. Copy Jesus and always be a servant.

Let go of your ego and better serve those around you.

September 2

Life is Your Test

And Moses said unto the people, Fear not: for God is come to prove you, and that his fear may be before your faces, that ye sin not. **Exodus 20:20**

Testing has been part of the human experience since the beginning of time. We are tested for our endurance, in morality, in our conscious, in what we learn in our profession, and a host of others. I remember when I first heard the word test in my early school years, and I was scared. All I knew was that I wanted to pass because I did not want to flunk! So I studied very hard to pass every test.

Testing has carried on into my professional career. Before I could be a superintendent, I had to pass the state test. Before I earned my doctorate, I had to pass my oral exam. Before I was admitted into the doctoral program, I had to score at a certain level on the GRE and pass the interview. Education has been one test after another. We have to show our competence and ability.

What I later came to realize was that the toughest tests are the tests of life. When I was 17 years old, I faced the test of having open heart surgery. Later on in life, I learned there would be more trials and temptations. When I failed a temptation test, not only did I suffer, but so did my family. When a child of mine failed a trial, I hurt along beside him. The tests of life coming from the job caused my blood pressure to sky-rocket. What I learned through it all is that I had to put my trust in God and trust him to see me through the trial and test.

Tests of life show how well you take instruction and correction, what you have learned, and what you will do in any given circumstance. Going through tests and trials is not fun, but they make you stronger, more empathetic, and willing to put your trust in God. Trials and tests help you mature as a Christian. Tests helped me get my priorities right. God comes first, family comes second, and the job comes last.

> *Where do I go, when the storms of life are threatening?*
> *Who do I turn to when those winds of sorrow blow?*
> *And is there a refuge in the time of tribulation?*
> *I go to the Rock, I know He's able, I go to the Rock.*
> –Dottie Rambo

Our problems are opportunities to discover God's solutions.
–Unknown

267

God's Mercy

When thou passest through the waters, I will be with thee; and through the rivers, they shall not overflow thee: when thou walkest through the fire, thou shalt not be burned; neither shall the flame kindle upon thee. **Isaiah 43:2**

When Isaiah wrote this passage, Israel was in captivity and he was talking about what people go through mentally, spiritually, and physically. Their floods were trials, their fires were temptations, and their rivers were testings. These were all Satan's attempts to destroy and overwhelm God's people.

Isaiah's words were a message of unmerited mercy for Israel. The people were in captivity because of their own stupidity and hard-heartedness. Because of God's mercy, he sent them a prophet who said, "God wants me to tell you that you belong to him."

Right now, you may be in the midst of your own troubled waters. You are so overwhelmed with a trial or temptation that is threatening to consume you. Remember, God will help you though because he has promised he would be with you. But also remember, you will go through trials because the Lord does not always calm the waters and does not always stay the floods or put out the fires. At the end of each trial, the seas are calmed. These trials make you stronger so you can bravely face the next trial.

As a superintendent, you may pray, dear Lord, why am I facing this trial? Why is my Board trying to fire me? Why are the teachers upset and unsatisfied? Why are parents complaining about how we are educating their children? Why is this administrator not loyal? How am I going to balance this budget? You can have a myriad of trials come upon you. I know of one superintendent that trusted his Chief Financial Officer but found out after he had to let him go, that the CFO failed to pay the state the retirement portion each year for the district. The district was in arrears for over $10 million. The superintendent tried to calm the teachers and the community, but he was figuratively crucified. He made it through the trial because he trusted in God's promise.

> *Some through the waters, some through the flood,*
> *Some through the fire, but all through the blood;*
> *Some through great sorrow, but God gives a song,*
> *In the night season and all the day long.*
> *–George Young*

I am a most noteworthy sinner, but I have cried out to the Lord for grace and mercy, and they have covered me completely. I have found the sweetest consolation since I made it my whole purpose to enjoy His marvelous Presence.
–Christopher Columbus

God's Army

Wherefore take unto ye the whole armor of God, that you may able to withstand in the evil day and having done so to stand therefore having your loins girt about with truth, and having on the breastplate of righteousness. And your feet shod with the preparation of the gospel of peace. Above all, taking the shield of faith, wherewith ye shall be able to quench all the fiery darts of the wicked. And take the helmet of salvation and the sword of the spirit, which is the word of God. Praying always with all prayer and supplication in the Spirit and watching thereunto with all perseverance and supplication for all sinners. **Ephesians 6:13-18**

How do you start your morning? There are some days you know will be full of meetings. It is on those days with the fullest agendas that you need to take extra time in the morning to prepare yourself. Perhaps some of these meetings will be with people who do not always work well together, or the issues have very divergent solutions and you know the meetings will not be easy. Superintendents have many days with hectic schedules and multiple groups of people. Some of the decisions that need to be made may also lead to unpopular solutions. Furthermore, crises happen in school districts that require your immediate attention and response.

So when is it best to prepare for an attack or difficult meetings? It would not be wise to prepare during the attack. Rather, it would be best to make preparations during peaceful times. Starting your day in prayer and asking for God's guidance and strength is one way to make preparations. Then, at the end of the day, it is important to repent of any wrongdoing, so that the devil has no chance to enter into your life.

It is good to remember all your blessings and thank the Lord for these blessings. Those are just a few ways to ensure that you are prepared for attacks.

I may never march in the infantry
Ride in the cavalry
Shoot the artillery
I may never fly o'er the enemy
But I'm in the Lord's army!
                                        –Unknown

We are troubled on every side, yet not distressed;
we are perplexed, but not in despair;
Persecuted, but not forsaken; cast down,
but not destroyed.
II Corinthians 4:8-9

Don't Hide God's Light

You are the light of the world. A city that is set on a hill can't be hid. Neither do men light a candle and put it under a bushel, but on a candlestick, and it giveth light unto all that are in the house. **Matthew 5:14-15**

The support of Christian friends should never be underestimated. One only has to let a fellow Christian know about a need and there will be an answer. There may be times when you ask for help, while at other times, you will be the one able to help. Jesus often showed us through His own examples. His first miracle was the fulfilling a need when a wedding celebration ran out of wine.

Many opportunities will be open to you as you watch for ways to help others in order to be a blessing for God. For many people, especially those who are not Christian, they may only understand Christianity by watching the Christians in the world. Hopefully, you will be the light that shows the way.

It is a reminder that we are not to hide our own light under a basket. It means we do not want to miss opportunities to help others and show the greatness of our Lord. This means we show contentment and obedience to God no matter what our circumstances. During the times of difficulty and challenges we may want to complain or question God. Yet, it is exactly these times when others watch our actions.

Are you ready to give support to others when you feel down yourself? It is those times when we most need to look to support others instead of dwelling on our own problems. Any time we need support, it is then that we need to lean on God and keep our focus off ourselves. Our Christian colleagues and friends can help us show light to a troubled world.

Let my life be a light shining out through the night,
May I help struggling ones to the fold;
Spreading cheer everywhere to the sad and the lone,
Let my life be a light to some soul.
                                                                        –J. R. Varner

And let us consider one another to provoke unto love and to good works.
Hebrews 10:24

Key to Deliverance

He brought me forth also into a large place; he delivered me, because he delighted in me. **Psalm 18:19**

When God delights in us, we are delivered. Do you need deliverance from lust, anger, temptation, bad habit, or trial? Do you need deliverance from a problem that's mental, spiritual, emotional, or physical? Remember, you are precious to Him and he delights in you!

In Song of Solomon 7:6, the Lord says of us, his bride, "How fair and how pleasant art thou, O love, for delights!" The Hebrew words in this verse are synonymous: fair means precious, pleasant indicates pleasure and delights. These three words describe our Lord's thoughts towards us, his bride. He looks at us and says, "How beautiful, sweet and delightful you are. You are precious to me, O love."

We, the bride, can confidently say, "I am my beloved's, and his desire is toward me" (7:10). These thoughts are found throughout the Psalms. "The Lord takes pleasure in them that fear him, in those that hope in his mercy" (147:11). "The Lord takes pleasure in his people: he will beautify the meek with salvation" (149:4).

I know of a superintendent who truly delighted in his employees and he would readily elevate those people who showed an aptitude for the promotion. When a person made a mistake, he would deliver them by counsel, retraining, or understanding. If an employee needed help, assistance, or counseling, the superintendent had "an open office and open ear." If the person needed to be let go and the superintendent had to recommend a "non-renewal," that employee would leave without having angry feelings because they knew that he went "beyond the call of duty" for them. His employees performed at their highest level for him because they knew he truly cared for them and their well-being.

> *I am my beloved and He is mine*
> *His banner over me is love*
> *He brought me to His banqueting table*
> *His banner over me is love.*
> –Unknown

Do what is right and the Lord will bring you to a wealthy place.

September 7

Who You Are: His Masterpiece

For we are his workmanship, created in Christ Jesus unto good works, which God hath before ordained that we should walk in them. **Ephesians 2:10**

There was a time in my life that I could not believe that I was a masterpiece of God because I was depressed and had no self-esteem. I knew God loved me and He saved me, but I did not think He really cared for me. Because no one cared for me, why would God? How could anyone love such a decrepit soul as I? I would read Scriptures like He loves me with an everlasting love and He accepts me. I just couldn't comprehend that He'll never leave me. Then, there is that wonderful passage in Ephesians 2:10 that reads "we are His workmanship."

I had read the Bible and saw "workmanship" and "masterpiece." Then, I would think that meant someone else as that can't be true about me. I struggled with it because of my past challenges and trials. How can I be a masterpiece when I have had so many struggles? One day while in prayer, the Lord finally showed me the answer to Paul's words, "That the God of our Lord Jesus Christ, the Father of glory may give unto you the spirit of wisdom and revelation in the knowledge of him: The eyes of your understanding being enlightened; that ye may know what is the hope of his calling, and what the riches of the glory of his inheritance in the saints." (Ephesians 1:17-18).

The enemy does not want you to see who you really are. He wants you to keep seeing yourself as who you were before you met Jesus. The enemy wants to keep you blind! Just like blind Bartimaeus, he was blind before he met Jesus and after he met Jesus, he could see. The enemy tries to remind you of your past. But now you can say, I am God's workmanship! I am his masterpiece! When you accept the Lord, you are redeemed, forgiven, and cleansed. God looks at you today as though you never once sinned as he has thrown your past sins into the sea of forgetfulness.

It was battered and scarred, and the auctioneer though it hardly worth his while
To waste his time on the old violin, but he held it up with a smile.
"What am I bid, good people", he cried, "Who starts the bidding for me?"
"Two dollars, who makes it three?"
"Three dollars once, three dollars twice, going for three,"
But, No, from the room far back a gray bearded man
came forward and picked up the bow,
Then wiping the dust from the old violin and tightening up the strings,
He played a melody, pure and sweet as sweet as the angel sings.
"One thousand, one thousand, Do I hear two?
Going and gone", said he. The audience cheered, but some of them cried,
"What changed its' worth?" And many a man with life out of tune
Is auctioned cheap to a thoughtless crowd, much like that old violin
But the Master comes, and the foolish crowd never can quite understand,
The worth of a soul and the change that is wrought
By the Touch of the Masters' Hand.
–Myra Welch

Today, you can say, "I am His masterpiece."

Dealing with Death

For God so loved the world that he gave his only Son, that whoever believes in him should not perish but have eternal life. John 3:16

Any superintendent who stays in the business long enough will inevitably have to deal with death. Since a district serves so many stakeholders, it is only a matter of time before we see the loss of a student, co-worker, parent, or community member. No matter what your position is in a school district, death is always tragic and difficult to deal with.

I was a high school principal the first time I had to deal with the death of a student. The young man's name was Kevin, and he was out hunting late one night with some other boys from school. I received the call from the city police chief that Kevin had been accidently shot and killed.

Kevin's death was particularly hard on the community, because Kevin was an honor student, incredible athlete, and extremely outgoing kid. In addition, he had 5 other siblings who either attended or graduated from our district. What made the matter even more complex was the fact that Kevin was black and the three boys he was hunting with were white.

A group emerged declaring that Kevin's death was a "murder" and a vicious racial "hate crime." At school the next day, students were angry and confused at all of the misinformation surrounding Kevin's tragic death. Late that afternoon, I received a call from Kevin's uncle. He asked if he could speak to the high school students about Kevin's accident. I knew his uncle well and agreed.

The next morning Kevin's family surrounded his uncle in support while he explained to the student body how much Kevin loved his school and his friends. He went on to explain that Kevin's death was an accident and that their family had forgiven the boys who he was hunting with. He asked the students to honor Kevin's memory by letting go of any hatred or blame they had in their hearts.

To this day, I look back with amazement at the Christian example Kevin's family displayed. During a time of incredible grief and sadness, they thought of others. They set an example for our community to follow on how to deal with the loss of Kevin.

As Christians, we can look toward Jesus as our example. The way He died shows us how to deal with death without placing blame on anyone, even on the ones who cause death. In Luke 32:34, Jesus said, " Father, forgive them, for they know not what they do." Death is simply a part of life. We can prepare for death by living according to God's word, and being good examples for others.

**We should want those around us to see us
living each day not as preparation for death,
but as preparation for eternal life.**

Slay Your Lions

Benaiah the son of Jehoiada, the son of a valiant man of Kabzeel, who had done may acts; he slew two lion-like men of Moab; also he went down and slew a lion in a pit in a snowy day. **1 Chronicles 11:22**

I was eagerly waiting and musing about the joys of Christmas. Then, I saw the snow. Even though the snow outside was beautiful, it was slippery and treacherous. I quickly remembered that many jobs still had to be done, even in these terrible conditions. Working in the snow is not easy, whether walking or driving.

A friend of mine fell on a snowy day and tore ligaments in his knee which required surgery and over a year of rehabilitation. You have to take extra care when you are out in the snow. Can you imagine fighting a lion in those conditions?

Do you know the valiant men and women in your school district who will "fight a lion in a snowy pit?" That has to be a person made of mettle and character. To slay a lion in a snowy pit, when you know the conditions are not good for fighting a man-eating beast, speaks volumes about that employees courage.

I had a Director of Auxiliary Services who "fought a lion in a snowy pit." He was not concerned about his safety, but would give of his all for the district and for me. In this particular community, we had a lion (community member) who was bent on destroying everything the district did and stood for. He would go into school buildings, find fault, and then send letters to the editor lambasting the school district, this director, and me. This director took on that "lion" and slew him. In the end, the community member was discredited and never bothered the district again. You need trusted, valiant men and women who are full of courage and integrity, and are not afraid to fight and slay the lion whatever the conditions might be.

> *Quit living as if the purpose of life is to arrive safely at death*
> *Quit holding out.*
> *Quit holding back.*
> *Quit running away.*
> *Chase the lion and kill it!*
> —Mark Batterson

**Stop running away from what scares you most
and start chasing the God-ordained opportunities that cross your path.**
—Mark Batterson

Only Believe

But when Jesus heard it, he answered him saying, Fear not: believe only, and she shall be made whole. **Luke 8:50**

We can't do things on our own. We have to be in perfect submission to Christ. God has everything under control and will take care of the situation. Jairus was in direct need of a miracle and had waited on God a long time only to see someone step in front of him.

How often have you prayed and only saw someone else receive the miracle and you felt like giving up? I do not know what you are facing today, but when we find ourselves in the same situation as Jairus, do not give up as Jesus eventually will make His way to your house as he did to Jairus' house when he calmly said, "Weep not; she is not dead, but sleepeth..Maid, arise." (v 52,54).

Your situation is not forgotten by Jesus. He knows all, sees all, and is touched by what troubles you. He is on His way to your house to take care of the situation and resurrect your dream.

I was watching an old Andy Griffith rerun and Barney was telling Andy "We have a situation!" He was tense, ready to react, and panicked. Andy was telling Barney that "It will work out ok and to relax." If he would have listened to Barney, they would have had a real problem on their hands. But, because Andy spoke common sense and did not listen, the problem was resolved.

How often as a superintendent do you have people coming to you and saying, "That won't work...", or "Let's do this now..." or "We've done that before..." or "We have a situation on our hands?" As a superintendent, I have wondered if I will ever get this done because I know it is best for children. But Jesus came along and the problem was solved.

In one instance, I had to wait 2 years and when the Board finally voted on the matter, it went through without any problems, faculty uproar, or community dissension. Remember, you were put in that position for a reason and God is there to direct and lead you. As with Jairus, Jesus is on his way to your job and home.

Fear not, precious flock, whatever your lot;
He enters all rooms, the doors being shut.
He never forsakes, He never is gone
So count on His presence in darkness and dawn.
–Paul Rader

Only believe, only believe; All things are possible, only believe.
–Paul Rader

Wise Use of the Rebuke

And he saith unto them, Are ye so without understanding also? Do ye not perceive, that whatsoever without entereth into the man, it can't defile him. **Mark 7:18**

As a superintendent, there will be times that you will have to rebuke, correct, or disagree with your administrators, which also means your central office administrators. How you rebuke that person takes tact and skill. If the rebuke is done the wrong way, you will end up with a disloyal and vindictive administrator. They will be like a deep silent UBoat ready to torpedo you at the first opportunity. Sometimes, the administrator will not take the rebuke kindly, but will "come around" after several days left alone.

An example of this is when I had a Director of Special Education. She was very articulate and had always received what she wanted. On this one occasion, she had come back from a state department meeting and was briefing me and the other central office administrators on the new changes.

She did not realize that I had been made aware of these coming changes. In the meeting, she kept saying that "the law says you have to do this…" Finally, after several minutes of this, I said to her, "please show us in the law where it says you have to do this." I went on to politely say that as I understand the law, and it is suggestions not mandates. Even though I chose my words carefully and used a soft voice, she did not take well to that comment. She quickly understood that I required correct information, not "spun" information. She worked with the district for 2 more years and then retired. I do not think she ever forgave me for that rebuke.

Biner and Pritchard in their book *Leadership Lessons From Jesus* wrote, "Good leaders use rebukes, especially the stinging ones, sparingly and strategically. They never use them to tear down or ridicule. They always show a positive purpose. Rebukes should hurt the leader as much as the one being rebuked."

Reprove not a scorner, lest he hate thee: rebuke a wise man and he will love thee.

Give instruction to a wise man, and he will be wiser
Teach a just man, and he will increase in learning. Proverbs 9: 8-9
It is better to hear the rebuke of the wise than the song of fools.
–Ecclesiastes 7:5

Wise leaders wait for the right moment to give a sharp rebuke,
and then move on.
–Briner and Pritchard

Yield Not to Temptation

There hath no temptation taken you but such as is common to man: but God is faithful, who will not suffer you to be tempted above that ye are able; but with the temptation also make a way to escape, that ye may be able to bear it.
I Corinthians 10:13

Temptation is a suggestion to sin, a reason for us to do something wrong. It arises from what we see, read, or feel. It is a lie straight from Satan. We sin when we yield to that temptation. In essence, temptation is an enticement to sin against the will of God. You are not tempted by God but when you are drawn away by your own lusts (James 1:13-15).

I will give you an example of falling to temptation and eventually sinning. When I was six years old, my folks drove to Lewiston, Idaho to Christmas shop. We entered this one store and, as young boys usually do, I was here and there from my parents in this small store. I noticed a big wire basket right by the cash register that was full of silver dollars.

I thought about that basket, but quickly found my mother as she was ready to check out. Again I saw the basket and I was tempted to take a silver dollar. At that point when no one was watching, I quickly took a silver dollar and put it in my pocket.

As the family drove home that night, 50 miles down the Clearwater River, my Dad saw the silver dollar and asked me where I got it. I quickly said, "I found it." My conscious was bothering me as not only did I steal a silver dollar, but I had to tell a lie to cover it up.

When we got home, I told Dad how I came in possession of the silver dollar. He asked me where I stole it from but I could not remember the name of the store. To say the least, I received an "old fashion seat warming."

There are times in the superintendency that you will be tempted to do something illegal, immoral or unethical. You might think that no one is watching you. But God does and you will be found out. Remember, do not ever put yourself in a situation that yields to the allures of temptation.

> *Yield not to temptation, for yielding is sin;*
> *Each victory will help you some other to win;*
> *Fight manfully onward, dark passions subdue,*
> *Look ever to Jesus, He'll carry you through.*
> –Horatio Palmer

Good habits result from resisting temptation.
–Old Proverb

Developing Future Leaders

And Joshua the son of Nun was full of the spirit of wisdom; for Moses had laid his hands upon him: and the children of Israel hearkened unto him and did as the Lord commanded Moses. **Deuteronomy 34:9**

Joshua was a strong leader with high integrity who encouraged the children of Israel to be strong and of good courage. He had learned from Moses. He was a faithful assistant to Moses and saw how he led the children of Israel for 40 years in the wilderness.

Moses was focused, had an inspiring shared vision, had faith and integrity, listened and moved when God told him so, was humble, challenged the process, took decisive action, enabled others to act, modeled the way, and encouraged the heart. Moses trained Joshua, Israel's future leader, by modeling and being consistent. He taught him that when God says He will open up the sea and give dry passage to the other side that it is time to move out and lead. He taught him how to take that bold first step.

Joshua learned these skills and demonstrated them. He was humble before he was a leader and he was willing to serve. He was a man of faith who trusted in God. He was a man of God's word, a man of prayer who put God first. He was a decisive leader both in military and governance. He had the highest integrity. He was committed as was his family when he said, "as for me and my house we will serve the Lord" (Joshua 24:5).

As a superintendent, you are in the position to develop future leaders for your school district. I was fortunate enough to work under Dr. Clarence Oliver before he retired in Oklahoma. Dr. Oliver's leadership legacy lives on by having a school named after him and many of his administrators moving on to the superintendency.

He began a principal's training program in the district and, from this program, he continually had quality principals moving into positions when they came open. His central office staff was staffed by principals who showed an aptitude for more responsibility. Mentoring and developing future leaders was a key to his success and legacy.

Do all the good you can, By all the means you can,
In all the ways you can, In all the places you can,
To all the people you can, As long as ever you can.
–John Wesley

The will to win is meaningless without the will to prepare.
–Joe Gibbs

Accomplishment Highlights

Josheb-Basshbeth, A Tahkemonite, was chief of the Three; he raised his spear against eight hundred men, whom he killed in one encounter. **II Samuel 23:8**

Your mighty men (men and women administrators) need a way to demonstrate their accomplishments just as David's mighty men listed their accomplishments. These mighty men fought for David for the betterment and deliverance of Israel just as your mighty men fight for your district for student improvement and achievement.

A superintendent of a large district recognized the value of having individual administrators manage themselves yet function as a team. At the end of the year, the superintendent set up a schedule for handling of accomplishment reviews. He wanted to review the accomplishments before the Board of Education in a special meeting.

The accomplishment highlight reviews covered all administrative levels. For each report, he looked for opportunities to provide reinforcement through handwritten comments. The superintendent also took advantage of the opportunity to coach by writing comments on the reviews. Since the comments were not made to every accomplishment, or on every report, they were restricted to accomplishments deemed exceptional to the superintendent. Therefore, each comment had special meaning to the individuals involved.

The superintendent then sent the accomplishment highlights back so the individual administrator could see what he had written. As a result of the superintendent's personal attention to the accomplishments of the past year, the setting of objectives for the coming year took on new significance.

Discussions of objectives for the coming year revolved around student achievement and school improvement. As soon as objectives were approved and correlated, the initial drafts of accomplishment highlights began to take shape. Individual administrators started to give serious thought as to what they wanted to be able to report at the end of the new year as their most significant contributions and to what evidence they would be able to present that they made it happen. Do you want administrators to be mighty for the school district? As David did, recognize their achievements and give them the glory.

Success is sharing sorrow, work and mirth
And making better God's beautiful earth
It's serving people, striving through strain and stress
It's doing your noblest for God – that's success.
–Berton Braley

To have quality highlights of your accomplishments,
you need a healthy form of skepticism
that can be summed up in these words:
Answer your questions but question your answers.

–Mark Sanborn

September 15

Trusting Your Calling of Leadership

And he said unto him, Oh my Lord, wherewith shall I save Israel? Behold, my family is poor in Manasseh, and I am the least in my father's house. **Judges 6:15**

It is an awesome calling when you are called to be a superintendent and you do not feel worthy. Gideon was the least in his father's house and on top of that, he came from a very poor family. He had very low self-esteem. He questioned God and was wondering if God made a mistake about calling him to lead Israel out of the hand of the Midianites.

Think about this, Gideon even put several fleece before God to see if it was truly God who was speaking. That shows his lack of self-confidence and low self-esteem. I would assume that Gideon was a middle child since he's the least in his father's house. Middle children, according to birth order researchers, can be shy, loners, and uptight. A positive trait of the middle child is that they are well-suited for management because of levelheadedness and the ability to be unbiased. God saw this positive trait in Gideon and through him delivered Israel.

Abraham Lincoln was a middle child and born to a poor family in a log cabin. When you look at Abraham Lincoln's life, you wonder how he could become one of America's greatest presidents. He lost jobs, failed in business, had a nervous breakdown, and was defeated every time he ran for a public office except when he won the presidency. God saw a different Abraham Lincoln and said, "This is the man I need to lead America during this time of unrest."

There was this superintendent who came from a poor railroader's family, was a middle child and who always worked hard to be accepted. When he received his doctorate, even his grandmother scoffed at it and was condescending. She said, "You mean that little squeaky runt received his doctorate, well that can't be nothing."

This superintendent kept his eyes on God and God led him to help out several multi-racial, troubled , Title 1 districts. Remember God can use you no matter what. Trust in him and have confidence. God is for you!

Living by faith, in Jesus above
Trusting, confiding in His great love;
From all harm safe in His sheltering arm,
I'm living by faith and feel no alarm.
                                        –J. L. Heath

If God is for you, who can be against you?

Redeemed

Therefore the redeemed of the Lord shall return, and come with singing unto Zion; and everlasting joy shall be upon their head: they shall obtain gladness and joy; and sorrow and mourning shall flee away. **Isaiah 51:11**

Webster's Dictionary defines "redeem" as "to buy back, to win back, to free from what distresses you, to free from captivity by payment, to release from blame or debt, to free from the consequences of sin."

I remember when I was a young boy we had a dog named Red. He was a mutt, a mixture of every dog in town. We loved that dog and thought the world of him. One day, he turned up missing. We went all over the small town hollering and calling his name, but there was no Red.

Red never showed up that night and we were all distraught. The next day, my dad said we were going to the Dog Pound to see if Red ended up there. Sure enough, as we entered the building we could hear his barking because he recognized the motor of the car. Dad had to pay a fee to get Red out of the pound.

He was so excited and happy when he was released you would have thought the he won the doggie lottery. I tell this story because this is an example of being redeemed. Red was redeemed and expressed great joy. My father paid the price for his redemption.

There are times during your career in which your school district might be put in "the Pound". Your district is put in the "pound" because it did not make the correct score on the standardized test. Therefore, the district is declared academically deficient by the state.

Threats come your way from the state on what they would do if you do not bring your school up to "acceptable." You file a lengthy appeal, make a trip to the state department of education with all of the documentation demonstrating why the school should be taken out of "the Pound," and attend the hearings.

After running you through the gauntlet, you win redemption for your district. As you drive home, you are euphoric, making phone calls back to the district to let them know the good news. Everyone rejoices as the district is redeemed! Now, your goal is to make certain your district never again gets put in "the Pound."

I'm redeemed by love divine
Glory, glory, Christ is mine
All to Him I now resign
I have been, I have been redeemed.
–James Rowe

If something is worth something, then sacrifice is nothing.
–Dan Gable

Job Hunting

Ask, and it will be given to you; seek, and you will find; knock, and it will be opened to you. **Matthew 7:7**

Did you know that in England at St. Cross Hospital, any person walking by, who chooses to ask for it, can knock on the door and be served a portion of bread? Whoever the person is, they simply have to knock and ask and the bread is given.

When I was looking for my first superintendent's job, I often thought of Matthew 7:7. I had applied at three districts. However, my family and I really had our eye on two of those three jobs. The two schools were in good locations, they were close to family, and the money was phenomenal. Well, I failed to get an interview at one of the schools I wanted, but I did land an interview at the other. I spent a lot of time in prayer before the interview and felt that God was preparing to open a door for me. In fact, to this day I do not think I have ever had a better interview. Unfortunately, I would not even make the finals.

It turned out the door that would open for me would be the third school on my list. It was a small district, a divided school board, far away from family, with very little money. I was disappointed, but I accepted the position. You see, I prayed for God to open a door for me and he did.

At the time, I could not understand why I did not get one of the other jobs, but after a couple of years I began to understand God's plan. The district at the top of my list (the one that did not give me an interview) ended up in financial trouble within a year and the superintendent they hired was fired before the end of his contract. The second district on my list went academically unacceptable the next year and their superintendent was fired mid-year.

What about that small district that offered me a job? Well, it turns out that district was located next to a larger city and within three years the district doubled in size. If fact, we grew so quickly that we had to build a new high school and new middle school before the end of my third year with the district. The school board was composed of seven strong Christian men who wanted good things for the school and students. When I took the job, I thought I had lost out on two better opportunities, but as it turns out, God put me in the best situation. Much like people that pass by St. Cross Hospital, I just had to ask.

The love of Jesus Christ is much like bread from St. Cross Hospital. The door is there ready to be opened, one has only to knock and ask for it. In John 14:6, Jesus says, "I am the way, the truth, and the life; no one can come to the Father except through me." Those who trust in Jesus will inherit eternal treasure and all that is required in return is for us to ask Him into our heart.

No matter what you are looking for, Jesus has the answer.

Peace With Your Enemies

When a man's ways please the Lord, he maketh even his enemies to be at peace with him. **Proverbs 16:7**

We all want to be at peace with our enemies and the secret seems simple: please the Lord. God owns everything and sees everything, so how is this accomplished? You have to be fully committed to the Lord, humble, surrendered to his will, and trust God. Everything you do will demonstrate your love for God. When you obey God's laws, you will be the "head and not the tail." The Lord will bless you beyond measure!

The first key to pleasing someone is to be totally honest. You can't please your spouse, boss, or friends if you are not honest. If you try to please less people, you will actually please more people because you will be seen as genuine. The second key is knowing people's likes and dislikes. You can't please your spouse if you do not know what they want or who they are. Therefore, you have to get to know them. The third key is putting them ahead of yourself. This is the Golden Rule, "Do unto others as you would have them do unto you." You love your neighbor as yourself.

Does this mean you will not have enemies? No! You will still have enemies just like we have enemies now, but you will not be at war with them. As a superintendent, you will have enemies and people that do not like you. They will try to make you fail. An example of this would be the teachers' union. It seems that their goal is not to work with administration but to get everything for the teachers. But remember, if your ways please the Lord, you will have a quality working relationship with them so that children in the district benefit. But remember, you can't become relaxed or get cocky, because this peace is not eternal.

Treat your people respectful, be honest, be humble, keep your word, and in essence, be a servant leader and you'll have peace in your district. When this happens, you will have less stress and more people will be satisfied with the district.

> *He drew a circle that shut me out –*
> *Heretic, rebel, a thing to flout*
> *But love and I had the wit to win:*
> *We drew a circle that took him in.*
>
> –Edwin Markham

We must reach out our hand in friendship and dignity both to those who would befriend us and those who would be our enemy.
–Arthur Ashe

Being Grateful to God

Rejoice and be glad, because great is your reward in heaven, for in the same way they persecuted the prophets who were before you. **Matthew 5:12**

Have you ever felt like that second grade student, who while saying his bedtime prayers utters, "God, thank you for not letting my Dad find out what I did in Mrs. Smith's class today. And thank you for letting me get the biggest slice of pizza at lunch. And a big thank you for not letting Mom miss the cookies I took from her kitchen. Amen!"

Even as adults, this behavior can characterize how we act during our Christian walk. Throughout the Bible we are warned not to put faith in money, success, or materials here on earth. The Bible teaches us to put our faith in Jesus and look forward to the rewards waiting for us in heaven. Matthew 5:12 reminds us to rejoice because great is our reward in heaven. Jesus teaches that ultimate happiness and wealth begin first in our hearts.

It is important that we thank the Lord in honest and genuine ways. We must thank Him for challenges in our lives, because it is through these challenges that we are able to grow spiritually and submit to His authority. We must thank Him for all of life's pleasures for all good things are given by Him. We must thank him for helping us live with an eagerness to follow His word. This is God's idea of prayer. It is important to thank God in times of happiness and grief, to ask him to help others, and to help us live in a way that brings Him glory and honor.

School superintendents should pray that God would help us to learn what being thankful is truly about. We should be grateful for the teachers and students we work with and come to work with joy in our hearts each day. It is important to realize that prayer is not just something we do at bedtime, but it is a way of life.

> *There is joy divine that is ever mine,*
> *Since the Lord has forgiven me;*
> *And I work and sign for my blessed King,*
> *By His grace I have been made free.*
> –Byron L. Whitworth

I thank God for my handicaps, for through them,
I have found myself, my work and my God.
–Helen Keller

How Long Will You Search for a Buried Treasure

The kingdom of heaven is like a treasure hidden in a field. When a man found it, he hid it again, and then in his joy went and sold all he had and bought that field. Matthew 13:44

If you found a map with a special mark and a story about the map that said there was buried treasure at that mark, would you search for the treasure? What things would make you continue to search? If someone you trusted gave you the map, you might be willing to search for a long time. Or if that trusted person had a small part of the buried treasure and a plausible story about the treasure, you might search longer. If the map was very clear with good details, then you might search a long time, or else, someone who has direct knowledge about the buried treasure could impact your decision to search longer for the treasure. I know good superintendents will search hard and long for the right curriculum to help their schools succeed.

I often wonder why people do not search for the gift of eternal life, provided by the death of Jesus for all our sins. The way is clearly described in the Bible. Jesus said, "I am the way, the truth, and the life. No man comes unto faith, but by me." John 14:6. We see glimpses of the treasure of eternal life when we see Christians on this earth. They have something unique, something that helps them be content no matter the occurrences in their life. They have learned a mature state of peace.

In the Bible, Paul even sat in a prison cell and said he could be content and praise the Lord. Paul said, "for I have learned, in whatsoever state I am, therewith to be content" Philippians 4:11. Christians know where the treasure is and are willing to share the directions to that treasure. The Bible has the clear way described for finding the treasure of heaven and it is given with good detail for any who want that treasure.

I hope all who are willing to search for the treasure of heaven and eternal life will follow the clear directions of the map, the Bible. It is not a buried treasure. Jesus rose from the grave and is preparing a place for all of us to enjoy heaven. We just need to accept Jesus as the Son of God and ask Him to forgive us for our sins.

Here in disappointment, we so sadly roam,
And earthly friends no longer speak one word of love.
But truly we have found contentment, Jesus promised us a home.
So we're looking for a city built above.
–Marvin Dalton

In Him are hid all the treasures of wisdom and knowledge. Colossians 2:3

Are You the Thorns, Rocks, or Good Soil?

A farmer went out to sow his seed. As he was scattering the seed, some fell along the path, it was trampled on and the birds of the air ate it up. Some fell on rock, and when it came up, the plants withered because they had no moisture. Other seed fell among thorns, which grew up with it and choked the plants. Still other seed fell on good soil. It came up and yielded a crop, a hundred times more than was sown. **Luke 8: 5-8**

Jesus often taught using parables. It was one of his ways to know who really wanted to learn about faith. If they were willing to search and question for the meaning in the parable, that means they wanted to grow in their faith. His disciples asked what it meant and He said, "The knowledge of the secrets of the kingdom of God has been give to you, but to others I speak in parables, so that, though seeing they may not see; though hearing, they may not understand." Luke 8:9-1. As I looked at this parable of the seed falling on the different conditions, I am reminded of perspectives.

My perspective was that I was good soil because I was reading the Bible, going to church, and trying to live a good life. But what if there was another perspective? If I was the thorn, perhaps my own actions of losing patience, talking about others, or omitting service to the Lord were thorns that would not allow others' seeds to grow. My actions could get in the way of others' growth in faith.

If I was the rock, my actions of not forgiving, holding grudges, or having unkind thoughts might lead others to not want to be a part of the Christian faith. These actions might hurt other young Christians so that they would not want to continue in the faith or would block their growth in the faith. The good soil would be showing the attitudes of Christ so that my own growth would help others and be a glory to God. The good nutrients of His Word would help me be strong and please the Lord in my actions.

Carefully examine all of Jesus' parables. His Word will help you grow in your faith. Then you will be able to share the good news of Christ while helping others grow in their faith. In this way, you are following the word of God.

This is the meaning of the parable. The seed is the word of the God. Those along the path are the ones who hear and then see on the devil comes and takes away the word from their hearts, so that they may not believe and be saved. Those on the rock are the ones who receive the word with joy when they hear it, but they have not root. They believe for awhile, but in the time of testing they fall away. The seed that fell among the thorns stands for those who hear, but as they go on their way they are choked by life's worries, riches and pleasures, and they do not mature. But the seed on good soil stands for those with a noble and good heart, who hear the word, retain it, and by persevering produce a crop. Luke 8: 11-15

White Fluff of Dandelions

Awake to righteousness, and sin not. I Corinthians 15:34

As I was walking, I saw a fluffy white head of a dandelion being blown across the driveway. It was barely touching the surface and appeared to glide along. It reminded me how beautiful things can seem, but are really dangerous. My late husband hated to see those dandelions growing in his well manicured lawn. At the first sight of a dandelion, he would immediately remove it by the roots. He wanted to remove it before it even had a chance to grow and develop the white fluffy head that would blow and spread more dandelion seeds.

There are times in our lives when we may see things that seem beautiful at first or at least not very dangerous, but if we were to partake in those areas, we could be leading ourselves to dire consequences also. Over-eating or eating the wrong foods may lead to poor diet or weight gain. A continued pattern of eating poorly will lead to poor health and other potential illnesses. Not exercising enough can seem more comfortable and easy, but may lead to poor health and dexterity.

It may feel good to sleep an extra hour in the morning instead of exercising, and yet our bodies need the exercise. Another area that may seem beautiful at first is the purchasing of new clothes, new jewelry, new cars, or new homes. There is nothing wrong with these purchases, but they can take us away from a prioritized life of giving. The use of our resources is important because there are people who need help and our resources could provide for them.

The continued lure of beautiful things could get in our way of doing the work of the Lord. This can lead to fewer opportunities presented to us to help others. It is spreading a life of not caring for our neighbors.

Though I am stubborn, sinful, weak and small,
And my Lord is power, strength, perfect one,
He still loves me the same, above it all,
In love he paid my ransom through his Son.

Therefore do not let sin reign in your moral body so that you obey its lusts, and do not go on presenting the members of your body to sin as instruments of unrighteousness; but present yourselves to God as those alive from the dead, and your members as instruments of righteousness to God. For sin shall not be master over you, for you are not under law but under grace. Romans 6:12-14.

September 23

It is Our Business

Brethren, if a man is overtaken in a fault, ye which are spiritual, restore such a one in the spirit of meekness; considering thyself lest thou also be tempted. Bear ye one another's burdens, and so fulfill the law of Christ. **Galatians 6:1-2**

How many times do we see fellow church members doing something we know is not helpful to them or may even be detrimental to them? Often, we do not want to pry in others' lives or we don't know how to broach the subject to them. We may even feel that it would be seen as judgmental if we stepped in when we are not perfect, either.

There are several samples in the Bible that remind us to be a help to others. We are reminded to walk together for safety and strength. Jesus sent his disciples out by twos (Mark 6:4). We also told to be a good example for others. And we are told to hold each other up and provide comfort.

It is our business to help others. Jesus said we were to take care of his sheep. That would mean we are to help our fellow Christians. There even may be times when we may be in need of help ourselves. It is our business to help humanity including the poor, widows, and those in prison. It is our business to confront our fellow Christians when they are doing wrong. We are to forgive each other.

Forbearing one another, and forgiving one another, if any man have a quarrel against any, even as Christ forgave you, so also do you. Colossians 3:13

Jesus even told us that "Moreover, if thy brother shall trespass against thee, go and tell him his fault between thee and him alone; if he shall hear thee, thou hast gained thy brother. But if he will not hear thee, then take with thee one or two more, that in the mouth of two or three witnesses every word may be established." Matthew 18:15-16. Jesus wants us to make sure that others have the opportunity to repent of their ways and receive forgiveness.

If a soul is backslidden in sin
And we ignore the cry
Then we will be held accountable
On judgment day.

Failing to help people in times of need,
physical or spiritual, magnifies our frailties.

Old Comfortable and Worn Out Shoes

Prove all things, hold fast that which is good. I Thessalonians 5:21

I have a pair of old walking tennis shoes that I use every day on my morning walks. The shoes are wearing out with little cushion left inside the shoe and worn soles on the outside. Yet, it is not easy for me to throw them away because they are very familiar to me, even though the shoes are starting to become uncomfortable. The shoes were expensive and I really do not look forward to going back to find a new pair.

There may be things in our faith and religious practices that have also become so familiar that we no longer question them. They may have become so familiar that I do not want to examine them, either. The Lord tells us to examine all things. And that we should hold to those things which are good. We need to reflect on our practices and beliefs as well as traditions to make sure there is a clear connection with the teachings of the Bible. There may be things we do as routine practices. The Lord does not want us to be lukewarm. He wants our passion and to have Him first in our lives. I do not want to routinely read the Bible, go to church, or pray in a passive manner.

We need to reflect on our practices and the traditions to make sure we are not following the comfortable way just because it is familiar. Do you read the Bible just because it is part of your daily routine? Or do you find new ways to really study the Bible so it impacts your daily life? Do you attend church just because you always have or do you attend so that you can worship your Savior? Are there things you learned as a child that may not have basis in the Bible? Some ideas are not reflected in the Bible, yet it is hard to examine those ideas and throw them out.

It would be more expensive to not examine faith and religious practices. My old tennis shoes will need to be replaced or my feet will start to ache because of the poor condition of the shoes. Have you held on to old wives' fables? Ask the Lord to help you erase them out of your life so you can live a more fulfilling life for Jesus.

Revive us again; fill each heart with Thy love,
May each soul be rekindled with fire from above.
Hallelujah! Thine the glory, Hallelujah! Amen;
Hallelujah! Think the glory, revive us again.
–John Husband

My faith may also need to be rejuvenated
so I am placing my Lord first in my life.
He will restore my oldness and routine ways
so that I have a full life with Him.

Be Strong

Strengthen ye the weak hands, and confirm the feeble knees. Say to them that are of a fearful heart, Be strong, fear not: behold, your God will come with vengeance, even God with a recompence; he will come and save you. **Isaiah 35:3-4**

We are living in perilous times. Nations are falling to unrest, Wisconsin teachers are taking to the streets to protest the Governor's proposal, states are billions of dollars in debt, and the national debt is in the trillions of dollars. In addition to this, there are more and more severe earthquakes (i.e. Haiti and New Zealand), record-breaking disastrous weather is everywhere from flooding in Australia to mudslides in California to snowfall in Oklahoma. The world seems like it is upside down.

At the local level, school superintendents have to make tough fiscal recommendations to their Board of Education because the state and federal monies are drying up. They have struggled to keep the district afloat and now the global world economy is turning their efforts upside down.

In the midst of a prior description of a wasteland and a coming prophecy of war and sickness, Isaiah speaks words of encouragement to the people of God. Today, this still speaks to us.

You may look at your past and see a wasted life. You may look toward the future and all you see is doom. You may look at your job and see all is hopeless. You may look to the future of the world and be in despair. But, take hold of another reality in the midst of your suffering: God will come to save you! So do not give up. Be strong. Do not fear. God was faithful in Isaiah's day, He will be faithful today.

I will not doubt though all my ships at sea,
Come drifting home with broken masts and sails,
I shall believe the Hand that never fails,
From seeming evil worketh good for me.
And though I weep because those sails are battered,
Still will I cry, while my best hopes lie shattered,
'I trust in Thee'
–Ella Wheeler Wilcox

The storm may be raging all around us but: He that dwelleth in the secret place of the Most High shall abide under the shadow of the Almighty. Psalm 91:1

Quit Deep Sea Fishing
(This title was part of a devotional given by Beth Moore with Living Proof Ministries)

Let not any iniquity have dominion over me. **Psalm 119:133**

How many of us have made mistakes in our past that are still an embarrassment to us? Even if no one knows about the mistake now, we still may feel regret that people would think differently about us if they knew.

Those are the times that the devil is working hard to convince us that the Lord could never love or care about us because of those awful sins. And yet, a guilty man hung on a cross beside Jesus and asked for forgiveness. Jesus told that guilty man that his sins were forgiven and that he would be with Jesus in paradise.

I hold on to that promise. Jesus said he would forgive me also if I confessed my sins. He said I was forgiven and that sin was no longer remembered. I needed to quit condemning myself. When I hold on to that sin, I am being self-centered again. I have to let go of my regrets and mistakes. My Lord had forgiven me. It is done and forgotten.

None of his sins that he hath committed shall be mentioned unto him if he turn from his sin and do that which is lawful and right. Ezekiel 33:14

I am reminded of a small child who had done something, perhaps broke a favorite vase or took something that did not belong to him. That child felt so awful that he did not even want to come out of his room. He was so sure that his parents would think he was a bad child. So he stayed in his room and felt miserable.

When what he really needed to do was tell his parents and not dwell on that mistake. At that point, he could not change the wrong. The damage had already been done. But sitting and worrying about the consequences or how awful he felt was not going to help either.

How many times do you go deep into your past to recall, relive, and reopen the terrible wrongs you have committed in the past? Those old mistakes and sins that seem to linger in your memory need to be in the deep sea and forgotten. Now, if you have not asked for forgiveness, it is time to do it.

There is no benefit to sitting in your room feeling miserable or worried about the consequences. You just need to go to the Lord in prayer, confess and then let it go. Do not hold unto that hurt because that is self-centered. Quit going deep sea fishing for your mistakes because there is nothing there. Jesus forgives, stands on your confessed sins, and then throws them away.

The Son of Man hath power upon earth to forgive sins. Luke 5:24

It All Belongs to God

But this I say, He which soweth sparingly shall reap also sparingly; and he which soweth bountifully shall reap also bountifully. Every man according as he purposeth in his heart, so let him give, not grudgingly, or of necessity, for God loveth a cheerful giver. **II Corinthians 9:6-7**

When I think of stewardship and tithing, I am reminded about everything belonging to God. Even things I have worked to gain and accomplish have been provided because the Lord gave me certain skills and abilities. The abilities are God-given. That is why everyone should be excited to give back to their Lord.

It pleases Him when His children share the gifts He has given them. Early in Genesis 28:22, we learn about giving a tenth of our bounty, as it says, "and of all that thou shall give me I will surely give the tenth unto thee." Cain and Abel also provided an early lesson on giving back to God. We are told in Genesis 4:3 that "Cain brought of the fruit of the ground an offering unto the Lord." Genesis 4:4 says, "And Abel, he also brought of the first things of the flock and the fat thereof. And the Lord had respect unto Abel and to his offering. But unto Cain and to his offering he had not respect. And Cain was very wroth, and his countenance fallen. And the Lord said unto Cain, Why are thou wroth? And why is thy countenance fallen? If thou doest well, shall thou not be accepted? And if thou doest not well, sin lieth at the door."

We can learn from these lessons. God desires our best in our offerings and he expects us to be free of sin when we make the offering that is best. When we are prosperous, God will accept the best of our offerings. He expects us to make the offerings in a simple manner. Therefore, we should not brag or point out our giving. We do not give so we can get credit, but to show our thankfulness for all God has given us. Romans 12:8 states, "He that giveth, let him do it with simplicity."

Being a cheerful giver pleases God
It satisfies the soul.
A selfish person will come to naught
But the cheerful giver will be made whole.

For unto whomsoever much is given of him shall be much required; and to whom men have committed much of him they will ask the more. Luke 12:48

Civility

Behold, how good and how pleasant it is for brethren to dwell together in unity! It is like the precious ointment upon the head, that ran down upon the beard, even Aaron's beard: that went down to the skirts of his garments; As the dew of Hermon, and as the dew that descended upon the mountains of Zion: for there the LORD commanded the blessing, even life for evermore. Psalm 133: 1-3

In a speech in Arizona, the president called for civility from all sectors of government and the public because he was seeing the disastrous effects of a factious society. This was coming from inflammatory rhetoric from legislators and blatantly false comments from news commentators who say such things as "Wisconsin's finances, the state is on track to have a budget surplus this year…I am not kidding." These false comments come from a lack of civility which breaks up unity and will destroy a nation. This lack of civility is carrying over to the presidential election with blatantly false statements by the mainstream media.

Just what is civility; civility is an act or utterance that is a customary show of good manners; courteous behavior; politeness. In sports' terminology it would be called "good sportsmanship." Practicing civility causes unity. In both large and small unities, those who do not continue as part of that unity are usually excluded in chiselly ways. The exclusion may come from one side or the other, but either way, the results are very disastrous to the unity. This is the "Babel Effect," which in essence causes the unity to break apart.

When the Psalmist described unity he used the "precious ointment …ran down the beard…that went to his garments." The precious ointment was made up of five ingredients (pure myrrh, cinnamon, calamus, cassia, and olive oil) of the highest quality. The formula was exact.

The priests and altar were anointed with this precious ointment. Myrrh is associated with deep feelings arising from the heart. Cinnamon, calamus, and cassia are from the bark of a tree or a plant and together they are ground into a fine powder with a rich fragrance. The olive oil is the carrier and energy for the release of the precious fragrances of Christ.

Dew is minimal after a cloudy day. Dew is also minimal after a cloudy night and during a windy day. The sun was shining but clouds between the sun and earth interrupted the flow of energy. Dew is an assurance of God's blessing to man on earth. Harmony among brethren is a delicate thing. The blessing of the dew of heaven is to be received and enjoyed in very peaceful conditions.

Civility comes from unity. Unity produces a sweet fragrance and produces conditions for quality relationships where communities can dwell together peacefully. Cloudy nights and days along with windy days can disrupt the civility in the superintendency. In times like these we need a Savior and that is Jesus Christ.

We can't do democracy without a heavy dose of civility.
–Mike Pence

Truth

If we say that we have no sin, we deceive ourselves, and the truth is not in us. If we confess our sins, He is faithful and just to forgive us our sins and to cleanse us from all unrighteousness. If we say that we have not sinned, we make Him a liar, and His word is not in us. I John 1:8-10

A majority of people think what they see on television, read in the newspaper, or hear second and third hand is the truth. Have you ever heard someone say, "I read it in the newspaper, it must be true or they wouldn't print it." I have witnessed numerous television and newspaper reporters, both locally and nationally, lie about their facts. One involved a long time staff member of the New York Times, one of the most recognized papers in the United States. Their reporter admitted that he falsified information frequently and purposely as a means of producing better articles.

I have also seen this type of deception destroy school administrative careers. A good friend of mine began his superintendent's career in a small East Texas district. He was a third generation school superintendent and excited to have his first opportunity. However, staff members in his district, as well as, community members began to falsify information about him to the extreme. They even went so far as to use tape recorded conversations that were later proven to be from someone else. Unfortunately, the dishonesty whirled out of control and he was forced to leave the district. These types of situations are common in school administration, and they leave a gullible and sometimes ignorant public, with no way of knowing what the truth is.

Where does truth exist? Do we actually believe that anything written in print or told to us by a third party is somehow truer? The Bible says, "if we say that we have no sin, we deceive ourselves, and the truth is not in us." We are all sinners and we are all capable of lying. But the lesson for all of us is: don't believe everything you read. There is only one source that is truth and it is the Holy Bible. Why do we waste so much time reading and listening to poorly reported news and gossip when we have the Good News that brings us hope?

I shall someday stand before my King,
My sins are blotted out,
With the ransomed host I then shall sing,
Praise the Lord, He forgave me and blotted out my sins.

Always tell the truth because it is easier to remember,
easier on your career, and pleasing to the Lord.

Holding God's Hand

For I the Lord, thy God, will hold thy right hand, saying unto thee, Fear not; I will help thee. **Isaiah 41:13**

It was a beautiful, sunny morning, so I decided to walk to the office. I lived about a mile from work and had to cross Highway 7, which was the major road through town. It was a four lane road with an extra turn lane. At the corner where I would cross Highway 7 was a gas station, and on the other side of the street was a fast food restaurant.

I looked both ways and walked out into the turn lane. I could see that the light up the street had turned green, and cars started to come. It was rush hour, and traffic was heavy. A large white bus stopped and the driver motioned for me to continue crossing; by that time, I had crossed four lanes of traffic. When I stepped out from in front of the large white bus, I noticed a car coming at a high rate of speed. I quickly thought, *This car isn't going to stop, and I can't go back,* because the white bus had started to move. So I took off in a sprint. I thought I had made it, but the lady driving the car, going about 45 mph, hit me and catapulted me onto the hood, where my head broke the windshield.

A crowd quickly surrounded me, and though I was dazed and bleeding, my only thought was that I needed to go to the office. A gentleman told me to wait for the ambulance. When the police officers and EMS arrived, they were utterly surprised that I hadn't been killed, paralyzed, or had any bones broken.

The ambulance took me to the emergency room, where they put stitches in my head in three different places, each having no more than four stitches. I was held overnight for observation and then released. When I told my son about the accident, he told my grandson, Matthew, that grandpa had been in an accident and was hurt.

That evening, Matthew told my daughter-in-law, "Tell grandpa that he needs to hold grandma's hand when he crosses the street." This made me laugh and then made me think. Sometimes an out-of-control "driver" in our profession will hit us. To make it through this world, we, as superintendents, need the Lord to hold our hands as we cross these dangerous streets.

> *Lord I can't even walk without You holding my hand*
> *The mountain's too high and the valley's too wide.*
> *Down on my knees, I learned to stand.*
> *Because I can't even walk without you holding my hand.*
> –Colbert & Joyce Croft

**The Lord is our friend who holds our hand,
and we need him every second of the day.**

OCTOBER

Breaking Habits

But I say unto you, That whosoever looketh on a woman to lust after her hath committed adultery with her already in his heart. **Matthew 5:28**

Several years ago, a prominent religious figure was twice exposed for shameful actions. Ashamed, alone, and afraid, he wrestled with a particular temptation, preached against this temptation, and prayed for the Lord to deliver him from it.

When did his problem escalate to the point of becoming a demonic lure to him? As a teenager, he started to look at pornographic magazines. This filled his mind with diabolic garbage and the enemy would use this lure on him in a moment of weakness. Ultimately, it drove him to destroy all he held near and dear.

Are the words from Matthew 5:28 enough to compel you to stop looking at pornography? Are you willing to still drink from the spring of sexual slavery? Sometimes, the consequences are hard to see but they come in the form of lost opportunities for real intimacy with your spouse. Your marriage is harmed every time you look for other comparisons as you will start to desire your mate less and less. You will start to become extremely critical of your wife, so you justify your actions to follow after other women. The sad part is that you will never know what your marriage could have become because you started to destroy its foundation by one visual turn-on at a time.

If this is you, turn to God in repentance and ask Him for a clean heart. Then go to your house and fulfill God's word by "loving your wives, just as Christ loved the church" (Ephesians 5:25).

> *Satan led my soul astray, from the straight and narrow way;*
> *But to Jesus I did pray, He heard my prayer,*
> *Rescued me that very day,*
> *Praise God I'm free, I've been set free by the grace of God.*
> —V. B. Ellis

Jesus is our only hope that we shall overcome. We may fall into sin; we may need to repent and be restored to favor with our Lord, but we shall also overcome.

Patient for Answers

Desire that you might be filled with knowledge of His will in all wisdom and spiritual understanding. **Colossians 1:9**

We have become accustomed to instant communication with high speed internet, text messaging, Facebook, email, and voice mail. We expect that our messages will be received quickly and that we should be able to have others respond to us as quickly. We can type a key word or Google a question on the internet to find several sites that will help us quickly get answers. Sometimes we expect that same reaction from God when we pray to Him. There are times God will tell us no and other times He may say yes. And other times we may get no response or we must wait for a response.

It has been my experience that when I was desperately in need of the Lord's strength, that is when the answers came quickly. Other times, my requests were not needed as quickly and did not come as quickly. The Lord did say, "In the day." I believe the Lord wants us to come to Him with any requests, but I also believe that he may want us to continue to do what we know is right. If there are times when we are conflicted about a direction then we need to examine His word.

Huge decisions should be made on whatever gives God the most glory. Again, we should start out with thanking God for everything He has already given and done for us. Then we can make known our requests, knowing that He knows what we need and what will be best for us. We may need to wait patiently for His direction and He may want us to continue working hard with no changes.

> *Patience in time of trouble,*
> *Trust and believe in Him*
> *And everything God has promised*
> *You will receive it right on time.*
> —D. McClurkin

Be careful for nothing
but in everything by prayer and supplication
with thanksgiving let your requests be made known unto God.
Philippians 4:6

A Wrinkle of Mine

To speak evil of no man, to be no brawlers, but gentle showing all meekness unto all men. **Titus 3:2**

The older I get and the more wrinkles on my face, the more I realize that my perception of time changes. Even though I exercise most days, my body still ages. There are some of my body parts that sag where there use to be tone. My physical body seems to get weaker. And yet my spiritual body seems to get stronger as I get older. It is the values I have come to understand that dictate a more gracious and gentle spirit.

The Lord's faithfulness to me when I do not deserve it makes me feel an overwhelming gratefulness. My spirit is a quiet soul that cares and is compassionate for those in need. So many people demonstrate a similar compassion that makes me see the Lord's power in our lives. I hope I wear the wrinkles of others to whom I have shown compassion and hopefully ease their burdens at times.

There are other times when my spirit is troubled, often because of situations that have happened to me or decisions I have to make. I know that there are different ways to perceive these situations. As a favorite supervisor once said to me, "I am not here to make you happy. Only you control that." There is some truth to his statement. There are times that things do happen and I can't control it or people say things that are hurtful. But I do have the choice to decide what to do about those situations and how to look at them.

Perhaps the people have so many of their own problems that they have no way to tell that they are hurting me. Or there is a grain of truth in what they say and I may need to reassess myself and ways I might change for my own growth. I can decide how I will perceive others' actions as well as decisions I need to make. I never want to hurt others, so I will always reflect on my own actions.

Dear God help me be stronger
Help me to process through my hurt
Help me to be the person that truly forgives and forgets
Help me to heal through all of life's pain.

For our light affliction, which is but for a moment, worketh for us a far more exceeding and eternal weight of glory. II Corinthians 4:17

Convenient Followers

Finally, brethren, pray for us, that the word of the Lord may have free course, and be glorified, even as it is with you. II Thessalonians 3:1

Do not turn away from needs of other people just because it is inconvenient. I am always amazed at the disciples for leaving their jobs and families to follow Jesus. It could not have been convenient for them. They were probably young adults helping out in the family business and getting ready to start their own family.

Even today, we have missionaries who leave their comfortable and familiar surroundings in order to spread God's word. It can't be convenient for them to leave everything they know, travel away from their family to areas that are very primitive and sometimes even dangerous. Even if we don't travel long distances for God, we may find that opportunities to serve God are not convenient for us either.

My church has many opportunities to serve God such as feeding our youth on Sunday nights, visiting members in nursing homes and shut-ins at home, service Sundays to do projects in the community, and volunteering with Houses for Humanity. All of these opportunities have regular schedules and the members can sign up when it is convenient in their schedules. But we also have opportunities that are unplanned. Some of these are helping with families who have a sick member or have experienced a death in the family.

These are times when the church community can step forward and help. It may not be convenient with the members' other obligations in their lives, but the illnesses and death were not convenient in the lives of our fellow church members. The Lord doesn't ask us to help just when it is convenient for us.

He wants us to be open to opportunities to help at all times.
It may not be on the mountain's height,
Or over the stormy sea;
It may not be at the battle's front,
My Lord will have need of me;
But if by a still, small voice He calls,
To paths that I do not know,
I'll answer, dear Lord, with my hand in Thine,
I'll go where You want me to go.
−Mary Brown

For we are his workmanship, created in Christ Jesus unto good works, which God hath before ordained that we should walk in them. Ephesians 2:10

Put Away Lying Lips

Wherefore putting away lying, speak every man truth with his neighbor: for we are members one of another. Ephesians 4:25

One day, a Sunday School teacher asked the students in his elementary class this question, "Would any of you tell a lie for a dollar?" The students said in unison, "No sir, Mr. Smith." "Would any of you tell a lie for ten dollars?" the teacher asked. "No sir, Mr. Smith," they all replied, shaking their heads. "Well would any of you tell a lie for $100?" The whole class was silent for quite a while. Then one little girl said, "No, Mr. Smith, I wouldn't, for when the $100 is gone, the lie is still there." "That is correct," said Mr. Smith. "When the money is all gone, the lie is still there.

Remember, the Lord has said that we must give an account for every word spoken. There is only one way which we can escape being judged for our lies. That is by telling Jesus all about them and asking Him to forgive us for them. And He has promised us that He would forgive us our sins as we confess them unto Him."

This story was about a Sunday School class and teacher but does that hold true with superintendents and other CEOs. Proverbs 12:22 says, "Lying lips are abomination to the Lord" and Proverbs 13:5 says, "A righteous man hateth lying." Proverbs 12:19 says, "The lips of truth shall be established forever." And, remember, DO NOT LIE is the 9th commandment. Vossler gives nine reasons superintendents should always tell the truth:

1. Truth is right and lying is wrong.
2. Lies will come back to haunt you.
3. Lies weigh you and others down.
4. Lies prevent you from developing as an administrator and person.
5. Truth enhances your reputation.
6. Truth will make true relationships for you.
7. You will feel better about yourself.
8. One truth, telling a lie makes the next one easier.
9. Your truth makes it easier for others to tell the truth.

Don't let lying lips separate you from God, from your family, your profession, and from your community.

Nothing between my soul and my Savior,
Naught of this world's delusive dream
I have renounced all sinful pleasure
Jesus is mine, there's nothing between.

It is through being truthful that you make needed changes
and accomplish many things you want in life.
–Bill Vossler

October 6

Fight the Extra Round

Be of good courage and He shall strengthen your heart, all ye that hope in the Lord. **Psalm 31:24**

When prize fighter James Corbett was asked what it takes to become a champion, he replied, "Fight one more round."

Did you know that: 1) Jim Abbot was a one-handed baseball player who overcame adversity and pitched on the U. S. Olympic team and for several years in the major leagues. 2) Thomas Edison, the great inventor, made 1000 unsuccessful attempts at inventing the light bulb before he succeeded. 3) Winston Churchill failed the 6th grade and was defeated in every election for public office until he became Prime Minister at age 62. He later wrote, "Never give in, never give in, never, never, never –in nothing, great or small, large or petty—never give in except to convictions of honor and good sense." 4) Abraham Lincoln was a failure as a businessman, impractical to be a successful lawyer and defeated in every attempt when running for public office except when he ran for President. 5) Albert Einstein did not read until he was 7 and he was described by teachers as mentally slow, expelled from school, and was refused admittance to the Zurich Polytechnic School. 6) Louis Pasteur was a mediocre student and ranked 15th out of 22 students in chemistry. 7) Henry Ford failed and went broke five times before he succeeded. 8) R. H. Macy failed seven times before his store in New York City caught on. 9) Vince Lombardi was described by an expert of only possessing minimal football knowledge and lacks motivation. 10) Michael Jordan and Bob Cousy were each cut from their high school basketball team. 11) Enrico Caruso was a factory worker who studied voice for 12 years before getting his first small break. 12) Gershwin composed 100 songs before he sold one and that was for $5.

When you look at the lives of those who you most admire, you will find out that they spent years climbing and surmounting obstacles, facing their deepest fears, learning from repeated failures, and rising above the predictions of those who said, "You'll never make it." They were like the little engine who said, "I knew I could."

Successful superintendents realize that success is sweat, perspective, dirt under your fingernails, holes in the knees of your pants, and worn out shoes. In essence, their success is blood, sweat, and tears. It is an inner discipline, a commitment, and a vision. It's bulldog tenacity.

Don't be discouraged if your dream has not come true. Keep pursuing it and pray over it daily. Study and learn. Grow by experience and keep working.

Too Many Sunsets Lie Behind The Mountain
Too Many Rivers My Feet Have Walked Through
Too Many Treasures Are Waiting Over Yonder
There's Too Much To Gain To Lose.
—Dottie Rambo

Victory always goes to the man or woman who's willing to "fight one more round."

Doing the Right Thing

Every way of a man is right in his own eyes: but the Lord pondereth the hearts.
Proverbs 21:2

The news for the past year in Wisconsin was about the Governor's proposal to curb the teacher's union's ability to negotiate job benefits raised teacher unrest and they tried to recall him through a special election. The union would still be allowed to negotiate salaries but that, in essence, would be all. The teachers and other unions cried "foul" and said that it's "union busting." The Governor said that it was because the state was three billion dollars in debt and one of the reasons was the union benefits.

Big name union leaders (such as the head of the AFL-CIO), other unions, community organizers, rabble-rousers and sympathizers came in from all over the nation and stormed the capital. The union sympathizers were either flown in, driven in, or bussed in. The protests were so hot that civility was lost with signs calling the Governor vicious names. Fourteen Democratic senators fled the state and were in Illinois so a vote couldn't be taken on the bill. The Democrats called them heroes and the Republicans called them cowards who were trying to circumvent democracy. The Governor campaigned on his promise to get the state out of debt. It was a mess and both sides thought they were right.

Every man has a high opinion of him/herself and their own ways, but they should consider, and keep uppermost in their mind, that God weighs and tests the hearts. Some people are very sincere and some are agitators.

As a superintendent, you will make a decision that you feel is best for the district and students but will raise people's emotions. You will have supporters, but if the noise of the non-supporters is loud, then it will drown out the voice of the supporters. You might feel all alone in your spirit but if you can go home, look in a mirror and say, "I've done what is right and students come first in all decisions," then your heart is right. Remember God sees all hearts.

> *Let me walk blessed Lord, in the way Thou has gone,*
> *Leading straight to the land above;*
> *Giving cheer everywhere, to sad and the lone,*
> *Fill my way every day with love.*
> –G. W. Sebren

That old law about 'an eye for an eye' leaves everybody blind.
The time is always right to do the right thing.
–Martin Luther King, Jr.

Again and again, the impossible problem is solved
when we see that the problem is only a tough decision waiting to be made.
–Robert Schuller

Cleaning off the Desk

He also that received seed among the thorns is he that hears the word; and the care of this world, and the deceitfulness of riches, choke the word, and he becomes unfruitful. **Matthew 13:22**

This morning, I woke up and my wife asked me if I was busy. I knew what that meant; she had chores for me to do. She wanted to clean up the office. What that means is that I have to make a choice in what I want to keep and what I want to throw away. Sometimes, I haven't looked at reports, studies, or policies for several months and they just lay there. But when I see them, I think that I will need it. So I let them lay on my desk in a pile. As the saying goes, "Out of sight, out of mind." My wife told me that I'm just like those "clutteraholics" on TV. We worked hard and cleaned out two storage boxes. This is a habit that I've gotten into and I have to work on keeping the office clean by filing and throwing away items that are old or outdated.

I also have to practice this at work. My desk gets so cluttered that I finally have to clean it all off. I say that I will keep it that way but in one week it is back to a mess. My goal is to keep it clean. I know that people judge you by how neat you keep your office which confirms a study that found a clean office was related to promotions.

This clutter happens to us in our personal life and spiritual life. We tend to get so cluttered in our lives and so there is no time for God or family. This clutter is, in essence, getting ourselves so involved in activities that we don't have time for God or family. When that happens, we have to throw away those things that are taking up unnecessary space and rearrange those that are important. We are spiraling out of control when we let excessive activities come into our lives. It pushes away God, our family, and friends. It's a downhill slippery slide. Ask God to help you take the clutter out of your life and to put Him first and your family second.

> *Have you cares of business, cares of pressing debt?*
> *Cares of social life or cares of hope unmet?*
> *Are you by remorse or sense of guilt depressed?*
> *Come right on to Jesus, He will give you rest.*
> –Charles Jones

Certainly this is a duty, not a sin. "Cleanliness is indeed next to godliness."
–John Wesley

Heavy Handed Supervision

And he spake to them after the counsel of the young men, saying, My father made your yoke heavy, and I will add to your yoke: my father also chastised you with whips but I will chastise you with scorpions. **1 Kings 12:14**

When King Rehoboam followed the advice of his young counselors instead of the old counselors, the people rebelled. He had to flee for his life from Jerusalem. Israel became split at that time and only the tribe of Judah followed King Rehoboam.

Experienced superintendents know that when they use a heavy hand for disciplinary measures, they will have negative results. For example, the superintendent who makes the most noise about principals or other administrators about being late to a meeting probably does not have a good track record himself. When a doctor's note is needed for every medical absence, absenteeism does not always decline but morale declines.

Safety measures are not always followed by lower level administrators whose superintendent threatens them with non-compliance. Why is this so? One good explanation for this paradoxical behavior is that extreme disciplinary measures can have the unintended effect of making employees feel less cared for and accountable.

Superintendents will benefit from the following suggestions: 1) Make your policies clear. 2) Rules should be explained by the superintendent. 3) Superintendents need to strive for employee cooperation. 4) Superintendents have to enforce rules evenly and fairly.

Many times, this is the mistake of new and younger superintendents. It is always wise to consult with older and more experienced superintendents. My mentor was Dr. Clarence Oliver, Jr. and his advice kept me "on the straight and narrow." Finally, always remember the Golden Rule, "Do unto others as you would have them do unto you."

> *There is joy divine that is ever mine,*
> *Since the Lord has forgiven me,*
> *I work and sign for my blessed King,*
> *He has grace I have been made free.*
> —Byron Whitworth

If your people are not loyal and there is low morale,
it's probably your leadership style.

Why Worry or Fret

The Lord is my shepherd I shall not want. **Psalms 23:1**

The Lord is our shepherd and as sheep leads us besides "still waters." Why do we, as superintendents or just people, want to worry about the situations in life? If God can feed the sparrows, he can provide for all our needs. The leading cause of stress is worry.

Worry is unscriptural and the opposite of faith. Worry is unhelpful and has never solved a problem. It can't change what happened yesterday or what is going to happen tomorrow. It will only mess up today for you. Worry is unhealthy.

Stress caused from worry is associated with all sorts of bodily ailments. The root cause of worry is our fear of losing control. Worry is an attempt to control the uncontrollable. Worry begins when we want to play God.

The shepherd protects the sheep and guides the sheep into safe places. The role of the sheep is to follow the shepherd.

He shall feed his flock like a shepherd: he shall gather the lambs with his arm, and carry [them] in his bosom, [and] shall gently lead those that are with young.
Isaiah 40:11

Worry is unnecessary if the Lord is your shepherd. "I am the good shepherd, and know my sheep, and am known of mine" (John 10:14). "My sheep hear my voice, and I know them, and they follow me" (John 10:27). As sheep, we will have to do the following to overcome worry:

a) Personally know the shepherd;

b) Listen to God; and

c) Do what God says…Obey! Remember, trust in a God who knows what lies ahead.

When trouble is in my way I can't tell my night from day,
When I'm tossed from side to side like a ship on a raging tide.
I don't worry, I don't fret my God has never failed me yet
Troubles come from time to time but that's all right,
I'm not the worrying kind because I've got confidence,
God is gonna see me through no matter what the case may be
I know He's gonna fix it for me.
–Andrea Crouch

God's secret … do life one day at a time.

Be Wise: Study Your Profession

The wisdom of the prudent is to understand his way: but the folly of fools is deceit. **Proverbs 14:8**

I was talking with the men's basketball coach at the university where I teach about the coaching process. He informed me that after every game the coaching staff comes in and watches the film to see where the team can improve. He also said that when they go into the locker room at half-time, adjustments are made. In addition to this, they scout other teams and watch films of those teams so he knows how to coach effectively against that opponent. He said, "I would be a fool if I didn't do that. My tenure as a coach would be very short as I would end up losing more often than winning."

Great philosophers and inventors continually worked to understand the ways of man. From Socrates to Plato to Edison to Einstein, these men sought to find the answer and understand the nature of man and the universe. They contributed much to the life and advancement of the 21st century man.

The effective superintendent of schools analyzes the data and communicates this with his stakeholders on how to narrow the "achievement gap" and how to continue to increase learning. This is especially true in our time of budget crunch. These prudent superintendents become "students" in all facets of schooling so that they can effectively lead their school. The foolish superintendent "shoots from the hip" and does not make himself a scholar of schooling.

King Solomon realized that a mark of being wise and prudent was to continually work towards improvement and to understand why things were like they were. He saw that people, whom he called "fools" tried to place the blame elsewhere, not work for improvement, and "spin" the truth. Paul wrote in II Timothy 2:15, "Study to shew thyself approved unto God, a workman that needs not to be ashamed, rightly dividing the word of truth."

We analyze and intellectualize
What we do not understand
We need God's wisdom in our hearts
Not the intellect of man
I wonder how almighty God
All knowing and divine
How He could care about my world
And give undivided time.
                                        –M S. Lowndes

A wise man can see more from the bottom of a well
than a fool can from a mountain top.
                                        –Unknown

Guarantees

Blessed is he that readeth, and they that hear the words of this prophecy, and keep those things which are written therein: for the time is at hand.
Revelations 1:3

How many of us like guarantees? I know superintendents always look at guarantees when they buy a product for the district. If we buy a product, we like to know that if it does not work then it can be returned and replaced. We can even buy an extended warranty for some products so that we are guaranteed to have it work or repaired at no cost. I see the commercials on television that offer your satisfaction or your money back guaranteed. All of these are done to assure us that we will be satisfied with the product. Other guarantees, we realize, are not sure things. If you gamble or buy lottery tickets, there is no guarantee that you will win anything. In fact, the odds are against you winning anything. There is no guarantee with those types of purchases or expenses.

The Bible gives us several guarantees. One is that when we read the prophecy in Revelations, we will be blessed. It makes me feel good to get blessings and guarantees. There are several other guarantees in the Bible. If I believe in Jesus as the one who died for my sins and accept him as my Savior, then I am guaranteed eternal life. Who would want to turn down eternal life? Even if you are not sure of the concept of eternal life, wouldn't you want to place your odds on that then to find out later that you were wrong? I like my extended warranty of eternal life.

Another guarantee is that the meek shall inherit the earth. "Blessed are the meek; for they shall inherit the earth" (Mark 5:5). The idea of being meek does not fit well with our society today. Many people admire those who have been powerful and make great investments for themselves—the type of great investments that make them rich materially on this earth. But that is not the type of investments or the character that is guaranteed anything in the Bible. "Be not thou afraid when one is made rich, when the glory of his house is increased: For when he dieth he shall carry nothing away; his glory shall not descend after him" (Psalms 49: 16-17). In fact, the Bible states that the first shall be last and the last shall be first. "If any man desire to be first, the same shall be last of all, and servant of all." Mark 9:35. God is looking for those who are meek and are willing to invest in the needs of others so that they may also be guaranteed eternal life.

I am reminded of the song "I Never Promised You a Rose Garden" when I think of guarantees. My Lord did not promise me that life on earth would be easy and that there would be no hurts. He did promise to be with me throughout any of those hurts and sadness. Further, He guarantees that in the eternal life there will be no sadness.

For the Lamb, which is in the midst of the throne shall feed them,
and shall lead them unto living fountain of waters:
and God shall wipe away all tears from their eyes. Revelation 7:17

Above Reproach

A bishop then must be blameless, the husband of one wife, vigilant, sober, of good behavior, given to hospitality, apt to teach. **I Timothy 3:2**

In 2007, the superintendent of Wayne Township, Indiana, negotiated a lucrative retirement package whenever he decided to retire. Just after he retired the Board realized how generous the superintendent's retirement package was—over $1 million. His retirement deal included a year's pay at $225,000 as well as contract provisions that provided hundreds of thousands more. In addition, the contract created a superintendent emeritus position that has been paying the superintendent $1,352 a day for 150 days since his retirement. Also, the contract provided for a onetime $15,000 stipend for "retirement planning." The board has issued a statement that said,

"We are disappointed in what we have learned is the financial impact of —-'s contract. We believe that his continued employment is not in the best interest of the school district, and today we asked for his resignation as superintendent emeritus."

During the superintendent's 15 years at Wayne Township, this superintendent had earned the Board and the community's respect. He was named superintendent of the year in 2010. A board member, not on the board in 2007 said, "It's a terribly difficult time because the superintendent did such terrifically wonderful things for Wayne Township."

A spokesperson for the district said, "Board members signed off on the provisions of the contract when it was opened in 2007 at the superintendent's request. But they did so without full knowledge of the information tucked into the lengthy documents that the superintendent asked them to approve at several meetings. The board didn't have the opportunity to get a full sense of the economic impact of the entire contract." The board trusted the Superintendent.

What makes this worse is that Wayne Township had to recently eliminate some programs, freeze administrators' pay, and reduce some teaching positions. This is not a new phenomenon with superintendents as a highly respected superintendent of the Russellville School District retired in 2006 with a healthy retirement package that even had the state legislators talking about it.

The Bible says that you are to have good behavior and, in fact, one translation use the words, "above reproach." Don't let greed, envy, selfishness, or any other negative trait cause you to lose your reputation from which you can never recover.

Yield not to temptation, for yielding is sin,
Each victory will help you, some others to win,
Fight manfully onward, dark passions subdue,
Look ever to Jesus, He'll carry you thru.
                                                        –H. R Palmer.

To hazard much to get much has more of avarice than wisdom.
                                                        –William Penn

Following the Voice of God

Now the Lord said to Abram, "Go from your country and your kindred and your father's house to the land that I will show you." **Genesis 12:1**

Abram lived in the land of Ur which is now the region of Iraq. All of his family was there. God told him to leave and go to a place he had never been and leave his family. The Lord told him he would make him a great nation and bless him. So, Abram obeyed God and left taking his wife and Lot, his grandson. Just think about leaving family and not being able to see them for a long time. That is a tough decision to make. This proves that Abram believed in and trusted God to direct and guide him.

In 1983, I left all my family who lived in the northwest and my wife and I moved to the Midwest. I had accepted an administrative job in a private school. I knew that if I left, it would be hard to "go back home" because we had five children and it was a long ways away. There were hard times along the way, but we learned to trust in God and in each other to help us over the bumps along the way. As I got close to retirement age, I asked my wife if she would like to retire back in the Northwest. She said that we can't because all of our children and grandchildren live in the Midwest.

As a superintendent, you will have to make a tough choice knowing that it might take you to a different state or a different position in life. That is when you "just trust God." I have heard young administrators say that they could not go to that state or move over there because it was too far from home. They have turned down some excellent jobs which they could have had if they had the courage to just "take the step." In whatever you do, trust God and believe in Him, he will direct guide your steps and direct your paths.

> *No matter what may be the test,*
> *God will take care of you;*
> *Lean, weary one, upon his breast,*
> *God will take care of you.*
> —W. S. Martin

Failure to follow God's voice will make you susceptible to worldly sirens.

Financial Diligence

In the house of the wise are stores of choice food and oil, but a foolish man devours all he has. **Proverbs 21:20**

The recent financial crisis brought a reality check to many of us. We can't continue to live like each year will bring us more than the last year. Proverbs 21:20 reminds me of the power that we amass when we live below our financial means. Are we devouring all that we have? Are we willing to learn to live so that we can create surpluses of our finances and resources?

A recent community forum discussed a proposal by the superintendent to add staff (five K-3 staff, five technology coaches, two principals and a police officer, a coordinator for the AVID program). The cost was estimated at $665,000. This was coming at a time when the district was facing as much as a $1.6 million in cuts this year. The school district to the north, of similar size, had to cut 27 positions from its classroom staff.

As a superintendent, you have to make certain you don't foolishly squander your district's resources. Sometimes, something might look right but isn't because you haven't looked at the big picture and the implications. If, in your own home, you use up all of your resources, you will end up filing bankruptcy. This is not wisdom.

Proverbs 8:12 (NIV) says, "I, wisdom, dwell together with prudence; I possess knowledge and discretion." Proverbs 8:23 says, "A prudent man foresees the evil, and hideth himself; but the simple pass on and are punished." A final Proverb says, "The rich ruleth over the poor and borrower is servant to the lender."

As with this superintendent above, too many people think you can buy now and pay later. This is not so! I was hired as superintendent of a district that was in financial distress because of this type of thinking. To get the district back in the black, I had to file a plan with the state department of education. This foolish spending caused us to close a school and to RIF several teachers. No one was a winner. Use financial diligence and be the leader God called you to be.

Manifest plainness,
Embrace simplicity,
Reduce selfishness,
Have few desires.

Economy is half the battle of life;
it is not so hard to earn money as to spend it well.
–C. H. Spurgeon

I Can

***Cast not away therefore your confidence, which hath great recompense of reward.* Hebrews 10:35**

Have you ever doubted yourself? If you have, then say, "I Can" and decide in yourself to be an achiever. The Little Engine had many trials and could not make it over the mountain. But he kept trying. Going up the mountain he puffed, "I think I can, I think I can, I think I can," and, when he reached the top, he went down the mountain saying, "I knew I could, I knew I could, I knew I could…" The Little Engine never gave up and believed "he could."

In Colorado, there is a flower that grows at the timberline called Saxifrage. This flower grows in and under conditions that you would think would be impossible to grow. The seeds of the plant lodges in the rocks and the roots go deep into the rock. Scientists in the beginning said, "It can't grow out of a rock." But it does, and the flower blooms in the Spring. In fact, the name of the plant Saxifrage means "rock breaker."

You, too, can be a rock breaker. Break out of acceptable limitations and from the negative naysayers. Just like this plant faces impossibilities, every person on this earth faces "impossible" situations. You will face "impossible" situations on your job and hear the voices of people who say, "That won't work, we've tried it before."

If you limit yourself to the standard limitations, then you will listen to the enemy who wants you to be "average." The Bible says you can "do all things through Christ." Look at all of the great inventors, they said "I CAN" instead of "I CAN'T."

I have assurance sweet, a solace most complete,
And I go onward singing His praise;
My Lord is at my side as my unfailing guide,
And He will keep me all of my days.
–Byron Whitworth

The difference between the impossible and the possible
lie's in a man's determination.
–Tommy Lasorda

Garden Growth

So then neither is he that planteth any thing, neither he that watereth; but God gave the increase. I Corinthians 3:7

In the early part of spring, I look forward to working in my flower gardens. I am always amazed that many small weeds sprout up from the hard ground. Many of my plants look dry and dead and yet, the weeds are green.

The plants first need to be cut back with the removal of the dead portions so that new growth will start again. As I pull out the weeds and cultivate the soil, I am reminded of God's work in my life.

God must also wonder when I show my immaturity in my Christian life, when I do not forgive quickly or I try to control things instead of allowing God to work. My weeds of pride and unrest seem to flourish in the hard ground of life.

I need to remember that God will continue to help me grow. He may have to remove the weeds around me. I need to ask Him to give me a heart that is willing to grow in His grace and show a life full of His glory.

As spring and summer advance, I am so awed by the beautiful flowers. The careful attention to watering and fertilizing has paid off. God also has plans for us, that if we allow He will share the beauty in His plans. He will reward our labor for Him. The reward, I believe, will be unique to each of His laborers. Plant your spiritual garden God's way.

Plant three rows of peas: Peace of mind; Peace of heart; Peace of soul
Plant four rows of squash: Squash gossip; Squash indifference;
Squash grumbling; Squash selfishness
Plant four rows of lettuce: Lettuce be faithful; Lettuce be kind;
Lettuce be obedient; Lettuce love one another
No garden without turnips: Turnip for meetings; Turnip for service;
Turnip to help one another
Water freely with patience and cultivate with love. There is much fruit in your
garden because you reap what you sow.
To conclude our garden we must have thyme: Thyme for God;
Thyme for study; Thyme for prayer.
–Unknown

But as it is written, eye hath not seen nor ear heard,
neither have entered into the heart of man,
the things which God hath prepared for them that love him. I Corinthians 2:9

Theo-Centered and Not Self-Centered

The Lord also will be a refuge for the oppressed, a refuge in times of trouble. And they that know thy name will put their trust in thee for thou Lord hast not forsaken them that seek thee. Psalm 9:9-10

Children's songs that I learned in Sunday school as a child still help me as an adult. When I am busy looking at myself and feeling sorry for myself because of earthly circumstances, I am reminded of a song, "Count your many blessings, name them one by one." I am sure, as a child, the song was just fun to sing because of the melody and the words did not carry the same meaning as they do to me as an adult.

It is now a gentle reminder that my focus belongs not on my troubles, or on myself even, but a realization that the Lord has given me many blessings and I should be thinking about Him. It is so easy to feel sorry for ourselves. But when we do center our thoughts on ourselves, we are not trusting God. We are not listening to our Lord as He tries to show us what He wants from us.

Hide not they face far from me, put not thy servant away in anger; thou hast been my help; leave me not, neither forsake me, O God of my salvation. Psalm 27:9

Job had severe troubles and his friends were not much help to him. His friends said he must have brought on his own troubles because of his sins. They even said that if God really gave him what he deserved because of his sins, it should have been worse. Those words did not help Job work through his sorrow.

His comfort came as he said he would trust in his Lord no matter what happened to him. He also had to take the focus from himself and center his thoughts on the Lord. If we are self-centered, then we are making decisions that are selfish and not connected to how we can help others and serve our Lord. The times we become self-absorbed, either in our misery or our plenty, are the times we are not giving God the glory. God wants our attention and passion. As a superintendent, does your comfort come from your trust in the Lord? If not, make that decision to turn everything over to Jesus.

> *Jesus, lover of my soul,*
> *Let me to Thy bosom fly,*
> *While the nearer waters roll,*
> *While the tempest still is high.*
> *Hide me, O my Savior, hide,*
> *Till the storm of life is past;*
> *Safe into the haven guide;*
> *Oh, receive my soul at last.*
> —Charles Wesley

Yea, they shall sing in the ways of the Lord
for great is the glory of the Lord. Psalm 138:5

Revealed

These shall make war with the Lamb and the Lamb shall overcome them, for He is Lord of lords, and King of kings and they that are with Him are called, and chosen, and faithful. **Revelations 17:14**

The word revelation means revealed. When I think of something being revealed, I think of something shown and made clear. People reveal the beauty of a precious stone covered in mud when they clean off the dirt. People reveal a priceless antique when they find it buried amongst the junk in an attic. People reveal their character by their actions over time. People reveal their dreams when they tell others about those hopes and dreams. People reveal their illness when they describe their symptoms to their doctor. People reveal their weaknesses and sins when they name the sins while asking for Jesus' forgiveness.

The word of God reveals the past, the present, and the future. There are clear signs given in the Bible to reveal God's purpose. We can understand those signs and God's purpose when we read the Bible. We can understand His word as He reveals it to us when we ask for that understanding of His word.

Jesus revealed to his disciples as well as the church at that time that He was the Christ. He continues to reveal that to people today. He shows how precious each of us are to him when He cleans away our sins. He shows how priceless and precious we are when he knows even the number of hairs on our head. He knows our character and our intentions as we serve others and Him with our gifts and service. He knows our dreams and inner thoughts. He knows our weaknesses and will provide us strength. He forgives our sins and loves us.

It is no secret what God can do
What He's done for others, He will do for you
With arms wide open He'll pardon you,
It is no secret what God can do.
–Stuart Hamblen

When it is evening ye say, It will be fair weather:
for the sky is red. And in the morning,
It will be foul weather today for the sky is red and lowering.
O ye hypocrites, ye can discern the face of the sky,
but can ye not discern the signs of the times. Matthew 16:2-3

Is Your Quiet Comforting?

And that you study to be quiet and do you own business, and to work with your own hands as we command you. **I Thessalonians 4:11**

If it is completely quiet in your house, is it a reflective time for you? Does the stillness amplify the outside, unknown noises of possible dangers or the inside noises of our own fears? Do you hear sounds that scare you? Do the sounds mean there are things than you can't see that will hurt you? I can remember when I was little and I would hear scratching on my windows at night. I was sure that something was trying to get inside my room and hurt me. It wasn't until I was older that I realized there were branches that blew against the window at times and other times there were leaves that blew against the window.

And the work of righteousness shall be peace, and the effect of righteousness, quietness, and assurance forever. Isaiah 32:17

The idea of sitting in silence still scares some people and even I do not like it at times. I am becoming more comfortable with the quiet and I even find that I appreciate the quiet at times. I have learned to listen for God's word in the silence. The quiet is appreciated after many family members have been together and there had been lots of noise in the house. When everyone leaves, a house can seem still and quiet. Those are times that it either feels lonely or like a relief from the loud noises.

Lead a quiet and peaceable life in all godliness and honesty. I Timothy 2:2

A quiet life is good and a way to enjoy peace. So when I find myself with quiet times, I remember that the Lord has blessed me with this time to be more reflective on His will and His goodness towards me. Superintendents also need that quiet time to refresh and reflect.

There is a quiet place
Far from the rapid pace
Where God can soothe my troubled mind
Sheltered by tree and flower
With Him my cares are left behind.
–Ralph Carmichael

The words of wise men are heard in quiet
more than the cry of him that ruleth among fools. Ecclesiastes 9:17

Jesus's Job

And it came to pass that after three days they found Him in the temple, sitting in the midst of the doctors, both hearing them, and asking them questions. And all that heard him were astonished at his understanding and answers. And when they say him, they were amazed: and His mother said unto Him, Son, why had thou thus dealt with us? Behold thy father and I have sought thee sorrowing. And he said unto them, How is it that ye sought me? Wist ye not that I must be about my Father's business. Luke 2:46-49

One of Jesus's jobs was to make the word of God clear for us so we could understand it. When he was young and starting his ministry, his parents had lost Him and then found in the temple. This is a first glimpse of Jesus' job.

Jesus taught by stories and parables. He taught in temples, near rivers, and mountains, on a lake, and large grassy areas outside. The stories he taught were often connected with familiar things so that people could more easily grasp the meaning. He used stories of nature, wildlife, birds, planting, and feasts. The stories of the prodigal son, the vineyard, the good Samaritan, the widow's mite, the unjust steward were taught so that we could know what was right. Jesus' job also was a model for how we should live and behave. He taught by his actions and his reactions to others that He met on his journey.

I must preach the kingdom of God to other cities also: for therefore am I sent.
Luke 4:43

Jesus also gave specific directions on how to live a good and faithful life. He provided specific ways to live. He described how we were to treat others and to trust in the Lord. He warned us of things to beware and not let into our lives. Jesus healed those who were sick. He calmed the waters and provided comfort to those in need. And he forgave the sinner. Jesus was a teacher, a doctor, a preacher, a counselor, a friend, a Savior. He continues to reach out to others to give salvation.

I came not to call the righteous but sinners to repentance. Luke 6:32

I've been reading, and I've been feeding, upon the precious Word of God.
Marvelous story, so full of glory; It is the path that Jesus trod.
He was man's deliverer, and sin forgiver, every problem He understood.
Everywhere He went, my Lord was doing good.
                                                            –Unknown

The spirit of the Lord is upon me,
because he hath anointed me to preach the gospel to the poor,
he hath sent me to heal the brokenhearted,
to preach deliverance to the captives,
and recovering of sight to the blind,
to set at liberty them that are bruised. Luke 4:18

Created to Glorify God

So God created man in his own image, in the image of God created he him; male and female created he them. **Genesis 1:27**

The song, "Born to Serve the Lord," by Bud Chambers, best describes why we were created.

> *From the dust of the Earth*
> *God created man*
> *His breath made man a living soul*
> *And for God so loved the world*
> *He gave his only Son*
> *And that is why I love Him so*
>
> *My hand were made to help my neighbor*
> *My eyes were made to read God's Word*
> *My feet were made to walk in His footsteps*
> *My body is the temple of the Lord.*
>
> *I was made in His likeness*
> *Created in His image*
> *I was born to serve the Lord*
> *And I can't deny Him*
> *I'll always walk beside Him*
> *I was born to serve the Lord*

This song has many truths. We were made by God and for God. We were born to serve God, but only when we are born again are we able to serve God. Because we are born to serve God, when we do not, we will be chastised. Samson is a very good example of this. Samson was born to call God's people back to God.

Man stands apart from all other living creatures because of his relationship to God. Everything had already been created when God created man. Man was the crown of the physical creation and was designed to rule over it. In all God's creation, only man was made in God's image and likeness.

The message of the Bible shows that God created man with a mind capable of communicating with God and thinking like Him. God wants us to be more like Him in both character and in composition. Our destiny is to be like Jesus Christ now is, as the glorified Son of God. Ephesians 2:10 (NIV) says, "For we are God's workmanship, created in Christ Jesus to do good works."

If God had wanted to be a big secret,
He would not have created babbling brooks and whispering pines.
                                                    –Robert Brault

Keep the Sabbath

Ye shall fear every man, his mother, and his father, and keep my Sabbaths: I am the Lord your God. **Leviticus 19:2**

When the Lord was giving the law to the children of Israel, he gave them the commandment to "keep the Sabbath." In the New Testament, Jesus proclaimed Himself at the Lord of the Sabbath. The Sabbath day is a day of rest as God Himself rested on the seventh day.

The Sabbath day was required to remind the children of Israel of their freedom from bondage and slavery. Jesus was not a legalist, but kept the Sabbath, which was the fourth commandment. Why is the Sabbath important?

The Sabbath was created so we could have communion with God.
It is a time of reverence and meditation.
It is a holy convocation where we meet and worship with others.
It shows God that we love, honor, and respect His authority.
The Sabbath is a time for singing.
The Sabbath is a time for prayer.
The Sabbath is a time for rest and not to buy or sell.
The Sabbath is a day of delight and rejoice in which we forsake our
thoughts and words for God's thoughts and words.

Sunday is our time of worship. Take time to go to church and praise your Creator. Have you let the cares of this life push God out? Have you let other people push God out of your life? Remember to keep the Sabbath and go to church. It will feed your spiritual man and revive your human body.

There is a song that is taught to the children in Sunday School. It encourages the children to go to Sunday School and later to church.

Everybody ought to go to Sunday School,
Sunday School, Sunday School.
The mothers and the fathers,
and the boys and the girls,
everybody ought to go to Sunday School.

A world without a Sabbath would be like a man without a smile,
like a summer without flowers, and like a homestead without a garden.
It is the joyous day of the whole week.

–Henry Ward Beecher

Lord's World Series

For by grace are ye saved through faith; and that not of yourself, it is the gift of God: Not of works, lest any man should boast. **Ephesians 2:8-9**

The Texas Rangers and the St. Louis Cardinals were playing each other in the 2011 World Series. The Rangers won their division whereas the Cardinals had to make the World Series via the wild-card route. The fans are excited because both teams are from the mid-west and it is a familiar World Series team (Cardinals) against a fairly new World Series team (Rangers). As a school superintendent, you always play in the world series but it is only the grace of God that helps you win. The following analogy was utilized from *Cathy's World Index* (2009):

Dr. School Superintendent and the Lord stood by to observe a baseball game. The Lord's team was playing Satan's team. The Lord's team was at bat, the score was tied zero to zero, and it was the bottom of the 9th inning with two outs. They continued to watch as a batter, named *LOVE*, stepped up to the plate. *LOVE* swung at the first pitch and hit a single, because 'Love never fails.' The next batter was named *FAITH*, who also got a single because *FAITH* works with *LOVE*.

The next batter up was named *GODLY WISDOM*. Satan wound up and threw the first pitch. *GODLY WISDOM* looked it over and let it pass—ball one. Three more pitches and *GODLY WISDOM* walked because he never swings at what Satan throws. The bases were now loaded. The Lord then turned to Dr. School Superintendent and told him He was now going to bring in His star player. Up to the plate stepped *GRACE*. Dr. School Superintendent said, "He sure doesn't look like much!" Satan's whole team relaxed and laughed when they saw *GRACE*.

Thinking he had won the game, Satan wound up and fired his first pitch. To the shock of everyone, *GRACE* hit the ball harder than anyone had ever seen. But Satan was not worried; his center fielder let very few get by. He went up for the ball, but it went right through his glove, hit him on the head, and sent him crashing on the ground. The roaring crowds went wild as the ball continued over the fence ... for a home run! The Lord's Team won!!!

The Lord then asked Dr. School Superintendent if he knew why *LOVE*, *FAITH* and *GODLY WISDOM* could get on base but couldn't win the game. Dr. School Superintendent answered that he didn't know why. The Lord explained, "If your love, faith and wisdom had won the game, you would think you had done it by yourself. Love, Faith and Wisdom will get you on base but only My Grace can get you Home."

> *There is grace for every need,*
> *Grace for you, grace for me, keeping true,*
> *Keeping free, precious saving grace indeed,*
> *Flowing from the throne above, Grace to cover all my sins.*
> –Unknown

**Grace is the unmerited favor of God toward all men
displayed in His general care for them.**

Needing To Be Rebalanced

Now when Daniel knew that the writing was signed, he went into his house; and his windows being open in his chamber toward Jerusalem, he kneeled upon his knees three times a day, and prayed, and gave thanks before his God, as he did aforetime. **Daniel 6:10**

I had just purchased tires, had them spin-balanced, and then took off for a trip to Florida. It was Spring Break and we were looking forward to visiting our son and watching a Spring Training baseball game. The car was driving excellently and the ride was smooth. My wife was in the outside lane and the car ahead of her straddled a piece of tire rubber in the road to miss it. My wife did not see it fast enough and she ran over it, hitting the tire rubber with our car.

After our visit we were driving back from Florida and I was driving. It was early in the morning and was still dark, when I also hit a piece of tire rubber in the road that I did not see. After that, the car started to ride like you were driving on a "washboard". When I got home, I took the car into the tire shop and sure enough, I had lost a balance-weight on the front tire. Those pieces of truck tire that we had ran over had knocked off the tire balance-weight. The tire store rebalanced the tires and now the car runs smoothly again.

How often is that like our job as a superintendent? We arrive at our office in the morning, and all of a sudden we hit a piece of "truck tire." We say, "Where did that come from?" Then later on that day, we hit another piece. Then the day starts "running" rough. These unexpected bumps, trials, tribulations, no matter how small, can cause our "car" to ride rough. That is when you need to go to the "Lord's tire shop and get your tires rebalanced." The Lord will put your day back on track if you let him.

> *Now let us have a little talk with Jesus*
> *Let us tell Him all about our troubles,*
> *He will hear our faintest cry,*
> *He will answer by and by*
> *Now when you feel a prayer wheel turning*
> *Then you'll know a little fire is burning*
> *You will find a little talk with Jesus make it right.*
> —Cleavant Derricks

Jesus is a friend who watches day and night.

God is Fighting Your Battle

So the people shouted when the priests blew with the trumpets: and it came to pass when the people heard the sound of the trumpet, and the people shouted with a great shout, that the wall fell down flat, so that the people went up into the city, every man straight before him, and they took the city. **Joshua 6:20**

God told Joshua to take Jericho. It was a formidable city with huge walls. The outer walls were six feet thick and 20 feet high. The inner wall was 12 feet thick and 30 feet high. From a military standpoint, it was practically impenetrable. He had sent spies into the land to inspect the weak parts of the city and see if anyone could help them.

They found one person who would help them and her only request was that she and her family would be saved. The Israelites laid siege on the city and marched around it six days. On the 7th day, they marched around the city seven times, the priests sounded the horns, and the people were ordered to shout. The walls of that great city collapsed.

How many times do we face a Jericho in our life and on our job? Our path to victory involves confrontation, confidence, and conquest. The Israelites had determination. We need to be like the Israelites and simply do it God's way.

What is the stronghold in your life or job that needs conquering? Some superintendents try so hard. When you fight that personal battle, it spills over to the job and when you fight the battles on the job, they spill over to your personal life. Come to Jesus and lay down your sword and say, "Lord, I can't do it, but you can." He will change your life. When this happens listen to and obey God as He will knock down your walls!

> *Joshua fought the battle of Jericho,*
> *Jericho, Jericho,*
> *Joshua fought the battle of Jericho,*
> *And the walls came tumbling down!*
> *Right up to the walls of Jericho*
> *They marched with spear in hand;*
> *"Go blow them ram horns," Joshua cried,*
> *"'Cause the battle is in my hand.*
> *–Anonymous*

Obstacles don't have to stop you. If you run into a wall, don't turn around and give up. Figure out how to climb it, go through it, or work around it.
–Michael Jordan

Opportunity

Then Samson called to the LORD and said, "O Lord GOD, please remember me and please strengthen me only this once, O God, that I may be avenged on the Philistines for my two eyes." And Samson grasped the two middle pillars on which the house rested, and he leaned his weight against them, his right hand on the one and his left hand on the other. And Samson said, "Let me die with the Philistines." Then he bowed with all his strength, and the house fell upon the lords and upon all the people who were in it. So the dead whom he killed at his death were more than those whom he had killed during his life. Judges 16:28-30

As a high school principal, I had the opportunity to oversee the senior leadership team. I wanted to challenge students to want to be a part of a team. Success is where preparation meets opportunity, so I reminded students of the importance of preparing for every single opportunity that comes their way. I also reminded them of the importance of servant leadership and the value in possessing such qualities as boldness and humility. During their lives they would be faced with critical "moments" and the hard work and preparation they put in before those "moments" come would translate into opportunities for success.

I remember a hot May evening in College Station, Texas. It was the final game of the Baseball Regional Finals. The score was tied with two outs in the bottom of the 7th inning. Dallas, a member of my senior leadership team, was at bat. Dallas was one of those students that you just enjoyed being around. I couldn't help but worry about the pressure he was facing as the entire season was now on his shoulders. Right before Dallas stepped to the plate, his dad grabbed my arm and said, "Hey, Dallas is trying to get your attention." I looked up and Dallas pointed to his chest and mouthed the words, "This is my moment!" It wouldn't be easy for Dallas as the pitcher on the mound had committed to the University of Texas. However, one thing was certain. One of these young men were about to own the "moment." Dallas had worked hard to prepare for this opportunity, and on this night, Dallas' hard work paid off. Dallas took a first pitch fastball over the left field wall and we won the game 2-1.

As a superintendent, we face game changing moments all of the time. Sometimes they deal with curriculum, finance, or construction. We are asked to "step up to the plate" and make the tough decisions. How can we prepare ourselves for those critical "moments?" Like Samson in the temple, we must submit to God and realize that, through Him, all things are possible. Letting God into our lives through daily prayer will help prepare us for whatever trials we might face. As educators we are blessed not only to have "moments, but also to create "moments" for students each and every day. I often find inspiration in a quote from Pat Conroy's book, The Prince of Tides:

> *She took my hand and squeezed it. "You sold yourself short. You could've been more than a teacher and a coach." I returned the squeeze and said, "Listen to me Savannah. There's no word in the language I revere more than teacher. None. My heart sings when a kid refers to me as his teacher and it always has. I've honored myself and the entire family of man by becoming one."*

Royal Family

And from Jesus Christ, who is the faithful witness, and the first begotten of the dead, and the prince of the kings of the earth. Unto Him that loved us and washed us from our sins in His own blood. And hath made us kings and priests unto God and His Father, to Him be glory and dominion forever and ever. Amen. **Revelations 1:5-6**

Many people are fascinated with royal families. We love to hear about their celebrations, ceremonies and even their troubles. The late Princess Diana's wedding was watched by viewers across the world. Many also watched the tragedy of her death. We have watched with interest as her sons have grown, gone to college, and served in the British military. We follow other royal families to observe their castles and palaces. And we may even watch to see how elaborately they furnish those palaces. Some people enjoy looking at the number of fancy vehicles they own. Other people enjoy the idea of having servants and help to complete tasks which we may get tired of completing on our own. When they are in a parade, we love to see their royal clothes and the pageantry of the parade.

In the United States, many watched Jackie and John Kennedy as if they were our version of royal family. Some people even called that time as Camelot. Perhaps it was the way they carried themselves or dressed that made people feel the Kennedys were like royalty. Or perhaps it was the wealth in their families or the famous people that surrounded them that made us think of them as a royal family.

Little girls often enjoy pretending to be princesses. It is fun for them to dress up in beautiful gowns, with long white gloves, necklaces, and a crown. The little girls may enjoy having royal tea parties with royal dainties. They enjoy thinking that there will be maids to wait on them, serve them, and take care of them. They may even believe that they will grow up to become a princess like Princess Diana or Princess Grace. This fascination with royalty seems to place the royal families as better people or people who have a better life.

Queen Esther in the Old Testament lived such a famous life in royalty, yet her beginnings were not royalty. "Now it came to pass on the third day, that Esther put on her royal apparel, and stood in the inner courts of the king's house; and the king sat upon his royal throne in the royal house, over against the gate of the house, And it was so when the king saw Esther the queen standing in the court, that she obtained favour in his sight." Esther 5:1-2 She needed to wait for the king to allow her to enter the inner court. She was then able to save Mordecai as well as later to save her fellow people.

Jesus has made it very clear that we also can be part of a royal family. He stated in Revelations that He would make us Kings and reign with Him.

> I'm a child of the King
> A child of the King
> With Jesus my Savior
> I'm a child of the King.
> –Harriet Buell

Jesus made it clear that we will be royalty.

A Storm is Coming

The Lord also thundered in the heavens, and the Highest gave his voice; hailstones and coals of fire. **Psalm 18:14**

What do you do when you hear a weather report that announces an approaching storm? It probably depends on the area in which you live as well as the type of storm. In the South, there are hurricanes and high winds that cause people to listen closely to the weather reports. The hurricanes are often tracked for many days in the ocean and the gulf before they actually are at the land.

The intensity of the hurricanes are monitored closely as well as the path of the storm. The backsides of the hurricanes seem to be the most violent. As weathermen watch the path, they are cognizant of the storm in relation to where people live. The hurricanes with the high winds can leave many places without power followed by high temperatures and/or devastating rains that cause havoc on damaged buildings and roofs.

In the Midwest, there are tornadoes that cause people to pay attention to the weather reports. The tornadoes can move very quickly and can be very unpredictable. But the damage can leave entire towns or areas destroyed. The conditions before a tornado often can lead the weathermen to watch carefully for tornadoes to form. The sky turns an off-yellow/green color and, many times, it becomes very still before it strikes. The birds do not even make a sound.

In the West, there are earthquakes. When the average temperature is increasing and water levels are rising and increasing the speed of flow, the weathermen start to watch for earthquakes. Earthquakes are very powerful and can cause massive damage to buildings. The ground shakes and buildings crumble. Often, it is the fires and power outages that cause more devastation.

The Bible tells that there will be an increase in many of these natural disasters during the end times. We do not know the date or time, but we are told to be ever watchful and to understand the signs. Revelations can be ominous and unsettling at times as we begin to think of the consequences mentioned in this book.

The first angel sounded, and there followed hail and fire mingled with blood, and they were cast upon the earth; and the third part of trees was burnt up, and all green grass was burnt up. Revelations 8:7

And yet, believers are not to be worried because the believers will be saved. What do we do when we hear the reports of more storms? It should be a reminder to us that the Lord's judgment will be final. There is a heaven and there is a hell. I want my family and friends to be with me in heaven. So as I prepare and watch for storms, I will want to know that God will protect me as well as those I love. I will want to tell them about the signs of God and His eternal salvation.

The Lord is my rock, and my fortress, and my deliverer;
my God, my strength, in whom I will trust;
my buckler, and the horn of my salvation, and my high tower. Psalms 18:2

October 30

Flee

And it came to pass, when they had brought them forth abroad, that he said, Escape for thy life; look not behind thee neither stay thou in all the plain; escape to the mountain, lest thou be consumed. **Genesis 19:17**

A devasting earthquake of over 9.0 on the Richter scale hit Japan. It caused a tsunami that killed thousands of people and ruptured a nuclear power plant. Japanese survivors said about the tsunami that there was nothing you could do "but run." Many people were killed in the aftermath caused from this earthquake, especially the sick and elderly.

From the earthquake came the tsunami, which killed many elderly people, unable to flee their homes in the villages along Japan's northeast coast. Next came the radiation, which forced a hospital to evacuate its patients, 14 of whom died as a result. For the sick and elderly, there was not enough prescription medicine. There was only a single kerosene heater available to heat a large drafty gym on a cold winter day. Medical supplies such as bandages, ointments and aspirin were scarce. One doctor said this about the elderly, "We feel very helpless and very sorry for them. The condition at the gymnasium was horrible. No running water, no medicine and very, very little food. We simply did not have means to provide good care."

I knew about a superintendent who had a tsunami hit him in his job. Everything was going great, the board just extended his contract, and he had a great evaluation. He fled his job and went to the Rock. To some, he looked like a coward, but only the brave are brave enough to run away when the tsunami is coming. Talking with people several years later, they marveled how he took the high road and the good things he had done in that district. Did it hurt him? Yes, but Jesus, our Rock, saw him though.

As with a tsunami, there is nothing else you can do but flee or leave. David had to flee Jerusalem when his son Absalom tried to overthrow and kill him. You have to flee earthly temptations and not look back. Superintendent, you might have to flee, just trust God and He will see you through. Just remember to "go to the Rock."

Where do I go, where do I go
When the storms of life are threatening
Who do I turn to when those winds of sorrow blow
And is there a refuge in the time of tribulation
Go to the rock, I know he is able, I go to the rock.
—Dottie Rambo

Don't look back after the Lord has told you to flee.

Bible Numbers

For ye are all the children of God by faith in Christ Jesus. **Galatians 3:26**

The Bible has many references related to numbers. And many of the numbers have specific significance. The number *one* represents our one true God. "There is one body, and one Spirit, even as ye are called in one hope of your calling; One Lord, one faith, one baptism, One God and Father of all who is above all, and through all , and in you all." Ephesians 4:4-6 The unity of believers in God is also seen with the number one. "Endeavoring to keep the unity of the Spirit in the bond of peace" (Ephesians 4:3). "There is neither Jew nor Greek, there is neither bond nor free, there is neither male nor female; for ye are all one in Christ Jesus." Galatians 3:28 "He that is joined unto Lord is one spirit" (I Corinthians 6:17).

The number *two* is given as a means to stay together to help each other and to add safety. Jesus instructed the disciples to go out and witness by twos, just as parents often instruct their teenagers to stay together and not walk alone, to make sure there are two together. "Two are better than one; because they have a good reward for their labor. For if they fall, the one will lift up his fellow; but woe to him that is alone when he falleth; for he had not another to help him up" (Ecclesiastes 5:9-10).

The number *three* represents the trinity of God; the Father, the Son, and the Holy Ghost. It also is used to represent strength. "And if one prevail against him, two shall withstand him; and a threefold cord is not quickly broken" (Ecclesiastes 5:12). The number *four* is often related to things of nature and all that is created. We have four seasons and four directions, four corners of the earth. In Genesis 4:1, God created light and saw that it was good. The number *five* represents the completion of the first day of creation. God created darkness he called night. Five is the creation plus another. This was needed so there would be victory over death. Five is, therefore, the unmerited favor of God which is grace. The number *six* represents the creation of mankind. It was on the 6th day God created man.

Seven stands for completion or perfection. There were seven churches who received letters of instruction on how well they were doing as well as shortcomings. There were seven lampstands representing the seven churches. "He that hath an ear, let him hear what the Spirit saith unto the churches" (Revelation 3: 13). The number *ten* is used as a reference to tithing. "And this stone, which I have set for a pillar, shall be God's house: and of all that thou shalt give me I will surely give the tenth unto thee" (Genesis 28:22). The number *twelve* is one of the perfect numbers. There were 12 disciples and 12 tribes of Israel. A number you must consider is yourself. Will you be one of God's people and have eternal life?

**Then Peter said unto them, "Repent, and be baptized
every one of you in the name of Jesus Christ
for the remission of sins
and ye shall receive the gift of the Holy Ghost. Acts 2:38**

November

November 1

Taking Advice from Others

Then King Rehoboam took counsel with the old men, who had stood before Solomon his father while he was yet alive, saying, "How do you advise me to answer this people?" And they said to him, "If you will be a servant to this people today and serve them, and speak good words to them when you answer them, then they will be your servants forever." But he abandoned the counsel that the old men gave him and took counsel with the young men who had grown up with him and stood before him. 1 Kings 12:6-8

In the spring of 2011, I promoted a young head coach to the position of athletic director. He was an outstanding coach and strong Christian role model. I knew that he was the best choice for our student athletes, but I worried how he would handle his new leadership role among the other coaches. He was extremely personable and had many friends on the coaching staff. During his first month on the job, our assistant baseball coach began making some rather "questionable" decisions. The new athletic director went to the head baseball coach to discuss the matter. After visiting with the head coach he decided to take no action. They were both his "friends" and they convinced him that nothing inappropriate was taking place. His decision to take their advice would create significant problems for our district later.

Afterwards, I asked him why he chose to ignore the problem. He explained that both coaches were his friends, and that he felt it was best to support their decisions. I took the opportunity to share with him the story of Rehobam. The people, led by Jeroboam, feared that Rehoboam would continue to tax them heavily, like his father Solomon. Jeroboam and the people promised their loyalty in return for lesser burdens. The older men counseled Rehoboam at least to speak to the people in a civil manner, and possibly meet some of their demands. However, the new king sought the advice from friends, who advised the king to show no weakness to the people, and to tax them even more. He proclaimed to the people,

"Whereas my father laid upon you a heavy yoke, so shall I add tenfold thereto.
Whereas my father chastised you with whips, so shall I chastise you with scorpions.
For my littlest finger is thicker than my father's loins; and your backs, which bent like reeds at my father's touch, shall break like straws at my own touch."

I explained to my young athletic director that the problem was that Rehoboam failed to listen to "wise" counsel. As Christians, our first priority is to please the Lord in our work, and then by His grace we will continue to honor God in all of our decisions. As leaders, many people are willing to give their opinion, but only by God's grace will we be granted the wisdom to separate the good advice from the bad. Do you take advise from wise men or friends?

I am not trying to micromanage your new position, but I want you to remember to be "friendly" not "friends" to those you now serve.

Always Prepared

So neither I, nor my brethren, nor my servants nor the men of the guard which followed me, none of us put off our clothes, saving that everyone put them off for washing. Nehemiah 4:23

Sanballat and Tobiah were extremely irate when they heard that the walls of Jerusalem were being rebuilt. They were so angry that they conspired to get other people to come up and go to war against the Israelites. This constant threatening produced constant preparedness by the Israelites.

For 52 days, none of the workers put off their clothes except for washing and taking a bath. They were alert 24 hours a day, seven days a week. They could not afford to let their guard down one minute as the enemy had assembled.

Are you prepared and ever vigilant as you go about your job as a superintendent? Lack of preparedness will cause you to stumble and allow your enemies to accumulate. A superintendent trusted his Director of Finance and, when the Director of Finance resigned, found out that he had not paid into the state several millions of dollars.

This superintendent is an upright person but let his guard down as his enemies were circling in the dark. It has become so bad that at the last board meeting a board member asked him for his resignation in an open meeting session. If you have found yourself in this situation, you do have time to turn things around, but the time will quickly evaporate.

Seek counsel from honest mentors and, from this day forth, seek purpose in your heart and always be prepared. You are the steward of the district. Live up to your title. As John Wooden said, "Always be prepared and always be honest." Emulate God who is always awake, watching.

> *All along on the road to the soul's true abode,*
> *There's an eye watching you;*
> *Every step that you take this great eye is awake,*
> *There's an all seeing eye watching you.*
> –J. M. Henson

We will always remember. We will always be proud. We will always be prepared, so we will always be free.
–Ronald Reagan

Choose Today

And if it seem evil unto you to serve the Lord, choose you this day whom ye will serve; whether the gods which your fathers served that were on the other side of the flood, or the gods of the Amorites, in whose land ye dwell: but as for me and my house, we will serve the Lord. **Joshua 24:15**

Joshua made a passionate plea to Israel to serve the Lord. Israel boldly stated that they would serve the Lord. What Joshua was doing was reminding Israel that they could not serve God and other gods. Choosing to serve God over false gods was the right choice. But what was Israel agreeing to do? What they were agreeing to do was to totally separate themselves from everyone else.

What about your decisions? You usually choose good, but is that because you decide to serve God? Have you also decided to cut off all else that is not worthy of God? Have you determined in yourself to follow a new course for your life? Are you keeping old acquaintances that are not ungodly because you are afraid to "burn your bridges"? Remember, if you serve God the way Israel said they would serve God, then there is no need for another way or god.

Choosing God demands that you cut off everything that is not what God wants for you in your life. This is not like choosing what you want to wear or eat when you could choose a satisfactory alternative. Have you chosen God or an appealing alternative? As a superintendent you are used to making the right choice. Use your courage to make the right choice for God.

> *Choose ye today whom you will serve;*
> *Will it be God or man?*
> *Well now the choice is yours,*
> *But you must choose ye this day whom you will serve;*
> *Without a moment to lose, you must choose.*
> —Marvin Winans

Never put a question mark where God has put a period.

Communication and Collaboration

Therefore came all the elders of Israel to the king to Hebron; and David made a covenant with them in Hebron before the Lord; and they anointed David king over Israel, according to the word of the Lord by Samuel. 1 Chronicles 11:3

Building a functioning quality team is the single most important thing a superintendent can do to achieve a successful school district. With the right attitude, this team will overcome almost any difficulty to succeed in achieving the district goals.

To achieve collaboration, the superintendent needs to behave as one of the team which is being collaborative, supportive, and friendly. Remember to do the following: a) celebrate all successes; b) share the good and the bad of financial results with all; c) align school goals with the district mission statement and strategies; d) regularly communicate policy, expectations, and results to every employee; e) share the strategic plan and vision to every employee; and f) develop a culture that encourages and rewards open communication and collaboration.

Effectively rising to the challenge of today's global economy and the increasingly collaborative horizontal relationships that characterize interactions (among administrators, teachers, parents, community, and business partners) demands a unified approach to communications and collaboration.

When David was anointed king, it was done in front of the elders of Israel. There was open communication and collaboration. Samuel recognized the need for high level open communication if Israel was going to accept David as king.

Have you had that high level open communication with your staff, teachers, and community? The Board might introduce you to the community and staff, but after you are hired it is your job to develop a culture of communication and collaboration. The prophets communicated with the people and with God. Jesus communicated to the people, his disciples and with God. In both of these examples, there was teamwork and communication.

Hear the blessed Savior calling the oppressed
O ye heavy laden come to Me and rest
Come no longer tarry, I your load will bear,
Bring Me every burden, bring Me every care.
                                        –C. P. Jones

When you communicate with God, he'll bless you and your job.

November 5

Giving God the Glory

And he said unto them, Look on me, and do likewise: and, behold, when I come to the outside of the camp, it shall be that, as I do, so shall ye do. **Judges 7:17**

Gideon was a man from a family that was, as some would say, "the lowest on the rung." Yet, God chose him even though he did not come from an elite or well-to-do family. Even Gideon was unsure of himself and questioned God's command. He laid a fleece out before the Lord to see if it was really God speaking.

Gideon gathered the men of Israel from the tribes of Manasseh, Asher, Zebulun, and Naphtali. Over 22,000 men showed up for war, but God said that was too many. When God got finished parrying down the men, there were 300 people left to fight the Midianites. After this victory, against all odds, the people of Israel wanted Gideon to be their king, but he refused, telling them that only God is their king.

How many times in our personal life or on the job do we seem to win a battle for the district or our family against all odds? We feel like we are on top of the world. The people, on that given day, would name a building after you or give you anything you ask. Be careful because a seed of pride enters in and, before you know it, everything comes falling down.

Solomon wrote in Proverbs 16:18, "Pride goeth before destruction, and an haughty spirit before a fall." Remember, when you win these victories that it is God who won them for you and not yourself. Do not let the people make you the king. Be humble and let the king be God. Gideon set the excellent example and made certain that the 300 men followed him. From this came the victory and Gideon gave God the glory.

> *Gideon had such an army of great men,*
> *But God looked at them and said, "They're too many."*
> *Gave some tests until three hundred men were left.*
> *With that number God would surely get glory.*
> *Though your many troubles seem to get you down*
> *Look for answers to your prayers and you will see*
> *God is really watching and will bless you too.*
> —Patsy Stevens

Always trust in God and He will see you through by winning the victory for you.

Hearing God's Call

And the Lord called Samuel, and he answered, Here am I. **I Samuel 3:4**

Samuel was a young boy when his mother gave him to the Lord. In the middle of the night, God spoke to Samuel but he did not recognize God's voice. Each time he thought it was Eli, the priest, who was calling him. Finally, after the second time of going to Eli and asking if he called him, Eli then realized it was the Lord calling Samuel so he said to him, if he calls again say, "Speak Lord, for thy servant heareth" (I Samuel 3:10).

Have you ever been in a place as a superintendent and after you have prayed you felt like you should do something, but did not quite know if it was the Lord speaking to you? Then, after several times of hearing his voice and continually having this urging it is the Lord, you say, "Speak Lord".

Do not feel like you did not hear the voice of God because even His disciples did not recognize His voice even when He was walking with them. Remember, the Lord does speak to us! This happened to two disciples when they were walking on the road to Emmaus after the resurrection of Christ. They did not realize it was Jesus who was walking and talking to them and they said, "Did not our heart burn within us, while he talked with us by the way and while he opened to us the scriptures" (Luke 24:32).

The Lord was calling Samuel to be a prophet in Israel. Eli's sons were evil and wicked so the Lord had to prepare someone else. Samuel was the prophet in Israel through the times of Saul and, later, King David. The Lord can be calling you and you just have to be quiet and still, and listen to the voice of God and answer. He just might be wanting you to make a difference in a new community and a school district!

Have Thine own way, Lord! Have Thine own way!
Thou are the Potter, I am the clay;
Mold me and make me, After Thy will,
While I am waiting, Yielded and still.
−G. S Stebbins

He walks with me and talks with me and tells me that I am His own.
−Austin Miles

Love the Lord Your God

In that I command thee this day to love the Lord thy God, to walk in his ways, and to keep his commandments and his statutes and his judgments, that thou mayest live and multiply: and the Lord thy God shall bless thee in the land whither thou goest to possess it. **Deuteronomy 30: 16**

During life's journey, we come to a fork in the road to choose between following the Lord or not following the Lord. There are five blessings you will receive from following the Lord. These are: 1) life and good things; 2) privilege to live and multiply; 3) blessings in the land of promise; and 4) long life on earth; 5) life for children.

As a superintendent, living your life for God with integrity will have positive results on your health, your job, and student achievement. This is because you are always doing what is right and God will bless you for doing that.

I know of several superintendents who, on the surface, looked like they were having a rough time in a district. During this time, they kept serving the Lord and giving God the glory in all things. They did not give the devil an opportunity to gloat because of their current circumstances.

Just because you are a Christian does not mean you will not go through trials but you realize that God has everything under control. After these superintendents left their respective district, people were still talking about their integrity and how they kept to the high road. Board members later were even saying they themselves had made a mistake.

During their tenures at their respective districts, and even after they left, student achievement rose and continued to rise. This was because educators who worked in the district knew they advocated the "effective education" and kept following what they had taught them through example, modeling, and professional development.

> *Praise Him! Praise Him! Jesus our blessed Redeemer!*
> *Sing, O earth His wonderful love proclaim!*
> *Hail Him! Hail Him! Highest archangels in glory,*
> *Strength and honor give to His holy name!*
> –C. G. Allen

If you want to truly be successful, love the Lord and walk in His ways.

My Wonderful Lord

And I was with thee withersoever thou wentest, and have cut off all thine enemies out of the sight, and have made thee a great name, like unto the name of the great men that are in the earth. ll Samuel 7:9

As superintendents, we face many obstacles, giants, problems, and situations. As a Christian, we have the comfort to know that God directs, protects, guides, and helps us. David certainly needed God's protection. God helped him defeat the giant, Goliath, protected him from his son, Absalom, when he tried to overthrow him, helped him in battles when he defeated the enemies of Israel, and protected him from Saul when he tried to kill him. God protected him and made him a great name. The Psalms is testimony of David's praise and when he said in Psalms 31:19, "Oh how great is thy goodness."

Dr. Oliver was a superintendent who had the union continually harass him during his l7 years as a superintendent. The teachers union ran full page adds against him, railed against him in open board meetings, and eventually got a community member elected to the Board of Education who was a sympathizer with the union.

After this board member was elected, Dr. Oliver retired within one year. During these years and his last year, he was very gracious and forgiving. He did not hold a grudge and treated everyone, even the antagonists, with utmost respect.

Who helped Dr. Oliver during this time? It was the Lord as Dr. Oliver was a Christian man and spent his time on his knees asking for God's protection and guidance. After Dr. Oliver left the district, he went on to become a Dean of a College of Education at a major university and the school district later named a new middle school after him. As the song writer wrote, "Wonderful, wonderful Jesus! He is my friend, true to the end."

> *He hideth my soul in the cleft of the rock*
> *That shadows a dry, thirsty land;*
> *He hideth my life in the depths of His love,*
> *And covers me there with His hand,*
> *And covers me there with His hand.*
> –Haldor Lillenas

My wonderful Lord, my wonderful Lord,
whom angels and seraphs in Heaven adore.

Walking in God's Statutes

Then will I give you rain in due season, and the land shall yield her increase, and the trees of the field shall yield their fruit. **Leviticus 26:4**

Walking with God and obeying Him will bring great reward to you. You will be fruitful in everything you do and touch. God will give you peace and you will not be afraid. People who desire to do you harm will flee before you. You will have plenty to live on and won't have to worry one iota. But if you do not follow the Lord, you will experience terror, sickness, sorrow, and you will work in vain because God will not be blessing you.

Trusting God allows us to put all of our cares upon him because he cares for us. Why should we worry or fret when God has everything under control? Sometimes we are out of step with God and we wonder why things just don't seem to be going right. That is when we have a "wake-up call" and get our priorities right. God becomes first place in our life.

As a superintendent, I used to put the job first, family second, and God last. After feeling like I was on a treadmill, I asked the Lord to forgive me and I started to put Him first and the job last. When I made that change, it was like everything I did turned to gold. God was guiding my every step and blessing me beyond measure. Do not let the cares of the job turn your life upside down. God wants to help you and is waiting for you to ask Him.

> *Tis so sweet to trust in Jesus, Just to take Him at His word;*
> *Just to rest upon His promise; Just to Know, "Thus saith the Lord."*
> *Jesus, Jesus, how I trust Him! How I've proved Him o'er and o'er!*
> *Jesus, Jesus, precious Jesus! O for grace to trust Him more.*
> –W. J. Kirkpatrick

He said if I would trust and obey he'd guide my steps all along the way,
that's why I'm walking in the favor of God.
–Harlon Burton

Your Spiritual Eye Sight

Then the Lord opened the eyes of Balaam and he saw the angel of the Lord standing in the way, and his sword drawn in his hand: and he bowed down his head, and fell flat on his face. **Numbers 22:31**

King Balak saw the people of Israel coming and was extremely fearful. He called upon Balaam to curse the children of Israel so they would not come and destroy his people. The King offered Balaam great riches and Balaam was seriously considering it.

Balaam did not obey God's word, so God sent an Angel of the Lord to block Balaam's path. Balaam was so blind that he could not see an "angel of the Lord" blocking his path, but his donkey did.

Balaam kicked, hit, and cursed the donkey three times. Finally, the donkey spoke to Balaam and said "What have I done to you that you would hit me these three times?" Balaam's heart was so corrupted that he talked to the donkey and did not even realize the donkey was talking back to him. Then the Lord opened Balaam's eyes and he saw the angel of the Lord.

I have seen where temptations and covetousness have corrupted a superintendent's heart. Bad choices were made and the superintendent usually gets fired or leaves in disgrace. When the "eye" of that superintendent is opened, they become extremely repentant.

Pray each day that the Lord does not have to "speak through the mouth of a donkey before you open your spiritual eyes." Arrogance, greed, covetousness, and envy will destroy your integrity and you will not be blessed. Do not make unethical decisions that will get you false honor and reward. Your "spiritual eyesight" will prevent you from falling into these temptations and this is done by following the will of the Lord.

There is naught to fear in the desert here
If Jehovah is leading you
Many foes you'll meet, but you'll still keep sweet, If Jehovah is leading you.
–Chesley Bray

Many a dangerous temptation comes to us in fine gay colors
that are but skin-deep.
–Matthew Henry

Always Be Upright

And Asa did that which was right in the eyes of the Lord as did David his father.
1 Kings 15:11

I was reading in the paper about a superintendent who had to resign from his position because of moral failure. Another superintendent was fortunate to keep his job, but he would have been fired if he did not resign. He had lied to the Board about working on his doctorate and had an affair with a district teacher which resulted in his divorce. Another superintendent was just indicted on embezzlement charges. I could go on about superintendents who made the wrong choices, but I will close with this example about a superintendent who was accused of embezzlement who had his name removed from a new building which was named after him, and is now spending years in prison. Finally, another superintendent was indicted on bribery and corruption charges for accepting gifts from a district vendor. Was their choice worth the shame?

Competency 1, Texas Standards reads, "The superintendent knows how to act with integrity, fairness, and in an ethical manner in order to promote the success of all students." This corresponds to ELCC Standard 5.0 which reads, "Candidates who complete the program are educational leaders with the knowledge and ability to promote the success of all students by acting with integrity, fairness, and in an ethical manner."

These superintendents, as described in the standards, always serve as an advocate for children. They promote the highest standard of conduct, ethical principles, and integrity in decision making, action, and behavior. They apply knowledge of ethical issues affecting education. In addition, they continually monitor accomplishments of the district to see if they are meeting district goals. Finally, they use everything within their power to support and implement the district's vision and goals. These superintendents are ethical role models.

Are you always doing what is right in the eyes of the Lord? Or are you letting temptations and lures turn your eyes to make a poor career-killing decision? If so, do what is right and the Lord will bless you in everything!

He leadeth me, O blessed thought!
O words with heavenly comfort fraught!
Whateve'er I do, where'er I be,
Still 'tis God's hand that leadeth me.
—W. B. Bradbury

Do not turn into the alluring door of evil temptation!

Determined to Trust God

Though he slay me, yet will I trust in him: but I will maintain mine own ways before him. **Job 13:15**

Job was determined to trust in God and maintain his own ways before Him, regardless of the outcome. Job thought his ways were righteous, for he confessed that God would be his salvation, and that the hypocrite could not come before Him. Concerning himself, he declared that he would be justified. Job had to plead his case because everyone was against him. He knew that if he held his tongue because of the hard-heartedness of his close acquaintances, he would die and give up the ghost. In other words, he must speak or die.

I know of a superintendent who was maliciously attacked by the media He was devastated. The only thing he could do was trust in God all the way through. Even his own mother told him that he should just admit that he did those things so it would pass. But he maintained his own ways as he knew he did nothing even close to wrong.

The whole community had turned against him because of the lies the newspaper reporter wrote and, like Job, had to fend for himself. He did not fight the newspaper, but he did talk to community members about the treacherous lies. In the end, he was vindicated. He did not do anything wrong and he trusted in God.

Do you feel when you have gone through a trial that God is far away? Do you have that trust in Him? Remember, take the attitude of Job, trust the Lord no matter what!

> *I know that He safely will carry me thru,*
> *No matter what evils betide,*
> *Why should I then care though the tempest may blow,*
> *If Jesus walks close to my side.*
> –J. L. Heath

Faith is a living, daring confidence in God's grace.
It is so sure and certain that a man could stake his life on it a thousand times.
–Martin Luther

Directing the Vision

And it came to pass, when they were gone over, that Elijah said unto Elisha, Ask what I shall do for thee, before I be taken away from thee. And Elisha said, I pray thee, let a double portion of thy spirit be upon me. ll Kings 2:9

Elijah was the mentor to Elisha and shaped his vision. At this time in Israel, Elijah was God's prophet who spoke God's word to the king. The most notorious king at this time was Ahab and his wife was Jezebel. They were so mad at Elijah that he went into hiding. Elijah mentored and taught Elisha the ways of God who later became the prophet of Israel. Just like Elijah helped shape Israel culture and train another prophet leader, a superintendent shapes the district culture, whether good or bad.

Elisha recognized Elijah was the master and decided he wanted to learn from the best. You too can find a super mentor superintendent or be that mentor to a future superintendent. The superintendent's effect on the district is tremendous. Be the best you can be so you can truly say, "I helped shaped this district and the students, teachers, and community succeeded."

A song writer wrote, "give of your best for the master." Copy the pattern of Elisha and pray for the Lord to give you that double blessing so you can truly lead your district and shape it into a high achieving district where outstanding student achievement is the norm. Elisha was focused to be the best for Israel.

Competency 2 of the Texas Standards reads, "The superintendent knows how to shape district culture by facilitating the development, articulation, implementation, and stewardship of a vision of learning that is shared and supported by the educational community." ELCC Standard 1.0 reads, "Candidates who complete the program are educational leaders who have the knowledge and ability to promote the success of all students by facilitating the development, articulation, implementation, and stewardship of a district vision of learning supported by the school community."

Each day I'll do a golden deed,
By helping those who are in need;
My life on earth is but a span,
And so I'll do the best I can.

–W. M. Golden

The painter will produce pictures of little merit
if he takes the works of others as his standard.
–Leonardo da Vinci

Favor with the King

And it was so, when the king saw Esther the queen standing in the court, that she obtained favour in his sight: and the king held out to Esther the gold scepter that was in his hand. So Esther drew near, and touched the top of the scepter. Esther 5:2

How did a young peasant Jewish girl become queen in Persia? How can you find favor that will transport you into the king's palace? We will all face Hamans in the world and all the trouble they stir up will give you an ulcer. Superintendents certainly understand this. Understanding how you live and find favor in a hostile world is hard. Esther reaped all of these benefits:

Esther found favor (2:17) so much that the King made her Queen.
Esther found favor (5:8) so much that the King offered up to half his kingdom.
Esther found favor (7:3) so much that her life and the lives of her people were saved.
Esther found favor (8:5) so much that the King wrote a law on her behalf for the Jews.

So how did Esther gain this favor? Favor comes:
To those who see life from God's perspective.
To those who pray and prepare themselves.
To those who act in faith which is faith in action.
To those who act favorably by being in the appropriate place, dressing appropriately and using appropriate words.

> *No one ever cared for me like Jesus;*
> *There's no other friend so kind as He.*
> *No one else could take the sin and darkness from me;*
> *O how much He cared for me.*
> —C. F. Weigle

Favor is the special affection of God toward you that releases an influence on you, so that others are inclined to like you, or to cooperate with you.
—Lance Wallnau

Fire

Seek the Lord and ye shall live; lest He break out like a fire in the house of Joseph and devour it, and there be none to quench it in Bethel. Amos 5:6

As I watch the weatherman say there is no rain in the future and the drought is continuing, I realize how easy a fire can spread across the land. Homes and acres of trees are quickly consumed in these wild fires. Many county authorities quickly enact "No Burning" bans in an attempt to protect the area from fires. But even with careful precautions, fires may start from dry areas and small embers.

Under these dry harsh conditions, the fires spread quickly and turn everything in its path to a black ashy powder. The fires roar across areas producing high levels of heat while leaving very little to be salvaged. Even the odor of the fire lasts a long time after the fire is extinguished.

Fires can also be good as they are used to cook food, but must be done carefully so you will not burn yourself. I can remember heating marshmallows on a stick over an open fire. The marshmallows needed to cool for a while or you would burn your tongue trying to eat them. I would blow on the marshmallow so it would be cool enough to eat.

When we burn our skin because of fire or something extremely hot, these burned areas become very painful. It takes soothing medicine and time to heal those burns. I can't imagine the torment of spending eternity with the pain from continual burning. That fear alone should cause anyone to turn away from hell.

In flaming fire, taking vengeance on them that know not God, and that obey not the gospel of our Lord Jesus Christ. II Thessalonians 1:8

The Bible also talks about fire in many different ways. Sometimes, the fire is seen as God's power. Other times, fire represents God's wrath. God often describes his judgment as a consuming fire, also. He will judge the wicked and even the devil will be thrown into the lake of fire. It will be God's fire that strikes against the evil of the devil.

The fire! The fire!
Gives victory over sing and purity within;
The fire! The fire!
The fire they had at Pentecost.
                                        –Wiegle

The sinners in Zion are afraid; trembling has seized the godless;
"Who among us can dwell with the consuming fire?
Who among us can dwell with everlasting burnings? Isaiah 33:14

God Holds the Future

Let the work of this house of God alone; let the governor of the Jews and the elders of the Jews build this house of God in his place. **Ezra 6:7**

Israel was given the permission to go back to Jerusalem and rebuild the temple by Cyrus, king of Persia. When the Jews arrived there to rebuild the temple, they were met with many obstacles. In fact, the opposition was so fierce, that Rehum wrote a letter against Jerusalem stating that the Jews are going to build up a "rebellious and bad city" and when they are finished, they will not pay tribute to the king. He went on to ask for permission to stop the Jews from building the city. The letter was read before King Artxerxes and an order was made to the Jews to cease from building.

A new king came to power, Darius, and a complaint was lodged against the Jews because they started to build the city again. King Darius did something different from his predecessors as he looked into the records and found that King Cyrus did order a decree to rebuild the city. King Darius then commanded that all of the people in the area assist and help the Jews rebuild Jerusalem and the temple.

What do we learn from this story? You, as a superintendent, will have factions rise up against you with lies, deceit, and tall tales about you. They will stop your progress in the district and hinder the vision for education of children. If you have a smart board, they will look into the records to find out if what is being said is false. I was visiting with a superintendent about a newspaper report which was scathing him in the newspaper with lies and half-truths. He had to keep his eyes focused on God to help him through this trial. God holds the future in His hands.

> *Dread not the things that are ahead,*
> *The burdens great, the sinking sand,*
> *The thorns that o'er the path are spread,*
> *God holds the future in His hands.*
> –James Vaughan

Satan's attack means another victory for God as God knows the outcome.

Judging

Judge not, that you be not judged. **Matthew 7:1**

How often are we quick to make judgments about people based on their appearance or actions? We see someone dressed poorly and we think they do not have money, and, thus, they are not worth our time or we treat them differently than someone who is dressed in expensive clothes. I can remember a wonderful activity a high school sociology teacher assigned his students. He asked the students to dress sloppy, make their hair messy, place stick-on tattoos to their arms and the girls to wear heavy make-up. Then, the students were to walk slowly around high-end department stores. On a different day, the students were to dress in the best clothes with well- groomed hair and walk into different high-end department stores.

The students reported the reactions of store clerks and other people in the stores. My daughter was one of those students and she was shocked by how people judged her and treated her differently based on her clothing and appearance. It had never occurred to her that how someone dressed would be a cause for judgments.

There are many times that superintendents have to make decisions that will require them to make certain judgments. It is important that they remember to base their decisions on the needs of the organization and not on certain appearances of people in the organization. The ability to use discernment wisely is a great gift from God. Solomon even asked for wisdom. And the Lord was pleased with his request. We too should want to have the wisdom to make the best decisions.

There are also times for leaders when people will come to the leader's office with personal needs and sometimes demands. Their actions and appearances may impact the leader's judgment. Therefore, it is important to be aware of potential biases so that leaders may treat everyone fairly.

Take a second and look in a stranger's life
Peer inside, think a thought, maybe you'll see strife
Judgments made from simple glances are often wrong we see
We should step back and with Christ's help look inside at "me."

Turn thou to thy God; keep mercy and judgment
and wait on thy God continually. Hosea 12:6

Listen to God: Give Me Ears to Hear

For since the beginning of the world men have not heard nor perceived by the ear, neither hath the eye seen, O God, beside thee, what he hath prepared for him that waiteth for him. Isaiah 64:4

God does not force us to listen to the spirit. But we will receive a blessing and his statement, "well done, good and faithful servant," when we listen and follow his word. When I walk in the morning, I walk alone so I have a chance to dwell on the day. It helps me plan my day and even express my thoughts and concerns to God. But, often, I am too busy planning, thinking, and talking silently to myself and not God. During that time, I sometimes forget to stop those things and I end up leaving God out of the conversation.

I am sure you have talked with some people or I should say had some people talk at you and you may have a hard time getting in any words. Or people are upset and they just launch into a tirade of what is upsetting them without giving you any chance to respond. It is at these times that we are forced to be silent and perhaps it is good that we remain silent so that we do not say inappropriate responses. Sometimes, people do need someone to listen to them. And, sometimes, we need time to think about a response so that it is calmly stated to an upset person. There are even times in church when during the prayer, my mind wanders off to other things besides listening to God or even giving God glory and praise. I need to conscientiously stop myself and redirect my mind back to a listening mode. The Lord is a wonderful listener, but I must also learn to listen to Him.

I love the Lord because he hath heard my voice and my supplications. Psalm 116:1

Preschool children even need that redirection back to listening modes. These small children often enjoy talking and asking questions. They spend less time listening if they have not received some training on listening. Adults also need to be taught to listen. Superintendents are often extroverts and that is why they have come to leadership positions. But they must also realize that they need to listen in order to understand the needs of others in the organization. They must have certain levels of sociability that show their concern to listen to others. God wants to lead us also so we can live our lives to his fullest design. Yet, we will need to train ourselves to be better listeners and to give God our attention and ears. Our minds are easily filled with cares of the earthly things in our lives. We must take the focus off ourselves and place it on the Lord. Train our minds to stop so our ears can hear the spirit.

> *In this world below there is one who loves me so*
> *And I'm talking talking of my Lord*
> *I can feel his hand and I know he understands*
> *And I'm walking walking with the Lord.*
> –J. D. Sumner

Hast thou not known? Hast thou not heard that the everlasting God, the Lord, the Creator of the ends of the earth, fainteth not, neither is weary? There is no searching of his understanding. Isaiah 40:28

Major Decisions

Yea, if thou criest after knowledge, and liftest up they voice for understanding; if thou seekest her as silver, and searches for her as for hid treasures; fear of the Lord, and find the knowledge of God. For the Lord giveth wisdom: out of his mouth cometh knowledge and understanding. He layeth sound wisdom for the righteous; he is a buckler to them that walk uprightly. He keepeth the paths of judgment, and preserveth the way of his saints. **Proverbs 2:3-8**

There are times when I feel overwhelmed with a number of major decisions. I don't mean the decisions between right and wrong. Those decisions are easy. It's the decisions that impact others' livelihood that require careful consideration and the decisions that have a major impact on our own lives. I am reminded that we are to turn to Jesus with any of our concerns.

Casting all your care upon him; for he careth for you. I Peter 5:7

He wants our prayers. He has shown us a way through his word. Jesus' way is easy and his burden light. It seems that my decisions should then be easy to make. I am not supposed to lean on my own understanding rather I am to search His ways.

Trust in the Lord with all thine heart; and lean not unto thine own understanding.
Proverbs 3:5

It should be easier to make the decisions based on this information. We should not hold onto our problems and decisions. We should let the Lord help us and repent our sins. One of my dear Christian friends does not think God cares whether he buys a certain house over another. Yet, I feel God should direct all of our major decisions. I feel that if we listen better or pray more, God will direct us. I tend to over analyze many decisions and that impacts my ability to take the word of the Lord to heart. I need to read the Bible and pray when I have to make major decisions. I also need to examine all aspects of the decision, but then, I need to make the decision and not waiver. The Lord wants us to make good decisions, but He wants us to make those decisions and not continually look for answers. At some point, we need to make the decision.

If any of you lack wisdom, let him ask of God that giveth to all men liberally, and upbraideth not; and it shall be given him. But let him ask in faith, nothing wavering. For he that wavereth is like a wave of the sea driven with the wind and tossed. James 1:5-6

Then, if the decision gives God glory, helps others, is something that would please God, and is an example of a Christian life, God will bless it. God will show me either through the Bible, the Holy Spirit, circumstances and/or other Christians, whether the major decision is best.

**Whether therefore ye eat, or drink, or whatever you do,
do all to the glory of God.I Corinthians 10:31**

Marvelous Grace

And he said unto me, My grace is sufficient for thee: for my strength is made perfect in weakness. Most gladly therefore will I rather glory in my infirmities, that the power of Christ may rest upon me. **ll Corinthians 12:9**

Is there something that attracts the marvelous grace of our Savior? Is it beauty, righteousness, healthiness, or our potential? No! It is our need, weakness and helplessness that attracts God's grace. "And they came unto him, bringing one sick of the palsy" (Mark 2:3).

This is a picture of absolute helplessness of a man without one bit of strength. He could not bring himself to Christ. That is you and me before we knew of Christ's power. Jesus stood before this sick man and did not even mention his weak condition. Jesus brought him before the Father clean and forgiven. He was accepted before he was healed. "When Jesus saw their faith, he said unto the sick of the palsy, Son, thy sins be forgiven thee" (Mark 2:5).

What a fantastic picture of the love of God! Here is a sick man who couldn't even utter a weak confession. "We are his workmanship, created in Christ Jesus" (Ephesians 2:10). The Pharisee, with all his good works and boasting, never attracted the grace of the Lord.

Show me the person who struggles against sin, one who is crushed beneath guilt, one who feels helpless and weak, and I will show you one who merits total grace. "But by the grace of God we are heirs of the King. Where sin abounds, grace much more abounds" (Romans 5:20).

Through faith in Jesus, your sins are forgiven. You now are sealed, accepted, and one with Jesus Christ and the Father! You are more than a conqueror, you are filled with Christ. You have the power to meet everything in your life. You are the apple of his eye!

> O this wondrous grace is for all the race,
> It is boundless and full and free;
> And I trust and cling to my blessed King
> Who by grace now is keeping me.
> –Byron Whitworth

The mystery of God's grace is that it never comes too late.

Meekness in Leadership

Now the man Moses was very meek, above all the men which were upon the face of the earth. **Numbers 12:3**

Exceptional superintendents share certain qualities like a strong personal ethic and a correct vision of the future. Frequently, great leaders emerge in response to a crisis as they attempt to achieve a bold new vision.

Moses played many roles throughout the book of Exodus, but some of his most memorable moments occur when he mediates between God and the Israelites. Time and again, Moses intercedes on behalf of the people, even when they have sinned, and puts his life in danger. Steadfast, unwavering support for your employees is the mark of a great leader.

Meekness is a tolerant and yielding spirit that says you do not insist on your own way. Many have looked upon meekness, humbleness, or the willingness to yield, with suspicion, loathing, and disdain. Meekness may seem too much like weakness or being wimpy. When Abram's and Lot's herdsmen quarrel, Abram graciously said to Lot, "Please let there be no strife between you and me, or between my herdsmen and your herdsmen; for we are brethren" (Genesis 3:8). Instead of pulling rank on his young nephew, he yields to Lot's choice, and for his meekness, he receives a much larger blessing.

Teachers and administrators appreciate meekness in a superintendent, just as customers appreciate a non-threatening, non-pushy sales representative. People do not naturally like to be "taught" or "sold on" anything. Through a meek spirit, a superintendent can inspire and facilitate the human natural desire to learn by engaging the employee's internal motivation.

A strong handed approach turns employees off and creates low morale. A humble, shepherd-like approach proves to be more practical and effective. In I Corinthians 10:23-24, it says that "nobody should seek his own good, but the good of others." Meekly yielding for the ultimate good does not mean weakness but instead strength, wisdom, and common-sense survival. A superintendent gave me a cartoon that graphically illustrates this: Two ornery donkeys tethered together by a single rope, each straining to reach opposite haystacks. Only when one donkey graciously yields do they both finally get enough to eat.

Give as it was given to you in your need,
Love as the Master loved you;
Be to the helpless a helper indeed,
Unto your missions be true.
–G. S. Schuler

Glances of true beauty can be seen in the faces of those who live in true meekness.
–Henry David Thoreau

Thanksgiving

In everything give thanks; for this is the will of God in Christ Jesus concerning you. I Thessalonians 5:18

What does God do for you and give you? He gives life, strength, guidance, food, air to breathe, a family, clothing, shelter, a job, children to teach, a district to lead. In essence, God gives you everything. We are to be thankful and give thanks. What happens when we have been given too much and forget to be thankful?

When we have been given too much, we can become unthankful. An unthankful spirit comes from self-reliance and the enemy of our soul, Satan. God warns us about being unthankful in Deuteronomy 8:11-16, 18 (NLT) which reads:

but that is the time to be careful! Beware that in your plenty you do not forget the Lord your God and disobey his commands, regulations, and decrees that I am giving you today. For when you have become full and prosperous and have built fine homes to live in, and when your flocks and herds have become very large and your silver and gold have multiplied along with everything else, be careful! Do not become proud at that time and forget the Lord your God, who rescued you from slavery in the land of Egypt. Do not forget that he led you through the great and terrifying wilderness with its poisonous snakes and scorpions, where it was so hot and dry. He gave you water from the rock! He fed you with manna in the wilderness, a food unknown to your ancestors[...] Remember the Lord your God. He is the one who gives you power to be successful, in order to fulfill the covenant he confirmed to your ancestors with an oath.

Being unthankful causes us to take people for granted, the ones we love the most, and makes us feel worse about others and life. Let a spirit of gratitude come on you. Use words like; "Thank you," "I appreciate you," "I love you," and so forth. These words go a long way. Finally, remember in this day and age in which we live to have Thanksgiving every day of your life. Superintendents need to be thankful for everything.

> *We gather together to ask the Lord's blessing,*
> *He chastens and hastens His will to make known;*
> *The wicked oppressing cease them from distressing,*
> *Sing praises to his name, He forgets not His own.*
> –Unknown

It is a good to give thanks unto the Lord.
–Unknown

Put Others Before Yourself

Let nothing be done through strife or vainglory; but in lowliness of mind let each esteem other better than themselves. **Philippians 2:3**

Have you ever worked for someone and they thought so highly of themselves that when you walked into their office you felt like you were "walking on God's turf?" In fact, they didn't even think their sweat reeked. I have and thoroughly disliked it. These superintendents were so full of themselves that people did not like to be around them. Some of these superintendents even treated fellow superintendents with disdain.

A superintendent in the Tulsa area kept other superintendents sitting in the outer office with his secretary until he "had time to visit" with them. When you went to a conference and he was there, he would ignore you unless you were in his inner circle. If you were in a meeting with him, he tried to exert his influence and be the "guru" of the topic. He felt the "sun rose and set in himself" and there was no one like him. Oh, his district would do some great things and he would let you know that it was he who was instrumental for these awards and accolades.

Another superintendent in the Tulsa area was just the exact opposite. He was humble, putting others ahead of himself, treating all with respect, and well respected by the community, his peers, and the state. When this superintendent retired, the district named a school after him and that was an embarrassment to him because he always gave all his workers the glory. He always said, "I can be no better than who works underneath me."

Paul said not to think better of yourself than you are. In verse four, he goes on to say that you should be concerned about the interests of others. There is the tendency to think that you are beter than others when you become a superintendent, but ask the Lord to keep you humble. This is done by always thanking God for all of the blessings he bestows upon you. If you put God first, your fellow man second and you last, then you will be successful as a superintendent.

> *And can it be that I should gain*
> *An interest in the Savior's blood?*
> *Died He for me, who caused His pain?*
> *For me, who Him to death pursued?*
> *Amazing love! how can it be*
> *That Thou, my God, shouldst die for me?*
> *Amazing love! how can it be*
> *That Thou, my God, shouldst die for me?*

Make the good of others the focus of your interest, strategy. and work.
You will find joy in making others better!

The Great Wedding Planner

Therefore shall a man leave his father and his mother, and shall cleave unto his wife; and they shall be one flesh. **Genesis 2:24**

So what does it take to plan a wedding? It takes time. Further, wedding planners will tell you that it requires a vision and organization. Weddings are based on style and beauty. Many brides will spend a large amount of time choosing their gown, flowers, cake, and bridesmaids' gowns. The wedding will need a date and time as well as a location and budget. Part of the preparation requires understanding what are the rules, restrictions, and procedures for the ceremony as determined by the pastor and church. The wedding party and guests will need to be identified. Anyone helping with a wedding usually wants to start by building a relationship with the bride and groom first. There will also be other relationship building between florist, the location, the caterers, photographers, musicians, and pastors. Invitations will need to be ordered and people invited to the wedding. The wedding couple will want to obtain a license as required by state laws. Many wedding planners recommend not waiting until the last minute for any of the aforementioned areas, but rather be organized and be prepared for the wedding day.

God's plan clearly connects weddings with His plan for our relationship with Him. The church is described as the bride with Jesus as the bridegroom. He spoke about heaven compared to a king who was preparing the marriage for his son. In Matthew 22, Jesus told about this king sending out his servants in order to invite people to a marriage banquet. The first group invited did not accept the invitation and went on with their own business. Some even killed the servants who had invited them. The banquet had great food with oxen and fatlings. The king sent servants out to invite others. As people came to the feast, they were expected to have a certain attire. The king noticed that one guest was not appropriately dressed. This inappropriately dressed guest was bound, and tossed into darkness where there was weeping and gnashing of teeth. Another example of the wedding is seen in Luke 14:8-9, 11, "when thou art bidden of any man to a wedding, sit not down in the highest room; lest a more honorable man than thou be bidden of him; And he that bade thee and him come and say to thee, Give this man place; and thou begin with shame to take the lowest room. For whosoever exalteth himself shall be abased; and he that humbleth himself shall be exalted."

At the wedding, we are not to assume we are chosen and deserve to be in any high place. An invitation to the wedding is an honor by itself and our focus is not on us but on the honoree, Jesus. Jesus has planned heaven to be the great wedding relationship with Him in glory.

The importance of weddings can be seen when Jesus' first miracle was performed at a wedding where he turned water into wine. "This beginning of miracles did Jesus in Cana of Galilee, and manifested forth his glory; and his disciples believed on him." John 2:11. Further, God's plan is finalized in Revelation 19:7 when He said, "Let us be glad and rejoice, and give honor to Him; for the marriage of the Lamb is come, and his wife hath made herself ready."

As a bride prepares for a wedding, prepare also for your job of leadership.

Drenched in the Love of God

Now the God of hope fill you with all joy and peace in believing, that ye may abound in hope, through the power of the Holy Ghost. **Romans 15:13**

Last weekend, my university where I work had a home football game and it was raining "cats and dogs." I wanted to see the game because it was only our second home game. I put on my rain jacket, leather hat, and went off to the game. The rain was coming down in buckets but I didn't mind because the temperature was 75 degrees and I was quite comfortable. After I entered the stadium, I climbed up to my seat and started to enjoy the game. My original intent was to stay until half-time, because of the rain, but I ended up leaving with still 3 minutes to go in the first quarter.

It had rained so hard that there were places in my rain coat that the water had found a way to come through. My leather hat, even though I had a hood, started to leak. I was so wet that I thought I might as well have just went over and sat in the pond outside the stadium. My underwear was also drenched, as were my socks.

Just think, if we as educators were willing to get fully immersed and give our all for the students, think of the learning that will take place. If parents are willing to get fully immersed with raising their kids, think of the learning that will take place. And if superintendents were willing to give of their all for the teachers and principals, think of the learning that will take place!

My immersion brought back memories of when I was baptized in Pend Oreille Lake. I was in grade school and I remember the water was icy cold. I was willing to get totally submersed because I wanted to demonstrate that I had given my all to my Lord and Savior. There is not one part of my being that I do not want to give to Jesus. If I am willing to get totally wet for a football game, I want to be totally willing to get submersed for Christ and be filled with His joy and peace. Jesus is coming soon! If you are not ready, why not ask Jesus to forgive you of your sins and to come into your heart?

> *Deeper, deeper though it cost hard trials,*
> *Deeper let me go!*
> *Rooted in the holy love of Jesus,*
> *Let me fruitful grow.*
> –C. F. Jones

You can't get better if you are not going to drench yourself to your profession.
As in sports, the player or team which dedicates itself to the game
is the winner.

My Soul Thirsts for You

I stretch forth my hands unto thee: my soul thirsteth after thee, as a thirsty land. Selah. **Psalm 143:6**

A sheriff and his deputy had caught an outlaw and were taking him across the arid hot Arizona desert to Yuma. Their water had run out and they had lost their horses. The outlaw knew the area and where water holes were, but would not tell them. He was laughing at them and said, "I will get out of these shackles and watch you drink sand." When a person gets so thirsty and in the desert, he will start to hallucinate and try to drink sand.

The three trudged on and finally the sheriff could go no further but told his deputy to keep going on. Maybe they would make it and bring back help. So the deputy and the outlaw kept going towards Yuma. It was hot and both were struggling. The outlaw kept up his heinous laughing and almost got away from the deputy, but wasn't successful. All of a sudden, they saw the horses coming back and they knew that they were saved because animals can smell water. But it was too late for the outlaw. He had become delirious and started to drink the sand before he died.

The horses did find the water and the sheriff and deputy were saved. They voraciously drank the water from the spring the horses found! Have you ever been that thirsty before? I have and the water tasted so good and was the most refreshing drink I could have ever had. This is the type of thirst that David had for the Lord! David continually sought and desired the Lord and likened this as a continual thirst for God. I desire the same and want to know so much about my Lord and Saviour, Jesus Christ. Do you? Only Jesus can satisfy your soul!

I thirsted in the barren land of sin and shame
And nothing satisfying there I found
But to the blessed cross of Christ one day I came
Where springs of living water did abound
Drinking at the springs of living water
Happy now am I, my soul He satisfied.
–John Peterson

O God, I have tasted Thy goodness and it has satisfied me and made me thirsty for more.
–A. W. Tozer

A Fool's Actions

A fool's mouth is his destruction, and his lips are the snare of his soul. **Proverbs 18:7**

*W*ebster's *Dictionary* says a fool is a person who acts unwisely or imprudently; is a silly person; a weak-minded or idiotic person. Psalms 14 and 53 give 12 characteristics of a fool which are:

> They say there is not God
> They live corrupt lives
> They do vile things
> They are without understanding
> They do not seek God and ignore Him
> They never learn from their ignorance
> They seek to destroy God's people
> They never pray
> They are overcome with dreaded fear
> They abuse and frustrate the poor

Jesus adds this to the list in Luke 12:

> They ignore their own soul
> They ignore their obligations to God

King Solomon adds to the list in Proverbs:

> They give full vent to their anger
> They are senseless and don't understand
> They despise wisdom and discipline
> They hate knowledge
> They detest in turning from evil

Now you can understand why a fool's mouth is his destruction. You can also identify who a fool is and whom to avoid. As a superintendent, you want people around you that desire knowledge and what is best for the school district. As it is said in Proverbs 19:8, "He that getteth wisdom loveth his own soul: he that keepeth understanding shall find good." Do you control your lips and do your administrators control their lips? As the saying went in the Navy, "Loose lips sink ships." Loose lips will sink your district and superintendency.

> *When all philosophies shall fail;*
> *This word alone shall fit;*
> *That a sage feels too small for life,*
> *And a fool too large for it.*
> —G. K. Chesterton

Behold, I have played the fool, and have erred exceedingly. Samuel 26:21

November 28

Never to Meet Again

And when he had thus spoken, he kneeled down, and prayed with them. And they all wept sore, and fell on Paul's neck, and kissed him, sorrowing most of all for the words which he spake, that they should see his face no more. And they accompanied him unto the ship. **Acts 20: 36-38**

Leaving behind loves ones is very hard, whether at death or moving away. The only difference is that death is final, but when you move, you have the opportunity to go back and visit.

Ben had resigned his superintendency and had taken a new superintendency several hundred miles away. The going away party was hard on him and his family. They were leaving behind people with whom they had become very close and a church in which they really loved. The people showed up in droves and wished him and his family the very best. They were happy for him and his new adventure, but the tears still flowed.

Ben had told me that he had planned to drive back every so often and visit, but that has been extremely rare. It has been nine years since he left that community and district and he has only been back once. He told me that he has several of those people on his email list, but that is about all of the contact he has with them. Then he reflected for a minute and said this, "You know, my intentions were good as I wanted to go back and visit, but because of my own family, grandkids, current job, and other things pulling at me, it almost makes it impossible." He went on to say, "In the future, if time permits, I would still like to go back and visit, but things have probably changed a lot."

This reminds me of when my brother passed away 12 years ago. He was 51 years old and we were very close. He lived in Denver and I was living in Kansas. Even though we were only able to see each other once a year, on vacation, we would talk weekly on the phone. When he died, that left a real void in my life as I knew I would never be able to see him again. It took me quite a few years before I could talk much about him because tears would come to my eyes and I would get choked up. My consolation prize is this: I know that I will someday meet him in Heaven! You will come across this as a superintendent, whether by a death in your family or in moving from a community. It will be hard but you will have precious memories!

> Soon we'll come to the end of life's journey
> And perhaps we'll never meet any more,
> Till we gather in heaven's bright city
> Far away on that beautiful shore.
> –A E Brumely

Goodbye may seem forever. Farewell is like the end,
but in my heart is the memory and there you will always be.
–Walt Disney Company

Joy and Excitement

For, lo, as soon as the voice of thy salutation sounded in mine ear, the babe leaped in my womb for joy. Luke 1:44

Thanksgiving is over and now the Christmas season is upon us. This is a joyous time and everyone is excited! Listening to the bells jingle, hearing the Christmas carols, seeing the manger scene, and the decorations brings joy to your heart. As a kid, this was my favorite time of the year. I enjoyed the prelude up to Christmas. The snows had come, I was able to sled outside and enjoy the winter season. I enjoyed shopping with my parents and buying Christmas gifts.

One time we were shopping in Lewiston, Idaho and the Salvation Army ringers were on the corner ringing for donations. They had left the kettle there and it was full of money, which I didn't realize. I ran up to it and turned it upside down and all of the money fell out. My folks helped me pick up the money and put it back in the kettle. They were not happy. When we got home that night, I received a good spanking. Did that stop the joy of the Christmas season in me? No! I was just as excited as before.

As superintendents, you may be excited about a test score, about your district being recognized in the state, about you receiving an award, or about a host of other good things happening to your district, but you will have your "kettle" turned upside down and then all of you, which includes the board members, administrators, and community has to help put the "coins" back in the kettle. A superintendent in the Tulsa area had his "kettle" turned upside down a few years ago when his football coach, who had won many 6A championships, was caught cheating by recruiting. It was a tough year for that district, but they all pulled together and were able to "put the coins back in the kettle" for the next year. Their pain was turned back into joy! The same is with us. Jesus has allowed us to put the coins back in the "kettle!"

Joy to the world, the Lord has come
Let earth receive her King;
Let every heart prepare Him room,
And Heaven and Nature sing
Joy to the Word, the Savior reigns
Let men their songs employ;
While field and flood, rocks, hills, and plains,
Repeat the sounding joy
No more let sins and sorrows grow
Nor thorns infest the ground
He comes to make His blessing flow
Far as the curse is found
He rules the world with truth and grace
And makes the nations prove
The glories of His righteousness,
And wonders of His love.
–Isaac Watts

Joy is the holy fire that keeps our purpose warm and our intelligence aglow.
–Helen Keller

Board Relations and the Political Arena

And the young men that were brought up with him spake unto him saying, Thus shalt thou answer the people that spake unto thee, saying, Thy father made our yoke heavy but make thou it somewhat lighter for us; thus shalt thou say unto them, My little finger shall be thicker than my father's loins. ll Chronicles 10:10

Texas Competency 4 reads: "The superintendent knows how to respond to and influence the larger political, social, economic, legal, and cultural context, including working with the board of trustees, to achieve the district's educational vision. ELCC Standard 6 reads: Candidates who complete the program are educational leaders who have the knowledge and ability to promote the success of all students by understanding, responding to, and influencing the larger political, social, economic, legal, and cultural context."

King Rehoboam, the son of King Solomon, had just taken over as king of Israel. The first step that King Rehoboam took after he became king was a judicial one. He wanted to cement the dissatisfied Ephramites to himself by being crowned king in their chief city. After the crowning, Rehoboam returned and started to attend to the affairs of being king.

The people came to him and asked for the burden to be lightened and requested certain changes in of the attitudes of the kings of the house of David. They agreed to be ruled by the house of David if they would only lighten the burden somewhat. The old men gave him counsel saying he should be king and lighten the burden for his subject, who would then willingly serve him. But when he consulted with the young men who had grown up with him, they advised Rehoboam to become harder on the people. When the people heard this hard speech and saw his haughty attitude, they rebelled.

This story has a sad ending. Because of Rehoboam's arrogance and harshness, the tribe of Israel split into Israel and Judah. You wonder why Rehoboam didn't listen to the wise advice from the old men. This is like board relations and the political arena in school districts. If you make the right choice, then the district will stay together and there will be a healthy climate in the district. The wrong choice is made by listening to the wrong people. You have to quickly learn who your board is, what makes them tick, and the political landscape of your community. This will help you be successful and keep your job. Ask the Lord to make you politically astute and alert with your board and community. So that you might be, as it is said in Matthew 10:16, "be wise as serpents and harmless as doves."

Lift me up above the shadows, plant my feet on higher ground,
Lift me up above the clouds, Lord, Where the pure sunshine in found.
—R E Winsett

Understanding the makeup of the board and community
will help you avoid landmines.

DECEMBER

Giving to the Poor

He that hath pity upon the poor lendeth unto the Lord; and that which he hath given will he pay him again. **Proverbs 19:17**

December is the time of year when we give gifts to people and show them our appreciation. God gave the best gift to us when He sent Jesus into the world. From the angels to the magi to the shepherds, all praised the Lord for this glorious gift.

In 1987, I was an assistant principal in Oklahoma and noticed that this one family was not going to experience a joyful Christmas. These five siblings came from a poor home and lived in low-income housing.

I got to know this family very well because the children were in my office quite often, usually in trouble. I would ask the mother to come to the school and visit with me so we could come to an agreeable solution on how to keep her children in the classroom and stay out of trouble. The mother was a tall, large lady with a demeaning look and her husband was in prison.

After those encounters, my heart went out to her children. I felt impressed to go to the Burlington Coat Factory and purchased 5 sweaters, one for each student. When they left school for Christmas Vacation, I gave them each a gift. I don't know what they did with those sweaters, but I felt that I had done the right thing.

As a superintendent, you will see a lot of needy students and you cannot begin to imagine their living conditions. These children wake up in the morning with only one thought on their mind: survival. The book of Proverbs says that the Lord will repay you for your good deeds. Throughout the year, remember the poor and help them in their plight. Remember, Jesus was born in a manger but was visited by the magi and given gifts.

We are made in the Creator's image
He richly gives to us all things to enjoy
When we give we are simply letting Him use our hands
To bring to others His happiness, blessings, and joy.
–Toni Doswell

You can't have a perfect day without doing something for someone who'll never be able to repay you.
–John Wooden

The Apple of God's Eye

He found him in a desert land, and in the waste howling wilderness; he led him about, he instructed him, he kept him as the apple of his eye. **Deuteronomy 32:10**

God found and sustained Israel in the wilderness. He led him about for 40 years. During these 40 years, God instructed Israel about the laws of God. Even though Israel would murmur and complain, God kept them as the "apple of his eye". He also kept Israel from falling into idolatry by exalting Him above all nations. Finally, God gave Israel material property. When you find favor with God, he will bless you beyond what you deserve or are worth.

Sometimes, as a superintendent, it seems that you are in a dry barren wasteland and the board and community is howling at you. You wonder if you will ever make it through, but, rest assured, you will if you put God first. Even though Israel wandered in the wilderness for 40 years, God did not let their shoes or their clothing wear out. He sustained them with meat and manna from Heaven. He also provided water for them in a barren land. This was because Israel had favor with the Lord. You can have favor, too, just put God first and give Him the glory.

A superintendent told me that she felt that her district was a wilderness. There was bickering, fighting, board turnover, and a newspaper that kept the turmoil going. Through it all, this superintendent gave God the glory and God brought her out to a better place.

I am the apple of His eye
I don't know the reason why
But goodness and mercy follow me
Because I'm the apple of His eye.
–Unknown

**Life doesn't always turn out the way we picture,
but God works in ways we can't see or imagine.**

Watch and Be Ready

Blessed are those servants whom the lord when he cometh shall find watching, verily I say unto you, that he shall gird himself, and make them to sit down to meat, and will come forth and serve them. Luke 12:37

How do you prepare for a trip or vacation? My preparation is defined by time periods. There are certain things I do when first planning a trip and other things I do right before my departure. For example, one of the first things I do when planning a trip is contact the people I want to meet to check their available schedule and then compare that with my availability for a trip. Then, immediately before my departure, I would check the house to make sure I turned off appliances and lights.

I usually have to check the coffee pot twice to make sure I turned it off. And I have been known to drive around the block, making sure a second time that I closed the garage door. In the middle time period of my preparations, I order the airplane tickets, find a dog sitter, choose clothing to pack, and try to lower the food supply in my refrigerator. I may even schedule some appointments before the trip. I want to be well-prepared for my trips.

Jesus told us to be prepared for him and to not be lazy, but rather to continue our work faithfully. We don't know the scheduled time of our departure from this earth or even the possible end of this earth. I think we often plan our days on this earth differently dependent on our age. The older we become, the more we realize our own mortality and, thus, we may be more conscious of serving the Lord each day. I hope that I have contacted those close to me about the need to believe in Jesus and accept Him as their personal savior because I want to see them in Heaven. I want to make sure that I have used my time and resources wisely as a servant of the Lord. I want to be ready for that trumpet sound!

There is coming a day, when no heart aches shall come,
No more clouds in the sky, no more tears to dim the eye,
All is peace forever more, on that happy golden shore,
What a day, glorious day that will be.
–Will Thompson

And that, knowing the time that now it is high time to awake out of sleep,
for now is our salvation nearer than when we believed.
The night is far spent, the day is at hand;
let us therefore cast off the works of darkness,
and let us put on the armour of light.
Let us walk honestly, as in the day,
not in rioting and drunkenness,
not in clambering or wantonness,
not in strife and envying.
But put ye on the Lord Jesus Christ,
and make not provision for the flesh,
to fulfill the lusts thereof. Romans 13:11-14

Having Courage During Adversity

I know where you dwell, where Satan's throne is; you hold fast my name and you did not deny my faith even in the days of Antipas my witness, my faithful one, who was killed among you, where Satan dwells. **Revelation 2:13**

The name Antipas is mentioned only one time in the Bible. There is an interesting story behind his name. In 92 A.D, Antipas was the Bishop of Pergamum assigned to that position by John the Apostle. The meaning of the name, Antipas, is "against all."

As a result of living faithfully in an evil environment, there were those in Pergamum who were losing their lives. Jesus mentioned one of their number by name: Antipas. According to a 10th century legend, Antipas was Bishop of Pergamum and was brought before an image of Caesar and told to confess that Caesar was God. When he refused, the Roman official said, "Antipas, don't you know that the whole world is against you?" to which he replied, "Then Antipas is against the whole world!" Antipas was then placed inside of a brass bull which was heated with fire until he was roasted to death.

I can visualize Antipas in a court room, people throwing things at him, shouting obscenities, his body badly beaten, and the courage it took for him to rise to his feet and say those words. Many times in my career I have prayed for such courage.

I have heard many school superintendents say, "It's lonely at the top" and never more so than when dealing with conflict or adversity. However, no matter the consequences, we always have a duty to do the right thing. We owe that to the community and students we serve.

> Upon life's boundless ocean where mighty billows roll,
> I've fixed my hope in Jesus, blest anchor of my soul;
> When trials fierce assail me as storms are gathering o'er,
> I rest upon His mercy and trust Him more.
>
> –Lewis E. Jones

Courage is being scared to death, but saddling up anyway.
–John Wayne

An Honest and Faithful King

The king that faithfully judgeth the poor, his throne shall be established for ever.
Proverbs 29:14

In Kouzes and Poser's research, they found that there are five essential leadership traits of successful leaders. These traits qualities are honesty, forward-looking, competent, inspiring, and intelligent. People want to follow an honest leader.

Years ago, many employees started out by assuming that their leadership was honest simply because of the authority of their position. When you start a superintendent position, you need to assume that employees will think you are dishonest. In order to be seen as an honest superintendent, you will have to go out of your way to display honesty. People now will not assume you are honest simply because you have never been caught lying. Finally, your decisions have to be immersed with justice, treating all equally.

An example of this was when I was a superintendent in Minnesota. The head of the support union came in to my office to introduce himself and meet me. He said, "So you're the new superintendent. You're probably like all other superintendents, a liar." That caught me off guard. I had to work hard to show that I was honest and treated the employees fairly and justly. Within the year, this union president was my biggest supporter.

One of the most frequent places where leaders miss an opportunity to display honesty is in handling mistakes. Much of a leader's job is to try new things and refine the ideas that don't work. However, many leaders want to avoid failure to the extent that they don't admit when something did not work. Then they stretch the truth, omit the truth, or spin the truth. That is the beginning of their downfall.

The superintendent that treats his employees with respect, sacrifices for them, emphasizes their good qualities, is humble, is prepared to follow, is willing to admit mistakes, and uses the same justice for rich or poor will have longevity in the community. Remember to follow the leadership style of Jesus: He lifted people up, He applied balm to the wounded hearts, His followers loved to follow Him, He had compassion on the multitude, He didn't turn anyone away, He was a servant, He got out amongst the people. Be a servant and get out amongst your people.

Great is thy faithfulness, O God my Father,
There is no shadow of turning with Thee;
Thou changes not, Thy compassion, they fail not
As Thou has been Thou forever wilt be.
−Thomas Chisholm

A good character is the best tombstone. Those who loved you and were helped
by you will remember you… Carve your name on hearts, not on marble.
−Charles H. Spurgeon

December 6

Add up your Securities

Therefore will not we fear, though the earth be removed, and though the mountains be carried into the midst of the sea. **Psalm 46:2**

One reason people have weak or little faith is due to a continual emphasis on their insecurities. As a result, they develop a haunting feeling that something bad is going to happen.

A cloud of ominous uncertainty constantly rests over them like dust did with Pigpen in the Peanuts comics. One can't mentally dwell upon insecurity without feeling insecure. Faith has great difficulty in taking root in a soil of insecurity. To counteract this dire situation and influence in your life, begin at once to dwell upon and emphasize the security factors in your life. Add up your "securities."

If you felt poor, but had a number of securities in the safety deposit box in the bank, you could go there, add them up and leave feeling pretty secure financially. Similarly, make a list of the dependable and secure factors with which you are surrounded. Such things as:

> The good earth, whose seedtime and harvest can be depended upon.
> The sun never fails to come back and shine through the clouds.
> You have the love of your wife or husband, the love of children.
> Your heart still beats.
> You can eat, walk and think.
> You have a steady job and a roof over your head.

Add to the above list and over it all write the words "Jesus Christ." As you habitually add up your securities, the feeling of insecurity will diminish. Your faith will grow stronger (Tom Leding Ministries, 2011). Scriptures to memorize are Psalm 18:2, Philippians 4:13, Isaiah 41:10, and Romans 8:28.

> *His oath, His covenant, His blood,*
> *Support me in the whelming flood.*
> *When all around my soul gives way,*
> *He then is all my Hope and Stay.*
> –Edward Mote

Always look at what you have left. Never look at what you have lost.
–Robert Schuller

Be Honest in Everything

Recompense to no man evil for evil. Provide things honest in the sight of all men.
Romans 12:17

If you always tell the truth, you will never have to worry about remembering what you last said. There is nothing more important that integrity and credibility. Lose those and you will have lost everything.

George Jones started out as a clerk in a grocery store. He quickly received the reputation as a hard-working, bright, and ambitious employee. His work ethic, manners, and easy-going personality were noticed by everyone. The trait that really caught his co-workers attention was his honesty. That came to the attention of Henry J. Raymond, the renowned journalist. Together, they started *The New York Times*.

Many years later, *The New York Times* waged a battle against "Boss Tweed" and his corrupt dynasty. Jones was offered under-the-table $500,000, which then was a lot of money, to go away and retire. Boss Tweed said, "You can live like a prince the rest of your days." Jones replied, "Yes, and know myself every day to be a rascal."

A superintendent told me she had a board president ask her to do something illegal for one of his friends. She told him that she would like to do that but she couldn't because it is illegal. After that, she never again received a vote in her favor from that board president. Her reputation and honesty meant more to her than pleasing a school board president.

> *I have to live with myself and so,*
> *I want to be fit for myself to know.*
> *I want to be able as days go by,*
> *Always to look myself in the eye.*
> *I don't want to stand in the setting sun,*
> *And hate myself for the things I've done.*
> *I don't want to keep on a closet shelf,*
> *A lot of secrets about myself;*
> *And fool myself as I come and go,*
> *Into thinking nobody else will know – the kind of man I really am.*
> –Unknown

Honesty is the first chapter in the book of wisdom.
–Thomas Jefferson

Being a Steward for the Lord

The silver is mine and the gold is mine, saith the Lord of hosts. **Haggai 2:8**

Jesus owns everything, yet he has entrusted this great wealth to us as his stewards. As a superintendent, you are trusted with making certain that the public monies are spent wisely. You will have all sorts of people knocking at your door to spend money for this and for that. Some of these people will be disguised as a board member who really are agenda-driven and are children of Belial. It is our duty to follow the example the Lord has given to us, which is to serve and to be diligent over what has been entrusted to you in your position.

Stewardship is a way of holiness and a way of imitating the Lord Jesus. Jesus came to do the will of His Father and not His own. He came to serve and give everything so we might have life abundantly. Why did he give so much when he owned everything? It is because of His unlimited love for us.

Why do you give so much of yourself for your school district? It is because of your love for children and your desire to see that they receive an optimum education, no matter the cost. At one board meeting, I said to the board, "The recommendations I make affect my children also because my children are in this school." Why would I make a recommendation or decision that would harm them? That doesn't even make sense.

All of the wealth is the Lord's and we are only His caretaker. In your district make all decisions as unto the Lord. Remember He owns everything and He will take care of you!

> *Jesus owns the cattle on a thousand hills,*
> *The wealth in every mine;*
> *He owns the rivers and the rocks and rills,*
> *The sun and stars that shine.*
> *Wonderful riches, more than tongue can tell -*
> *He is my Father so they're mine as well;*
> *He owns the cattle on a thousand hills -*
> *I know that He will care for me.*
> —John Peterson

Stewardship is what we do after we say, "We Believe."

Keep Holding On

Looking unto Jesus the author and finisher of our faith; who for the joy that was set before him endured the cross, despising the shame, and is set down at the right hand of the throne of God. **Hebrews 12:2**

Jennie Wilson wrote the song, "Hold to God's Unchanging Hand." She had experienced spinal problems when she was four and was confined to a wheel chair until she died at age 56. She didn't get to attend school, but was taught at home. While at home and later on in her life, she wrote over 2,200 texts. She put all of her faith and trust in God and with her words have encouraged countless people.

Joni Eareckson Tada had a diving accident when she was a teenager in which she broke her neck. She became a quadriplegic and confined to a wheel chair. After two years of rehabilitation, she emerged, like a butterfly out of a cocoon, determined to help others. Her words and encouragement have helped many people.

These are two examples of women who have overcome their handicap and have been an encouragement to many people throughout the years. Jennie's songs are sung in churches today and Joni has written several books and can still be heard on the radio where she hosts "Joni and Friends." If you are experiencing difficulty or have become so depressed and discouraged that you don't know which way to turn, then remember to "Hold to God's Unchanging Hand."

> *Time is filled with swift transition*
> *Naught of earth unmoved can stand*
> *Build your hopes on things eternal,*
> *Hold to God's unchanging hand.*
> *Trust in Him who will not leave you,*
> *Whatsoever years may bring,*
> *If by earthyl friend forsaken,*
> *Still more closely to him cling.*
> *Covet not this world's vain riches*
> *That so rapidly decay,*
> *Seek to gain the heavenly treasure,*
> *They will never pass away*
> *When your journey is completed,*
> *If to God you have been true,*
> *Fair and bright the home in glory,*
> *Your enraptured soul will view.*

Stay strong and weather the storm, you'll make it through. Prayer is not overcoming God's reluctance, but laying hold of His willingness.
–Martin Luther

The beginning of anxiety is the end of faith, and the beginning of true faith is the end of anxiety.
–Georg Mueller.

We are one "hearing" away from victory.

Dealing with Change

Meditate upon these things; give thyself wholly to them; that they profiting may appear to all. I Timothy 4:15

Superintendents know that they will have a difficult time when they introduce change to their employees. They will make enemies of all those who have done well under the old system, and only lukewarm defenders among those who are not sure how well they will do under the new one. Resistance to progress is universal. The reason for this is because people feel like they are lost and change is one of the biggest stressors there is. Therefore, change seizes every generation by the throat and attempts to stop all forward movement.

In 1553, Admiral Richard Hawkins recorded while he was at sea 10,000 men under his command died of scurvy. He also noted that oranges and lemons completely cured it. But his observations went unheeded for 200 years during which time thousands of sailors needlessly died.

In 1753, James Lind, a British Naval surgeon, published a book saying that scurvy could be eliminated with lemon juice. He even cited case histories to prove it. But instead of being honored, he was ridiculed by the Lords of the Admiralty and by the leading physicians of that day. In fact, his advice was ignored for another 40 years. It wasn't until his death in 1794 that a Naval Fleet was supplied with orange juice before a voyage. On that 23 week voyage, there wasn't one reported case of scurvy. Even so, another 10 years passed and thousands more died, before regulations were enacted requiring sailors to drink a daily ration of lemon juice. With that enactment, scurvy finally disappeared from the British Navy.

Do not let complacency, prejudice, or the fear of change, rob you of all that God intends you to be. Spence Johnson (1998) wrote in his book, *Who Moved My Cheese,* how people will utterly fail before they allow change to take place.

The six important lessons on change in this book are:
1. Change happens
2. Anticipate change
3. Monitor change
4. Adapt to change quickly
5. Change
6. Enjoy change.

When you accept Christ as your personal savior, you become a changed person in Christ with your name written in the Lamb's book of life!

> *There's a new name written down in glory, and it's mine, yes it's mine*
> *The white-robed angels sing the story, "A sinner has come home;"*
> *With my sins forgiven I am bound for heaven,*
> *Never more to roam.*
> —Austin Miles

Growth means change and change involves risks;
stepping from the known to the unknown.

December 11

God Encounters

But when he saw the multitudes, he was moved with compassion on them because they fainted, and were scattered abroad, as sheep having no shepherd.
Matthew 9:36

A man was walking to church and saw four young boys hanging out on a street corner. As he was going by, he visited with them and invited them to go with him. They did and went with him each Sunday thereafter. These four boys became the main group of his Sunday school class that he began to teach.

Many years later, the Sunday school teacher's friends decided to throw him a birthday party. They thought it would be nice to contact the four boys to see what had come of them and invite them to write a special letter to their old Sunday school teacher. Their letters were shockers, to say the least. One boy had become a missionary to China, one was president of the Federal Reserve Bank, one was a private secretary to President Herbert Hoover, and the fourth was President Hoover himself. As the Ray Boltz wrote in his song, "Thank you for giving to the Lord, I'm so glad that you gave."

Be aware and alert! God-encounters can happen at any time especially when you're on your way to doing something else. Being insensitive to the Spirit of God will cause you to miss a real blessing, a chance to grow, and an opportunity to put God first in your life. As a superintendent, you do not know the influences you will have on the students in your district.

Jesus left Heaven to walk the road that humans walk. He didn't puff himself up and set up a kingdom in each town and say, "This is my place, if you want to see Me come here." He was like the good Samaritan (Luke 10:33). He went to the shopping places, to their places of business, and to their homes. He "went through the towns, preaching the gospel and healing everywhere" (Luke 9:6). Everywhere he went, he was doing good.

Rescue the perishing, care for the dying,
Snatch them in pity from sin and the grave;
Weep over the erring one, lift up the fallen,
Tell them of Jesus the mighty to save.
–W. H. Doane

The moment your compassion is activated, stop!
You may be on the verge of a God-encounter!

Jesus Understands Your Circumstance

Rejoice greatly, O daughter of Zion; shout, O daughter of Jerusalem: behold, thy King cometh unto thee; he is just and having salvation; lowly, and riding upon a donkey, and upon a colt the foal of a donkey. **Zechariah 9:9**

The prophesy came true when Jesus rode into Jerusalem on a donkey. He was hailed and people cried, "Blessed is he that cometh in the name of the Lord; Hosanna in the highest" (Matthew 21:9). The people spread their coats on the road for Him and waved palm branches which was the customary practice in parades for conquerors and great princes. It was shortly after this triumphant entrance into Jerusalem that Jesus was arrested, tried, and crucified.

Jesus knew no sin and lived an upright life. Yet, even after he triumphantly entered into Jerusalem, he was arrested and tried. The leaders sought to find false witnesses against Him, but could find only two.

When He was brought before Pilate, He did not answer the charges of the false witnesses such that Pilate marveled at Him. Finally, Pilate said he could find no fault in Jesus, but then asked the leaders who he should release, Jesus or a murderer. The leaders, like community organizers, stirred up the crowd so much that they made the most grievous and errant choice of their lives, they asked for a murderer to be released and a righteous man to be crucified.

Has it ever been like that for you on your job? A neighboring superintendent was being hailed by the board and city as an exemplary leader. The district just finished building projects and received exemplary ratings in their achievement. Then a chillingly evil board member stirred up the crowd so vigorously because of a lie told by an evil and incompetent assistant superintendent of finance, that the board suspended this upright and good man. The board went on to fire the superintendent even after the district had achieved greatness.

Keep looking to Jesus for your help and example since he overcame the grave. You, too, will overcome your circumstance or trial that you may be going through. Jesus has a better place waiting for you.

O when I come to the end of my journey,
Weary of life and the battle is won;
Caring the staff and the cross of redemption
He'll understand and say, "Well done."
–Roger Wilson

In the darkest hour our soul is replenished
and given strength to continue by our Lord.

Leave Your Burden with the Lord

For, lo, the wicked bend their bow, they make ready their arrow upon the string, that they may privily shoot at the upright in heart. **Psalms 11:2**

Have you ever had your enemies and naysayers start attacking you? It seems that everyone is against you and no one sticks up for you. I know of a superintendent who had this happen to him. He was viscously beat up in the media, almost on a daily basis, by an unscrupulous reporter who was a front for the teacher's union.

It got so bad that the superintendent didn't want to go into his office or even answer his phone because he did not want to run into this reporter. What he was accused of was based on utter falsehoods and half-truths. He went to the pastor of his church to find help, but no one from the church stepped forward except one lady. A deacon told him that everyone is afraid of this villainous reporter and they didn't want to see their names on the front page of the newspaper. The superintendent was upright in heart and arrows were being shot at him by the evildoers.

Another superintendent just resigned his position after a board member organized rabble-rousers accusing him of financial incompetence. Again, these were based on half-truths and lies. This superintendent had an assistant superintendent of finance who failed to pay the state monies that was due. A board member and an assistant superintendent of finance rabidly attacked him so hard that he resigned his position. He only asked that the board clear his muddied name.

Both of these superintendents were Christian men and left their burden on the Lord. They needed His help to fight their battles. You will face situations in life where people will get so angry that they will blatantly slander you. They will not only want you to be fired, but also want to destroy you and assassinate your career. When these things happen, put your cares and burdens on the Lord. Remember to stand strong when adversity hits, for when the storm clouds come in, the eagles soar while small birds take cover.

> *When you enemies assail and your heart begins to fail,*
> *Don't forget that God in heaven answers prayer,*
> *He will make a way for you and will lead you safely through;*
> *Take your burden to the Lord and leave it there.*
> –C. A Tindley, Jr.

Every evening, I turn my worries over to God.
He's going to be up all night anyway.
–Mary C. Crowley.

Mastery Over the Wilderness

And immediately the Spirit driveth him into the wilderness. **Mark 1:12**

Jesus was baptized by John the Baptist and a voice coming out of Heaven said, "Thou art my beloved son, in whom I am well pleased" (Mark 1:11). Jesus had just heard His father's voice and all of sudden He was in the wilderness. When you are on the mountain top, you will later have valley experiences just as Jesus did when he was driven into the wilderness.

In the wilderness with the wild beasts, Jesus was tempted by Satan. Jesus not only became Master over Satan, demons, and all their works, but also became Master of the wild beasts and had immunity from their poisons.

Christ alone grappled with Satan. He had no fellow worker with him which demonstrated the strength of Jesus. He alone was able to overcome Satan, the father of all liars, without any assistance. To have mastery over the wilderness, you have to:

1. Know that Satan is your enemy and he desires nothing but misery and destruction for you.
2. Know that all men are subject to temptations.
3. Know the hopes of success. God set Christ before us as a pattern of trust and confidence so we will not fear the temptations of Satan.
4. Know the use of instruction to the people of God. The wilderness experience taught three lessons: comfort, patience, and obedience.
Bring comfort to those who need it. Their troubles will not always last. They may be tried and tested, but "joy comes in the morning."
Patience teaches that we must be contented and undergo our course of trial, as Christ patiently continued.
Obedience means following Christ's example. He submitted to the Holy Spirit while Satan tempted him. If you would look for the conflict to cease then, do as Christ did, carry it humbly to God.
5. Know that you have to carry your conflict faithfully to God while still opposing sin and Satan. The more you give in to Satan, the more you are troubled and tempted by him, and your misery is increased. But if you repel his temptations, he will leave and the angels will minister unto you!

> *Tis the grandest theme thru the ages rung,*
> *Tis the grandest theme for a mortal tongue*
> *Tis the grandest theme that the world ever sung*
> *Out God is able to deliver thee.*
> –W. A Ogden

**The Lord Jesus Christ was pleased to submit himself
to an extraordinary combat with the tempter for our good.**

Playing With Your Authority

The king's heart is in the hand of the LORD, as the rivers of water: he turneth it whithersoever he will. **Proverbs 21:1**

Doug Sisk remembers when he was a rookie relief pitcher for the New York Mets and he heard a rumor that he might not make the team. The equipment manager came and told him that manager George Bamberger wanted to see him. Bamberger said to him, "Sorry, I can't keep you. Report to Tidewater. Do you have anything that you want to say?" Doug said he didn't have anything to say and that Bamberger then said, "That is good because that's not how it is. You're staying." Doug's teammates had congregated outside of the office listening to the prank and broke up with hysterical laughter. Doug made the team and performed very well.

In education, there is a fine line between nice and too nice. You want your employees to respect you and respect your authority. However, you don't want to come off like "the tail instead of the head." There are a couple of things you can do to preserve your reputation of being a great person while still showing authority and commanding respect.

Be friendly, but not friends. There is a code of conduct between friends and there is a code of conduct between superintendents and employees. Once you cross the friendship line and your employees feel like you are personal friends, they will naturally become confused. Things that a friend is likely to "sweep under the rug" a superintendent has to address. The confusion of these boundaries often gets nice superintendents a reputation of "not being in control and a dufus."

Joking and kidding by the superintendent doesn't usually go over very well and you come across as a "dufus" leader! You are the leader and have to set the right example and model the behavior you desire from your employees just as Christ modeled the right and proper behavior for us.

> Give of your best to the Master; Naught else is worthy His love
> He gave Himself for your ransom, Gave up His glory above,
> Laid down His life without murmur; You from sin's ruin to save;
> Give Him your heart's adoration, Give him the best that you have.
> —Mrs. Charles Bernard

You do not lead by hitting people over the head - that's assault, not leadership.
—President Eisenhower

Secret Sins

In the day when God shall judge the secrets of men by Jesus Christ according to my gospel. Romans 2:16

After a great sports blowout, it is hard for the team to practice for the next game because the team members feel so elated and that they are invincible. It is at this time that a lot of teams will stumble and lose their next game to an inferior opponent. The same is true in the Christian walk, after a great victory or blessing from the Lord, we tend to let our guard down and then Satan comes to steal it away.

There are many times that Israel fought and won a great victory but because of a person's secret sin they were routed in their next battle. The secret sin of Achan caused Israel to lose a battle, cost him the lives of his family, and his life.

What is a secret sin? That is a sin that you try to hide as you know what you did is wrong. Examples are hiding sexual impurity, pornography, greed, theft, murder, lying, adultery, disobedience, addictions, and so forth. A secret sin starts when you see something you shouldn't do or see, you covet that item, you take it, and then you hide it.

Many of us have sins that just make us shudder to think about if someone found out about them. Richard Exley writes, "If you are living in secret sin, your heart hurts. You despise yourself. Shame has made you sick and you have little or no energy. Fear eats your belly and depression dogs your days. You feel trapped and you are tempted to run away, but where can you go to escape yourself. To get rid of this secret sin, you have to confront it and confess it."

How many times have we ignored God's warning signs which are the checks to our spirit? He knows that if we continue down this path, then the bridge will run out and death is guaranteed. If you are trying to overcome a secret sin and can't, maybe it is because you are trying to handle this secret sin on your own. God wants you to rely on the believers He has brought into your life as well as His strength to overcome your secret sin. The following is a prayer of deliverance from your secret sin:

Jesus Christ, I confess and I proclaim that You are the Lord of my life and that the stripes You bore on the Cross at Calvary has established You as my Redeemer. By my faith in Jesus Christ and my belief that You are able, I petition You to purify my soul from darkness and to deliver me from my secret sin (name it). In the name of Jesus Christ, I submit my dark and evil secret sin into Your hands, Father, for a work of purification, redemption and deliverance to take place. Thank you Lord Jesus for delivering me from this bondage and secret sin and for throwing my secret sin away as far as the east is from the west. In Jesus' name, I pray. Amen.

Satan wants you to keep your sins secret.

Spirit of Adoption

For ye have not received the spirit of bondage again to fear; but ye have received the Spirit of adoption, whereby we cry Abba, Father. **Romans 8:15**

When you become a child of God, you have not received a spirit of slavery to relapse again into fear and terror, but you have received the Spirit of freedom and, thus, can break all bondages. The Spirit of adoption is the Spirit and nature of God. It is strongly affirmed in this passage that the children of God are emancipated from the spirit of bondage, the present and woeful condition of all the unregenerate.

Very few of the children of God realize the possession and largeness of their birthright. Few rise to the privilege of their adoption. Few walk in a large place and by the sunny jubilant stream from God. This is evidence that they have "not received the spirit of bondage again to fear."

"But you have received the Spirit of adoption." The Spirit of adoption is the same as the Spirit of God. He imparts the nature of the Father to all His children which make up the family of God. Man can only confer his name and his inheritance upon the child he adopts but God gives a divine inheritance. This divine inheritance results in a regeneration so we can manifestly be the "children of our Father who is in heaven."

There is not a need, or an anxiety, or a grief which is not all your own. His adoption of you, an act of his spontaneous and most free grace, pledged Him to transfer all your individual heart aches and trials to Himself.

Superintendent, you are a child of God and adopted into His family. Rejoice in Him and put all fears behind you.

I trust in God wherever I may be,
Upon the land or on the rolling sea,
For, come what may, from day to day,
My heavenly Father watches over me.
                              –W. C. Martin

Adoption into God's family gives you the love and support from God.

Telling the Story of Christ

And He said unto them, Go ye into all the world, and preach the gospel to every creature. **Mark 16:15**

My brother-in-law and sister-in-law, Wes and LeeAnn Reed, just came back from Papua New Guinea where they spent 25 years with the Yopno people. These people now have the Word of God in their own language and tongue.

During these 25 years, schools were developed to teach the people their own language, how to read it, and how to write it. These schools would have never been developed if it had not been for two people who felt the call to go into the jungle region to translate the Bible into the language of the people. This was important because most people who read do not read in Yopno. They are probably fluent in Tok Pisin or some of them in English. Now, the Yopno people will be able to read the Bible in their own native tongue.

When new children come into your school district from other countries, teaching them and working with them in love is, in essence, "telling the story of Christ" through you actions. My wife is a school nurse in a Title 1 school and because of her kind treatment of the children, when they see her in a store or at a fast-foods drive-in they will always say hello, want to hug her, or shake her hand. She gets embarrassed, but the children truly know that she genuinely cares for them. The parents are so appreciative because they know that someone does care.

Are you telling the story of Christ through your actions? Are your employees telling the story of Christ through their actions? Do children and all patrons feel welcome at their school and in your district? Let your actions always glorify Christ.

> *I love to tell the story of unseen things above,*
> *Of Jesus and His glory, Of Jesus and His love;*
> *I love to tell the story, because I know it's true,*
> *It satisfies my longings as nothing else can do.*
> –W. G. Fischer

**Start telling the story of Christ through your actions
and see the big changes come.**

The Environment of Grace

And God is able to make all grace abound toward you that ye always having all sufficiency in all things may abound to every good work. **II Corinthians 9:8**

What is grace? It is the seemingly effortless beauty or charm of movement, form, or proportion. It is a disposition to be generous or helpful, show mercy, and show clemency. It is also a favor rendered by one who doesn't need to do so. It can be simply defined as "God's unmerited favor." Grace is a gift from God.

I worked for a superintendent in Oklahoma and he was a very gracious man. It was a joy to work under him in that school district. We did not deserve his favor, especially the teachers who gave him a horrible time through their union affiliation. He treated everyone with the utmost respect and compassion. This was recognized by the community and when he retired after 17 years of service, a middle school was named after him. Even the teacher's union had to finally acknowledge his greatness.

Another example of grace in action is Raytown School District. The district incorporated a system of staff support and care that is provided when teachers need it the most, during or just after a crisis incident. This support includes regular team support meetings, individual staffing support, a crisis help line, and the availability of counselors. Preliminary results indicate that when the GRACE model of discipline is implemented, results can be dramatic. For example, one middle school reported an 80% drop in office referrals from a team of eighth-grade teachers who previously had had the highest number of suspensions in their school.

Have you brought an environment of grace to your district? If not, it will be extremely beneficial to the students, teachers, and all patrons.

THE BENEFITS OF GRACE

We are...
Saved by grace
Forgiven by grace
Sustained by grace
Healed by grace
Liberated by grace
Restored by grace
Used by grace
Transformed by grace
Give by grace
We are to live by Grace
Grow in Grace
Express Gratitude for Grace

Grace is the free, undeserved goodness and favor of God to mankind.
–Matthew Henry

The Tornados of Life

For I am persuaded, that neither death, nor life, nor angels, nor principalities, nor powers, not things present, nor things to come, nor height, nor depth, nor any other creature, shall be able to separate us from the love of God, which is in Christ Jesus our Lord. **Romans 8:38-39**

The death toll from the 2011 monster tornado in Missouri was 139. That was the deadliest year for tornadoes since 1950, based on an assessment of figures from the National Weather Service. The tornado death toll for 2011 was 520. Until then, the highest recorded death toll in a single year was 519 in 1953. There were deadlier storms before 1950, but those counts were based on estimates and not on precise figures.

Horatio Spafford wrote the hymn "It Is Well With My Soul" after several traumatic events in his life. The first was the death of his only son in 1871 at the age of four, shortly followed by the great Chicago fire which ruined him financially (he had been a successful lawyer). Then, in 1873, he had planned to travel to Europe with his family on the S.S. Ville du Havre, but sent the family ahead while he was delayed on business concerning zoning problems. While crossing the Atlantic Ocean, the ship sank after colliding with a sailing ship, the Loch Earn, and all four of Spafford's daughters died. His wife, Anna, survived and sent him a telegram saying, "Saved alone." Shortly afterwards, as Spafford traveled to meet his grieving wife, he was inspired to write the words to the song "It is Well With My Soul" as his ship passed near where his daughters had died.

When the tornados of life come, which they will, whether you are a superintendent or a support person, remember nothing can separate you from the love of Christ. Paul was whipped, beaten, stoned, suffered shipwreck, in perils of water, and in perils of everyone from false teachers to his own brethren. Paul only gloried in the cross, gladly going through these trials for Jesus Christ. As Paul said, "when I am weak, then I am strong" (ll Corinthians 12:10).

> *And Lord, haste the day when my faith shall be sight,*
> *The clouds be rolled back as a scroll;*
> *The trump shall resound, and the Lord shall descend,*
> *Even so, it is well with my soul.*
> –Horatio Spafford

I will always glory in the cross as I know my Redeemer lives.

December 21

The Wages of Covetousness

When I saw among the spoils a goodly Babylonish garment, and two hundred shekels of silver, and a wedge of gold of fifty shekels weight, then I coveted them, and took them; and behold they are hid in the earth in the midst of my tent and the silver under it. Joshua 7:21

Covetousness and greed are interrelated. Greed is the desire for material wealth, ignoring the realm of the spiritual, and is also called covetousness. One definition calls covetousness extreme greed. St. Thomas Aquinas, in his Summa Theologica, said of greed: "It is a sin directly against one's neighbor, since one man cannot overabound in external riches without another man lacking them. It is a sin against God, just as all mortal sins, inasmuch as man condemns things eternal for the sake of temporal things." This sin cost Judas Iscariot his eternal life.

Greed and covetousness is a weakness that afflicts almost every person. It is an area that is actively promoted by Satan as he knows they believe that money is their passport to doing anything and going anywhere. The longing to be rich or to have more money is a primary reason for acts of crime.

Covetousness is probably the biggest sin in the United States today. Colossians 3:5 calls covetousness "idolatry." Philippians 3:18-19, "that they are the enemies of the cross of Christ: Whose end is destruction, whose God is their belly, and whose glory is in their shame, who mind earthly things." America is spoiled rotten to the extent that people have no gratitude whatsoever anymore and it has become a land of lust and greed. The love of money has led to every evil imaginable. I Timothy warns, "For the love of money is the root of all evil..."

Superintendents also fall prey to the temptation of covetousness. You can google superintendents and *covetousness/greed* and see the shame that many have heaped upon themselves and their families. A superintendent in Indiana, former superintendent of the year, is now trying to restore his lost reputation because of greed. Another superintendent in West Virginia was forced to resign as the paper said this about him, "This was a man so full of himself that he saw nothing wrong with charging taxpayers of the poorest state in the nation mileage for hundreds of luncheon trips from the Capitol to restaurants a couple of miles away." These superintendents have forgotten that they are stewards of the public's moneys and trust. They do all they can to line their pockets. Pray that you don't fall into the temptation and trap.

O What a happy soul am I!
Although I can't see,
I am resolved that in this world
Contented I will be.
–Fanny Crosby

If you are not satisfied with a little, you will not be satisfied with much.
–Unknown

Tithing

Ye are cursed with a curse: for ye have robbed me, even this whole nation. **Malachi 3:9**

One of the first mentions of paying tithes was when Abraham paid his tithes to Melchizedek, King of Salem, who was a priest of God. Abraham had just come back from a victory and King Melchizedek blessed him and Abraham paid him a tenth of the spoils.

God owns everything and it is by His goodness and mercy that He blesses us with the needs of our life. God does not need our tithes, but we need to give it to Him because God is teaching us the law of reciprocity. In addition, if we don't tithe, we rob God (Malachi 3:8). You will not be blessed and your finances and blessing will cease. Your gold will be in "bags with holes." Robbing God puts you under a curse.

What are the benefits of tithing? You will receive many blessings from God and your storehouses will be full and running over. Tithing is a continual reminder that God is your source. Christians fail to tithe because of unbelief, fear, greed, selfishness, and lack of correct teaching.

I know of a CEO who failed to tithe because he was in debt that he reasoned with himself that he just could not afford it. He ended up going so far in debt that now he lives like a pauper, trying to pay off the massive debt even though he makes six figures. He told me he learned the error of his ways and has started tithing and giving back to the Lord. His situation is slowly turning around. When you tithe, your money stretches further and you will be blessed by God.

Remember, tithing opens the windows of heaven, your crops won't be destroyed, and God's blessings will be recognized by everyone. If you want God's blessings, start tithing.

If you want to be blessed,
Pay your tithes and your offerings
If you want more, give it to the poor.
And the Lord will give it back to you.
                                        –Shirley Caesar

The money and the time you give to Jesus
are the best indicator of how much you love Him.

December 23

You're No Accident

According as he hath chosen us in him before the foundation of the world, that we should be holy and without blame before him in love. **Ephesians 1:4**

You were in God's mind before you were in your mother's womb. Your parents did not create you, God did. Even though the famous pro-abortionist Richard Dawkins says that you are on this earth by chance when a sperm meets an egg. This may be true, but he forgets that a new life is so much greater than scientific fact. God may have set the scientific order of reproduction in place and left it up to mankind's emotions and actions to start the process, but our life comes from the breath of God.

Tim Tebow was born in 1987 and is the Heisman-winning quarterback. His parents were missionaries to the Philippines when Tim was conceived. His mother suffered a life-threatening infection while pregnant and her unborn baby suffered a severe placental abruption. Doctors recommended that his mother abort him to save her life, but she refused. Tim was carried to term and both he and his mother survived.

It doesn't matter how you were conceived. God created you. He didn't allow you to be aborted, miscarried, stillborn, or die of crib death. Those events didn't take you because God has a purpose for your life. When you were abused as a child, He never took His hand off you. He is the One who brought you to accept Jesus as your Lord and Savior. He is the One who raised you up in spite of every attempt of the enemy to destroy you, diminish you, defame you, or discourage you.

The fact is, if you hadn't gone through what you have been through, you would not be the person you are today. He has been in the process of creating you, molding you, refining you, and perfecting you, since the moment He first thought of you. He gave you your own personality, your own abilities, and your own identity in Christ. This was so that you will uniquely praise Him, give to Him, serve Him, and love Him.

> *From the dust of the earth my God created man-*
> *His breath made man a living soul;*
> *And God so loved the world He gave His only Son,*
> *And that is why I love Him so!*
>
> *My hands were made to help my neighbor,*
> *My eyes were made to read God's word.*
> *My feet were made to walk in His footsteps,*
> *My body is the temple of the Lord.*
>
> *I was made in His likeness, created in his image,*
> *For I was born to serve the Lord.*
> *I will not deny Him, I will always walk beside Him,*
> *For I was born to the serve the Lord.*
> —Bud Chalmers

Rejoice, you are His unique creation and He loves you.

Friendship

Let us hold fast the profession of our faith without wavering; (for he is faithful that promised); And let us consider one another to provide unto love and to good works; not forsaking the assembling of ourselves together, as the manner of some is; but exhorting one another; and so much the more, as ye see the day approaching. Hebrews 10:23-25

What does it mean to be a friend to a fellow Christian? Jesus shared the meaning of His parables with his friends, the apostles, who were closest to him. Further, he walked with them. He ate with them. In other words, He shared time with them.

Many of our churches are full of older people who have limited capacity to get out of their homes very often. Yet, do we stop and consider them? Jesus wants us to be faithful to them and assemble with them. If they can no longer make it to church, then we should go to them. We need to think about ways to share our time with them. It can be as simple as stopping for a cup of coffee and sharing of stories. Or it can be remembering them when an event comes to town. Perhaps they would enjoy the event also.

There was a quilt show at our local Civic Center and I immediately thought of an elderly friend. I thought she might enjoy seeing the quilts. We were able to put her walker in my trunk and have a wonderful time at the event. I learned more about her as she talked of family members who liked to quilt as well as family members who enjoyed antiques and would appreciate the quilts. I am always amazed at how close I feel to someone when we have shared some time together. I learned more about them and they learned more about me. It helps bring a connection of care for each other.

A great example of friendship is seen in the Bible between David and Jonathan. In I Samuel 18:1, we learn of this close friendship. "And it came to pass, when he had made an end of speaking unto Saul, that the soul of Jonathan was knit with the soul of David and Jonathan loved him as his own soul." Are you the kind of friend that will give your royal best to your friend? Jonathan gave David his own robe, his sword, and his bow. He gave David the royal status as well as the weapons that he could use for protection. Jonathan later would save David's life.

As a superintendent, you need to have close colleagues and friends who you can share with and fellowship with. This is necessary as we need this communion as we need communion with Jesus.

Two are better than one: because they have a good reward for their labour. For if they fall, the one will lift up his fellow; but woe to him that is along when he falleth, for he hath not another to help him up. Ecclesiastes 4:9-10

Friendship with Jesus, fellowship devine
Oh what blessed sweet communion,
Jesus is a friend of mine.

A friend is that person that you want to spend time with and that you trust when you tell about your life, sorrows and happy events.

Christmas: Foretelling of Christ's Birth

For unto us a child is born, unto us a son is given: and the government shall be upon his shoulder: and his name shall be called Wonderful, counselor, The mighty God, The everlasting Father, The Prince of Peace. **Isaiah 9:6**

The angels sang and the shepherds rejoiced when Jesus was born. His birth trumpeted the fulfillment of the prophecies. There were many predictions and are as follows:

> He would be born in Bethlehem (Micah 5:2)
> He would have the right genealogical address (Isaiah 11:1, Jeremiah 23:5,6)
> He would come from a miraculous birth (Isaiah 7:14)
> Royalty would worship him (Isaiah 60:3, Psalm 72:10)
> Mourning would follow his birth (Jeremiah 31:15)
> He would have a connection to Egypt (Hosea 11:1)
> He would have a uniquely praise-worthy name (Isaiah7:14)

> *Far away in Bethlehem, a baby boy was born;*
> *Born with neither riches nor fame,*
> *Yet Wise Men came from all around to bring to Him gifts,*
> *And peace was felt by all who heard His name.*
> *Angels watched Him as He slept, and gently rocked His bed;*
> *Their voices signing softly in His ear; His mother and His father both gave thanks to God*
> *For the greatest gift of all, their Son, so dear*
> *They knew His life upon this earth would not be filled with wealth,*
> *They also knew He would encounter strife;*
> *But most of all, they knew that He would be a loving Child,*
> *And teach the love of God throughout His life.*
> *At Christmas, as we celebrate this Birth of Jesus Christ,*
> *Let's keep in mind the truth of Christmas Day;*
> *For it's not the Christmas wrappings, nor the gifts that lie within,*
> *But our gift of love to others in every way* (Unknown)

George Truett said it best in a short statement, "Christ was born in the first century, yet he belongs to all centuries. He was born a Jew, yet He belongs to all races. He was born in Bethlehem, yet He belongs to all countries."

CHRISTMAS is C-hrist's H-istoric, R-emarkable I-ncarnation S-tory, T-elling M-essiah's A-waited S-alvation.

–Jose Cabajar.

The Price for Avarice

Shall not all these take up a parable against him, and a taunting proverb against him, and say, Woe to him that increaseth that which is not his! How long? And to him that ladeth himself with thick clay. Habakkuk 2:6

Grimm's *Fairy Tales* tells a story about "The Fisherman and His Wife." In this fairy tale, a fisherman catches a large fish and the fish asked the fisherman to let him live. Because the fish knew how to talk, the fisherman let it go. When he got home, his wife asked him if he caught anything today. He said he caught a fish and it was an enchanted prince, so he let it go. The fisherman's wife asked him if he asked for anything and the man said no. So, at the pleading of his wife he went back and called the fish.

The fish appeared and the fisherman said his wife doesn't want to live in a filthy shack. When the fisherman went back home, there was a beautiful cottage, but his wife wasn't satisfied. She sent the fisherman back to ask for a stone palace. When he got home, there was a stone palace.

When his wife woke up in the morning, she wanted to be king so after much nagging, the fisherman went and called the fish and told him his wife's request. He went home and his wife was made King. His wife then wanted to be an Emperor, then a Pope, and then, finally, to be like God. So, each time he went to the fish and made the request for his wife. When he told the fish that she wanted to be like God, the fish told him to go home. He found her sitting in a filthy shack again.

Greed will kill a nation, a community, and a school district. Look how food prices and gas prices are drastically rising. For food, you could say natural disaster, crop failure, commodity speculation and so forth drive up the price, but one factor that drives up the price is greed. Great world empires including Bablyon, Medo-Persia, Greece and Rome were destroyed by greed. As they became more powerful, powerful people became greedier. Governor Christie of New Jersey was so upset about the greed of superintendents that he called one out by name. Choose to live above the temptation of greed and ask the Lord to test your thoughts and motives.

Greed will take you back to the filthy shack!
For nothing good have I, whereby Thy grace to claim,
I'll wash my garment white, in the blood of Calvary's Lamb.
Jesus paid it all, all to Him I owe;
Sin had left a crimson stain; He washed it white as snow.
                                        –John Grape

Follow the example of Jesus who wasn't greedy and gave His all for you!

Erase the Negative

For he that touches you, touches the apple of the Lord's eye. **Zechariah 2:8**

Several people let past statements, hurts, and events replay over many times. They replay those negative aspects instead of pressing erase and allowing God to heal them. The Bible talks directly about the caustic power of words. Our Lord wants to provide the healing and He wants us to let go of these hurtful phrases.

When I walk around public places, I am always upset when I hear a parent berating a child. I understand the need of discipline. But I never understand the need to ever call someone bad names or telling them they are awful. It makes no sense to hear those negative phrases.

Children as well as Christians are the apple of the Lord's eye. He is hurt when we are hurt. He feels our pain when the hurtful words are attacked at us. Jesus understands the hurt. It must have been extremely hurtful to Jesus when he was taunted and sarcastically called the "King of the Jews", when he really was a king.

The following references in the Bible show the negative power of words.

In Jeremiah 9:3, "And they bend their tongues like their bow for lies; but they are not valiant for the truth upon the earth; for they proceed from evil to evil, and they know not me, saith the Lord."

Psalms 140:3, "They have sharpened their tongues like a serpent; adders' poison is under their lips."

Psalms 57:4, "My soul is among lions, and I lie even among them that are set on fire, even the sons of men, whose teeth are spears and arrows, and their tongue a sharp sword."

Psalms 50:19, "Thou givest thy mouth to evil, and they tongue frameth deceit."

Psalms 73:8-9, "They are corrupt, and speak wickedly concerning oppression, they speak loftily. They set their mouth against the heavens and their tongue walketh through the earth."

We are reminded in several places within the Bible to also monitor our own words so that they do not cause hurt to others. The idea of words being harmful are clearly presented when the double-edged sword is used to represent words. God reminds us that, "I will reprove thee, and set them in order before thine eyes. Now consider this, ye that forget God, lest I tear you in pieces, and there be none to deliver" (Psalms 50:22). God was talking about those who used hurtful words.

As leaders, it is our job to protect any of our employees and students. This protection includes hurtful words. Whether you have been on the side of the attack from words or have seen the hurt of words, help others know they are valued and the Lord has a purpose for the apples of His eye.

Words which do not give the light of Christ, increase the darkness.
–Mother Teresa

God Said NO!

For this thing I besought the Lord thrice, that it might depart from me. II Corinthians 12:8

I asked God to take away my habit.
God said, No!
It is not for me to take away, but for you to give it up.

I asked God to make my handicapped child whole.
God said, No!
His spirit is whole, his body is only temporary.

I asked God to grant me patience.
God said, No!
Patience is a byproduct of tribulations; It isn't granted, it is learned.

I asked God to give me happiness.
God said, No!
I give you blessings; Happiness is up to you.

I asked God to spare me pain.
God said, No!
Suffering draws you apart from worldly cares and brings you closer to me.

I asked God to make my spirit grow.
God said, No!
You must grow on your own, but I will prune you to make you fruitful.

I asked God for all things that I might enjoy life.
God said, No!
I will give you life, so that you may enjoy all things.

I asked God to help me LOVE others as much as He loves me.
God said, Great, you finally have the idea. (unknown)

> *To the world you might be one person,*
> *But to one person you just might be the world'*
> *'May the Lord Bless you and keep you,*
> *May the Lord Make his face shine upon you,*
> *And give you Peace......Forever'*

This day is yours, don't throw it away.

Jesus Reaches and Touches Us

Blessed be God, even the Father of our Lord Jesus Christ, the Father of mercies, and the God of all comfort; Who comforteth us in all our tribulation, that we may be able to comfort them which are in any trouble, by the comfort wherewith we ourselves are comforted of God. For as the sufferings of Christ abound in us, so our consolation also aboundeth by Christ. And whether we be afflicted, it is for your consolation and salvation, which is effectual in the enduring of the same sufferings which we also suffer; or whether we be comforted, it is for your consolation and salvation. II Corinthians 1:3-6

Have you ever been hurt? Then someone reaches out and touches your shoulder or arm in a gesture of comfort and sympathy. It is a moment that helps you understand that someone else cares and shares in your pain. As we see others suffering, we must find ways to reach out to them and help them. Sometimes, a touch will help while other times there are different ways to help.

My Sunday School class often finds projects to help the community. We have a Women's Shelter in our town. Many of us bring our shampoos and soap from stays at hotels while on vacation, and share them with the Women's Shelter. We have made quilt bags that we fill with these soaps and other personal hygiene necessities that battered women have left behind as they left their homes to find safety.

My church also has service Sundays when the church members sign up to help with projects around town. We have painted houses, planted flowers and plants at Nursing Homes, decorated rooms at Nursing Homes, planted and weeded gardens for the city, and made wheelchair ramps. All of these projects help us reach out and touch others that need our help.

My church also has a variety of groups that help our members. We have a group for those grieving, another group of young moms, a groups that visits our house-bound members, a group that adopts college students, a group that has celebrations for those in our Nursing Homes. Again, we are reaching out to fill the needs of our members and touch them in ways to help them feel comfort. "Therefore we were comforted in your comfort: yea and exceedingly the more joyed we for the joy of Titus, because his spirit was refreshed by you all." II Corinthians 7:13

> *He touched me, oh He touched me,*
> *And oh the joy that floods my soul,*
> *Something happened and now I know,*
> *He touched me and made me whole!*
> —Gloria Gaither

Reaching out does help other people,
but it also provides a great feeling
for those who were doing the reaching out.

Overcomers

Great is our Lord, and of great power: His understanding in infinite. The Lord lifteth up the meek: He casteth the wicked down to the ground. **Psalms 147: 5-6**

Many of us don't want trouble or pain to come our way. Yet, it is just these troubles and pains that challenge us and determine if we put our trust in God and become overcomers. It is not just surviving, but it is also learning how we can grow stronger and overcome with the help of our Lord. Without any troubles, there is nothing to overcome.

I find myself closest to God when there is no way that I can overcome something on my own. It is when I have to turn to Him in order to survive. Even though there are many times I have overcome immense pains and sorrows by the grace of God, I still find myself easily slipping into a questioning state at a new sorrow or pain. Or, I have difficulty letting go of an old hurt. I have seen the miraculous and, yet, I am surprised when I find myself questioning a new trouble or hurt. It is as if I can't even remember all God is capable of doing when I am stuck in the present concerns.

For this is the love of God, that we keep his commandments: and his commandments are not grievous. For whatsoever is born of God overcometh the world: and this is the victory that overcometh the world, even our faith. 1 John 5:3-4

We should know that victory has been won by Jesus. He has overcome all and we need to just keep our faith in him and the knowledge that he has overcome. As we learn to overcome our hurts and sorrows, we can claim God's victory. It was a victory won with Jesus' own life. God gave His own son so we could have that victory. Our Lord will help us remember that we can overcome. And as we become overcomers, we have contentment and peace.

> *Encamped along the hills of light, Ye Christian soldiers, rise.*
> *And press the battle ere the night shall veil the glowing skies.*
> *Against the foe in vales below let all our strength be hurled.*
> *Faith is the victory, we know, that overcomes the world.*
> –John H. Yates

These things I have spoken unto you, that in me ye might have peace.
In the world ye shall have tribulation; but be of good cheer;
I have overcome the world. John 16:33

Be Strong and of Good Courage

Be strong and of a good courage: for unto this people shalt thou divide for an inheritance the land, which I sware unto their fathers to give them. Only be thou strong and very courageous, that thou mayest observe to do according to all the law, which Moses my servant commanded thee: turn not from it to the right hand or to the left, that thou mayest prosper withersoever thou goest. **Joshua 1:6-7**

The dictionary defines "courage" as bravery, boldness; and the word "strong" as powerful. What the Lord meant was to be powerful and very brave. Let's look at some examples of Bible heroes. *Joshua* was strong and of good courage as he needed this to subdue the land. The people of Israel were ready to accept him when he showed that he would keep faith with God and give them good leadership. *Job* had to endure severe trials. He was wracked with pain while, at the same time, having to listen to the wisdom of his "comforters." Job is a demonstration of the suffering world of mankind and their final deliverance and inheritance.

Gideon showed strength of endurance and courage coupled with his total trust and faith in God when God whittled the number of his army down to three hundred. We take so much for granted and it is refreshing to read how God dealt with Gideon. The culmination of the victory, how they took up strategic places, how they had lamps in their pitchers and trumpets in their hands, and ,at a command from Gideon, they broke the pitchers while holding the lamps in their left hands and the trumpets in their right hands. Every man stood his ground and the whole enemy host fled in terror. *David's* life is full of examples. Here was a strapping young lad who was no match for such an antagonist. Goliath derided him and scorned those who sent him. David took the sling he used to protect his father's sheep from the lions and bears. He was confident when he was face to face with Goliath. David came out against Goliath in the name of the Lord of hosts whom Goliath defied.

Elijah showed tremendous courage and dependency on the Lord. He had to go before Ahab and Jezebel to prophecy before them. He boldly faced the 800 prophets of Baal before the masses and believed God for the miracle. *Jeremiah* had a very unpleasant mission to perform, but he carried on, determined to follow the leading of the Lord. Judged by his own estimate of himself, he was feeble and his mission a failure. But, in the hour of need and duty, he was an iron pillar against the whole land. He is a noble example of the triumph of the moral over the physical nature.

Daniel, an innocent man wrongfully condemned, was thrown into the lion's den by jealous men. He demonstrated complete trust and confidence in the Lord which emboldened his courage he showed when he was confronted by the vicious lions. His exultant reply when the king went to visit him the next morning was, "My God hath sent his angel."

How do these reflections affect us? Are we being strong and very courageous in our present, everyday experiences? Do we trust sufficiently? Are we bold enough to come to the throne of heavenly grace to get the necessary strength to assist us in our trials and difficulties?

What an ennobling thought,
That the God of the universe has called us to be joint-heirs with his son.
Just as he dealt with the heroes of faith;
He dealt with them by fighting their battles,
Preparing the way for them,
Cheering, encouraging, and fortifying them when they lost hope;
So does he deal with us if we are willing and obedient.

Courage is looking fear right in the eye and saying,
"Get out of my way, I've got things to do as the Lord is on my side."

CPSIA information can be obtained at www.ICGtesting.com
Printed in the USA
LVOW08s0140020514

384089LV00002B/2/P